T0398760

Place Branding

Place branding as a field of research is still in a state of infancy. This book seeks to address this, offering a theory of place branding based on the tourist experience, keeping in mind the roles of stakeholders, both public and private organisations and DMOs in managing the place brand.

Place Branding: Connecting Tourist Experiences to Places seeks to build a customer-based view of place branding through focusing on the individual as a tourist who travels to undertake a memorable experience. The place is the key creator of this experience, which begins well before the travel-to and ends well after the travel-back. Individuals choose the places where to go, collect information on them, ask for advice and suggestions from fellow travellers, give feedback when they come back and talk a lot about their experience, spreading word-of-mouth. The book enables readers to understand how the tourist experience can be managed as a brand. Readers are exposed to a variety of problems, methodological approaches, and geographical areas, which allows them to adapt frames to different contexts and situations.

This book is recommended reading for students and scholars of business, marketing, tourism, urban studies and public diplomacy, as well as practitioners, business consultants and people working in public administration and politics.

Pantea Foroudi is Senior Lecturer in Branding at Middlesex University, London, UK.

Chiara Mauri is Professor of Business Economics at LIUC – Università Carlo Cattaneo, Castellanza, Italy, and Adjunct Professor at Università Bocconi, Milan, Italy.

Charles Dennis is Professor of Consumer Behaviour at Middlesex University, London, UK.

T C Melewar is Professor of Marketing and Strategy at Middlesex University, London, UK.

Place Branding
Connecting Tourist Experiences to Places

**Edited by
Pantea Foroudi, Chiara Mauri,
Charles Dennis and T C Melewar**

Routledge
Taylor & Francis Group

LONDON AND NEW YORK

First published 2020
by Routledge
2 Park Square, Milton Park, Abingdon, Oxon, OX14 4RN

and by Routledge
52 Vanderbilt Avenue, New York, NY 10017

Routledge is an imprint of the Taylor & Francis Group, an informa business

© 2020 selection and editorial matter, Pantea Foroudi, Chiara Mauri, Charles Dennis and T C Melewar; individual chapters, the contributors

The right of Pantea Foroudi, Chiara Mauri, Charles Dennis and T C Melewar to be identified as the authors of the editorial material, and of the authors for their individual chapters, has been asserted in accordance with sections 77 and 78 of the Copyright, Designs and Patents Act 1988.

All rights reserved. No part of this book may be reprinted or reproduced or utilised in any form or by any electronic, mechanical, or other means, now known or hereafter invented, including photocopying and recording, or in any information storage or retrieval system, without permission in writing from the publishers.

Trademark notice: Product or corporate names may be trademarks or registered trademarks, and are used only for identification and explanation without intent to infringe.

Library of Congress Cataloging-in-Publication Data
A catalog record for this title has been requested

ISBN: 978-1-4724-5592-5 (hbk)
ISBN: 978-1-315-60056-7 (ebk)

Typeset in Sabon
by codeMantra

Visit the eResources: www.routledge.com/9781472455925

Contents

Contributors

Awele Achi
The Open University Business School, The Open University, Milton Keynes, UK

Ogechi Adeola
Lagos Business School (Pan-Atlantic University), Lagos, Nigeria

Elena Ageeva
Middlesex University London, UK

Tuğra Nazlı Akarsu
Middlesex University London, UK

Marco Alderighi
Università della Valle d'Aosta, Italy

Magda Antonioli Corigliano
Bocconi University, Italy

Sunny Bose
IBS Hyderabad (ICFAI Foundation for Higher Education), India

Marco Cioppi
University of Urbino "Carlo Bo", Italy

Giovanni Paolo Crespi
Università degli Studi dell'Insubria, Italy

Charles Dennis
Middlesex University London, UK

Mauro Dini
University of Urbino "Carlo Bo", Italy

Magdiel Y. Espinal R.
Middlesex University London, UK

Cristina Fona
University of Leicester, UK

Mohammad M. Foroudi
Foroudi Consultancy London, UK

Pantea Foroudi
Middlesex University London, UK

Robert Ebo Hinson
University of Ghana and University of the Free State Business School

Saheb Imani
Member of Material and Procurement Management, National Iranian
South Oilfields Company, Ahvaz, Iran

Eleonora Lorenzini
Politecnico di Milano, Italy

Giada Mainolfi
University of International Studies of Rome, Italy

Samuel Marfo
Department of Marketing and Entrepreneurship, University of Ghana
Business School

Vittoria Marino
University of Salerno, Italy

Reza Marvi
Middlesex University London, UK

Anna Marsanasco
Bocconi University, Milan, Italy

Chiara Mauri
Università Carlo Cattaneo – LIUC, Italy

Dominic Medway
Institute of Place Management, Manchester Metropolitan University,
Faculty of Business and Law, Manchester, UK

T C Melewar
Middlesex University London, UK

Cristina Mottironi
Bocconi University, Italy

Alireza Nazarian
University of Roehampton, UK

Bang Nguyen
University of Southern Denmark, Denmark

Tonino Pencarelli
University of Urbino "Carlo Bo", Italy

Cristina Scarpocchi
Università della Valle d'Aosta, Italy

Simone Splendiani
University of Perugia, Italy

Kathryn Swanson
Consultant, N. Plymouth, MN, USA

Kayhan Tajeddini
Sheffield Hallam University, UK

Gary Warnaby
Institute of Place Management, Manchester Metropolitan University, Faculty of Business and Law, Manchester, UK

Part I
Introduction

1 Place branding
Connecting tourist experiences to places

Pantea Foroudi, Chiara Mauri, Charles Dennis, and T C Melewar

Introduction

Two texts can be considered as seminal contributions to the place branding literature, both published in 2002: the book *Destination Branding*, edited by Morgan, Pritchard and Pride, and the special issue "Nation Branding" of the *Journal of Brand Management* (vol. 9, issue 4). The authors of the first book are two academicians and one practitioner (Pride); the editor of the special issue (Anholt), who is neither properly a practitioner (being qualified as "one of the UK's best-known international marketing thinkers," p. 1) nor an academician, writes in his Foreword, "To be plunged back in the world of academia after nearly 18 years in the world of 'practice' has reminded me sharply of both its attractions and its limitations." Of the 19 contributors to the special issue, roughly half are academicians, many are practitioners, a few are politicians (one is a ministry); of the academicians, approximately half are professors of marketing, while the others work in history, in arts, and in tourism.

This beginning qualifies immediately place branding as a multi-faceted field, a cross-road between academicians of many disciplines, practitioners working in private companies and public institutions, and politicians.

Actually, the topic was anticipated almost 10 years before 2002, when in 1993 two books were published: *Marketing Places: Attracting Investment, Industry, And Tourism To Cities, States and Nations*, written by Kotler et al., and *Product-Country Images: Impact and Role in International Marketing*, edited by Papadopoulos and Heslop. The fact that Kotler appears as an author on the topic is in itself a clear signal that place marketing and branding are significant fields, and had already developed a body of knowledge that could be packaged in a book for larger dissemination.

Another significant landmark is the article Nation-brands of the twenty-first century (Anholt 1998), which, assigning the status of brands to some countries and not to others, opened a new stream of inquiry with clear political implications. Simon Anholt has indeed developed a toolkit that public policy-makers can use to measure the strength of their place's brand and to understand its components. In his continuous effort to build and spread the knowledge on place branding, in 2004 he created the journal *Place Branding and Public Diplomacy*, which, together with the *Journal of Place Management and Development* (founded in 2008) and the latest *Journal of Destination Marketing and Management* (founded in 2012), nurture and broaden the debate involving a growing number of contributors (Table 1.1). The SCImago Rankings shown in Table 1.1 can be segmented not only by journal but also by country, a clear sign of the relevance of the geographic dimension also in scientific literature.

In the same years in which the debate grows, we see the appearance of the first destination brands indexes and rankings. While they do not seem to be much used in academic publications, nonetheless they have the merit to raise the attention of the stakeholders involved in managing places, and to put in the spotlight that the brand dimension of a country can be a key factor for its competitiveness. The publication of these rankings has an interesting positive effect: the particular position of a country in a rank can be the starting point of a demanding, long and complex process of rethinking the place as a brand to improve its score, and even to develop new indexes.

Following the low ranking of South Korea, 33 out of 50 in 2008 Anholt-GfK Roper Nation Brands Index, the government of South Korea decided to take action in order to climb up the rankings. In January 2009, President Lee Myung-bak, who made upgrading South Korean nation brand one of the priorities of its mandate, created the Presidential Council on Nation Branding, which consisted of 47 members: 34 civilian members and 13 government officials (including 8 ministers).

> We are one of the most technological advanced nations, and the first images evoked by foreigners are strikes and street protests. If our country wants to be considered an advanced country, we must work hard to improve its image and its reputation.
>
> (Dinnie 2010; Schwak 2016)

Table 1.1 Ratings of journals involved in the debate on place branding (in parenthesis the year of foundation)

Journals	SJR[a] (2017)
Journal of Destination Marketing & Management (2012)	1.148
Journal of Brand Management (1993)	0.640
Journal of Place Management and Development (2008)	0.35
Place Branding and Public Diplomacy (2004)	0.30

a SJR = Scimago Journal Rank.

The Chairman of the Council announced in March 2009 that the goal of the Presidential Council on Nation Branding was to raise South Korea's ranking in the index of 18 spots in 4 years, reaching rank 15 by 2013. The goal was not reached, and in 2014 South Korea ranked 27 out of 50.

This process of branding places, which involves a very large number of public and private stakeholders, has been the topic of many case studies, published in academic journals. The increasing availability of newer and newer experiences to tell is probably one of the reasons why the literature has been focused on descriptive cases (Muñiz Martinez 2012) and has been scarcely involved in developing a theoretical framework (Gertner 2011; Hanna & Rowley 2011). The consequence is that "Place branding still lacks a clear and commonly accepted theoretical framework that would structure and guide its practical application and fill the evident gap between existing theory and practice" (Ashworth et al. 2015, p. 2). The field is very much practitioner-led, and sees an absolute predominance of articles of qualitative nature based on the authors' personal opinions, and paradoxically the scarcity of empirical research (Gertner 2011). Practice has been abundant, while theory has lagged behind.

Besides country brand indexes, rankings, and case studies, another stream that has been developing through the years is the distinction between branding different geographical units: nations (Dinnie 2008; Marino & Mainolfi 2013), regions and cities (Anttiroiko 2014; Dinnie 2011; Kavaratzis & Ashworth 2010; Kavaratzis et al. 2015), small cities (Baker 2012), glocal and virtual identities (Govers & Go 2009), and other hybrid units (Zenker 2015). If on one side it is true that identities of different classes require dedicated attention, we believe that the critical issue is not to see these concepts as separate units, but rather to integrate the branding of a nation with that of its regions, cities or even parts of the city. As well as companies have to organize hierarchically their product portfolio to develop an effective brand architecture strategy, the stakeholders involved in branding different geographical and physical identities must investigate their hierarchy, which is not only a matter of physical size, neither of administrative boundaries.

The difference between applying the brand relationship spectrum (Aaker & Joachimsthaler 2000; Keller 2014) to brand a portfolio of products and a portfolio of geographical units is that place branding appears to be an organic concept springing from the routine behavior of a large variety of stakeholders (residents, tourists, firms, public institutions, investors, etc.), but most of them are not aware of their effective contribution to the equity of the place (Medway et al. 2015). What's more, while images of places evolve over time, the place's past can continue to exert a strong effect on its current image (Govers & Go 2009) so that this image appears as a stereotype emerging from the many activities, behavior, political and economic issues in which a place has been involved in its past history (Boland 2008). In this perspective, place images may be hard to change in a short time: "Paris is about style, Japan about technology, Switzerland about wealth and precision, Rio de Janeiro about carnival and football, Tuscany about the good life, and most African nations about poverty, corruption, war, famine and disease," noted Anholt in 2007 (p. 1). We do not know if these stereotypes still hold today, but it is certainly true that it is very tough for a country to convince people living in other countries to stop thinking in frames and start seeing the place the way it really is (Kotler & Gertner 2002). What is even more is that these clichés affect how people treat other close places, as it may be true for South Korea and North Korea, or for South Africa compared to the African continent.

In its relatively short life, place branding has evolved in different stages, where each stage was not substituting the old one, but rather co-existed (Kavaratzis & Ashworth 2010), so that the topic becomes more and more multidimensional and multi-faceted, and the delimitation of the field is still rather blurred (Gertner 2011).

"Rethinking place branding" was the call for action of Kavaratzis et al. in 2015, and each chapter of their book was dedicated to the re-thinking of something related to the place: the concept, the image, the physical communication, and the sense of place. Even if someone was questioning whether talking and theorizing about place branding could be a waste of time (Medway et al. 2015), we have made the call ours, and this book is the result of the contributions of all the scholars who have answered the call.

The innovative perspective of this book is told in the second part of the title: Connecting tourism experiences to places. The reinterpretation of the relationship between people and brands as brand experiences brought about by the experience economy (Pine & Gilmore 1998, 1999) and by the experiential marketing orientation (Schmitt 1997, 1999) has had a strong impact on tourist behavior, which is more and more interpreted as a travel and visitation experience (Morgan et al. 2010; Richtie et al. 2011). Understanding the nature of tourism experiences can add significant value to academicians and practitioners, since offering tourisms memorable experiences is the essence of tourism management: what matters to visitors is places that provide attractive experiences for them. From each place, they may visit for any reason, tourists expect something special, real and authentic, something that engages their senses and touches their heart. They want to live an experience that is worth to be lived, remembered and told.

This book is organized in five parts: an introductory part, a second part dedicated to the tourist experience, a third section focused on customer-based place branding, a fourth part centered on destination brand management, and a concluding section on actual trends and future challenges for place branding.

After this introductory chapter, Chapter 2 is an overview of tourism trends and challenges. From 25 million international arrivals in 1950 to 1,326 billion in 2017, tourism has been one of the world's fastest growing economic sectors, and it is projected to increase to 1.8 billion by 2030. The greater availability of international tourism locations segmented by different motivations and behavior makes very hot the place branding issue: where are people going, and what are the motivations behind the choice of destinations to visit?

Visitors' length of stay at a place varies between tourism segments, hence also by the same experience of the place. In Chapter 3, a survival analysis of a sample of tourists in a summer mountainous region allows to identify the profile of tourists who stay for longer periods at a place, which greatly helps public bodies in choosing the best targets for their place branding strategy. One of the key conclusions of the chapter is that to stimulate tourism segments to spend more time at a place, the offer should be more diversified to satisfy their different motivations and preferences.

In the same vein, Chapter 4 suggests that the place branding of a winter mountain destinations should go beyond mountain, snow and ski. An extensive research conducted in three locations reveals the existence of different segments, differentiated in terms of activities they practice and the time dedicated to each activity. Branding geographies such as mountain areas cannot be based only on physical assets and on sport activities but requires going beyond the landscape to understand its meaning for different tourist segments.

The formation of the image of a place is heavily influenced by the social media, in particular by the content provided by the same visitors who are experiencing the place. Chapter 5 explores the content generated by tourists through their pictures posted on Flickr and compares this content to the one communicated by the local destination management organization through photos posted on Facebook. The analysis of the differences between the perceived and the projected image of the place reveals new opportunities to reinforce the strategy of place branding, satisfying the propensity of return tourists to experience all the areas of a place, and not only the hotspots.

Place image is a component of customer-based brand equity, and in Chapter 6, Bose et al. develop a new scale to measure place image.

Tourists' interpretation of a place is influenced by traveler orientation, that is, by tourism operators' knowledge of travelers' needs and by their promptness in satisfying them. Chapter 7 analyzes this relationship and investigates how digital marketing can shape it. Chapter 8 moves a step forward on place image, exploring the nation brand perception of Ghana and suggesting new avenues to redefine Ghana as an attractive country for tourists and investors.

The tourism experience is an experience of loyalty, reputation, satisfaction, and passion towards the place, which is shaped not only by tourism operators but also by new emerging forms of accommodation born with the sharing economy. One of these is peer-to-peer websites, and Chapter 9 attempts to shed light on their impact on the way tourists choose and book a destination.

The sense of distinctiveness of a place that nurtures the place brand identity is embedded in its cultural heritage. Cultural music is a typical expression of the place brand identity, and Chapter 10 describes how musical events supported by the local community of Dominican Republic can be very effective in communicating the sense of the place.

Not only music but also TV series and movies can be very effective to promote the place brand image and also to attract new segments of tourists, who are driven by the will to experience in person what they saw at the movie. Chapter 11 explores the phenomenon of film-induced tourism, and how it has an impact on the authentic identity of a city.

In its history of almost 20 years, place branding has become a recurrent strategy for many places, whose local governments have created dedicated functions responsible for the development and promotion of the place brand, and have developed specific activities to implement the place branding process. Chapter 12 attempts to integrate all these experiences and develops a country-branding framework that may be used as a benchmark, a reference model to fix all the activities and their sequence to implement an effective place branding strategy.

The websites of official tourism departments are not only a source of information for tourists who are deciding the destination to visit but also one key ingredient of the place branding strategy. Chapter 13 analyzes and compares the tourism websites of the 28 member states of European Union, with the goal to verify how destination managers use the Internet to communicate the values, the unique characteristics, and the strengths that distinguish their nations by thus persuading tourists to choose that nation as their holiday destination.

In the same vein, Chapter 14 examines the impact of a destination website on the place image, culture, and identity.

Chapter 15 is a focus on the strategic role of local networks in shaping the place identity, and, specifically, on the relationship between wine and food tourism, and place identity.

Chapters 16 and 17 conclude the book. Chapter 16 investigates the role that virtual data collection techniques can play in capturing the place customer experience. Virtual technologies and applications offer significant potential for enhancing the study of the tourists who experience places. Chapter 17 is a window on the actual challenges in place branding and the emerging issues and trends. Contested places and identities, new and emerging place brands, un-sustainable destinations, and digital place brands are the major themes that, while they are widely debated today, will shape the future research in place branding.

References

Aaker, D.A., & Joachimsthaler, E. (2000), "The Brand Relationship Spectrum: The Key to the Brand Architecture Challenge", *California Management Review*, vol. 42, no. 4, 8–23.

Keller, K.L. (2014), "Designing and Implementing Brand Architecture Strategies", *Journal of Brand Management*, vol. 21, no. 9, 702–715.

Anholt, S. (1998), "Nation-Brands of the Twenty-First Century", *Journal of Brand Management*, vol. 5, no. 6, 395–406.

Anholt, S. (2007), *Competitive Identity: The New Brand Management for Nations, Cities and Regions*, Basingstoke: Palgrave Macmillan, UK.

Anttiroiko, A.-V. (2014), *The Political Economy of City Branding*, Abingdon: Routledge.

Ashworth, G. J., Kavaratzis, M., & Warnaby, G. (2015), "The Need to Rethink Place Branding", in Kavaratzis, M., Warnaby, G., & Ashworth, G.J. (Eds.). *Rethinking Place Branding*, Springer International Publishing.

Baker, B. (2012), *Destination Branding for Small Cities*, Portland, OR: Creative Leap Books.

Boland, P. (2008), "The Construction of Images of People and Place: Labelling Liverpool and Stereotyping Scousers", *Cities*, vol. 25, no. 6, 355–369.

Dinnie, K. (2008), *Nation Branding. Concepts, Issues, Practice*, Oxford: Elsevier. New edition in 2015 (Routledge).

Dinnie, K. (2011), *City Branding: Theory and Cases*, Hampshire: Palgrave Macmillan.

Gertner, D. (2011), "Unfolding and Configuring Two Decades of Research and Publications on Place Marketing and Place Branding", *Place Branding and Public Diplomacy*, vol. 7, no. 2, 91–106.

Govers, R., & Go, F. (2009), *Place Branding. Glocal, Virtual and Physical Identities, Constructed, Imagined and Experienced*, Basingstoke: Palgrave Macmillan UK

Hanna, S., & Rowley, J. (2011), "Towards a Strategic Place Brand-Management Model", *Journal of Marketing Management*, vol. 27, no. 5–6, 458–476.

Kavaratzis, M., & Ashworth, G. (2010), "Place Branding: Where Do We Stand?", in Ashworth, G., & Kavaratzis, M. (Eds.), *Towards Effective Place Brand Management: Branding European Cities and Regions*, Cheltenham, UK: Edward Elgar Publishing.

Kavaratzis, M., Warnaby, G., & Ashworth, G. (Eds.) (2015), *Rethinking Place Branding: Comprehensive Brand Development for Cities and Regions*, Cham: Springer.

Kotler, P., & Gertner, D. (2002), "Country as Brand, Product, and Beyond: A Place Marketing and Brand Management Perspective", *Brand Management*, vol. 9, no. 4–5, 249–261.

Kotler, P., Haider, D., &Rein, I. (1993), *Marketing Places. Attracting Investments, Industry, and Tourism to Cities, States, and Nations*, New York: The Free Press.

Marino, V., & Mainolfi, G. (2013), *Country Brand Management. Esperienze internazionali a confronto attraverso la ricerca qualitativa*, Milano: Egea.

Medway, D., Swanson, K., Delpy Neirotti, L., Pasquinelli, C., & Zenker, S. (2015), "Place Branding: Are We Wasting Our Time?", *Journal of Place Management and Development*, vol. 8, no. 1, 63–68.

Morgan, M., Lugosi, P., & Ritchie, J.R.B. (2010), *The Tourism and Leisure Experience: Consumer and Managerial Perspectives*, Vol. 44, Bristol: Channel View Publications.

Morgan, M., Pritchard, A., & Pride, E. (Eds.) (2002), *Destination Branding: Creating the Unique Destination Proposition*, Oxford: Butterworth-Heinemann.

Muñiz Martinez, N. (2012), "City Marketing and Place Branding: A Critical Review of Practice and Academic Research", *Journal of Town and City Management*, vol. 2, no. 4, 369–394.

Pine, J. B. II, & Gilmore, J.H. (1998), "Welcome to the Experience Economy", *Harvard Business Review*, vol. 76, 97–105.

Pine, J. B. II, & Gilmore, J.H. (1999), *The Experience Economy. Work is a Theatre & Every Business a Stage*, Boston, MA: Harvard Business School Press.

Richtie, J.R.B., Sun Tung, V.W., & Richtie, R.J.B. (2011), "Tourism Experience Management Research: Emergence, Evolution and Future Directions", *International Journal of Contemporary Hospitality Management*, vol. 23, no. 4, 419–438.

Schmitt, B. (1997), "'Superficial Out of Profundity': The Branding of Customer Experiences", *Journal of Brand Management*, vol. 5, no. 2, 92–98.

Schmitt, B.H. (1999), *Experiential Marketing: How to Get Customers to Sense, Feel, Think, Act, Relate to Your Companies and Brands*, New York: The Free Press.

Schwak, J. (2016). National identity in an era of Global Competitiveness: the case of South Korean nation branding, in Paper presented at the Second Euro-academia International Conference Identities and Identifications: Politicized Uses of Collective Identities, Florence, Italy.

Zenker, S. (2015), *Inter-Regional Place Branding: Best Practices, Challenges and Solutions*, Heidelberg: Springer.

2 Tourisms and tourists
Where are people going?

Cristina Scarpocchi

Learning outcomes

At the end of this chapter, readers should be able to:

1 Understand the size and significance of international tourism.
2 Appreciate the patterns and trends of domestic, regional, and international tourism.
3 Understand basic definitions and criteria utilized to measure tourism.
4 Be able to appreciate some of the main contemporary forms of tourism.
5 Be able to identify some of the macro-level factors that affect the development of tourism.

Introduction

In recent decades, tourism has experienced persistent growth and deepening diversification, making it one of the world's fastest growing industries at the global level. The globalization of tourism is the consequence of more general trends of growing economic globalization and technological innovation in communications and transportation (Keller, 1996). Tourism activity is both the cause and effect of globalization. One of the main elements of tourism globalization entails the geographic aspect. Globalization involves intra-regional and inter-regional travel, and extending tourism on a worldwide scale: the movement of tourists both for the number of people traveling and the geographic spread of where people travel has continued almost unabated since the end of World War II. From 25 million in 1950, international tourist arrivals have grown steadily to reach 1.4 billion arrivals in 2018. This growth is projected to continue, and according to UN World Tourism Organization (UNWTO) forecasts, international tourist arrival is expected to increase to 1.8 billion by 2030 (Glaesser et al., 2017).

Multiple reasons exist for the growth in international and domestic travel, the main background factors of which are demography (e.g., population growth and migrant flows), culture (e.g., leisure, fashion, hedonism), economy (e.g., discretionary income), technology (e.g.,

Information and Communication Technologies (ICT), high-speed transport systems), environment (e.g., nature and climate), and institutions and politics (e.g., liberalization, global tourist operators). The critical factors recently contributing to embed tourism into the lifestyle of a growing number of consumers in industrialized, and more significantly, in emerging economies are increasing disposal incomes and available time for travel, better lifestyles of larger segments of the world population, the lower cost of travel, the continuing reduction of travel times, and mass media globalization that has contributed to cross-cultural contamination and exchanges and above all to increased awareness of the outside world (Urry, 2002; Cooper and Hall, 2008). Additional aspects include greater availability of international tourism locations segmented by different tourism behavior, the consolidation of the recovery in key destinations affected by previous crises, increased connectivity and increased visa facilitation, and, in the last 10–20 years, the growing interest of many global corporations in investing in the tourism sector (Brondoni, 2016: 11).

However, it is to be noted that, despite the extension of tourism demand throughout the world and the increase in intra- and inter-regional travel, many people are still traveling only locally or are not familiar with international tourism.

This chapter will focus on international tourist flows, patterns and trends, including a range of the main factors that determine the patterns, flows and trends of contemporary tourism, focusing on the macroscale spatial aspects, whereby the movement of people will be examined in aggregate form. The description of aggregate flows and patterns will be complemented looking at different forms of tourism (i.e., broad account of tourism) defined on the basis of activity and motivation.

Research background

Tourism is characterized by its complexity: it is a multi-sectoral activity involving multiple stakeholders, as well as a complex geographical pattern of supply and demand, which is continuously evolving; it can be viewed as a social, economic or environmental phenomenon, whereby material and immaterial aspects are strictly interwoven. As a result, tourism has attracted the attention of researchers from a wide range of disciplines, including geography, economics, marketing, business management, sociology and anthropology.

While tourism is intrinsically based on the movement of people through time and space, either between their home and destinations or within destination areas, the study of tourist flows has been the subject of relatively little academic enquiry. The understanding of tourist movements and the factors that influence the time/space relationships that tourists have with destinations has profound implications for tourism product development, infrastructure and transport facilities, the commercial sustainability of the tourism industry, and the management of social, environmental, and cultural impacts of tourism. Being able to trace and forecast tourist flows, and the spatial patterns of tourist movements between destinations and within a destination, can help tourism policy-makers, planners and tourism industry actors to provide better services and facilities for tourists as well as for residents. Further, an understanding of the factors that affect tourist movement, such as market access, time availability, and socio-demographic characteristics, can help the industry to manage the impacts of tourism attractions, as well as to develop new products to respond to changing demand (McKercher and Lew, 2004: 36).

However, the intuitive appeal of using secondary statistical data faces limitations and challenges posed by the still diversified landscape of the concepts, definitions, and criteria adopted to measure and account for global tourism flows, expenditures, and behaviors. These challenges can contribute to explain the tendency to produce increasingly sophisticated statistical summaries, together with an attempt to identify meanings, causes, and the variability, and culturally situated nature of changing tourism behaviors. A growing body of research has therefore developed multi-scale quanti-qualitative approaches to understand the factors shaping the movement of tourists between their home and destination merging macro-level analysis of flows with micro-level account of consumer preferences and behaviors shaping the contemporary tourism sector.

The tourism industry in the global economy

Tourism is not a clear-cut sector but an all-embracing and pervasive domain of service and industrial activities (Wahab and Cooper, 2001: 5). A tourism industry is defined as any industry that produces a tourism commodity, that is, any good or service for which a significant portion of demand comes from persons engaged in tourism as consumers. In assessing the economic impact of tourism, travel is often accounted together with tourism as a multi-faceted industry with many components including travel distribution, transportation and infrastructure, tourism facilities such as accommodations, food and beverage establishments, and support services (Cooper and Hall, 2004: 27), the core of which draws together all of these into a conceptual commonality that is defined as "the tourist experience."

Travel and tourism have persistently grown since the end of World War II, with respect to the number of people traveling as well as the geographic spread of from and to where people travel. Over the years, travel and tourism have transformed into one of the world's largest industries, both for its direct and indirect impacts on the economy, contributing significantly to global GDP, with 3.2% of global GDP generated by directly induced impacts and 10.4% by indirectly induced impacts. According to the World Travel Tourism Council's (WTTC), between 2010 and 2017, the travel and tourism industry has performed better than the global economy, being the fastest growing broad economic sector globally, overtaking manufacturing, retail and wholesale, and agriculture.

The economic relevance of tourism is evident also in terms of employment. Tourism is a labor-intensive sector that has become a major source of job creation at all skill levels. Worldwide, tourism is estimated to account for one in ten jobs, including direct, indirect, and induced jobs as referenced at the beginning of this chapter. Tourism can have a significant multiplier effect, creating employment in related sectors such as agriculture, construction, maintenance, retail, handicrafts or financial services. According to UNWTO and the International Labour Organization (2014), one job in the core tourism industry of accommodation creates about one and a half additional (indirect) jobs in the tourism-related economy. In 2017, 3.8% of total employment was directly supported by travel and tourism, rising to around 9.9% when considering direct, indirect, and induced. This means that almost one out of ten jobs is referred to tourism and travel. In the European Union, most recent data account 9% of the total employment to be generated by tourism (UNWTO, 2018: 9).

Many countries rely on tourism as a primary source for generating revenues, employment, infrastructure development, and private sector growth. For this reason, tourism development is encouraged particularly among the developing countries around the world, when other forms of economic development are not commercially viable (WTTC, 2017).

An account of basic definitions

Given the relevance of tourism in different domains, and also in view of understanding the data and information collection systems, it becomes important to outline a clear set of terminology. The measurement of tourism involves conceptual and analytical challenges. First of all, the challenges are related to the nature of tourism, especially when considering its economic implications and impact. Understanding fundamental and internationally agreed definitions and concepts used in the context of travel and tourism industry provides an essential framework from which most discussions on the industry are based. Standardized definitions help insure that all parties are speaking about the same term or concept, reducing the room for variables. This is essential for tourism developers from different regions and countries to discuss travel and tourism matters, as well as for having a more standardized framework for statistical data collection and analysis. In addition, having standardized definitions enables planners to use comparable data to make more informed business decisions. However, exact definitions cannot be taken for granted. For the first half of the twentieth century, tourism visitor arrivals were barely recorded by many countries and, when they were recorded, methods varied by countries. It was not possible to effectively compare the total number of visitors. Statistically, there are significant variations between countries with respect to defining tourist activity as well as in collecting tourism data making it difficult the comparison between countries and historical series of data.

At the UNWTO's conference on tourism statistics, held in 1991, tourism was defined as comprising "the activities of a person traveling outside his or her usual environment for less than a specified period of time and whose main purpose of travel is other than exercise of an activity remunerated from the place visited," where "usual environment" is intended to exclude trips within the areas of usual residence and frequent and regular trips between the domicile and the workplace, and other community trips of a routine character; where "less than a specified period of time" is intended to exclude long-term migration; and "exercise of an activity remunerated from the place visited" is intended to exclude only migration for temporary work (cited in Chadwick, 1994: 66).

The conference in 1991 has also led the way in establishing a list of definitions for general use and a set of resolutions and recommendations relating to tourism concepts, definitions, and classifications. The following definitions are based on the UNWTO classifications and explain the various types of visitors (UNWTO, 1995: 17).

Tourism: The activities of persons traveling to and staying in places outside their usual environment for not more than one consecutive year for leisure, business, and other purposes.
Tourist (overnight visitor): Visitor staying at least one night in a collective or private accommodation in the place visited.
Same day visitor (excursionist): Visitor who does not spend the night in a collective or private accommodation in the place visited.
Traveler: Any person on a trip between two or more locations.
Tourists and tourisms are also defined according to four different characteristics, which help to classify and hence measure activity.
Time, that is, as discussed above, how long someone is away from their place of permanent residence will affect their statistical and general description. For example, if undertaking a trip that does not require an overnight stay before returning the person would be classified as a day-tripper or excursionist. If undertaking an extended trip, for example, of over 12 months, a person may be classified as a migrant.
Space (distance), that is, how far does a person travel before being classified as a tourist? In some jurisdictions, a minimum travel distance is required before being classified as a tourist. Such an approach can differentiate tourism from localized leisure or other travel behavior such as commuting.

Boundary crossing, that is, crossing a national border, can enable a person to be classified as an international tourist arrival and/or departure depending on where a person is in the tourism system. Boundaries are also significant for the development of domestic and regional tourism figures. According to the WTO, international tourism differs from domestic tourism and occurs when the traveler crosses a country's border.

Purpose of travel: The identification of the range of purposes for travel and its application to tourism is very important as it reflects the development of new forms of tourism products, such as medical tourism, health or well-being tourism, sport tourism, educational tourism, business and meetings tourism as well as more "traditional" leisure tourism. In addition, trips are more and more characterized by multiple purposes of travel.

Forms and category of travel: Just as there are different types of visitors, there are different forms and categories of travel which take place, varying by traveler, destination, and motive for travel, such as international versus domestic travel, intra-regional versus inter-regional travel, as well as inbound versus outbound travel.

According to the UNWTO, international tourism differs from domestic tourism and occurs when the traveler crosses a country's border. Not every international traveler is a visitor, however. The traveler is a visitor only if the trip takes him or her outside the usual environment: for example, workers who cross borders for employment are not considered visitors.

Regarding regional travel, three main types of criteria are commonly used to identify a region in tourism research: (i) geographical location, (ii) administrative areas, and (iii) a combination of location and criteria of a more physical nature (e.g., "the Pacific Basin"). The term inter-regional travel refers to travel among various regions, whether in regions found within the same province or state, a country, or various regions throughout the world. Intra-regional, on the other hand, refers directly to travel contained within the same defined region, whether domestic or international such as travel between countries of East Asia.

Tourism flows are also defined in relation to a given area: for example, domestic region, country, or group of countries, whereby domestic tourism involves residents of the given area traveling (as visitors) only within that area; inbound tourism those non-residents traveling as visitors in the given area; and outbound tourism, involving residents traveling as visitors in an area other than the given area.

Macro-trends in contemporary tourism

The boom in international tourist arrivals around the globe is relatively new. Despite its long history and that fact that a small number of people have traveled to distant lands for centuries, tourism did not become a truly global phenomenon until the development of commercially viable jet aircraft capable of trans-oceanic flights in the 1950s (Smith, 2004: 25). In 1950, 25 million people crossed an international border. In 1960, nearly 70 million international arrivals were recorded. By 1970, this figure had grown to 160 million. In 1980, international arrivals totaled more than 280 million. By 1995, international tourist arrivals in all destinations were over 563 million. The overall trend of international tourism shows a steady increase since 1995, except for two major slowdowns in 2003 and in 2009 for the financial crisis. The year 2018 and 2017 recorded the highest growth in international tourist arrivals (7%) since the 2009 global economic crisis, with an uninterrupted growth not recorded since the 1960s, and well above UNWTO's long-term forecast of 3.8% per year for the period 2010–2020 (UNWTO, 2011). A total of 1.4 million international tourist arrivals were recorded in destinations around the world, some 90 million more than in 2016.

Outbound and inbound international tourism: a regional perspective

Despite the significant scope of domestic travel, especially for those countries where the large size is combined with availability of income and leisure time, the global industry of tourism is increasingly driven by international travel. The international movement of tourists is not evenly spread around the globe. Tourism is subject to a range of influences and factors that determine its relative distribution. Flows are not random but are patterned and show a certain degree of "inertia," which can be observed in the great deal of year-to-year stability in aggregate travel patterns (Williams and Zelinsky, 1970: 563). International tourism has historically been concentrated in North America and Europe, both for origin and destination of the flows. Traditionally, the industrialized economies of Europe, the Americas, and Asia and the Pacific have been the world's major source markets for international tourism. However, over recent years, emerging economies in Asia, Central and Eastern Europe, the Middle East, Africa, and Latin America have shown fast growth driven by rising levels of disposable income. If Europe still remains the world's largest source region for outbound tourism, generating almost half of the world's international departures, the share of Asia and the Pacific has been increasing rapidly, currently generating one out of four international trips.

Regarding inbound flows, Europe is also the top destination region, with 51% of the total arrivals (671 million) in 2017, and an average growth of 3% per year since the 1990s. The Asia Pacific region is the second ranked, with 324 million arrivals, 25% of the total, and a 6% growth. Latest data show the American continent recorded 207 million arrivals, equal 16% of the global figure, and 3% growth. Africa and the Middle East follow with 63 and 58 million, respectively (6% and 5% of the arrivals), and a growth of 9% and 4%.

By region, Africa and Europe are the regions with a more substantive and above average growth, with North Africa and Southern Mediterranean Europe leading arrivals, due to the strong demand for destinations along the Mediterranean coasts.

In Europe, 2017 marked the eighth year in a row of sustained growth in Europe, the world's most visited region. Growth in arrivals was mirrored by receipts which also increased 8%. Travel demand increased from virtually all Europe's source markets, both inside and outside the region, fueling inbound growth across Europe. The recovery of the Russian outbound market, in particular, benefitted many destinations.

By subregion, Southern Mediterranean Europe leads results in arrivals and receipts, driven by the recovery of Turkey and the continued strength of other traditional and emerging destinations. Italy and Spain reported an increase of 6 million arrivals each.

In Western Europe, growth was led by top destinations France and Belgium, recovering from a slight slowdown of previous years for security incidents. Destinations in Central and Eastern Europe also experienced solid growth, thanks to increased outbound demand from Russia. All destinations in Northern Europe reported growth, including the United Kingdom, the subregion's largest destination, the attractiveness of which was improved by the depreciation of the British pound which made the destination more affordable.

International tourist arrivals in Africa have increased by 9% and receipts almost at the same pace (+8%). Results were mainly driven by the continued recovery in North Africa and the solid growth in most destinations of Southern Mediterranean, after the temporary slowdown due to political instability. Tunisia continued to rebound strongly in 2017 with a 23% growth in arrivals, while Morocco also enjoyed better results after weaker demand in the previous year. Growing demand from European source markets and a more stable environment contributed to the subregion's positive results. In sub-Saharan Africa, positive performance continued in large destinations Kenya, Côte d'Ivoire, Mauritius, and Zimbabwe. The subregion's top destination, South Africa, reported slower growth in arrivals in 2017, but a strong increase in receipts. Island destinations of Seychelles and Cabo Verde all experienced double-digit growth in arrivals, benefiting from increased air connectivity.

The growth in Asia and the Pacific (+6%) is the result of a solid intraregional demand, especially from China, the Republic of Korea, and Australia. The growing purchasing power in emerging economy markets, increased air connectivity, more affordable travel, and enhanced visa facilitation are the main reasons for this growth and continue to support tourism from within and outside the region.

In North-East Asia, the largest subregion in Asia, results were positive overall. Solid growth was recorded in many destinations, led by Japan, which registered its six straight year of double-digit figures in the number of tourist arrivals. On the other end, the Republic of Korea suffered a decline, especially due to a decrease in arrivals from China.

Of all Asian subregions, South-East Asia experienced the highest growth, with an additional 9 million international tourists in 2017. Growth across destinations was fueled by robust demand from North-East Asian origin markets. Vietnam recorded the fastest growth in arrivals, while Thailand, the subregion's largest destinations, registered additional 3 million arrivals, due to improved air connectivity and visa exemption program.

In South Asia, the increase is largely driven by India, the subregion's largest destination, which benefited from increasing demand from western source markets and simpler visa procedures.

Oceania reflects solid growth in Australia and New Zealand, fueled by robust demand from North-East Asian source markets, the United States, and the United Kingdom.

Arrivals to the Americas have increased by 5%, although receipts showed a slight slower growth. In South America, the outbound travel from Argentina and the rebound of Brazil contributed to the growth in neighboring destinations: Chile, Colombia, Ecuador, Paraguay, and Uruguay. Central America recorded positive results in almost all destinations in terms of arrivals, led by Nicaragua, especially linked to a strong demand from regional markets.

North America, which currently accounts for two-thirds of both international arrivals and receipts in the region, recorded positive growth in arrivals in 2017 but slower growth in receipts.

In the Caribbean, results show some different patterns, with some destinations recording robust growth such as the Dominican Republic and Jamaica, and others in a phase of decline for natural events, mainly due to the strong hurricanes that affected many islands in 2017.

The Middle East shows signs of significant recovery from previous years, with 13% increase in income generated by international tourism. Results were fairly mixed across destinations, with strong rebound in some and sustained growth in others, partly counterweighted by a few destinations reporting declines. Egypt led growth both in absolute and relative terms in arrivals, rebounding strongly from previous years. Visitor numbers rebounded from both traditional markets in Western Europe and emerging markets in Central and Eastern Europe, the Middle East, and Asia. Promotional efforts and a return of confidence contributed to this recovery. Bahrain, Jordan, and the Holy Sites in Israel also recovered steadily, while the United Arab Emirate of Dubai and Lebanon continued to grow at a sustained pace.

Receipts and expenditures at regional level

The interest in international tourism has always been strong, primarily for economic reasons, as this form of tourism plays an important role in trade and monetary flows among nations. While domestic tourism has been somehow overshadowed by the interest in international tourism, international and domestic tourism do relate to each other. Travelers' choices change depending on circumstances, and domestic tourism can be substituted for international tourism and vice versa under the influence of external factors, such as relative growth in real incomes, price differences between countries, and international political conditions. Over the past few decades, in many Western countries, domestic holidays were largely replaced by outbound holidays, due to the rise in living standards and discretionary incomes, while developing countries have seen sharp increases in domestic tourism (UNWTO, 1995: 34).

In addition to outbound and inbound tourist flows, another way to measure tourism is through tourism expenditures and receipts. Tourism expenditure refers to the amount paid for the acquisition of consumption goods and services, as well as valuables, for own use or to give away, for and during tourism trips. It includes expenditures by visitors themselves, as well as expenses that are paid for or reimbursed by others. Tourist expenditure is an important measure of international tourism demand.

China continues to lead global outbound travel in terms of expenditure. Tourism expenditure from the United States, the world's second largest source market, increased by US$ 13 billion compared to 2016 (+9%), the largest increase in absolute terms among the top tourism spenders. The Russian Federation showed a sharp increase of 30% after a few years of decline. All other source markets among the top ten recorded increases, with the Republic of Korea, Italy, and Canada. However, a recent change in accounting for tourism expenditures.

For inbound travel-related financial flows, when assessing total exports at global level, international tourism ranks third after chemicals and fuels and ahead of automotive products. Also, in many developing countries, tourism is the top export category. International tourism receipts in destination countries increased by 4.9% in real terms (UNWTO, 2017), mainly due to the outbound demand from both traditional and emerging markets, drove growth in global receipts, coupling the positive trend recorded globally in international tourist arrivals.

By region, the Middle East is the first one for the growth rate in receipts, also because of the recovery of some destinations after weaker results in 2016, when flows the security situation. Tourism receipts' growth was significant also in South and South-East Asia, as well as in Southern Mediterranean Europe and North Africa.

Forms and products

Since the turn of the twenty-first century, tourism as an industry has achieved a higher profile in the public consciousness especially in advanced economies than ever before. Momentary setbacks—or *wildcards*

(Cooper and Hall, 2008: 55)—due to international conflicts, economic recession, and outbreaks of contagious disease have all proven transitory with respect to tourism growth at the global scale, although their destination, community, and firm effects remain significant. Regional and local changes in consumer confidence and travel behavior and corresponding shifts in travel patterns, such as a reported growth in "staycations" and more local travel, have, in the main, been short term as economic conditions improve in generating regions (Hall, 2010a). Existing data and forecasts suggest a clear increase in the number of travelers in the coming decades as well as a significant overall growth in the tourism sector worldwide. While the information presented here has focused on global travel trends and international tourist flows, it is important to note that domestic tourism is also expected to expand continuously, opening up more destinations and source markets in the future. The data also underscore how the rapid expansion of the sector is increasingly being driven by growth of the tourism markets in emerging economies, as well as an increase in the number of first-time travelers.

Statistics on worldwide tourism arrivals are dominated by a high proportion of intra-regional and domestic travel. The first perspective relates to the evolution of international tourism worldwide, as it is faced with a growing amount of new destinations in emerging regions, the impact of globalization and of the new technologies as well as the increased travel facilities at a lower cost.

UNWTO estimated in its study "Tourism 2020 Vision," published in 2000 that, while in the 1990s, the market share of Europe's inbound tourism represented 60%; due to the ever-increasing levels of destination competition outside the region, this percentage is expected to decrease to 46% by 2020. The analysis shows that while Europe will remain the world's largest tourist receiving region by some considerable margin, it is losing its market share. The reason is that Europe continues to grow but at a slower pace compared to other regions: for the period 1995–2020, Europe's growth rate is foreseen to be of 3%, while other regions such as East Asia and the Pacific or South Asia are expected to grow during this period by 6.5% and 6.2%, respectively.

Travel is organized individually: rather than going for the organized trips, tourists ever more prefer the *do it yourself* through Internet, low-cost airlines, and multi-purpose web-based platforms (such as Kayak, Skyscan, etc.). For transportation, consumers prefer to travel by car, coach, or train, instead of using planes. With regard to accommodation, apartments, country houses, and the like are used by an increasing number of tourists, instead of hotels.

The reasons people desire to travel are multiple and often combined. In 2017, more than half of international tourist arrivals (53% or 632 million) were motivated by holidays, recreation, and leisure-related travel. In the same year, business and professional travel accounted for

14% of all international tourist arrivals, and another 27% traveled for other reasons such as visiting friends and relatives (VFR), religious reasons, and health treatments. The purpose of travel for the remaining 6% of arrivals was not specified. According to UNWTO forecasts, trends will remain largely stable into 2030, when it is projected that leisure, recreation, and holidays will represent 54%; business and professional travel 15%; and VFR, health, religion, and other purposes 31% of all international arrivals.

In the area of leisure travel, a significant and growing number of people, especially those who travel frequently, now approach tourism with different expectations. Rather than simply going on sightseeing tours and relaxing at pool side, these tourists search for more meaningful or intense experiences. For and increasing number of tourists, a holiday has become an investment rather than a simple form of consumption (Brondoni, 2016: 18). Part of the reason for these newer expectations of travel lies in the development of the tourism industry itself. As tourism has grown and matured, it has become increasingly sophisticated and creative in the range of products and services it offers, including destinations. Tourism suppliers are constantly innovating ways to differentiate themselves from other suppliers and stand out in the market. This innovation is part of the natural process of product development, where the accumulation of knowledge and experience enables suppliers to modify and improve their products. This has direct impact on the proliferation of multi-faceted forms of tourist products within the same destination. As defined by UNWTO, a *Tourism Product* is a combination of tangible and intangible elements, such as natural, cultural, and man-made resources, attractions, facilities, services, and activities around a specific center of interest which represents the core of the destination marketing mix and creates an overall visitor experience, including emotional aspects for the potential customers. A tourism product is priced and sold through distribution channels and it has a life-cycle. The changing and multifaceted nature of tourism products which is shaping contemporary tourism is

Differentiation of vacation types, the competitive proliferation of new destinations, the creation of demand bubbles in traveler preferences, and the growth of softer forms of tourism (B&B, rent-a-house, sharing accommodation, etc.) overall constitute new dimensions that stress the quality of the tourist experience.

Forecasts of international tourist arrivals predict an average of 3.3% increase until 2030. In absolute numbers, international tourist arrivals are expected to increase by almost 43 million a year on average between 2010 and 2030 compared with an increase of 28 million a year during the period from 1995 to 2010. At this rate, international tourist arrivals worldwide are expected to reach 1.5 billion by 2020 and 1.8 billion by the year 2030 UNWTO.

From a regional perspective, Asia and the Pacific is expected to witness the strongest growth in tourist arrivals, with a prospected increase by 331 million over the 2010–2030 period (expected) to reach 535 million in 2030 with a growth of 4.9% per year. Tourist arrivals are also expected to double in the Middle East and Africa (from 50 million to 134 million) in the period from 2010 to 2030. In contrast, projections suggest that growth in Europe (from 475 million to 744 million) and the Americas (from 150 million to 248 million) will be slower compared with the projections for other regions.

Moreover, emerging economy destinations are expected to experience nearly twice as much growth in international tourist arrivals (+4.4% a year) as advanced economy destinations (+2.2% a year), exceeding the total number of arrivals in advanced economies before 2020. As a result, it is expected that in 2030, 57% of international arrivals will be in emerging economy destinations (compared to 30% in 1980), and the remaining 43% will be in advanced economy destinations (vs. 70% in 1980).

Conclusions

Globalization constitutes a number of processes and challenges for tourism. First, tourism flows are directing to new destinations, reflecting a shift in the traditional divides between the Global North and South, and the Global East and West (Hall et al., 2014). However, while there is no doubt of the growing scale of domestic and international tourism centered on countries such as South Korea and China, the globalization of tourism remains highly uneven. The predominant trend is toward macro-regionalization: most of the principal destinations of the expanding outbound Chinese tourism market are to be found in Asia, while most of the leading destinations for European tourists are other European countries. Additionally, the most significant spatial reordering has so far been confined to East and Southeast Asia, and there are still large parts of the world's population, particularly in sub-Saharan Africa, who do not participate in any form of activity as tourists, let alone international tourists (Williams et al., 2014).

References

Brondoni, S.M. (2016). Global Tourism Management, Mass, Experience and Sensations Tourism. *iSymphonya. Emerging Issues in Management* 1, 7–24.

Chadwick, R.A. (1994). Concepts, Definitions and Measures Used in Travel and Tourism Research, in Ritchie, J.R.B. and Goeldner, C.R. (Eds.). *Travel, Tourism and Hospitality Research: A Handbook for Managers and Researchers.* New York: John Wiley, 65–77.

Cooper, C. and Hall, C.M. (2008). *Contemporary Tourism: An International Approach.* Oxford: Butterworth-Heinemann.

Glaesser, D., Kester, J., Paulose, H., Alizadeh, H. and Valentin, B. (2017). Global Travel Patterns: An Overview, *Journal of Travel Medicine*, 24(4), 1–5.

Hall, C.M. (2010). Changing Paradigms and Global Change: From Sustainable to Steady-State Tourism. Tourism Recreation Research, 35(2), 131–143.

Hall, C.M., Williams, A.M. and Lew, A.A. (2014). Conceptualizations, Disciplinarity, Institutions, and Issues, in: Lew, A.A., Hall, C.M. and Williams, A.M. (Eds.), *The Wiley Blackwell Companion to Tourism*, Chichester: John Wiley & Sons Ltd.

Keller, P. (Ed.) (1996). *Globalisation and Tourism*. St. Gallen: AIEST.

McKercher, B. and Lew, A. (2004). Tourist Flows and the Spatial Distribution of Tourists, in Lew, A.A. et al. (Eds.), *A Companion to Tourism*. London: Blackwell Publishing, 36–48.

Smith, S.L.J. (2004). The Measurement of Global Tourism: Old Debates, New Consensus, and Continuing Challenges, in Lew, A.A. et al. (Eds.), *A Companion to Tourism*. Oxford: Blackwell Publishing, 25–35.

UNWTO (1995). Concepts, Definitions, and Classifications for Tourism Statistics. Technical Manual No. 1. Madrid.

UNWTO (2011). *Tourism Towards 2030/Global Overview*. Madrid: World Tourism Organization.

UNWTO (2017). *Tourism Highlights*, 2017 Edition, Madrid.

UNWTO (2018). *Tourism Highlights: 2018 Edition*. Madrid: World Tourism Organization.

World Travel and Tourism Council (2017). *Benchmark Report 2017*. World Summary.

Urry, J. (2002). *The Tourist Gaze*, 2nd edn. London: Sage Publications.

Wahab, S. and Cooper, C. (Eds.) (2001). *Tourism and Globalisation*. London: Routledge.

Williams, A., Hall, C. M., & Lew, A. (2014). Theoretical and Methodological Challenges for Tourism. Just Out of Sight or Just Within our Reach?, in: Lew, A.A., Hall C.M. and Williams, A.M. (2014). *The Wiley Blackwell Companion to Tourism*. Chichester: John Wiley & Sons, 625–634.

Williams, A.V. and Zelinsky, W. (1970). On Some Patterns in International Tourist Flows. *Economic Geography* 46(4), 549–567.

Part II
The tourist experience

3 Visitor's experience and other drivers of length of stay at a destination

Marco Alderighi, Giovanni Paolo Crespi, and Eleonora Lorenzini

Learning outcomes

At the end of this chapter, readers should be able to:

1 Understand the main issues concerning tourist behavior.
2 Identify and classify the key drivers of length of stay.
3 Acquire the ability to apply a survival analysis model.
4 Explain the meaning of the estimated coefficients from a survival analysis model.
5 Explore a case study of summer holidays in Aosta Valley.

Introduction

We investigate the main attributes affecting tourists' length of stay at a destination. Based on the most recent literature on tourist behavior, we group the main drivers into (1) tourist's socio-demographic profile (age, gender, education, composition of the party, and income), (2) holiday frame (motivation, planning, accommodation, distance, and mean of transport), and tourist's experience of the place (on site activities and satisfaction). We show how to empirically measure the effect of key drivers through survival analysis and we apply this methodology using data coming from a customer satisfaction survey. Understanding the key drivers that influence the duration of tourists' stay is paramount for public bodies to define strategies in terms of (1) the type of tourism product they want to promote and offer, (2) the use of tourist facilities, and (3) the type of tourism demand they aim at attracting.

Research background

The study of tourist behavior covers different topics such as holiday budget allocation, choice of period of the year, place, accommodation, activities to be performed, as well as length of stay. Although it has been unanimously recognized that each of these aspects is related to the other, current literature has also clarified that the main drivers of the tourist behavior may have different effects on each of the above issues. A few examples clarify the point. The distance between the residence of a tourist and a possible destination has a negative impact on the likelihood to visit the destination but in many cases plays a positive role on the length of stay. Larger income usually implies larger resources allocated to holidays (holidays are normal goods). Therefore, it usually induces tourists to visit farther places and to stay in superior accommodations. However, richer people may spend a shorter period in a given destination than people having lower income.

In light of these findings, there are two ways to tackle the problem. The first one is to assume that tourists are involved in sequential decisions. For example, first s/he chooses whether to go on holidays or not. Second, s/he chooses how much time to spend. Third, based on its budget allocation, s/he chooses the best destination among feasible ones. Within this framework, a tourist has to choose the mean of transport, the activities to be performed, thus defining per day's cost, and, for given holiday budget, the length of the stay. A major concern involving this modeling choice is that the results of the analysis are strongly affected by the sequence of decisions. Why we should expect that people's stay depends on a budget choice and not the opposite? It is also reasonable, for instance, that depending on the appeal of a place, tourists can choose a shorter or a longer stay, that is, allocating a smaller or a larger amount of budget to that holiday.

The second way to tackle the problem is to assume tourists choose all the above-mentioned aspects simultaneously. In this case, since a comprehensive model is too complex to be developed and measured, researchers have often preferred to circumscribe their research object to one aspect of the consumer behavior and to estimate a reduced form of the general model. In this case, the interpretation of the impact of each driver on, say, the length of the stay must be carefully interpreted, keeping into account that it is jointly determined with all other choices.

In what follows, we focus only on one aspect of tourist behavior: the length of stay. In terms of the first view, the interpretation is that tourists have already chosen the other attributes of the stay and we show as this choice affects the decision on the length of stay. In terms of the second view, we discuss a reduced form of the decision process where tourists consider all the other aspects jointly. In the next sub-section, we classify the main drivers of the length of the stay into three groups: (1) tourist socio-demographic profile (age, gender, education, composition of the party, and income), (2) holiday frame (motivation, planning, accommodation, distance, mean of transport), and (3) tourist experience of the place (on site activities and satisfaction).

Although the first two sets of variables are extensively investigated in previous papers (for a review, see Gokovali et al., 2007; Hennessey et al., 2008), the last group of variables has received less attention in literature and constitutes the most original part of this work.

Each sub-section is organized in two parts. The first part is theoretical and offers a review of the underlying relations between the length of stay and its main drivers. The second part is an application to the model of the survival analysis (the methodology presented in the previous section of this chapter). Before concluding, it is worth mentioning that empirical results presented across studies show high degree of homogeneity. Our empirical findings, obtained from a customer satisfaction survey hold in Aosta Valley in summer 2008, are an additional confirmation of main-stream theory of length of stay.

Tourist's socio-demographic profile

A first set of drivers affecting the length of stay is provided by visitors' attributes. Among the most relevant are age, gender, education, compo-sition of the party, and income. As far as these socio-demographic char-acteristics are concerned, we have the following expectations concerning their impact.

Age

There are three main reasons why length of stay is related to age. The first one is that tourists who are employed are more likely to have shorter spells because of their job schedule, while students and retired people are more flexible to schedule longer spells (Alegre & Pou, 2007). The second one is that tourists' willingness to visit various destinations is often decreasing with age; consequently, older people are more likely to have longer stays. Third, younger people usually have lower holiday budgets to spend. This is particularly true when considering people that have been working only a few years. The combination of these factors suggests that it is likely that age has a non-linear effect on the length of stay. Roughly speaking, we can expect length of stay to decrease up to some age class and then to increase again.

Gender

We have not an a-priori indication concerning the effect of gender from the literature. Thus, we are not excluding that it could play a role, but we have not a theory to suggest what it can be. The reason why this driver has not received any attention is that often the composition of the party is mixed (simultaneous presence of males and females). In this case, the length of the stay as well as many other attributes of the holi-day are likely to be arranged together. Thus, this driver may have some effects, especially in those cases in which people travel alone; there is only one person who has decided about the holiday; or, finally, in the case in which the composition of the party includes only one gender.

This critique only partially applies to the variable age, since couples or groups of friends usually tend to be the same age.

Income and education

We discuss these two variables together since they are strongly and positively correlated.[1] Before proceeding in the analysis, it is worth noting that the way in which these two variables tend to affect the length of stay is partially different. Nevertheless, both yields to very similar conclusions in term of travel behavior and we expect to observe a shorter stay in the presence of rich and highly educated people. We start to explain the causal link between income and length of stay. Among different explanations, the first one is related to the nature of holidays as a good. Since they are assumed to be normal goods (i.e. there is positive demand-income elasticity), the number of days spent on holidays usually increases with income. However, income also positively affects the decision of going on holidays and the choice of the number of trips (number of destinations consumers wish to visit). Consequently, the duration of a single stay may also reduce. In addition to this, we expect working age tourists to have mostly a stable spell of holidays, because of job constrains, no matter the income; while older (retired) tourists might decrease the length of stay on specific location, the richer they are, in order to increase the number of locations visited per holiday.

A second explanation comes from the fact that larger income induces people to increase the quality more than the quantity. If the second effect dominates the first one, tourists having larger income are more likely to stay in a destination for a shorter period. Third, larger income means a higher value of time and therefore interest for new experiences. Also this factor reinforces the interest of richer people in visiting different places and having a shorter stay (Martínez-Garcia & Raya, 2008). Finally, if we assume that people love varieties, that is, they prefer to visit many places, since travel costs have a large incidence for low income tourists, we expect that richer people tend to have a larger number of trips and therefore a lower length of stay at each location.

Education is a factor often accounted for to study the demand of cultural goods. In Alderighi and Lorenzini (2012), it has been emphasized that cultural attractions, and more generally new experiences, are characterized by increasing return of satisfaction. Thus, through the accumulation of cultural capital, people tend to be addicted, and they are more likely to show a larger demand for this kind of recreational activities. Since more educated persons are usually more prone to be involved in such activities, they are also more likely to demand more new experiences. Therefore, we expect more educated people to move more than others, in search of a broader offer and a variety of cultural attractions and new experiences, and hence to shorten the spell spent in a given location. In addition to this, the link between education and length of stay is often mediated by other factors. As already mentioned, a negative relation between education and length of stay may be a consequence of the fact that it is positively related to income. Another way in which education affects the length of stay is what the tourists look for her/his holidays. Usually more educated people are much more interested in cultural activities or to visit a place for prestige and therefore they tend to stay less (a more detailed explanation will follow in the next paragraphs).

Composition of the party

Composition of the party has a large impact on the length of the stay. Literature on the field seems to agree that tourists having babies or small children are more likely to stay a longer time, because each trip involves a more complex organization and difficulties. Similar explanation applies to parties traveling with grand-parents or seniors (Fleischer & Pizam, 2002). On the contrary, people traveling alone can freely organize their holidays and are expected to spend shorter spells in a given place. Greater per day's costs faced by large parties, especially families, are also adduced as a motivation for a negative correlation between party size and length of stay (Alegre & Pou, 2007). However, the apparent puzzle can be solved by noting that the two factors affect different aspects of tourist behavior. The former usually influences the duration of the stay so that a larger family tend to stay more at a destination, while the latter usually influences the decision to go on holidays.

Holiday frame

A second set of drivers that affect the length of stay is provided by holiday attributes. The most relevant ones are motivation, how the holiday has been organized (booking and accommodation), distance of the residence, and the mean of transport.

Holiday motivation

Not all tourists share the same motivation and preferences. Following McIntosh and Goeldner (1995), they can be classified in different groups such as physical (relaxation and sport), cultural (visiting historical places, tasting local cooking, and meeting new cultures), interpersonal (meeting friends and new people), and prestige. The effect of tourist motivation on the length of stay has received little attention in literature, with some notable exceptions focusing on specific issues such as the behavior of golf players (Hennessey et al., 2008), or that of price sensitive travelers (Martínez-Garcia & Raya, 2008). With regard to the broad categories mentioned above, it is likely that people looking for physical entertainment and interpersonal tend to spend much more time in a place, while those aiming to do new experiences, as in the cultural tourism, are typically moved by prestige and will program shorter spells. As far as the first factors are concerned, the utility a sport or spa-oriented tourist gains from his/her stay depends on activities that can be repeated several times during the sojourn. On the contrary, cultural activities or prestige, as we have mentioned before, require new experiences to gain or to tell and therefore force tourists to visit different destinations. Roughly speaking, once an exhibition has been visited, the location exhausts its utility.

Booking

Different booking choices have a non-linear impact on the length of stay and tend to be affected by other drivers in a very complex way.[2] Indeed, booking happens at the end of a decisional process involving the choice of the destination, the mean of transport, and the expected expenditure. Hence, the level of intermediation of specific tourism destination strongly affects the final decision. Usually, the interpretation is not unique. On one hand, people buying a package should tend to spend a shorter period of time with respect to others since their per day's cost of stay is on average higher due to intermediary costs. On the other hand, tourists planning by themselves may be induced to a shorter visit because of larger uncertainty about the stay. In addition to this, as far as the booking of package holidays is concerned, it has been pointed out that in some cases the distribution of the stay may be multi-modal, with all time length condensed around 1-week or 2-week stay (Alegre et al., 2011).

Accommodation

The length of stay at a destination is thus a negative function of the cost per day's stay. To better understand the role of cost per day's stay, it is worth mentioning the model proposed by Dubin and McFadden (1984) on the joint consumer consumption of goods and its application to tourism sector by Alegre and Pou (2007). The length of the stay depends on the flow of activities that tourists can perform during their holidays. Thus, once a tourist chooses a given destination, a type of accommodation and activities, s/he has determined her/his per day's cost of stay. Finally, budget constraints, the maximum time available for holiday purposes, and cost per day's stay jointly determine the length of stay. Therefore, people who stay in villas and apartments tend to have a longer stay than those accommodated at hotels, and likewise, people staying in hotels with a larger number of stars usually stay less than those staying in lesser hotels.

Place of residence of travelers

The origin of the traveler has a significant impact on the length of the stay (Alegre & Pou, 2007; Gokovaly et al., 2007; Martínez-Garcia & Raya, 2008). Tourists living in different countries have diverse culture, peculiar habits, and differential exposure to promotional campaigns. In addition to these idiosyncratic factors, it is important to identify a driver which is not specific to a single origin-destination relation: the distance. People living closer to the tourism destination are more likely to organize shorter visits since the travel cost is lower. Thus, we expect a positive relation between distance and number of days spent in the tourism destination (Silberman, 1985).

Moreover, people sometimes want to visit more than a tourism destination, that is, they want to tour (Santos et al., 2015). This happens especially in the summer period, where weather conditions facilitate to move from one place to another. People coming from farther destinations are more likely to visit a location as part of a tour, since they are willing to visit most important attractions in the surrounding areas, and because the possibility to revisit the broad region, where the location is included, is less likely to occur. Thus, with this respect, the larger the distance, the shorter is the time spent at a specific destination.

Finally, it is also worth mentioning that the size of the city of residence could also affect the decision to stay on holiday (and, in case, the length of stay) since cities with high density induce people to escape from the town (Eymann & Ronning, 1997).

Mean of transport. The mean of transport is another driver of the length of stay. People using a private mean of transport enjoy greater freedom of movement and, therefore, are more likely to visit more than one destination during the same holiday. Hence, the spell at a single destination is likely to be shorter when using private transportation.

Tourist's experience of the place

A third set of drivers affecting the length of stay is given by the tourists' experience and satisfaction at the destination.

Customer satisfaction

This driver has received less attention from tourism literature on the length of stay so that we ground our theoretical considerations on another piece of literature in a closely related field. Li et al. (2015) have recently developed a conceptual framework that accounts for tourist decision to visit a place. They identify three different steps to be fulfilled to take a decision. At the end of each step, a tourist may decide to go to the next step or to stop; the completion of the third step is thus the tourist's decision to visit the place.

In the first step (tourism awareness), prospective tourists receive/collect information and news about a destination. In the second step (tourism affection), the prospect tourist invests time and emotions to build a personal image about its stay at the destination. In the last step (choice), tourist chooses whether to visit the destination or not. This conceptual framework poses much emphasis on the role played by tourism affection and favorable image as a key step to induce tourists to visit the destination. Indeed, a positive image of the destination affects the decision to visit the place and determine tourist behavior including tourism expenditure and the decision to visit and to re-visit a destination (Cárdenas-García et al., 2016). Moreover, a favorable image of the destination has a positive effect on satisfaction (Chi & Qu, 2008) and increase the probability of staying longer at the destination (Gokovali et al., 2007; De Menezes et al., 2008).[3]

On-site activities

The possibility to undertake different activities is the last driver of the stay, we are taking into consideration. In general, we expect a positive relation between the undertaking activities and the duration of the stay (Davies & Mangan, 1992). Indeed tourists that are planning to perform a larger number of activities tend to stay more. However, activities are related to the destination image as well as to the motivation of the stay. With regard to the last attribute, we have already noticed that tourists having cultural interests tend to stay shorter so that the specific impact of undertaking cultural activities on the length of stay may be negative or insignificant. On the contrary, other activities, such as sports, may positively affect the length of the stay (Hennessey et al., 2008).

Survival analysis techniques

How much time a tourist will spend at a certain location? How does this change according to the experience at the location? How does the length of stay vary according to the age of the tourist or the distance from home? How transportation options affect the length of stay? These topics can greatly affect the management of tourist facilities. However, to answer those questions, we need to build an empirical model where the regress is a duration variable: namely, the length of stay.

This kind of variable is continuous, positive, and refers to a concatenated sequence of decisions, making unsatisfactory the application of the standard linear regression model.

Since the seminal papers by Kiefer and Neumann (1979), Narendranathan and Nickell (1985), and Kiefer (1988), the economic literature on survival analysis has become a well-established tool to deal with problems involving duration data (such as studies on unemployment duration, time between trades in financial markets, occupational mobility). More recently, the same techniques have been successfully proposed to study the determinants of length of stay in tourism management (Gokovali et al., 2007).

Roughly speaking, to estimate the spell at the location means to study the unconditional probability of an event to take place at time t (say to leave the location at time t). Standard regression analysis requires to specify the probability function $f(t) = \Pr\{\text{leave at day } t\}$. However, this approach requires considering simultaneously different possibilities of leaving. More trivially, we can think of the probability of extracting the first red ballot from a box equally filled with black and red ballots after t trials without replacement. To do so, we need to consider all the possible failures before t-th drawing.

Alternatively, survival analysis suggests focusing on conditional probability $\lambda(t) = \Pr\{\text{leave at day } t \mid \text{stay lasted } t-1 \text{ days}\}$ (i.e. the probability of leaving the location at day t, given the vacation has already lasted $t-1$ days). Likewise, in our ballot game, we have the conditional probability of drawing a red ball, given $t-1$ black balls have already been drawn. Still, we need the probability of drawing the first red ball at t-th drawing, but now, we can consider a sequence of conditional probabilities $\lambda(t) = \Pr\{j\text{th ballot red} \mid \text{ballots } 1...j-1 \text{ black}\}$ as $j = 1,...,t$. Each conditional probability has the advantage to focus on just one ballot.

The conditional probability of leaving the location at day t, given the stay has already lasted t days, $\lambda(t)$ is known as hazard function. From a statistical point of view, the two approaches are actually equivalent: given $f(t)$, $\lambda(t)$ can be computed and vice versa, but from an economic point of view, that is from the possible interpretation of the model, to study hazard functions allows for a broader class of behavioral interpretations that can hardly be modeled through a given probability distribution. Indeed, different hazard distributions have pros and cons: if we choose a normal or log normal probability distribution, then the hazard function will be very complex, while if we choose a Poisson distribution, then the hazard function will be too simple and with an unattractive features, e.g. it is memoryless. Nevertheless, the statistical equivalence allows us to apply known econometric techniques (e.g. partial likelihood) to estimate the parameters without caring about the exact distribution. More formally, let T be the continuous random variable, with values in an interval $[0, t^*]$, that represents the spell of the vacation. We denote the distribution function by $F(t) = \Pr(T < t)$.

The corresponding density function is

$$f(t) = \frac{dF(t)}{dt}$$

Both F and f identify a specific distribution. As we want to study the duration of stay, we are more interested in the survival function $S(t) = 1 - F(t) = \Pr(T \geq t)$ that represents the probability the spell is longer or equal t time units.

Since the random variable is continuous, in a survival analysis framework we are interested in the probability that the spell ends h time units after t, for h very small. The hazard function can be defined as

$$\lambda(t) = \lim_{h \to 0^+} \frac{\Pr\left(t \leq T \langle t + h | T \geq t\right)}{h} = \frac{f(t)}{S(t)}. \tag{1}$$

Equation (1) represents a continuous version of the argument presented with discrete number of days. The hazard function measures the probability that the spell ends shortly after t. In the general framework, this is a function of the duration t itself. Therefore, if $\lambda'(t) > 0$, we have a positive duration dependence, that is, the probability the spell ends will increase with the length of the spell. On the contrary, $\lambda'(t) > 0$ denotes a negative duration dependence as the more a tourist stays at some location, the longer he/she would stay. Finally, if $\lambda'(t) > 0$, that is the hazard function is constant, then the probability to end shortly after t the spell is not affected by the overall duration.

Constant hazard functions are related to exponential distribution with parameter $k > 0$: $F(t) = 1 - e^{-kt}$. Therefore, we also have $f(t) = ke^{-kt}$ and $S(t) = e^{-kt}$. By direct calculation, we obtain $\lambda(t) = k$ that provides a memoryless process. Some drawbacks arise with such an assumption. Mostly mean and variance of the distribution cannot be adjusted separately.

Alternatively, another common specification for the distribution of T in survival analysis is the Weibull distribution, depending on two parameters, $k > 0$ and $\alpha > 0$, that lead to a family of hazard functions of the form: $\lambda(t) = k\alpha t^{\alpha-1}$.

Depending on the value of α, we can recognize whether we have a positive ($\alpha > 1$) or negative ($0 < \alpha < 1$) duration dependence in our model. We also remark that the exponential distribution is a special case of Weibull one, with $\alpha = 1$. Other choices of distribution can be used in order to represent non-monotonic hazard functions, but a complete overview is above the topic of this chapter. In order to define the model to be tested by our data, we need a more general formulation of the (non-negative) hazard function:

$$\lambda(t) = \exp\left\{g(t, x_1, x_2, \ldots, x_n; \beta)\right\},$$

where $t, x_1, x_2, \ldots, x_n$ are the explanatory variables, while β is a vector of $n + 1$ parameters.

When estimating the model, in ordinary regression models, one would expect, at least at first, that the explanatory variables affect the distribution of the dependent variable by moving its mean around. However, such an interpretation is no longer clear in survival analysis, where two major approaches can be outlined. The Proportional Hazard (PH) specification entails that the regressors affect the hazard function multiplying it by a positive scale factor. Alternatively, in the Accelerated Failure Time (AFT) specification, the regressors rescale the time axis in the model. For our purposes, the PH specification seems more appropriate and, besides, it is now mostly accepted in the tourism management literature on the length of stay (Gokovali et al., 2007; Barros et al., 2010). In PH framework, the regression model can be specified through the hazard function:

$$\lambda(t,x,\beta,\lambda_0) = \lambda_0(t)\exp\{\beta_1 x_1 +,\ldots,\beta_n x_n\},$$

where $\lambda_0(t)$ is the baseline representation of the hazard function, corresponding to $\exp\{\beta_1 x_1 +,\ldots,\beta_n x_n\} = 1$. As a common practice, regressors are measured so that this happens at their mean value, so that $\lambda_0(t)$ can be easily read as the probability of instantaneously ending the spell at time t for the average tourist. Note that also $\lambda_0(t)$ is normally unknown and needs to be estimated, yielding to Cox's PH model. Alternatively, a specific parametric form such as an exponential can be assumed. Since in exponential distribution, the hazard function is constant, the baseline hazard function would be $\lambda_0(t) = k$. Likewise, assuming Weibull's distribution, we have $\lambda_0(t) = k\alpha t^{\alpha-1}$.

Another feature of this model is that it is assumed that explanatory variables define a coefficient that does not depend on the duration and multiply the baseline hazard. The coefficients can be interpreted as the constant proportional effect of the corresponding regressor on the conditional probability of leaving the location at time t. Indeed:

$$\beta_i = \frac{\partial \ln\lambda(t,x,\beta,\lambda_0)}{\partial x_i}.$$

Therefore, the sign of the coefficient defines the direction of the effect of the explanatory variable on the conditional probability of concluding the spell at time t. A positive value of β_i denotes that increasing the value of x_i results in a greater probability of concluding the vacation, while negative values suggest it is more likely to extend the sojourn. Before concluding, it is worth mentioning some other peculiarities of econometric models regressing a duration.

First, sampling data may be an issue. If the survey is conducted along a given period, recording the duration of the spell between two dates, some spells may be truncated, either they started before the beginning of the survey (left-censored) or they will end after (right-censored). Moreover, some of the exogenous variables, the determinants of the length of stay, may change during the vacation spell, a feature that in standard regression analysis is not accounted for. Finally, we need "inherent aging process": see, for example, Gokovali et al. (2007). Using time as dependent variable restricts possible model specification. Since only positive length of stay is possible, a linear regression could easily yield negative fitted values, especially for short-term holidays.

Data

Aosta Valley is a region of 128,230 inhabitants and 3,263.25 km^2 in the Italian Alpine Arc at the border with France and Switzerland. The GDP for 2009 was 4,183.2 million euros, on which tourism services and activities account for about 22%. Aosta Valley is mostly a winter destination, but the rich offer in terms of cultural heritage and open air activities, like excursions, trekking, and sport facilities, attract tourists also in summer season. In 2008, the regional tourism office collected data with a survey to explore the level of satisfaction experienced by tourists visiting Aosta Valley in summer and to identify levers to improve the destination branding for the summer season.[4]

Data were collected at the lodging structures. The survey considered only tourists who have spent one or more nights in local hotels. For each party, one questionnaire was distributed. In case of incomplete answers to the question about length of stay, the questionnaires have been discarded. Of the 3,037 questionnaires initially collected, 2,788 were used in the analysis. Some sparse missing values on the other variables (<1%) are replaced with a randomization procedure. For some analyses, we restrict the sample to only consider tourists that have already visited Aosta Valley in the last 5 years. In this case, the size of the sample is 2,043 observations.

Table 3.1 provides the main statistics of the variables considered in the analysis, which are mainly dummies. An exception is the dependent variable and those concerning different aspects on the on-site satisfaction. To reduce the influence of outliers, we have decided to restrict the regress and in the range 1–40 days.[5] A second set of variables that are not binary is about tourist satisfaction and they refer to the sub-sample of 2,043 observations. They have been built on a 4-point Likert scale, where 0 means strongly unsatisfied and 3 means strongly satisfied. The choice of an even-numbered scale moves on the need to force respondents and excluding the fact that an indifferent option is available.

In Figure 3.1, we present the graph of the survival function for the dependent variable with respect to the whole sample. The survival function describes the fraction of tourists remaining at destination for a certain amount of time (number of days). Before we move to the next section, we should point out that in our analysis there are no problems with data censoring of the time variable.

Table 3.1 Descriptive statistics of the sample

Variable	Mean	Std. dev.	Min	Max
Duration of the stay	8.451937	7.197819	1	40
Male	0.577834	0.493993	0	1
Age				
18–30	0.163199	0.369614	0	1
31–40	0.232783	0.422681	0	1
41–50	0.236729	0.425151	0	1
51–65	0.247848	0.431841	0	1
>65	0.119441	0.324364	0	1
Education				
Primary	0.078192	0.268522	0	1
Secondary	0.140961	0.348044	0	1
College	0.167504	0.373492	0	1
University	0.395624	0.489072	0	1
Master	0.119082	0.323943	0	1
PhD	0.098637	0.298228	0	1
Composition of the party				
Couple w/o others	0.400287	0.490044	0	1
Children	0.068508	0.252661	0	1
Adolescent	0.187231	0.390167	0	1
Relatives	0.047346	0.212416	0	1
Alone	0.188307	0.391027	0	1
Friends	0.015782	0.124653	0	1
Motivation				
Rest and relaxation	0.392755	0.488451	0	1
Sport	0.098996	0.29871	0	1
Searching for new cites	0.206958	0.405198	0	1
Stay with the family	0.079627	0.270763	0	1
Culture	0.034075	0.181453	0	1
Multiple interests	0.113702	0.317505	0	1
Other motivations	0.073888	0.261636	0	1
Booking				
By myself	0.753587	0.430999	0	1
On the site	0.183644	0.387263	0	1
Package holiday	0.062769	0.242591	0	1
Number of stars				
1 star	0.035868	0.185994	0	1
2 stars	0.300574	0.45859	0	1
3 stars	0.464491	0.498827	0	1
4 stars	0.199067	0.399371	0	1

(Continued)

Variable	Mean	Std. dev.	Min	Max
Place of residence				
Piedmont	0.141679	0.348783	0	1
Lombardy	0.184362	0.387848	0	1
Liguria	0.107604	0.309935	0	1
Lazio	0.055595	0.22918	0	1
Toscana	0.063128	0.243236	0	1
Emilia-Romagna	0.053085	0.224243	0	1
Rest of Italy	0.168221	0.37413	0	1
France	0.087159	0.282119	0	1
UK	0.023673	0.152055	0	1
Belgium	0.016858	0.128762	0	1
Spain	0.016499	0.127408	0	1
The Netherlands	0.015782	0.124653	0	1
Germany	0.02439	0.154285	0	1
Switzerland	0.019727	0.139087	0	1
Rest of Europe	0.009684	0.097949	0	1
US - Canada	0.006456	0.080105	0	1
Rest of the world	0.006098	0.077862	0	1
Mean of transport				
Car/Bike	0.898494	0.302052	0	1
Train	0.025825	0.158641	0	1
Coach	0.037303	0.189537	0	1
Airplane	0.03264	0.177724	0	1
Other	0.005739	0.075551	0	1
Activities on the site				
Nature	0.915352	0.278408	0	1
Sport	0.501435	0.500088	0	1
Culture	0.829986	0.375713	0	1
Entertainment	0.497131	0.500082	0	1
Gastronomic tour	0.78264	0.412524	0	1
Satisfaction on the site				
Nature	0.783925	0.454485	0	3
Sport	0.384087	0.491703	0	2
Culture	0.612207	0.468673	0	3
Entertainment	0.335994	0.428138	0	3
Gastronomic tour	0.649839	0.500073	0	2

Results

Table 3.2 summarizes the main results of the survey analysis. To correctly interpret the estimates, note that a negative sign means, all things equal, a longer stay. Because all the regressors are coded as dummy variables, the estimated coefficients must be interpreted as the impact of a shift from the reference category to a given category. Model 1 presents the estimated results considering the main socio-demographic variables.

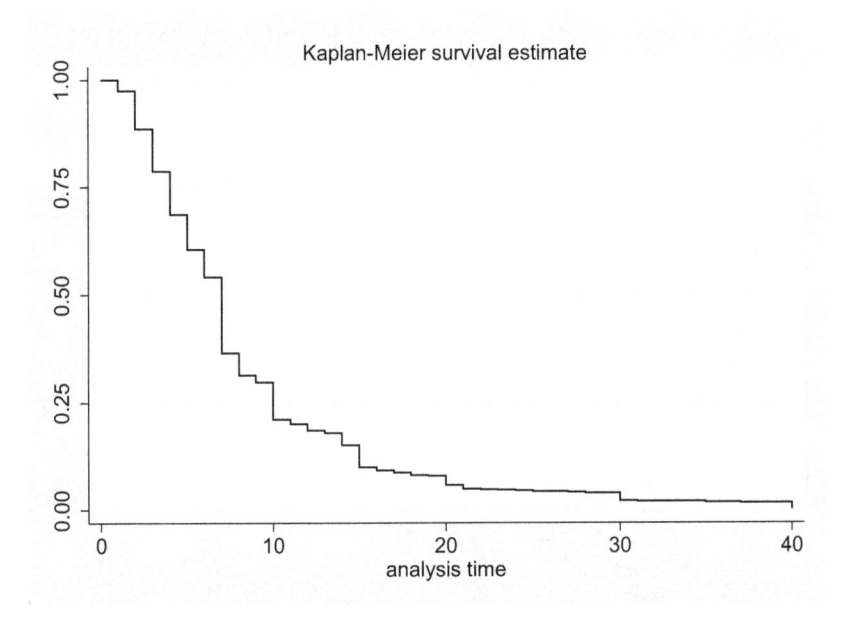

Figure 3.1 Kaplan-Meier survival curve.

Models 2–4 include some extension. In order to study the role of age on the duration of the stay, we choose people belonging to the class 31–40 as a reference category. It means that the coefficients associated to the other classes measure the positive or negative differential with respect to this category. Consistently with the theoretical analysis, we find a positive relation between age and the time spent at a destination. The coefficients of the classes 41–50, 51–65 and >65 have a negative sign (longer stay). Moreover, we find that tourists of class 18–30 show a negative sign confirming that students stay a longer period than the reference group. Incidentally, it is worth noting that in Models 2–4, where we are considering a richer specification, the sign of the coefficient remains negative, but it is smaller in magnitude and not significant at 10% level.

The coefficients referring to educational levels draw a trend moving from primary and secondary experience to higher educational levels, which confirm that more educated people tend to stay less on a single vacation. Finally, we find that larger parties tend to stay longer at a destination.

The results of the empirical analysis about the set of variables grouped as Holiday frame are displayed in columns 2–4 of Table 3.2. The estimates largely confirm the theoretical predictions described. When tourists are motivated by cultural aspects as well as by searching for new attractions, they are likely to spend a shorter period. There is not

Table 3.2 Estimates

Variables	Model 1		Model 2		Model 3		Model 4	
	Coeff.	Std. dev.	Coeff.	Std. dev.	Coeff.	Std. dev.	Coeff.	Std. dev.
Male	0.079**	(0.039)	0.087**	(0.040)	0.139***	(0.047)	0.139***	(0.047)
Age								
18–30	−0.125*	(0.064)	−0.058	(0.066)	−0.094	(0.080)	−0.055	(0.079)
31–40	Reference category							
41–50	−0.112**	(0.056)	−0.155***	(0.057)	−0.145**	(0.069)	−0.133*	(0.069)
51–65	−0.325***	(0.057)	−0.347***	(0.058)	−0.377***	(0.069)	−0.373***	(0.069)
>65	−0.853***	(0.072)	−0.874***	(0.074)	−0.976***	(0.087)	−0.943***	(0.086)
Education								
Primary	Reference category							
Secondary	0.001	(0.086)	−0.005	(0.087)	0.044	(0.100)	0.027	(0.100)
College	0.104	(0.076)	0.108	(0.077)	0.176**	(0.088)	0.191**	(0.089)
University	0.108	(0.084)	0.022	(0.085)	0.019	(0.099)	0.041	(0.099)
Master	0.200**	(0.089)	0.078	(0.091)	0.156	(0.108)	0.141	(0.108)
PhD	0.429***	(0.093)	0.189*	(0.097)	0.199*	(0.116)	0.222*	(0.116)
Composition of the party								
Couple w/o others	Reference category							
Children	−0.219***	(0.051)	−0.149***	(0.053)	−0.161**	(0.063)	−0.148**	(0.062)
Adolescent	−0.175**	(0.076)	−0.090	(0.078)	−0.122	(0.095)	−0.123	(0.095)
Relatives	−0.219***	(0.050)	−0.176***	(0.052)	−0.209***	(0.060)	−0.215***	(0.060)
Alone	−0.207**	(0.092)	−0.187**	(0.095)	−0.148	(0.110)	−0.164	(0.110)
Friends	0.035	(0.050)	0.022	(0.052)	0.075	(0.062)	0.071	(0.062)
Colleagues	−0.030	(0.154)	−0.133	(0.160)	0.089	(0.180)	0.141	(0.179)
Motivation								
Rest and relaxation	Reference category							
Sport			−0.118	(0.073)	−0.110	(0.088)	−0.040	(0.088)

Searching for new cites		0.182***	(0.053)	0.239***	(0.067)	0.216***	(0.066)
Stay with the family		0.053	(0.078)	0.015	(0.089)	0.050	(0.089)
Culture		0.443***	(0.110)	0.510***	(0.146)	0.535***	(0.147)
Multiple interests		−0.092	(0.067)	−0.043	(0.079)	−0.082	(0.079)
Other motivations		0.060	(0.079)	0.016	(0.093)	0.043	(0.092)
Booking						
By myself	Reference category					
On the site		−0.061	(0.053)	−0.135**	(0.061)	−0.128**	(0.061)
Package holiday		0.036	(0.088)	0.078	(0.116)	0.074	(0.117)
Number of stars						
1 star	Reference category					
2 stars		0.144	(0.108)	0.280**	(0.126)	0.237*	(0.125)
3 stars		0.495***	(0.107)	0.606***	(0.126)	0.596***	(0.125)
4 stars		0.825***	(0.113)	0.936***	(0.132)	0.943***	(0.131)
Place of residence						
Piedmont	Reference category					
Lombardy		−0.057	(0.068)	−0.074	(0.073)	−0.074	(0.073)
Liguria		0.049	(0.078)	0.066	(0.084)	0.087	(0.084)
Lazio		−0.014	(0.098)	−0.021	(0.117)	−0.051	(0.117)
Toscana		0.080	(0.095)	0.128	(0.115)	0.097	(0.115)
Emilia-Romagna		0.019	(0.098)	−0.033	(0.113)	−0.036	(0.113)
Rest of Italy		−0.094	(0.073)	−0.084	(0.085)	−0.073	(0.085)
France		0.451***	(0.089)	0.439***	(0.103)	0.440***	(0.102)
UK		0.415***	(0.139)	0.557***	(0.172)	0.597***	(0.173)
Belgium		0.112	(0.160)	0.129	(0.200)	0.140	(0.200)
Spain		0.411**	(0.162)	0.381*	(0.220)	0.381*	(0.221)
The Netherlands		0.165	(0.168)	−0.089	(0.243)	−0.025	(0.242)

(Continued)

Variables	Model 1		Model 2		Model 3		Model 4	
	Coeff.	Std. dev.	Coeff.	Std. dev.	Coeff.	Std. dev.	Coeff.	Std. dev.
Germany			0.434***	(0.137)	0.346*	(0.206)	0.299	(0.206)
Switzerland			0.836***	(0.149)	0.940***	(0.170)	0.941***	(0.170)
Rest of Europe			0.679***	(0.207)	0.762***	(0.253)	0.730***	(0.254)
US - Canada			0.347	(0.270)	0.534	(0.448)	0.561	(0.450)
Rest of the world			1.061***	(0.255)	0.663	(0.422)	0.923**	(0.420)
Mean of transport								
Car/Bike	Reference category							
Train			0.096	(0.125)	0.121	(0.153)	0.126	(0.153)
Coach			0.142	(0.111)	−0.020	(0.137)	−0.003	(0.138)
Airplane			−0.248**	(0.116)	−0.320**	(0.160)	−0.397**	(0.160)
Other			0.319	(0.273)	0.599**	(0.294)	0.586**	(0.294)
Activities on the site								
Nature					−0.356***	(0.088)		
Sport					−0.199***	(0.052)		
Culture					0.028	(0.066)		
Entertainment					−0.268***	(0.050)		
Gastronomic tour					−0.070	(0.061)		
Satisfaction on the site								
Nature							−0.115**	(0.059)
Sport							−0.137**	(0.056)
Culture							0.063	(0.059)
Entertainment							−0.176***	(0.062)
Gastronomic tour							−0.036	(0.055)
Observations	2.788		2.788		2.043		2.043	

Note: ***1% significance level, **5% significance level, and *10% significance level.

a statistical difference between people booking by themselves and those choosing a package even if holiday packages show a tendency toward a shorter stay. Indeed, people who directly book their accommodation on the site tend to stay less, probably because it may be part of a tour. Number of stars have a significant and negative effect on the stay in all the three models. The place of residence shows that there is not a significant difference among Italians, while people coming from abroad show attitude to shorter stay. Such evidence, in the case of the Aosta Valley, should confirm that the stay is part of a larger tour, where Aosta Valley is one stop. The estimates do not provide any statistical difference among means of transport, with the only exception of people coming by airplane, who tend to spend a longer period.

Models 3 and 4 present the empirical analysis on experience and satisfaction of activities. Before commenting the results, it is worth noting that, to conduct the analysis, we restrict the sample of tourists to those who have already visited the destination in a previous holiday. Because it is uncommon that tourists modify the length of stay after being on holidays, by relying on experienced travelers, we focus on the behavior of those who, at the time they were planning their holiday, had a clear image of the destination. Thus, the choice on the length of stay depends also on the expected activities and satisfaction.

All the variables concerning the activities on the site and the satisfaction show a positive and significant sign, as we predicted in our theoretical framework. Exceptions are cultural activities and gastronomic tours that turn out to be not significant.

Future research directions

The analysis can be extended to study how the duration of stay is affected by the presence of attraction factors as well as by the existence of close tourism destinations. In this case, the customer survey design should include tourism geographical areas having product similarity and/or spatial proximity with the one the researcher is going to analyze. For example, future research on duration of stay in the Aosta Valley should comprise the whole of the Alpine region because of product similarity and Piedmont and Lombardy because of spatial proximity.

Conclusions

Survival data analysis has been applied on data collected from a customer satisfaction survey to study the main factors affecting the duration of stay in a mountain tourism destination. Our estimates suggest that highly educated childless foreign couples, aged between 31 and 40, and culturally motivated, are more likely to spend a longer period in the same tourism destination (Aosta Valley).

Information on tourist composition and their decision on the stay can help public bodies to define their place branding strategy. Because tourists are often interested in new experiences, being more acquainted on the duration of the stay can be useful to identify the type of tourism product they want to promote and offer (Gokovali et al., 2007). In particular, for tourism segments staying for longer periods, the offer should be more diversified. Moreover, the same argument can be applied to optimize the use of tourist facilities (Ritchie & Crouch, 2003). Finally, in order to increase the attractiveness of the place, new information on stays can be helpful to re-define the type of tourism demand they aim at attracting (Goodall, 1988).

Key construct definitions

Customer satisfaction survey: It is usually understood as the process of discovering whether or not a company's customers are happy or satisfied with the products or services received from the company. The survey can be conducted face to face, over the phone, via email or internet, or on handwritten forms. The goal of the survey is to decide whether or not changes are needed to achieve higher level of satisfaction of customers.

Length of stay: In official statistics about tourism, the length of tourism trips (involving at least one overnight stay) falls into two categories:

1   long tourism trips are trips with at least four overnight stays;
2   short tourism trips are trips with one to three overnight stays.

Accordingly, the average length of stay for a number of tourism trips is calculated by dividing the total number of nights spent by the total number of tourism trips.

Survival analysis: It is a set of methods for analyzing data where the outcome variable is the time until the occurrence of an event of interest. The event can be death, occurrence of a disease, marriage, divorce, departure from a location, and others. The time to event or survival time can be measured in days, weeks, years, and others.

For example, if the event of interest is the departure from a touristic location of a tourist, then the survival time can be the time in days until that person check-out from the location, hence the length of stay.

Notes

1 Indeed, it is a common practice in empirical survey to use education (and/or occupation) as a proxy of income, when interviewees are expected not to reveal their income.

2 Ferrer-Rossell et al. (2014) find that tourists booking a package (including the hotel and the trip) stay longer than tourists booking by themselves if the trip is offered by a low-cost carrier but not a legacy carrier.

3 The result of comparing tourists' experiences in a destination visited and expectations about the destination determines the tourist satisfaction (Pizam et al., 1978; Kotler et al., 1996).

4 Other studies base their empirical analysis on tourist surveys (Silberman, 1985; Alegre et al., 2011).

5 Contrary to many studies where the dependent variables are censored, in our model we have considered the full distribution. To be precise, most of the interviewed persons have reported a duration of the stay smaller or equal to 40 days. Only three interviewed persons have been reported a length of stay larger than 40.

References

Alderighi, M., & Lorenzini, E. (2012). Cultural goods, cultivation of taste, satisfaction and increasing marginal utility during vacations. *Journal of Cultural Economics*, 36(1), 1–26.

Alegre, J., Mateo, S., & Pou, L. (2011). A latent class approach to tourists' length of stay. *Tourism Management*, 32(3), 555–563.

Alegre, J., & Pou, L. (2007). Microeconomic determinants of the duration of stay of tourists. In *Advances in modern tourism research* (pp. 181–206). Physica-Verlag Heidelberg.

Barros, C.P., Butler, R., & Correia, A. (2010). A length of stay of golf tourism: A survival analysis. *Tourism Management*, 31, 13–21.

Cárdenas-García, P. J., Pulido-Fernández, J. I., & Pulido-Fernández, M. D. L. C. (2016). The influence of tourist satisfaction on tourism expenditure in emerging urban cultural destinations. *Journal of Travel & Tourism Marketing*, 33(4), 497–512.

Chi, C. G. Q., & Qu, H. (2008). Examining the structural relationships of destination image, tourist satisfaction and destination loyalty: An integrated approach. *Tourism Management*, 29(4), 624–636.

Davies, B., & Mangan, J. (1992). Family expenditure on hotels and holidays. *Annals of Tourism Research*, 19(4), 691–699.

Dubin, J. A., & McFadden, D. L. (1984). An econometric analysis of residential electric appliance holdings and consumption. *Econometrica: Journal of the Econometric Society*, 52(2), 345–362.

Eymann, A., & Ronning, G. (1997). Microeconometric models of tourists' destination choice. *Regional Science and Urban Economics*, 27(6), 735–761.

Ferrer-Rosell, B., Martínez-Garcia, E., & Coenders, G. (2014). Package and no-frills air carriers as moderators of length of stay. *Tourism Management*, 42, 114–122.

Fleischer, A., & Pizam, A. (2002). Tourism constraints among Israeli seniors. *Annals of Tourism Research*, 29(1), 106–123.

Gokovali, U., Bahar, O., & Kozak, M. (2007). Determinants of length of stay: A practical use of survival analysis. *Tourism Management*, 28(3), 736–746.

Goodall, B. (1988). How tourists choose their holidays: An analytical framework. In Goodall, B., & Ashworth, G. (Eds.). *Marketing in the tourism industry (RLE Tourism): The promotion of destination regions* (pp. 1–17). London: Routledge.

Hennessey, S. M., MacDonald, R., & MacEachern, M. (2008). A framework for understanding golfing visitors to a destination. *Journal of Sport & Tourism, 13*(1), 5–35.

Kiefer, N. M. (1988). Economic duration data and hazard functions. *Journal of Economic Literature, 26*(2), 646–679.

Kiefer, N. M., & Neumann, G. R. (1979). An empirical job-search model, with a test of the constant reservation-wage hypothesis. *Journal of Political Economy, 87*(1), 89–107.

Kotler, P., Makens, J., & Bowens, J. (1996). *Marketing for hospitality and tourism.* Upper Saddle River, NJ: Prentice Hall.Li, H., Zhang, Z., & Goh, C. (2015). Analyzing non-participation in domestic tourism: A combined framework. *Journal of Travel & Tourism Marketing, 32*(4), 454–473.

Martínez-Garcia, E., & Raya, J. M. (2008). Length of stay for low-cost tourism. *Tourism Management, 29*(6), 1064–1075.

McIntosh, R. W., Goeldner, C. R., & Ritchie, J. B. (1995). *Tourism: Principles, practices, philosophies* (7th Ed.). John Wiley and Sons.

De Menezes, A. G., Moniz, A., & Vieira, J. C. (2008). The determinants of length of stay of tourists in the Azores. *Tourism Economics, 14*(1), 205–222.

Narendranathan, W., & Nickell, S. (1985). Modelling the process of job search. *Journal of Econometrics, 28*(1), 29–49.

Pizam, A., Neumann, Y., & Reichel, A. (1978). Dimensions of tourist satisfaction with a destination area. *Annals of tourism Research, 5*(3), 314–322.

Ritchie, J. B., & Crouch, G. I. (2003). *The competitive destination: A sustainable tourism perspective.* Wallingford: CABI.

Santos, G. E. D. O., Ramos, V., & Rey-Maquieira, J. (2015). Length of stay at multiple destinations of tourism trips in Brazil. *Journal of Travel Research, 54*(6), 788–800.

Silberman, J. (1985). A demand function for length of stay: The evidence from Virginia Beach. *Journal of Travel Research, 23*(4), 16–23.

4 Beyond mountain and snow

Holiday experiences in winter mountain destinations

Chiara Mauri

Learning outcomes

At the end of this chapter, readers should be able to:

1 Understand how tourists spend their leisure time at a destination.
2 Comprehend the complexity of the motivations behind tourists' choice of a winter mountain destination.
3 Apply segmentation techniques to segment tourists on the basis of the activities they practice.
4 Develop tourism packages addressed to different targets.
5 Understand the role of destination management organization and tourism operators in promoting the attractiveness of a destination.

Introduction

The aim of this chapter is to understand the factors that contribute to create effective tourism experiences at a winter mountain destination. A preliminary qualitative analysis with six focus groups revealed that tourists, both skiers and non-skiers, engage in many different activities during their holidays; their days are full of activities, because they want to live a complete and authentic experience of the place. A survey made in three locations shows that while mountain and snow are key elements to attract tourists, once there, visitors engage in different kinds of activity, and many of them do not ski. After a literature review on mountain tourism, an empirical research on tourists' behavior and preferences is conducted in three mountain destinations: Courmayeur and Pila in Italy and Chamonix in France. Results offer useful insights for destination management organizations and tourism operators to develop holiday packages targeted to different segments.

Research background

The search for authenticity has been attracting increasing attention in marketing and consumer behavior literature: consumers increasingly decide whether to buy or not a product depending on its perceived genuineness (Boyle, 2004; Gilmore & Pine, 2007; Pine & Gilmore, 2008). This is the case also for the choice of tourism destinations (Cohen, 1988; Wang, 1999; Taylor, 2001; Yeoman, Brass & McMahon-Beattie, 2007). The concept of authenticity in the tourism literature is not new and has evolved from "objective" authenticity (MacCannell, 1973) to "constructive" authenticity (Hobsbawn & Ranger, 1983), and, more recently, to "existential" authenticity (Wang, 2000). While objective authenticity has to do with the intrinsic originality of the object, constructive authenticity is related to the deliberate construction of displayed objects as authentic by tourists or service providers. Existential authenticity, instead, is not associated at all with the actual object displayed but is connected with the tourists' inner state of being, a feeling of self-authenticity triggered by the experience lived in a particular setting.

If authenticity has become an important reason in the choice of places to visit, one possible way of increasing the perceived authenticity of a place is to focus on its experiential component (McIntosh & Prentice, 1999), stimulating visitors to explore all facets of the place. A genuine, true, real tourism experience (Grayson & Martinec, 2004) is the one capable of integrating the four realms of entertainment, education, escapism, esthetic (Pine & Gilmore, 1999); hence, it must encompass all the activities and offerings that a place may offer. If to distinguish from competition, destinations should sell experiences rather than products (Morgan, Lugosi & Ritchie, 2010; Pencarelli, 2017); the distinctive attractions of the destination should be cleverly assembled into packages able to represent authentic experiences of the place. Since tourists may choose a single destination for different reason, tourism operators may configure different experiences for different tourist segments, but always safeguarding the quest for authenticity. The risk in selling experiences is in fact that of creating staged experiences that are perceived as too superficial, commercial, or artificial, and therefore, not satisfying the customers' search for authenticity (Boswijk, Thijssen & Peelen, 2007). As Binkhorst and Den Dekker (2009) argue, the risk of inauthenticity can be avoided through the "co-creation" of tourism experiences, inviting visitors to interact with tourism operators to create their own unique experience.

In this setting, it would seem that holiday packages are not in line with modern tourists' desires and expectations; however, holiday packages' sales are increasing (Wong & Lee, 2012; Räikkönen & Honkanen, 2013).[1] Traditionally, package holidays have been considered as a rational choice to maximize and optimize holidays: they enable people to travel safely while minimizing transportation or hygiene worries (Enoch, 1996) and offer the benefits of ex-ante expense planning, pre-defined quality standards, and qualified personnel assistance (Morrison, 2013). Holiday packages are especially attractive to the growing segment of thematic tourism (e.g., sport, nature, gastronomic, and heritage tourism) (Stamboulis & Skayannis, 2003); in this perspective, a holiday at a winter mountain destination can be considered thematic tourism because it is usually imagined as ski holiday. However, climate changes are posing serious challenges to winter mountain destinations, forcing ski resorts to review their offer, to diversify their activities and to promote other activities complementary to skiing (Rosson & Zirulia, 2018). Joly and Ungurueanu (2018) report that some low-altitude villages that were once ski resorts have already abandoned their skiing infrastructure and are investing in activities that do not depend on snow.

If on one side, the use of artificial snow can be a solution to maintain the attraction of winter ski resorts, above all for those high on above sea level; on the other side, artificial snow goes against the demand of authenticity both for skiers and non-skiers, also because it creates a sense of fake in the mountain panorama (Osti & Cicero, 2018). Packaging attractions into authentic tourism experiences can be an effective solution not only to respond to the growing demand for authenticity but also to address the issue of long-term sustainability for winter mountain destinations (Dornier & Mauri, 2018).

In mountain destinations located in the Alps, winter tourism mainly coincided with ski tourism (Pechlaner & Manente, 2002), but new trends in tourist behavior have emerged at the end of the Nineties: preference for shorter and repeated holidays, decreased time spent in holiday planning, diversification of mountain sports, increase in "slow" sports (e.g., snowshoe walks, dog- or horse-drawn sledge rides, winter trekking), emergence of alternative extreme sports (e.g., heli-skiing, ice climbing, freestyle skiing, ski mountaineering), rising interest in health and nature tourism, and growing demand for vibrant and entertaining night life (Skipass Panorama Turismo, 2018).[2] While the worldwide skier market is showing a trend upward, the global Western skier market is flattening or even decreasing, and Italy and France are no exception (Vanat, 2018). Moreover, the non-sport component of mountain tourism is becoming more and more important: most tourists seem to enjoy the "relax" associated with mountain tourism and its "nature" component. Only one-third of visitors cite sports as the reason why they choose mountain destinations (Skipass Panorama Turismo, 2012).

Given these trends, it is timely for mountain destinations to "reinvent mountain tourism" (Flagestad & Hope, 2001), to broaden their offer to go beyond ski and snow, and include those attractions that allow to experience the place in all its authentic facets so that tourists feel fully immersed and involved (Carù & Cova, 2007). This transformation calls into question the place brand identity and positioning, which for Alpine destinations are heavily based on mountain and snow. Mountain, snow, and ski are key elements of the place branding physique (Kapferer, 2012), and hence of its brand identity, but the place positioning and image should be able to tell a story of the place that goes well beyond mountain and snow, which nonetheless are the heart and soul of the place. To understand how a place can update its positioning while keeping its heritage, an empirical research has been run in three mountain places located in the Alps: Courmayeur, Pila, and Chamonix. The three places are very close, located on two sites of Mont Blanc: the Italian and the French side.

Objectives of the research, study field, and methods

The empirical research has three main objectives:

1   To investigate whether tourists think of winter mountain tourism mainly as ski tourism.
2   To investigate how winter mountain tourists spend their holiday at the destination.
3   To segment winter mountain tourists according to their preferences for different bundles of activities.

The study was conducted in three Alpine mountain stations: Courmayeur and Pila (located in Aosta Valley, Italy) and Chamonix (Haute-Savoie, France). Courmayeur is one of the most renowned Italian mountain destinations, and its altitude of 1,224 meters above sea level allows for many kinds of alternative activities. Chamonix has been chosen for similar reasons, being the first among the best ski resorts in France[3] and the tenth station worldwide in terms of average annual skier visits (Vanat, 2018). Courmayeur and Chamonix, besides being very close, are both élite destinations; hence, their portfolio of activities goes well beyond skiing, offering many alternatives to "all ski." The third location, Pila, was chosen because the characteristics of its location make it a typical "all ski" destination; tourists who choose Pila should be skiers who like to dedicate most of their time to ski, and hence, less prone to spend time on other activities. In this context, Pila can work as a benchmark for understanding the different weight of the various activities included in a tourism package winter holiday.

The research applies a mixed design, qualitative and quantitative. The qualitative method consists of five focus groups with winter mountain tourists, where participants discuss how they spend a 3-day holiday at their typical destination; two focus groups involved Courmayeur as the destination (20 participants in total), and the other three involved Chamonix (18 participants in total). The explorative qualitative analysis was needed because of the lack of research on package holidays connected with winter mountain tourism. The technique of focus group discussion was preferred over individual interviews: in focus groups, the participants explain themselves to each other and compare their experiences (Morgan, 1996), which helps to remind them of insightful details.

The quantitative research is a survey to measure tourists' preferences for specific activities. The qualitative research was done at the beginning of the 2015–2016 winter season (end of November), and the survey was repeated at the three destinations—Courmayeur, Chamonix, and Pila—in two winter seasons: 2015–2016 (Courmayeur and Pila) and 2016–2017 (Chamonix). The questionnaires have been submitted through multiple channels: self-administered interviews at ski schools and hotels, emailing lists, social media, links on tourist web pages, QR code printed on cards left in hotels, house agencies, and ski schools. The sizes of the three samples are 273 respondents in Courmayeur, 254 in Chamonix, and 105 in Pila.

Qualitative research

The five focus groups were structured in three parts:

1 *Slide show.* In the first part, images of different mountain panoramas, of typical mountain activities, and of alpine winter atmospheres were projected as a slideshow. Images and sounds acted as multisensorial stimuli to facilitate participants' retrieval of mountain atmosphere (Delamont & Jones, 2012); after the show, participants were invited to share personal experiences related to their winter mountain holidays.

2 *Collage of 3-day holiday.* In the second part, participants had to plan a 3-day holiday at Courmayeur/Chamonix choosing from a list of specific activities adapted to the location and located within a 90-min drive, each activity paired with the time and total cost required. The activities were grouped in categories, identified in advance integrating the Madrigal and Kahle's (1994) list with Moscardo et al.'s (1996) list and adapting them to the locations, using as source the official websites of the local Tourism Departments. Each category was assigned three to four options to represent the breadth of the portfolio of activities in terms of time, price, and accessibility. Participants were asked to develop a collage, and then to review it in case of bad weather. Figure 4.1 shows the poster with all the options available in Courmayeur: participants had to configure a 3-day holiday cutting and pasting their preferred options according to their time-length and cost.

3 *Discussion of the collages.* In the last part, participants discussed their collage, explained in details how they spent a typical day at their most preferred location, and indicated the single activity they would never give up.

The final result of the five focus groups was a set of 38 collages of the bundles of activities that tourists chose for a 3-day winter holiday, with good and bad weather, and a list of the 38 activities that participants were not willing to give up.

1 h: Break or aperitivo downtown - Courmayeur	3 h: Casino – 45 minutes drive from Courmayeur	2 h: Ice skating – Courmayeur Price: according to time	4 h: Thermal bath at Pré Saint Didier - 10 minutes drive from Courmayeur Entrance fee: 49,00€	6 h: Downhill - Courmayeur Price: 45,00€/day
1 h: Shopping typical products - Courmayeur				
1 h: Alpine Museum – Courmayeur 5€, children 1,50€		4 h: Fenis castle - 40 minutes drive from Courmayeur Entrance fee: 5,00€, children free		
1 h: Shopping mountain sports-good - Courmayeur	3 h: Typical dinner in restaurant/chalet - Courmayeur		4 h: Winter Eco Trail – Courmayeur Price: 25,00€	
1 h: SPA/Massage/Swimming pool - Courmayeur				
2 h: Christmas tree lighting with food and music - Courmayeur	3 h: Astronomic observatory- 40 minutes drive from Courmayeur Entrance fee: 12€, children 6€	3 h: Wine tasting – 30 minutes drive from Courmayeur Cave du Vin Blanc de Morgex e de la Salle		6 h: Eliski - Courmayeur Price: 120,00€
2 h: Torch-light procession - Courmayeur				
2 h: Snow walking - Courmayeur	3 h: Foire des Glaciers/Tradeshow- 20 minutes drive from Courmayeur	3 h: Sledog with coffee break or aperitivo – Courmayeur Price: 100,00€	6 h: Forte di Bard – 50 minutes drive from Courmayeur	4 h: Cross country ski - Courmayeur Price: only in case of renting
3 h: Bread show, with local cheese and wine - Courmayeur	2 h: Sledding – 30 minutes drive from Courmayeur	2 h: Kitchen school - Courmayeur		

Figure 4.1 Poster with all options (Courmayeur).

Quantitative research

The activities that emerged from the focus groups were used to configure different winter holiday packages, which were administered to a sample of tourists to better understand their preferences for specific bundles of activities. The quantitative research was structured as follows:

1 Definition of package holiday components, derived from the focus groups.
2 Design of eight different kinds of package holidays and of their composition through the orthogonal array technique.
3 Design and administration of a questionnaire to a sample of winter mountain tourists;
4 Data analysis and interpretation:

    a Identification of tourists' most preferred activities during their winter mountain holidays.
    b Segmentation of tourists according to their attitude toward winter mountain tourism through factor analysis and cluster analysis.
    c Identification of preferences for different activities through conjoint analysis in each segment (Green & Srinivasan, 1978, 1990).

Discussion of results

Results from the focus groups

Figure 4.2a and b shows the bundles of activities of 10 + 10 collages related to Courmayeur and Chamonix.

Tourists' days are full of activities, but the bundles of activities are very different. Seven tourists over ten ski, but only for two to three of them ski is the number one activity (30%–40% of the total time): after ski, skiers dedicate a significant amount of time to other snow sports (snowshoe walks, trekking, skating), to wellness (spa and thermal bath), and above all to food and beverage. Food and beverage is the activity that takes most of the time on average (22%–23%), is included in all bundles but one, and is the most preferred activity by 25% of the tourists in both locations. Tasting and eating typical local food is a loved and recurring theme: winter mountain tourists underlined the differences between everyday life in the city and holiday time referring to how they consume food, and the time dedicated to food. Holiday means buying local food since very early in the morning at breakfast; it means eating local specialties, purchasing in small specialty stores, choosing local restaurants, and preparing local receipts. Food and beverage emerges as a key ingredient of the place experience: food, shops, restaurants, receipts, personnel, and

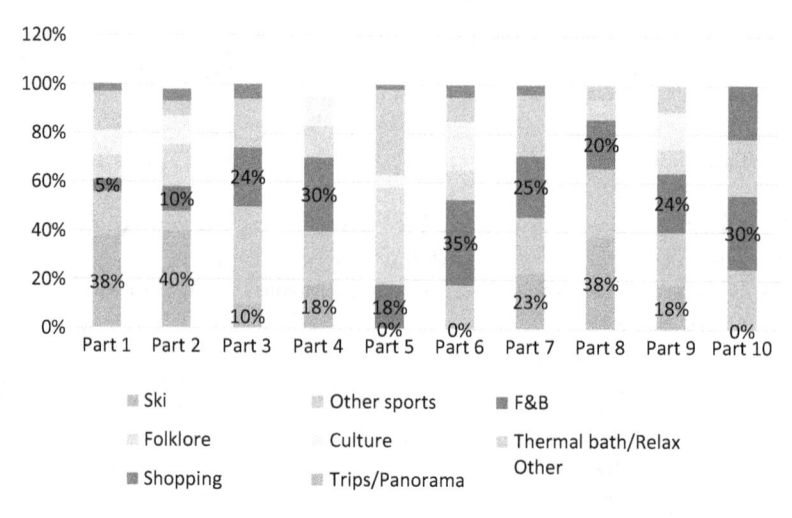

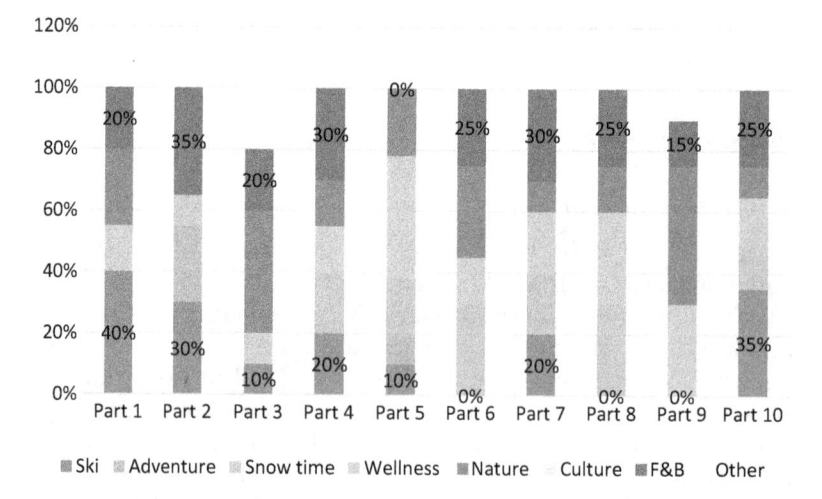

Figure 4.2 Bundles of activities of a 3-day winter mountain holiday (percentage of time).

producers all together create a unique world that is a story to tell, a story that has a great stake in qualifying the place brand.

> When I am there, I start the day going out to the local bakery to buy the local black bread, and then I prepare breakfast which is very different from what we usually have at home. The bread, the jam, the milk, the yogurt: they all are made here.

Even if we are in a hotel, we do not like to have dinner there. When we finish skiing, and maybe after a couple of hours at the local thermal bath, we look for a restaurant to taste real local food, made there. Local, I mean, not a star-rated restaurant. We like to discover small restaurants, typical of the place.

When I go to bed I am so tired, but happy and satisfied with the day.

Participating in local cultural events or visiting local attractions is more a wish than a fact; its importance increases in case of bad weather, but time spent is very low for Chamonix and not very much for Courmayeur (10% on average). Cultural activities were never mentioned as the most preferred, and many subjects seemed not to be aware of all the opportunities that local cultural attractions could offer.

As soon as we arrive, we check on the Internet to find all the events that are planned to coincide with our stay, and we select one or two to attend, particularly in case of bad weather. These events allow you to understand the real spirit of the place.

These comments, collected via the focus group discussions, reveal tourists' desire to fully experience the authenticity of the place: even on short-break holidays, tourists try as much as they can to combine objective authenticity (the snow, the food, the restaurant, the spa) with constructive authenticity (the breakfast ritual) to reach an inner state of existential authenticity, to be completely immersed in the place to live out a memorable experience.

Results from the quantitative research

Results of the three surveys show that the link between winter mountain tourism and ski is not as strong as it is often assumed, particularly in élite places such as Courmayeur and Chamonix. Tourists' interest in skiing appears dichotomous, with over 90% of respondents concentrating in the tails of the distribution: either they like or they do not like skiing. A different picture is that of Pila: Pila is an all ski resort that can be reached only by cableway, hence tourists who choose Pila; it is because skiing is their primary goal (Figure 4.3a). Tasting local food and beverage is instead an experience that the great majority of tourists like in all the three locations (Figure 4.3b) and is strongly connected to purchasing local food and visiting local factories (enogastronomic tours). Second for overall preference are activities related to health and wellness, and to walking in the nature to experience the landscape. These three activities—F&B, health, and wellness and closeness with nature—represent an interconnected set of gratifications that connect very well with the beauty of the Alpine places. The best representation of this "three in one" holistic experience of the place is taking a thermal bath in the open air with the view of Mont Blanc, and eating local food after the bath at the same spa. In this perspective, they represent the physical facets

(a) Skiing

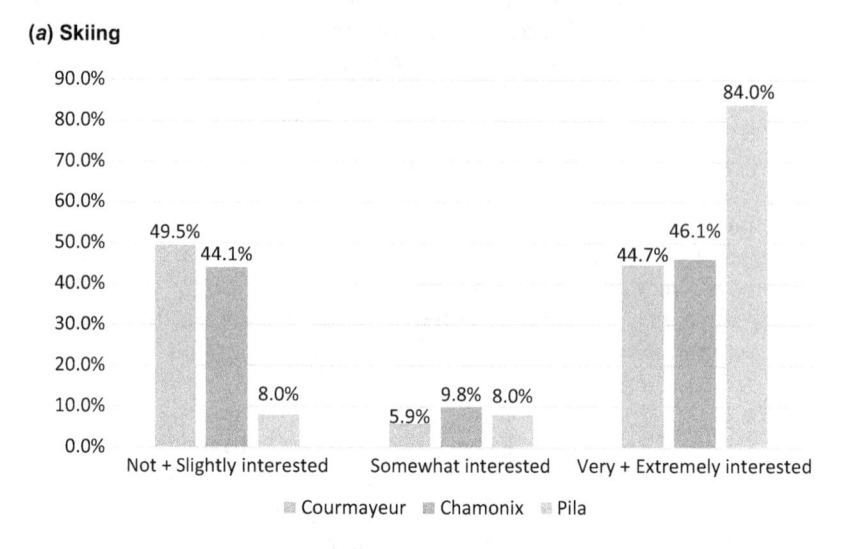

(b) Local Food & Beverage

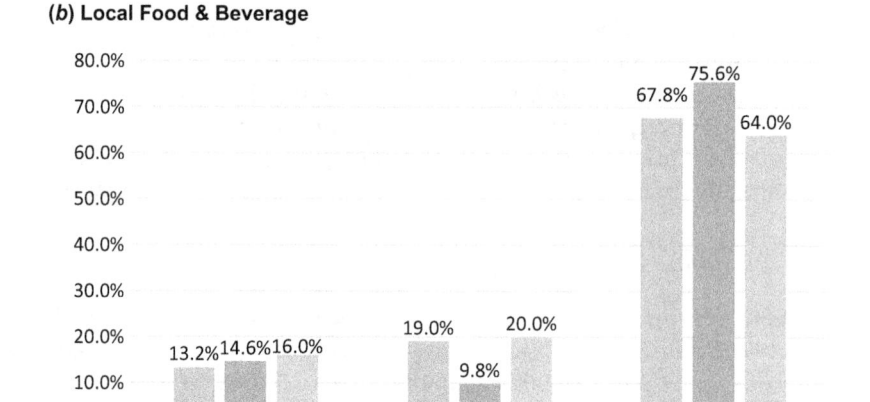

Figure 4.3 Frequency distributions of tourists' interest toward skiing and food and beverage (three locations).

of the place brand identity (Melewar, 2003; Kapferer, 2012), and hence key ingredients of the place brand positioning and image.

Ski instead is a segmenting activity: its average importance overall hides the highest variance among all activities. Pila is a niche station by itself, because it is chosen almost exclusively by skiers.

Culture, folklore, and other activities related to snow show average ratings above ski but very low variances, because the ratings are concentrated around the average, hence they appear a minor part of the place

	Factor 1 Relax	Factor 2 Boredom	Factor 3 Classic: snow sport	Factor 4 Fun and friends	Factor 5a Exploration	Factor 5b Contact with nature
Courmayeur	X	X	X	X		X
Chamonix		X	X	X	X	
Pila	X	X	X			

Figure 4.4 Factor structure in the three locations.

brand identity and image. Winter mountain tourism goes well beyond ski and snow: tourists give higher rates to activities related to local food, well-being, and intimate contact with nature. Taken all together, these activities configure a holistic set on which the DMO of the place can build and develop the place brand image. Even many passionate skiers rate tasting local food higher that skiing!

Tourists' preferences for specific activities may vary according to their attitude toward winter mountain tourism, which may depend on their motives and motivations to visit the place (Crompton, 1979; Dann, 1981; Fodness, 1994). Respondents in the three samples were asked to rate their attitudes on a 15-point Likert scale, and their rates have been analyzed applying factor analysis (Varimax rotation). The results show some commonalities and differences in the three locations. In both Courmayeur and Chamonix, data are summarized by five factors, which explain 69% of the total variance, while data related to Pila are summarized by three factors. The details of the three analysis[4] are out of the scope of this chapter; what is more relevant are the insights that emerge from the comparison of the three locations (Figure 4.4).

Two factors emerge in all the three locations: "Classic," that is, active life related to practicing snow sports, and "Boredom." If the first factor was expected, the second was a surprise, even if anticipated in the focus groups, in which some participants were describing their winter mountain holidays as monotonous and boring. To the best of our knowledge, tourism has never been associated to boredom, but rather to leisure (Morgan, Lugosi & Ritchie, 2010), above all given its interpretation as an experience to be lived, remembered, and told. On the one side, tourism per se is mostly interpreted as a positive, leisure, and exciting experience (Carr, 2002), while on the other side boredom has often been analyzed more as a feeling that stimulates tourism rather than a feeling perceived while practicing it (Iso-Ahola & Weissinger, 1990; Lee & Crompton, 1992; Ryan & Glendon, 1998). Tourism can be considered an unstructured time, or at least a time very different from the daily routine, especially when the choice of the destination has been determined more by pull than by push factors, more by others than by the tourist him/herself. One of the items with high loadings on boredom is in fact the motivation of accompanying family and friends.

Relax is appearing only in the two Italian locations (full immersion in the nature, break from daily routine, relax, family time), while "Fun and friends" shows up only in the two élite locations. The fifth factor is different in two élite locations: a push to visit new places and explore the place in Chamonix and a more intimate contact with nature in Courmayeur.

The application of cluster analysis on the factors scores of respondents reveals the existence of different segments of winter mountain tourists in the three locations: four in Courmayeur and Chamonix and three in Pila. To avoid a tedious comparison of all the details for the three locations, we focus on their similarities and differences.

The largest segment for two locations is the segment of skiers: 60% in Pila and 39% in Courmayeur. Skiers in Chamonix are less clearly identified and are distributed in two segments: classic winter mountain tourists, who spend their holiday with family and friends (33%), and dynamic tourists (29%), proactive visitors who like to take part in all activities that the place offers. The second segment appearing in the three locations is that of "Companions": they are tourists who have come to the mountain to accompany family and friends; their attitude toward winter mountain tourism is often not positive, and they describe mountain as dangerous, boring, tiresome, and expensive. Nonetheless, they take part in many activities, particularly those related to local traditions and food and beverage. This segment is not small: 10% in Pila, 19% in Chamonix, and 23% in Courmayeur. The other segments are different because they are related to the characteristics of the place, but they have one element in common: they all like the beauty of the place and the total immersion in the nature.

The final step of the quantitative research was to determine the preference for different activities of each segment. The five most recurring activities in each place were combined into eight 4-day packages applying orthogonal array, and each package was given a title related to the breadth and depth of the offer (Figure 4.5). No package included travel and accommodation and all packages allowed individuals to plan the different activities at their will without a pre-defined schedule, so as to co-create their own holiday (Suvantola, 2002; Prahalad & Ramaswamy, 2004; Ferrari, 2006; Lugosi, 2008).

Package	Ski	Other snow sports	Wellness	Food & beverage	Culture
Sport	Yes	Yes	No	No	No
Classic	Yes	No	Yes	No	No
Beyond ski	No	Yes	No	Yes	No
Relax	No	No	Yes	Yes	No
Myths and traditions	No	No	No	No	Yes
A different Courmayeur	No	Yes	Yes	No	Yes
Traditions on the snow	Yes	No	No	Yes	Yes
Total Courmayeur	Yes	Yes	Yes	Yes	Yes

Figure 4.5 Eight packages (Courmayeur).

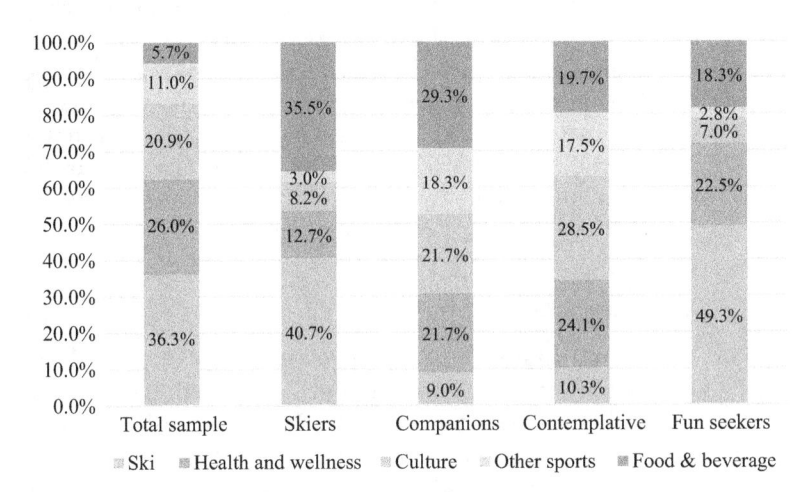

Figure 4.6 Importance of different activities: total sample and four segments (Courmayeur).

Respondents had to rate their interest for each package on a five-point scale, ranging from "Not interested" to "Extremely interested."

A conjoint analysis operated on the total sample and separately on the different segments reveals that the interest for different activities is significantly different between the segments (Figure 4.6).

While overall skiing has the highest importance (36.3%), the situation changes when referred to the four segments. The two segments who give the highest importance to skiing (the "Skiers" and the "Fun seekers") represent 50% of the total sample, but the other two segments are much less interested in skiing and prefer to practice other activities. Second to ski overall is health and wellness (26%), whose importance is relatively high in all segments but skiers. Culture gains importance for the segments of "Companions" and "Contemplative," together with other snow sports. Finally, Food and beverage appears as a key ingredient in all segments: it is the most important activity for the "Companions," and it is second to ski for the skiers. To confirm these results, a simulation was operated to estimate the choice shares of tourism packages configured on the basis of the part-worth utilities of the different activities resulted from the conjoint analysis, at the levels of both the total samples and of the segments. Five new packages have been tested:

– Food and beverage + health and wellness;
– Food and beverage + health and wellness + culture;
– Ski + other snow sports + food and beverage + health and wellness + culture;
– Other snow sports + food and beverage + health and wellness;
– Only ski.

Even applying different simulation models,[5] the most preferred package is the first one, which does not include ski, and the least preferred is the third, which includes all activities. The package "Only ski" has a choice share of 20%–24% in all the segments, and a share of 100% in the segment of skiers only when applying the First Choice model. This simulation is a further test of the importance of skiing as the classic discipline of winter mountain holidays, but reveals that there is a lot more beyond snow and ski to build an effective tourist experience.

Future research directions

There are winter mountain tourists who experience boredom during their holiday; most of them are "Companions," who go to the mountain to accompany their relatives and/or friends. To the best of our knowledge, tourism has never been associated to boredom, but rather to leisure (Morgan, Lugosi & Ritchie, 2010). On the one side, tourism per se is almost always interpreted as a positive, leisure, and exciting experience to be lived, remembered, and told (Carr, 2002); on the other side, boredom has often been analyzed more as a feeling that stimulates tourism rather than a feeling perceived while practicing it (Iso-Ahola & Weissinger, 1990; Lee & Crompton, 1992; Ryan & Glendon, 1998; Kim et al., 2012). Given the non-small size of this segment (10%, 12%, and 23% in Pila, Chamonix, and Courmayeur, respectively), it would be interesting to explore more in-depth the actual behavior of these individuals and to understand if the activities they engage in during their holiday may alleviate their boredom.

Almost the totality of tourists involved in the research were living in the same country of the destinations involved (Italy and France); hence, a possible extension is to analyze the behavior of foreign tourists, a growing segment of Alpine places who are heavier buyers of holiday packages (Räikkönen & Honkanen, 2013).

A third direction is the extension of the research to summer mountain tourism, which shows some commonalities with winter mountain tourism but also significant differences.

Conclusion

"Winter" adds an important characteristic to a mountain geography: the snow. It is very difficult to think of a winter mountain place without the snow, and the great majority of pictures of mountain places include the snow. Snowy landscapes are often associated to downhill skiing, as a sort of default activity: people who go to the mountain in winter are skiers or are interested in skiing. The place brand image and positioning of these geographies (Pike, 2011) are heavily based on snow and skiing, which appear very often also in summer advertising campaigns. Skiing is one of the key activities that attract tourists to the mountain in winter season, but while its practice in the global Western market is flattening or even decreasing, the climate change is creating serious challenges to ski resorts, particularly those located at low altitudes. These resorts must find new avenues to maintain their attractiveness, investigating the motivations and the benefits that tourists are looking for when choosing a mountain destination for their winter holidays. These motivations and searched benefits can be the basis on which to rethink the place branding, its concept, image, communication, and the sense of the place (Kavaratzis, Warnaby & Ashworth, 2015). Branding geographies such as winter mountain places cannot be based anymore only on a physical asset (snow in the mountain) and on a sport activity (ski) but should be oriented to the creation of new meanings able to tell the essence of the place, its spirit, personality, and narrative. The sense of place should combine the physical aspects of the setting with the meaning that tourists attach to it, through their relationships with their family and friends and with the local community, and the emotional and symbolic benefits they derive from being there.

The focus of branding winter mountain destinations is not simply a physical or symbolic representation of the landscape but requires to go beyond the landscape to understand its meaning for different segments of tourists, and hence to integrate multiple offers to attract multiple audiences (Warnaby & Medway, 2010). The results of the empirical research in three winter mountain destinations have significant implications for all the stakeholders involved in developing and managing the tourist experience. The empirical research has shown the potential of the new "snow tourisms," new forms of thematic tourisms. While attracted by mountain and snow, tourists show different interests toward the activities that the place may offer. The scarcity of snow is a further element that forces a rethink of the ski-centric image of alpine destinations to preserve and even augment their attractiveness, possibly opening the door to new tourists. Even the most passionate skiers who choose "all ski" destinations like Pila are not looking solely for high-quality ski slopes and modern ski systems: they want to experience other elements of the place that make it unique and worth visiting, above all local authentic food and beverage. The boundaries separating skiers from other tourists are becoming blurred (Beedie & Hudson, 2003) because skiers are far from being one only segment.

In summary, winter mountain destinations should offer a wide spectrum of activities to attract a growing number of tourists and to allow them to co-produce their own holidays combining elements that make the specific destination unique. Tourism packages can be an effective way to connect mountain tourism with other types of tourism that can be practiced in the same place and that at the same time can respond to special interests such as food and wine, culture, etc. (Stamboulis & Skayannis, 2003; Uriely, 2005), but it is clearly important to preserve the sense of enchanting alpine atmosphere.

Key construct definitions

Winter mountain destinations: Mountain areas are divided into seven classes, based on altitude and slope. Mountain places as ski resorts are classes 3–5 (elevation 2,500–3,500, 1,500–2,500, and 1,000–1,500, respectively). Within these destinations, seasonality is a major issue, particularly for those that rely on winter tourism. The global warming, with its associated scarcity of snow, is creating serious challenges to winter mountain places, particularly to those at lower elevation. Some low-altitude villages that were once ski resorts have already abandoned their skiing infrastructure and are investing in activities that do not depend on snow.

Search for authenticity in tourism: Authenticity in tourism can be considered from different perspectives: objective, constructive, and existential. Objective authenticity is related to the intrinsic originality of the object; constructive authenticity has to do with the deliberate construction of the displayed objects as authentic by tourists or service providers; existential authenticity is connected with the tourists' inner state of being, a feeling of self-authenticity triggered by the experience lived in a particular setting. Authenticity has become an important reason in the choice of places to visit, and one possible way of increasing the perceived authenticity of a place is to focus on its experiential component, stimulating visitors to explore all facets of the place.

Tourism package: Tourism packages are organized trips following pre-determined programs involving several activities and services. Since tourists are interested in different activities, the distinctive attractions of the destination should be configured into packages targeted to different segments. The tourism package should not be 100% pre-determined in all details but should allow tourists some freedom to co-create the place experience.

Tourist segmentation: Visitors of a destination can be segmented using many different bases and techniques, whose choice depends on the goal of the segmentation. For the purpose of configuring the most effective tourism packages to attract different segments, tourists can be segmented using as basis the motivations to visit the place, and/ or the amount of time they spend in different activities, and the activities they like most.

Conjoint analysis to study tourists' preferences: Conjoint analysis is a statistical technique that can be used to investigate tourists' preferences for different activities offered by a destination and included in holiday packages. It consists of six main steps: (1) identification of the activities (or attributes) to be included in the package, (2) definition of the levels for each activity, (3) definition of the number of packages (profiles) to be rated or ranked by a sample of tourists, (4) survey to a sample of tourists who are asked to rank or rated the different packages, and (5) analysis of results and identification of the utilities for different activities included in the package.

Notes

1 Revenue in the worldwide package holiday segment amounted to US$169,624 million in 2018 and is expected to grow in the years 2019–2023 at a CAGR of 5.9%. Source: www.statista.com.
2 Skipass Panorama Turismo is the only Italian Mountain Tourism research center. The latest study (2017–2018) is based on a panel of 61 Italian mountain destinations.
3 "Top best ski resort in France", *Snow Magazine*, December 2015; Alexander, L. (2017), "8 Top-Rated Ski Resorts in France", *PlanetWare*.
4 Further details can be asked to the author.
5 The three models are First Choice, Bradley-Terry-Luce, and Logit.

References

Beedie, P. & Hudson, S. (2003). Emergence of mountain-based adventure tourism. *Annals of Tourism Research*, 30(3), 625–643.

Binkhorst, E. & Den Dekker, T. (2009). Agenda for co-creation tourism experience research. *Journal of Hospitality Marketing & Management*, 18(2/3), 311–327.

Boswijk, A., Thijssen, T. and Peelen, E. (2007). *The experience economy. A new perspective*. Amsterdam: Pearson Education.

Boyle, D. (2004). *Authenticity: Brands, fakes, spin and the lust for real life*. London: Harper Perennial.

Carr, N. (2002). The tourism–leisure behavioural continuum. *Annals of Tourism Research*, 29(4), 972–986.

Carù, A. & Cova, B. (2007). *Consuming experience*. Abingdon: Routledge.

Cohen, E. (1988). Authenticity and commoditization in tourism. *Annals of Tourism Research*, 15(3), 371–386.

Crompton, J.L. (1979). Motivations for pleasure vacation. *Annals of Tourism Research*, 6(4), 408–424.

Dann, G.M.S. (1981). Tourism motivation: An appraisal. *Annals of Tourism Research*, 8(2), 187–219.

Delamont, S. & Jones, A. (2012). *Handbook of qualitative research in education*. Cheltenham: Edward Elgar.

Dornier, R. & Mauri, C. (2018). Conclusions: Managing tourism sustainability in mountain destinations. *Worldwide Hospitality and Tourism Themes*, 10(2), 267–273.

Enoch, Y. (1996). Contents of tour packages: A cross-cultural comparison. *Annals of Tourism Research*, 23(3), 599–616.

Ferrari, S. (2006). *Modelli gestionali per il turismo come esperienza: emozioni e polisensorialità nel marketing delle imprese turistiche*. Padova: CEDAM.

Flagestad, A. & Hope, C.A. (2001). Strategic success in winter sports destinations: A sustainable value creation perspective. *Tourism Management*, (22)5, 445–461.

Fodness, D. (1994). Measuring tourist motivation. *Annals of Tourism Research*, 21(3), 555–581.

Gilmore, J.H. & Pine, J.B. (2007). *Authenticity: What consumers really want*. Boston: Harvard Business School Press.

Grayson, K. & Martinec, R. (2004). Consumer perceptions of iconicity and indexicality and their influence on assessments of authentic marketing offerings. *Journal of Consumer Research*, 31(2), 296–312.

Green, P.E. & Srinivasan, V. (1978). Conjoint analysis in consumer research: Issues and outlook. *Journal of Consumer Research*, 5(2), 103–123.

Green, P.E. & Srinivasan, V. (1990). Conjoint analysis in marketing: New developments with implications for research and practice. *Journal of Marketing*, 54(4), 3–19.

Hobsbawn, E. & Ranger, T. (1983). *The invention of tradition*. Cambridge: Cambridge University Press.

Iso-Ahola, S.E. & Weissinger, E. (1990). Perceptions of boredom in leisure: Conceptualization, reliability and validity of the leisure boredom scale. *Journal of Leisure Research*, 22(1), 1–17.

Joly, M. & Ungureanu, E.I. (2018). Global warming and skiing: Analysis of the future of skiing in the Aosta Valley. *Worldwide Hospitality and Tourism Themes*, 10(2), 161–171.

Kapferer, J.N. (2012). *The new strategic brand management. Advanced insights and strategic thinking*. London: Kogan Page.

Kavaratzis, M., Warnaby, G. & Ashworth, G. (eds.) (2015). *Rethinking place branding: Comprehensive brand development for cities and regions*. London: Springer.

Kim, J.H., Ritchie, J.R.B. & McCormick, B. (2012). Development of a scale to measure memorable tourism experiences. *Journal of Travel Research*, 51(1), 12–25.

Lee, T.-H. & Crompton, J. (1992). Measuring novelty seeking in tourism. *Annals of Tourism Research*, 19(4), 732–751.

Lugosi, P. (2008). Hospitality spaces, hospitable moments: Consumer encounters and affective experiences in commercial settings. *Journal of Foodservice*, 19(2), 139–149.

MacCannell, D. (1973). Staged authenticity: Arrangements of social space in tourist settings. *American Journal of Sociology*, 79(3), 589–603.

Madrigal, R. & Kahle, L.R. (1994). Predicting vacation activity preferences on the basis of value-system segmentation. *Journal of Travel Research*, 32(3), 22–28.

McIntosh, A.J. & Prentice, R.C. (1999). Affirming authenticity: Consuming cultural heritage. *Annals of Tourism Research*, 26(3), 589–612.

Melewar, T. C. (2003). Determinants of the corporate identity construct: A review of literature. *Journal of Marketing Communications*, 9(4), 195–220.

Morgan, D.L. (1996). Focus groups. *Annual Review of Sociology*, 22(1), 129–152.

Morgan, M., Lugosi, P. & Ritchie, J.R.B. (2010). *The tourism and leisure experience: Consumer and managerial perspectives*. Bristol: Channel View Publications.

Morrison, A.M. (2013). *Marketing and managing tourism destinations*. London: Routledge.

Moscardo, G., Morrison, A.M., Pearce, P.L., Lang, C.T. & O'Leary, J.T. (1996). Understanding vacation destination choice through travel motivation and activities. *Journal of Vacation Marketing*, 2(2), 109–122.

Osti, L. & Cicero, L. (2018). Tourists' perception of landscape attributes in rural tourism. *Worldwide Hospitality and Tourism Themes*, 10(2), 211–221.

Pechlaner, H. & Manente, M. (ed.) (2002). *Manuale del turismo montano. Prospettive, cambiamenti e strategie di management*. Milano: Touring University Press.

Pencarelli, T. (2017). Marketing in an experiential perspective: Toward the "experience logic". *Mercati & Competitività*, 2(2), 7–14.

Pike, A. (ed.) (2011). *Brands and branding geographies*. Cheltenham: Edward Elgar.

Pine, B. & Gilmore, J. (1999). *The experience economy: Work is theatre and every business a stage*. Boston: Harvard Business School Press.

Pine, B. & Gilmore, J. (2008). The eight principles of strategic authenticity. *Strategy & Leadership*, 36(3), 35–40.

Prahalad, C.K. & Ramaswamy, V. (2004). Co-creation experiences: The next practice in value creation. *Journal of Interactive Marketing*, 18(3), 5–14.

Räikkönen, J. & Honkanen, A. (2013). Does satisfaction with package tours lead to successful vacation experiences? *Journal of Destination Marketing & Management*, 2(2), 108–117.

Rosson, S. & Zirulia, L. (2018). A hedonic price model for ski lift tickets in the dolomites. *Worldwide Hospitality and Tourism Themes*, 10(2), 222–235.

Ryan, C. & Glendon, I. (1998). Application of leisure motivation scale to tourism. *Annals of Tourism Research*, 25(1), 169–184.

Skipass Panorama Turismo (2012). Report 2012, Italian Observatory of Mountain Tourism (www.skipass.it/osservatorio)

Stamboulis, Y. & Skayannis, P. (2003). Innovation strategies and technology for experience-based tourism. *Tourism Management*, 24(1), 35–43.

Suvantola, J. (2002). *Tourist's experience of place*. Farnham: Ashgate.

Taylor, J.P. (2001). Authenticity and sincerity in tourism. *Annals of Tourism Research*, 28(1), 7–26.

Uriely, N. (2005). The tourist experience: Conceptual developments. *Annals of Tourism Research*, 32(1), 199–216.

Vanat, L. (2018). *2018 international report on snow & mountain tourism*, 10th edition. www.vanat.ch.

Wang, N. (1999). Rethinking authenticity in tourism experience. *Annals of Tourism Research*, 26(2), 349–370.

Wang, N. (2000). *Tourism and modernity: A sociological analysis*. Oxford: Pergamon.

Warnaby, G. & Medway, D. (2010). Semiotics and place branding: The influence of the built and natural environment in city logos. In Ashworth, G., & Kavaratzis, M. (eds.), *Towards effective place brand management*. Cheltenham: Edward Elgar, 173–190.

Wong, J.-Y. & Lee, W.-H. (2012). Leadership through service: An exploratory study of the leadership styles of tour leaders. *Tourism Management*, 33(5), 1112–1121.

Yeoman, I., Brass, D. & McMahon-Beattie, U. (2007). Current issue in tourism: The authentic tourist. *Tourism Management*, 28(4), 1128–1138.

5 Assessment and measurement of destination image through user-generated content

Chiara Mauri and Anna Marsanasco

Learning outcomes

At the end of this chapter, readers should be able to:

1 Understand the factors that contribute to the formation of destination image
2 Understand the role of social media in shaping the image of a destination
3 Apply user-generated content (UGC) to analyze destination image
4 Use network maps and geo-maps to analyze destination image
5 Identify avenues to strengthen the image of a destination

Introduction

The aim of this chapter is to investigate the role of social media in shaping a destination image from an innovative perspective: the analysis of pictorial materials posted by Destination Management Organizations (DMOs) and visitors on photo-sharing websites.

Photos published on social media are used by visitors to document and share their experiences; hence, UGCs can be used to study tourists' perception of a place image.

Interesting work is the one of Stepchenkova and Zhan (2013), who compare the pictorial materials published online and the DMO's visual materials. The research presented in this chapter applies Stepchenkova and Zhan (2013)'s method to study the image of Milan.

After a literature review, empirical research is conducted by comparing the photos that tourists publish on Flickr and those published on the website of the local municipality.

Results reveal insights on tourists' behavior, and the comparison with the DMO's documentation opens new avenues to strengthen the image of the city.

Research background

Social media represent a powerful tool in order to get information about perceptions of the destination visited and the type of activities undertaken by visitors. Social media appear as an essential application both to preserve and to express the tourist's experiences through images, comments, geo-localization (Latorre-Martízen & Iñiguez-Berrozpe 2014). Furthermore, contents are shared not only with family and friends but also with strangers, thus creating a dense network of information. Social media become technological mediators in the creation and diffusion of the image of a tourist destination (Latorre-Martízen & Iñiguez-Berrozpe 2014), and as non-official promotional communication, they show a higher impact on destination image than official promotion. For these reasons, DMOs need to constantly check whether the image shared is consistent with the information provided by the destination itself (Stepchenkova & Zhan 2013).

The deep bond between visual culture and modern tourism (Cheung et al. 2011; Domšić 2013) has led to the decision of focusing on photo-sharing social media. According to Latorre-Martínez and Iñiguez-Berrozpe (2014), the emergence of social media totally devoted to images stresses the importance of image as a mean of expression and communication. By using photo-sharing websites as a source, our analysis will be limited to a selected group of tourists because the majority of tourists who post their photos online tend to be young (Lo et al. 2011).

The following section presents a brief examination of the two streams of literature that have contributed to this research: the concept, formation, and measurement of destination image, and UGC as a source of data to study destination image.

Destination image

Conceptualization and attributes

Since nations, cities, and regions are competing with each other to attract their rightful share of the global tourism market, it is important for destinations to establish a recognized and valued tourism position and image in the market (UNWTO 2007) because a positive image increases the likelihood of commercial success or failure of the destination (Dominique & Lopes 2011; Gartner 1993).

The importance of destination image is twofold. On the one hand, it is a salient factor in tourists' decision-making process of where to travel, as tourists have limited information on potential destinations. On the other hand, destination image influences post-purchase behavior and tourists' satisfaction, which in turn impact on the willingness to return in the future and on word of mouth (Gallarza et al. 2002; Phillips & Jang 2010); eventually, a positive destination image leads to destination loyalty (Kim et al. 2013).

Definitions of destination image are many (Gallarza et al. 2002). Terms such as "impression," "perception," or "mental representation" of a tourist destination are generally used in order to conceptualize destination image (San Martìn & Rodrìguez del Bosque 2008), but differences emerge when determining its components. The most cited contribution is the one by Echtner and Ritchie (2003), who portray a comprehensive examination of the definitions provided in major studies. Destination image is frequently described as a list of attributes, but Echtner and Ritchie suggest that destination image consists of both attribute-based and holistic-based components. They develop a framework that distinguishes not only between these two views but also between functional and psychological characteristics. Considering the attribute side, tourists have numerous perceptions of the characteristics of a destination, both functional, such as climate and nightlife, and psychological, such as friendliness of people and general safety. From a holistic perspective, the functional impression consists of the mental picture of destinations' physical characteristics, whereas the psychological characteristics could be described as the atmosphere or feeling of a place. It is the attributes of the destination's resources and attractions, as well as the feeling and emotion component that contributes to motivating tourists to visit the destination (Dominique & Lopes 2011; Phillips & Jang 2010). While Manhas et al. (2016) have shown that the affective construct has more impact on building destination image than the cognitive one, Garner (1993) added a third component: the conative image, namely the action component, which depends on the image developed during the cognitive stage and evaluated in the affective stage. Images of destinations can also range from those based on common functional and psychological traits to those based on more distinctive or even unique features. The former are the traits that can be used to compare destinations, in general, while the latter might become distinctive symbols of each specific destination.

The formation of destination image

Understanding how a destination image is formed can assist destination promoters in developing appropriate destination images for the target markets (Gartner 1993; McCartney 2008). By portraying the complexity of image formation, Gartner (1993) identifies seven agents that have an active role in this process: (1) advertising developed by destination areas promoters (e.g. television, radio, brochures), which has a strong influence on destination image; (2) information provided by organizations who have interest in the travel decision process, such as tour operators; (3) recognizable spokespersons; (4) articles or reports from an unbiased source with no vested interest in increased travel to the destination; (5) autonomous agents such as news and popular culture; (6) unrequested information received from individuals who have been in an area or believe they know what exists there; and (7) word of mouth.

Image is thus shaped by many sources of information, from promotional literature to opinions of others and general media. Furthermore, by actually visiting the destination, its image is affected and modified based on first-hand information and experience (Echtner & Ritchie 2003). Gunn's model (1988) is frequently mentioned for its validity to express the role of external and internal sources of information in the image formation process (Gunn, in Echtner and Ritchie 2003). This model identifies seven phases of the travel experience (1) accumulation of mental images about vacation experiences, (2) modification of those images by further information, (3) decision to take the vacation trip, (4) travel to the destination, (5) participation at the destination, (6) return home, and (7) modification of images based on actual experience. Gunn labels the destination image formed in the first phase "organic image," since it is based on non-commercial sources. In the second phase, termed "induced image," tourists start to get an image from commercial sources, while in the last stage image is shaped by the actual experience. A similar conceptual model developed by Manhas et al. (2016) points out three components of destination image related to three stages of consumption: pre-consumption, during-consumption, and post-consumption. The last phase represents the satisfaction/dissatisfaction response, tourists' positive/negative world-of-mouth, and their intentions to revisit. This phase is of critical importance, as these post-consumption responses influence other tourists' pre-consumption images. This model highlights that individuals have an image also prior to departure (Echtner & Ritchie 2003) and that visitors and non-visitors differ in their destination image.

Phillips and Jang (2010) add empirical evidence to the difference between first-time visitors and repeated visitors' destination image. The results of their research show that both cognitive and affective image improve after the actual experience of the city (NYC), in the sense that the visitation of New York acts as a step for confirming tourists' prior beliefs.

So far, the factors influencing destination image discussed are related to the type of information sources used by tourists, as well as to their direct experience. In addition to these factors, many other authors in the tourism literature have highlighted the psychological (e.g. motivation) as well as socio-economic (e.g. age, education) characteristics as key constructs in the image formation process (Gallarza et al. 2002). Tourists' psychological motivations significantly influence the affective components of destination image. Individuals have a more favorable affective image of the destination when the emotions related to the place coincide with their motivation or benefits sought (San Martin & Rodrìguez del Bosque 2008).

Also, cultural background plays a key role in influencing the image construct (McCartney, 2008). In tourism research, culture has been examined according to the tourist's geographical origins: in this sense, it has been established that tourists from different countries have heterogeneous cultural values, and consequently, a different perception of the same tourist destination (Dominique & Lopes 2011; San Martìn & Rodrìguez del Bosque 2008). According to San Martìn and Rodrìguez del Bosque (2008), the shorter the cultural distance, or the higher the degree of similarity between the tourists' values and the ones embedded in the tourist destination's culture, the more favorable is the cognitive/affective image of the tourist destination.

The uncertainty-avoidance trait that characterizes some national cultures also affects the type of information sources used in the formation of a destination's pre-visit image (Frías et al. 2012). Those individuals who use a source consistent with their culture will obtain information best suited for their needs and will consequently develop a more positive attitude toward the destination. Strictly linked to the cultural resources, the destination image formation is affected by the political and legal system of the country (Manhas et al. 2016). These contextual variables, both social and political, may be the main forces determining which tourist destination to visit (San Martìn & Rodrìguez del Bosque 2008).

Assessment and measurement of destination image

The important role of destination image, in terms of both understanding travel behavior and designing effective tourism marketing strategies, stresses the need to develop methodologies that accurately measure this concept (Echtner & Ritchie 2003). In their review of destination image research, Gallarza et al. (2002) elaborate taxonomy of the methodologies used in research starting from 1980. The taxonomy shows a predominance of quantitative methods, which has led to a focus on attribute-based components rather than holistic and unique components. Quantitative methodologies are easy to administer, facilitate the comparison between different destinations, and produce results with a high degree of generalizability, but since they limit the possible answers, it may result in difficult to measure holistic impressions as well as unique traits of a destination. Most frequently, qualitative techniques are applied as a preliminary step in order to elicit the relevant attributes and dimensions, which are then inserted in a structured protocol to investigate images (Jenkins 1999). Thus, on the one hand, unstructured methodologies allow the development of a complete list of attributes, and on the other hand, structured methodologies allow for a reaching of statistical significance. In this perspective, a mixed qualitative-quantitative approach is suggested as an effective solution to exploit the benefits of each method as well as to extend the breadth and range of inquiry (San Martìn & Rodrìguez del Bosque 2008).

The role of user-generated content (UGC) in destination image

UGC refers to media contents created or produced by the general public rather than by paid professionals and shared publicly (Bright et al. 2008; Xiang & Gretzel 2010). Although the concept is not recent, Web 2.0 has enabled ordinary consumers to communicate with and influence a wider audience, adding a new dimension to destination marketing (Govers & Go 2005). Tourism organizations cannot ignore the development of UGC, peer-to-peer web applications, and virtual communities as consumers perceive them as more trustable than professional guidebooks or travel agency (Akehurst 2009). Many DMOs have recognized the potentiality of UGC as a transparent source of information (Xiang & Gretzel 2010); for instance, they have included blogs on their official web pages.

According to Akehurst (2009), those who post online are the ones who tend to search travel information from others who engage in similar activities; hence, it is undeniable that the key role of UGC in shaping the image elaborated in the first phases of Gunn's stage model. Furthermore, the very fact that social media are updated frequently and include a lot of hyperlinks leads search engines such as Google to index social media pages more and more frequently (Xiang & Gretzel 2010). Thus, when looking for information on the Internet, tourists will inevitably be affected by UGC, a process described by Cheung et al. (2011) as "democratization of the image creation and dissemination."

The fact is that UGCs are affecting the destination image dimension and its formation has led several authors to adopt UGC as a method of measuring destination image. Despite the time, energy, resources, and cost required to locate relevant UGC information and extract meaningful insights (Akehurst 2009), few researchers have tempted to do so. By comparing comments and meta-tags from official websites of agritourism farms and selected nationwide tourist offers' comparison sites, Stepaniuk (2015) states that UGC can be used effectively in destination image analysis. An additional case is that of Serna et al. (2014), who analyze the opinions on social networks using a text-mining tool in order to compare the projected image developed by the DMOs and visitors' perceptions.

Of fundamental importance for the present research are the works of Stepchenkova and Zhan (2013), who elaborate a comparison between the pictorial materials published online and the DMOs' visual materials, and of Latorre-Martínez and Iñíguez-Berrozpe (2014), who defend the use of image-focused social media as a first-hand source to discover the type of tourists, the most visited places, and the months with greatest tourist influx.

Methodology

Analysis of pictorial material

Pictures are sources of a great amount of information; they appear as a direct representation of reality, a true reflection of places (Domšić 2013). Albers and James (1988) identify two main components of a photograph: the content and the composition. The former refers to the signs captured in a photo, whereas the latter refers to the way in which these signs are linked to each other. Starting from these components, different approaches can be applied in order to interpret photographs. While the metonymic perspective interprets the sign as they appear, the metaphoric approach goes beyond the mere appearances, treating the signs as symbols whose meaning lies outside the picture. Finally, a picture can be interpreted through a historic or sociologic perspective that seeks to understand the relationship between the image and the context in which it is created (Dorfles & Pinotti, 2009).

Different from a text, which requires some thoughts and reflection, a picture is instantaneous. While traditional snapshot has usually been taken at special places and occasions, digital snapshots tend to extend the range of sites for photography (Dong-Hoo, 2010). Digital cameras have allowed people to photograph "recklessly" and "unconditionally" without consideration of the cost of film and printing and to capture every moment of their experience.

Stepchenkova and Zhan (2013) identify two methods for examining photographs: quantitative method or content analysis and qualitative method or semiotic analysis. The former considers the photo as attribute-based, and it is concerned with describing the appearance of certain themes and attributes. The outcomes are the frequency of a certain attribute, its co-occurrence with others, and the clustering of attributes. Co-occurrences of focal elements in a photograph are an important factor in describing a dataset because they allow understanding the key associations related to an experience. Content analysis has been used mainly to study textual content, but it can be applied to images, maps, sounds, and other works of art (Krippendorff 2004; Neuendorf 2002).

The semiotic analysis considers the picture as a whole and does not "break" it in its attributes. In this context, both the content and composition of a picture are examined in order to extract the intended message. As such, this analysis is characterized by a high degree of interpretation and hidden content, but its integration with content analysis creates more critical, richer, and complex interpretations (Domšić 2013).

In the present work, content analysis has been selected as the main approach due to its ability to manage qualitative material in a systematic, verifiable, and replicable way.

Category development and data coding

Pictorial materials can be transformed into analyzable representation by applying a coding process (Krippendorff 2004), which should result in good meaningful content categories. The categories chosen have to be mutually exclusive and exhaustive in order to assure that the results represent the dataset of pictures completely and unambiguously. First, we reviewed the relevant literature to develop a list of functional and psychological attributes generally used to measure destination image (Table 5.1). Looking at the number of authors who have investigated each attribute, it is clear that research has focused more on functional rather than psychological attributes of destination image.

This list of attributes can be considered a basis for the category definition in the coding process, with the caution that the importance of attributes is related to the destination type (Echtner & Ritchie 2003). The coding process takes place when observers, readers, or analysts interpret what they see, read, or find, and then state their experiences in the formal terms of analysis (Krippendorff 2004).

The first step in the coding process is to identify an exclusive and exhaustive list of destination attributes. Stepchenkova and Zhan (2013) analyzed separately a sample of photos from the two databases to develop a list of categories, which were compared and integrated (Neuendorf 2002). The following step consists of assigning the photos to the

Table 5.1 Attributes used by researchers to measure destination image

	Echtner and Ritchie (2003)	Gallarza et al. (2002)	Jenkins (1999)
Scenery/natural attractions	13	19	12
Hospitality/receptiveness	11	20	10
Climate	8	12	10
Cost/price levels	9	16	8
Nightlife/entertainment	8	17	8
Sports facilities/activities	8	16	7
Shopping facilities	5	15	10
Personal safety	4	10	10
Different cousin/food/drinks	7	15	7
Restful/relaxing	5	12	9
Historic site/museums	6	18	7
Accommodation facilities	5	14	8
Different customs/culture	7	7	6
Tourist sites/activities	8	8	4
Local infrastructure/ transportation	7	8	4
National parks/wilderness areas	7		3
Architecture/buildings	7		3
Beaches	6		3

categories, allowing multiple classifications, depending on the complex nature of the picture (Stepchenkova & Zhan 2013).

After a pilot test on a sub-sample of the total dataset to prove the coding scheme, a coding guidebook is developed with detailed rules in order to make the process reliable and replicable.

Presentation of the case study

The current research uses Milan as a case study. In Anholt's City Index, the Brand Milan is strongly associated with fashion, design, shopping and "design lifestyle": "Milan's contribution of fashion to the world is considered by an enormous margin to be the greatest contribution of any city in any field" (Anholt 2006, p. 26). Milan also occupies a significant position in the country's tourism sector, together with Rome and Venice. In the past three years, Milan had more visitors than Rome; the almost ten million visitors in 2018 make tourism a booming industry for the city, and Milan becomes the 15th city in the Mastercard's 2018 Global Destination Cities Index. According to De Carlo et al. (2009), the city is the second most important Italian destination in terms of overnight stays and the average expenditure of foreign tourists is higher than in other large Italian destinations. At the same time, Milan reveals a crucial weakness: its seasonal tourism is strictly linked to business travel, as is proven by the high number of people traveling alone.

The current positioning of Milan can be attributed to its model of tourist development, where the players operate as atoms without exploiting possible benefits that they could gain by creating synergies within a unified destination strategy. De Carlo et al. (2009) recommend that Milan should include culture at the very core of its strategy to strengthen the positive elements of the city image and to slacken the bond with its business-oriented current positioning. A recent research conducted by Ipsos (2015) revealed Milan's twofold soul: on the one hand, the city is linked to business and production, on the other, it has a cultural and creative identity. The data show that foreigners perceive the city as creative, rich in culture, and welcoming, whereas Italians perceive it as hard-working, expensive but also dynamic and international. The research also confirms the positive impact of Expo 2015, which has contributed to the positive image of Milan.

Method of empirical research

Data collection

The first decision to face was related to the choice of the most suitable database for the DMO's pictorial materials and the photo-shared social media.

For the former, we chose Milan official website www.turismo.milano.it. The website contains a photo gallery whose photos are shared between the tourist's and the municipality's websites with a predominance of promotional photos (ContattaMI section on the website). Of the initial 1,049 photos,[1] 136 were doubles of the same image and thus were withdrawn, 58 were deleted as they consisted of banners and press-related images, 91 were excluded because of their bad quality or because they were irrelevant to the locality, 141 were deleted because they represented exclusively paintings and/or sculptures, and 20 were historic photos. The remaining 603 photos were filtered again in order to obtain a smaller database. The photos were organized in groups based on the month of publication, and a proportional number of photos were randomly deleted[2] from each group so as to have all months equally represented. We finally obtained 500 photos (Tourism Website Database).

Flickr was chosen.as the photo-shared social media. Actually, the first decision was to focus on Instagram because of its larger penetration, but starting June 1, 2016, the Application Programming Interface's policy changed and restricted to pre-selected scopes.

Flickr, on the other hand, has been widely used for research, mainly because of its accessibility, size, and links to other social media (Stepchenkova & Zhan 2013). Flickr offers a search engine called "World Map" that shows the most relevant photos based on geo-localization and tags of interest, but, despite this tool, a specific web application was developed in order to create a database that could best fit our research.

The first step was to choose the parameters of the research, in particular, the period of time and the tags of interest. As regards the former, all the photos from September 1, 2015 to August 31, 2016 were considered. For the tags of interest, following Stepchenkova and Zhan's study (2013), the "travel" tag was thought to indicate that images were posted by travelers rather than by residents. Since the research carried out on the web application resulted in a smaller database compared to the Tourism Website database, we developed a methodology using Google Adwords in order to come up with other similar tags. By doing so, we could develop a database as close to the reality studied as possible. Using the planning tool for keywords displayed in the Google AdWords page, we reviewed the 702 ideas linked to "travel" under the travel and tourism category, and compared the results with Google Trends. The initial words were "travel," "traveling," "vacation," "tourism," "trip," "holiday," and "destination." The words "traveling" and "destination" are less frequent than "tourism," and thus they were not included in the tag's list, whereas we added the equivalent Italian worlds "viaggio," "viaggiare," "turismo," and "vacanza." The final dataset includes 454 photos (Flickr Database).

Category development and data coding

The following step consisted of choosing a sufficient number of categories to be mutually exclusive and exhaustive in order to assure that the results represented the dataset of pictures completely and unambiguously. First, a subset was created of approximately 10% of both databases. Using Stepchenkova and Zhan's list of categories (2013) as a starting point, we adopted a combined approach in which we analyzed separately the samples of photos and developed a list of categories that were then integrated. Some categories (for example, "People," "Architecture Buildings," "Tourism Facilities") were kept the same, while others were adapted to the city environment (for example, "Nature Landscape" was changed into "Green parks"). Finally, new categories were developed so as to express the unique attributes of Milan: "University Academy," "Design Fashion," and "Church."

In order to further assess the reliability of the list of attributes and prove the coding scheme, a pilot test was undertaken on two randomly selected sub-samples, with two independent judges. The reliability coefficient was calculated for each category, namely the percentage of photos for which the coders agreed on the presence or absence of a particular category. All the categories were proven to meaningfully describe the dataset; hence, they were included the coding guidebook. Table 5.2 lists the final categories.

Table 5.2 List of categories

Stepchenkova S., & Zhan's list	Our list (City of Milan)
Nature landscape	Green parks
People	People
Archeological sites	Monuments
Way of life	Nightlife
Traditional clothing	
Architecture buildings	Architecture building
Outdoor/adventure	
Wildlife	
Art object	Museum art objects
Tourism facilities	Tourism facilities
Urban landscape	Urban landscape
Domesticated animals	
Plants	
Festival and rituals	Festivals and rituals
Leisure activities	Leisure activity
Food	Food
Country landscape	Country landscape
Transport infrastructure	Transport infrastructure
Tour	
	University academy
	Design and fashion
	Church
Other	Other

Results

Attribute frequency

The first objective of our research was to detect the most frequent attributes and the differences between the perceived and the projected images. First, the probability of each attribute to appear in each database was calculated as the frequency of that attribute divided by the total number of photos of each database. Second, a chi-square analysis for each category revealed if there was a significant distance between the two databases. Table 5.3 summarizes the results in order of the total number of pictures.

Milan is represented as a city of arts and culture: architecture buildings, the "church" (Duomo), monuments take a large share of the photos in both databases, but with significant differences in the two databases. The photos published on the Tourism Website tend to represent more green areas, people, architecture and buildings, museums and art object, country landscape and universities and academies. On the other side, visitors focus more on tourist attractions such as monuments and churches. Within the latter, the large majority of photos (97.5%) are taken to the Duomo cathedral. This result is in line with De Carlo et al.'s findings (2009): their survey revealed that Milan's preeminent emblem is the Duomo (75% of their interviewees). Also "Design and fashion" is considered more relevant by visitors compared to the Tourism Office.

Table 5.3 Category frequency: comparison between DMO and Flickr's databases

	DMO (500)	DMO (%)	Flickr (454)	Flickr (%)	Tot	Tot (%)	Chi-square	P value
Architecture building	219	43.8	153	33.7	372	39.0	10.203	0.001
Church	57	11.4	163	35.9	220	23.1	80.519	0.000
People	107	21.4	61	13.4	168	17.6	10.401	0.001
Urban landscape	72	14.4	81	17.8	153	16.0		
Museum art objects	104	20.8	21	4.6	125	13.1	54.672	0.000
Monuments	46	9.2	70	15.4	116	12.2	8.615	0.0003
Green parks	74	14.8	7	1.5	81	8.5	56.139	0.000
Festival rituals	35	7.0	35	7.7	70	7.3		
Transport infrastructure	22	4.4	35	7.7	57	6.0		
University academy	50	10.0	6	1.3	56	5.9	32.433	0.000
Food	9	1.8	19	4.2	28	2.9		
Country landscape	21	4.2	0	0.0	21	2.2	19.497	0.000
Design and fashion	4	0.8	20	4.4	24	2.5	12.611	0.000
Leisure activity	14	2.8	5	1.1	19	2.0		
Tourism facilities	4	0.8	12	2.6	16	1.7		
Nightlife	8	1.6	6	1.3	14	1.5		
Other	11	2.2	28	6.2	39	4.1	9.552	0.000

Aggregated maps

The purpose of constructing destination image maps is to obtain a visual summary of the data and a better understanding of the attributes that tend to appear together in the photos. The maps are an effective tool to compare the Tourism Website and Flickr databases. If any two attributes are independent of one another, the number of their co-occurrences is binomially distributed. A z-score statistic was calculated as the difference between the number of actual and expected co-occurrences of two attributes divided by their standard deviation and was compared to the critical z-score from a normal distribution (1.96 at the significance level of 0.05). Larger z-scores in absolute value would indicate that the two attributes tend to appear together in photos. On the contrary, larger and negative z-scores mean that if an attribute is in the photos, it is unlikely that the other would appear as well.

All the categories with a frequency <3% were excluded, with the only exception of "Leisure activity" in the Tourism Website database (2.8%) because we would have lost significant associations (this category is significantly linked with both "People" and "Transport infrastructure"). Also, the category "Others" was excluded from the analysis. Figure 5.1 shows the graphical representations of results. The colored bubbles portray the most frequent categories for each database, whereas the numbers shown on the segments between bubbles represent the actual co-occurrence of the two attributes linked and the respective z-score. Only links with z-score >1.96 are shown.

The Tourism Website's map shows that the most frequent attributes are "People," "Architecture buildings," and "Museum art objects." There are no links between the three largest bubbles, meaning that they are not associated statistically. The pairs "People"-"Museum art objects" and "People"-"Architecture Buildings" are negatively associated (their z-scores are respectively –2.51 and –2.23), which means that people are rarely associated both with "Museum art objects" and with "Architecture buildings." The map shows the positive associations between "People" and "Festivals rituals" and between "People" and "Leisure activity." Another group consists of the positive associations between "Transport infrastructure" and both "Leisure activity" and "Urban landscape." For instance, there are photos promoting car-sharing and bike lines around Milan as well as inaugurations of new underground stops. The same figure displays the positive relations between "Green parks" and "Country landscape," and between "Architecture buildings" and "University academy." The former is composed of photos of farms and abbeys in Milan's province, whereas the latter is represented mostly by photos showing the external parts of universities or libraries, promoted as buildings worth to visit. Finally, the map shows three stand-alone categories: "Museum art objects," "Church,"

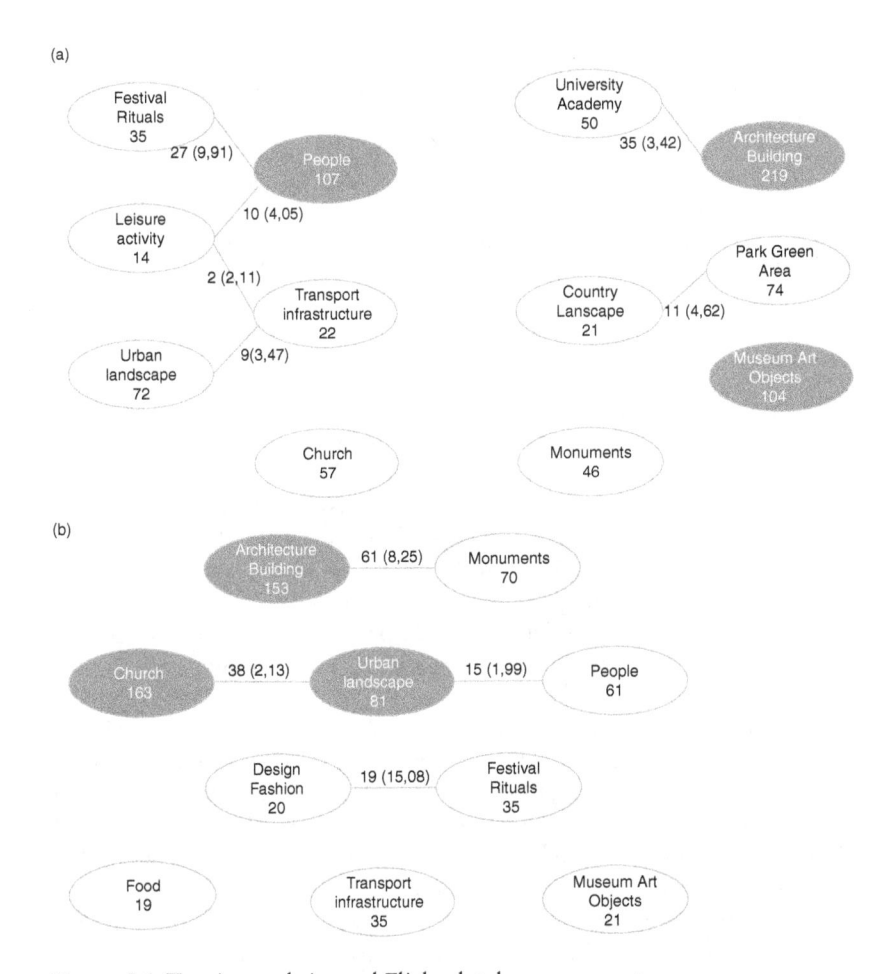

Figure 5.1 Tourism website and Flickr database: aggregate maps.

and "Monuments." The categories "Monuments" and "Architecture Buildings" had co-occurrence of 26, but the z-score was slightly lower the threshold (1.37).

The Flickr aggregated map is simpler than the Tourist Website map. The most frequent attributes are "Architecture buildings," "Church," and "Urban landscape." The last two are positively associated, indicating that visitors tend to photograph churches within their urban setting, such as the view from the top of Duomo. "Urban Landscape" is also weakly linked with "People" (their z-score is slightly >1.96). The map also displays the positive relation between "Architecture buildings" and "Monuments" as well as between "Design and fashion" and "Festival rituals." The latter consists mainly of photos taken during the Design Trade Fair (Salone del Mobile), which takes place every year around

April. Finally, there are three stand-alone categories: "Food," "Transport infrastructure," and "Museum art objects." The first category is rarely depicted in combination with other elements, with the exception of "People" (four photos only). For "Transport infrastructure," tourists frequently picture trains at Stazione Centrale; despite that, this category and "Architecture buildings" are not statistically associated. Finally, within the category "Museum art objects," the photos mainly focus on street art paintings, with few exceptions showing people at art expositions (three photos) or the external part of museums (five photos).

Geo-maps

Geographical distribution maps allow understanding of the differences between the projected and the perceived image of different areas of Milan. The city was divided into nine municipalities, and each photo was assigned to one of these areas. For the Tourism Website database, by looking at the description next to each photo, we were able to associate it with a specific area of Milan in 83.4% of the cases; the other photos were excluded. The same process was followed for the Flickr database relying on attached tags or titles; 20.5% photos were excluded because we could not identify the location. Figure 5.2 shows the two corresponding maps.

Area 1 represents more than half of the photos projected by the Tourism Office (59.7%) and 72% of the photos of the Flickr database because the majority of tourist attractions are located in this area. In the Tourism Website database, the less represented areas are areas 7 and 5 (1.9% and 2.4%, respectively), followed by areas 8, 2 and 4 (2.9%, 3.1% and 5.0%, respectively); areas 3, 6 and 9 are almost equally divided (6.5%, 7.4%, 11.0%). In the Flickr map, the less represented areas are 4, 6, 5, 3, and 7 (from 0% to 3%), and the remaining areas are almost equally represented at around 6%–7%. Most of the areas differ in the two groups of photos. For instance, Area 2 is overrepresented in the Flickr database, because travelers tend to photograph Stazione Centrale (17 photos) since it is a historical building with a high level of daily traffic. Area 4, which in the Tourism Website database is represented by parks, art galleries and few other points of interest, is not represented at all in the Flickr database.

Tags frequency

In addition to the analysis of pictorial materials, we investigated the tags associated with Flickr's photos. Tagging is gaining high popularity because of its potentiality of sharing and communicating information as well as organizing photos. In their quantitative study on tags on Flickr, Nov and Ye (2010) state that depending on the types of audience, people

(a) Tourism Website

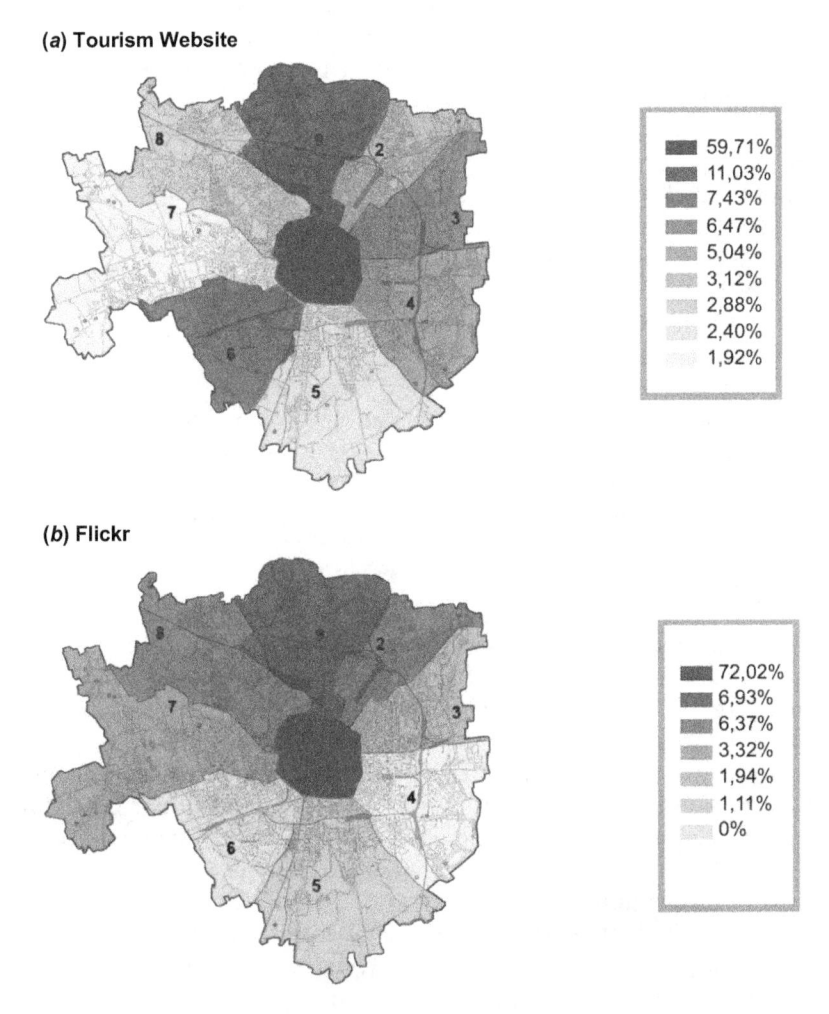

59,71%
11,03%
7,43%
6,47%
5,04%
3,12%
2,88%
2,40%
1,92%

(b) Flickr

72,02%
6,93%
6,37%
3,32%
1,94%
1,11%
0%

Figure 5.2 Tourism website and Flickr geo-maps.

seek different objectives. If the audience is "the Public," tags are used so that the whole of Flickr's community can find the images. The authors found that being a public Flickr user, the social presence (such as the number of contacts) and the number of photos published on profiles was positively associated with tagging level.

As expected, results reflect the ones found in the pictorial analysis. First, the tags "#architecture" and #building" and tags related such as "#modernarchitecture" or "#housing" are among the most frequently used by tourists to describe their photos. Also, the "Church" (symbolized by the Duomo) and "City landscape" categories are repeatedly described by different tags. "Monuments" and "People" do not receive the same importance that they had in the pictorial analysis. The former is represented by the tags "#landmark" and "#monument," whereas the latter can be associated with "#martinaway," "#travelblogger," "#travelbloggers." Furthermore "#expo" is the only tag that can be linked with the "Festival rituals" category. In relation to the cultural trait of Milan, "Museum art objects" is portrayed by a few tags such as "#culture," "#art," and "#decoration." Finally "#design" terms the "Design and fashion" category. Differently from the results obtained in the previous sections, the categories "Transport infrastructure" and "Food" are not described by tags.

An extremely interesting insight into the present analysis is that Milan is seen as a city to explore. The new tourists who are visiting Milan seem to be repeat tourists: the first time they come for business, then they come back to visit the city. Leisure tourists are relatively new for Milan, and the Tourism Administration is targeting this segment inviting them to explore the city. The tags "#exploring," "#adventure," and "#explore" confirm De Carlo et al.'s (2009) results that Milan is perceived as a dynamic city in which "doing" and "discovering" are valued.

Discussion

The results of the research allowed us to obtain a general view of the perceived and a projected image of Milan. The methodology applied used content analysis as the main technique, followed by a statistical comparison of the frequency of categories and construction of both aggregated maps and geographical maps. Tags related to the photos confirmed most of the previous findings and revealed additional information meaningful for understanding the city image. By combining the results obtained in the two databases, the three categories that best describe Milan are: "Architecture buildings," "Church," and "People." These attributes are statistically different between the two databases: the first and third attributes are more frequent in the Tourism Website database, whereas travelers tend to photograph more churches, and especially the cathedral. Duomo is a recurring visual motif among tourists.

For the "People" category, the difference between the two databases is due to the fact that the photos published on the Tourism Website are shared among the Municipality's and the Tourism's websites. Most of the subjects portrayed in this database are new politicians and/or institutional events. The 35 photos coded just in this category confirm this statement because they mainly picture politicians in their offices. The three most frequent attributes not only statistically differ in the two databases, but they are also portrayed differently, as it is shown in the two aggregated maps. For instance, tourists tend to take pictures of the building that have historical value, such as Castello Sforzesco or Galleria Vittorio Emanuele, whereas, on the Tourism Website, the photos representing buildings are related to universities and public libraries.

Travelers tend to take photos either from the square in front of the cathedral or from the top of it, showing the urban landscape, and people are often photographed in a generic urban context. On the contrary, in the Tourism Website database people are showed while performing sports activities or during events. The chi-square test shows that only seven categories are equally represented in the two databases; one of them is "Nightlife," whose frequency is surprisingly very low. Despite the fact that Milan is considered a young city, with many tourists 18–34 years old (De Carlo et al. 2009), the frequency of "Nightlife" is <3% in both datasets, and thus, it is not shown in the aggregated maps. A possible interpretation is that young people do not want to be seen as tourists when experiencing Milan's nightlife, and thus they do not tag their photos as #travel, #vacation, #tourism, #trip or #holiday. Furthermore, they would probably rely on peers' advice or blogs rather than on the official tourism website in order to find places to go out during the night, as the former is perceived more trustworthy (Akehurst 2009).

An additional interesting finding is related to the "Festival rituals" category. Despite the fact that it does not statistically differ in the two databases, at a closer look, the internal composition diverges. In the Tourism Website database, the photos are related to music festivals (11 photos) or institutional events (9 photos), while the photos published on Flickr and coded within this category are related to worldwide events such as the Expo (11 photos) and the design fairs (22 photos).

Milan is really seen as intimately entwined with fashion and design (De Carlo et al. 2009). Within the category "Design and fashion," travelers seem to be more interested in the design rather than in the fashion trait of Milan. Both the pictorial and tag analysis reveal that Flickr users were involved in the design fair: most of the photos coded in this category portray design objects exposed in the fair. Since Milan is also strongly linked to fashion events, as it is stressed in the Anholt City Index (2006), the absence of this attribute in the Flickr database could be ascribed to the fact that people who participate in fashion events do not want to label themselves as tourists. De Carlo et al. (2009) confirm that only 10% of tourists suggest an association with fashion. This category is underrepresented in the Tourism Office website vs the Flickr database: there are only four photos coded as "Design and fashion."

A possible explanation is that Milan has a seasonal pattern of tourism activity, dictated mainly by trade fairs, but the Tourism Administration is adopting a strategy to enhance the cultural heritage of the city, as recommended by De Carlo et al. (2009). This strategy seems to be effective, as tourists share photographs of monuments (15.4%) and churches (35.9%). Among the former, tourists tend to take pictures of Castello Sforzesco (24 photos) and the Galleria Vittorio Emanuele (26 photos). The only aspect regarding the cultural sphere that does not appear valued by tourists is "Museum art objects" (4.6%). Thus, this strategy allows a slackening of the bond with Milan's business-oriented positioning and, at the same time, a satisfying of tourists' interests and expectations.

Additional considerations regarding the Tourism Office's strategy can be drawn by looking at the frequencies recorded in Table 5.2. The Tourism Website database shows more photos coded as "Country landscape," "Green parks," and "University academy," evidence of the Tourism Office's strategy to promote not only the city but also its hinterland. This promotional strategy can be tracked also within the "Church" category. While the majority of photos coded in the Flickr database portray the Duomo, the photos posted in the Tourism Website portray almost 30 different churches across the city. The geographical maps give additional proof of this strategy developed by the Tourism Office. Compared to Flickr's map, fewer photos are geo-localized in area 1 (12% less), and the rest is distributed across the other eight areas of Milan.

As regards the "Country landscape," only the Tourism Office shows areas in the Milanese Province, whereas in the Flickr database there are zero photos. This result is in line with De Carlo et al. (2009), who state that tourists tend to visit the city rather than its metropolitan area. These are the reasons that drove us to consider only the city of Milan when we had to develop the geo-maps. Finally, the under-representation of "Green parks" in the Flickr database respects De Carlo et al.' finding (2009) that Milan is perceived as a city that lacks green spaces.

The category "Food" is equally represented in both databases. Despite the fact that Milan is felt to represent the apogee of Italian food (De Carlo et al. 2009), this attribute is not fully developed by the Tourism Administration: its frequency is <3%, and hence it is not represented in the aggregated map. Since travelers seem attracted by the culinary offer of the city, the Tourism Office should allocate more importance to this trait. Finally also the "Transport infrastructure" is equally represented by the Tourism Office and by travelers, with the typical orange tram and the bike-sharing BikeMi.

A final consideration deals with the aggregated maps. The overall number of significant associations is lower in both databases compared to the one found by Stepchenkova and Zhan (2013). This may be due to the exploring's aspect that characterizes Milan, as it emerged in the tag analysis, while Peru has routes that are common among tourists. For instance, the so-called Gringo Trail, which is common among American tourists, includes the most famous attractions: Lima, Ica, Arequipa, Puno, Cusco. Furthermore, while it was easier to classify the photos posted in the Tourism Website since they were more structured and planned, the Flickr photos showed a high degree of diversity that can be ascribed to the "discovery" nature of the city.

Future research directions

Previous research has found that people who post online tend to be young; hence, they do not represent the totality of tourists. An in-depth analysis of the Flickr users could be interesting additional research that could provide DMOs with useful insights.

A second avenue for future research is the integration between content analysis and semiotic analysis: when used in conjunction, these investigations create more critical, richer and complex interpretations of pictorial representations, revealing insights regarding the general feeling and atmosphere of the city as well as the friendliness of the people or perceived safety.

An additional topic for future research could be to conduct the same analysis on different pictorial materials, such as brochures and website, and/or different social media, to detect whether the DMOs' strategy is consistent among different promotional channels, and to get a well-rounded picture of tourists' perceptions.

Conclusion

The empirical study contributes to the analysis of Milan's image and suggests practical implications for the Tourism Administration. Overall, the Tourism Office presents a rounded image of the city by posting photos of all the areas of Milan, including the less touristic ones. Furthermore, the projected image of the city is linked with its cultural and academic traits, which helps to dampen its business-oriented positioning. This is the reason why, even among the festivals and rituals, the Tourism Office does not promote the trade fairs in favor of less known events detached from the business' sphere.

The analysis of the photos posted on Flickr allowed for the identification of two patterns in tourist behavior. If on one side, visitors are interested in the most famous touristic attractions such as the Duomo and architecture buildings, which are mainly located in area 1 of Milan; on the other side, they also explore the city. Compared to other Italian cities, Milan seems to have a lower number of attractions, but many have to be discovered, and the strategy of the Tourism department is to stimulate the curiosity of the visitors.

The theoretical implications of the present study belong to the significant role of UGC in both shaping and measuring the destination image. Both the deep bond between tourism and visual materials, and the increasing relevance of photo-sharing social media have led us to the decision of focusing on photos posted online. Studying the photos posted online reveals insights regarding the during-consumption and post-consumption phases of the traveling journey; the latter is critical both for understanding tourists' intention to revisit and to attract new visitors.

Key construct definitions

Destination image measurement: The image of a destination can be measured focusing on attribute components or holistic and unique components. The first approach requires the development of a list of attributes of the destination, which are then analyzed using quantitative techniques; the second is more qualitative in nature and can be used either as a first step to identify the attributes of the destination or as a stand-alone method.

Pictorial material as a source to study destination image: Pictorial materials both offline and online are a very rich source to study destination image. Photos published on brochures and websites, as well as on social media, such as Facebook, Flickr, Instagram, and Pinterest, can be analyzed using many different techniques. In this work, content analysis on a sample of photos selected by different databases allowed to identify the categories represented in the pictures, their frequency of occurrence and co-occurrence, thus giving insights on the intended and perceived positioning of the city.

Destination image maps: Destination image maps are networks that allow for an obtaining of a visual summary of the data of interest and a better understanding of the attributes that tend to appear together in the photos.

Geographical distribution maps: Geographical distribution maps allow for an understanding of the differences between the projected and the perceived image of different areas of a destination. In this work, the city has been divided into nine municipalities, and each photo was assigned to one of these areas on the basis of the description written by the Tourism Office and the tags used by tourists.

Notes

1 Website last updated on May 2016. The photos were collected on August 2016, in three sections lasting around six hours each.
2 After having assigned a number from 1 to 500 to each photo in the Tourism Website database and from 1 to 454 in the Flickr database's photos, we used the Excel formula that gives random numbers in the selected interval.

References

Akehurst, G. (2009). User generated content: the use of blogs for tourism organisations and tourism consumers. *Service Business*, 3(1), 51–61.
Albers, P. C. & James, W. R. (1988). Travel photography: A methodological approach. *Annals of Tourism Research*, 15(1), 134–158.
Anholt, S. (2006). The Anholt-GMI city brands index. How the world sees the world's cities. *Place Branding*, 2(1), 18–31.
Bright, L. F., Daugherty, T., & Eastin M. S. (2008). Exploring consumer motivations for creating user-generated content. *Journal of Interactive Advertising*, 8(2), 16–25.

Cheung, C., McKercher, B., Law, R., Lo, I. S., & Lo, A. (2011). Tourism and online photography. *Tourism Management*, 32, 725–731.

De Carlo, M., Canali, S., Pritchard, A., & Morgan, N. (2009). Moving Milan towards Expo 2015: designing culture into a city brand. *Journal of Place Management and Development*, 2(1), 8–22.

Dominique, S., & Lopes, F. (2011). Destination image: origins, developments and implications. *Pasos*, 9(2), 305–315.

Domšić, L. (2013). Touristic photography and the construction of place identity: visual image of Croatia. In *Advance in environment, ecosystem and sustainable tourism*, Proceedings of the 11th international conference on sustainable tourism and cultural heritage. Brasov: WSEA Press, 277–282.

Dong-Hoo, L. (2010). Digital cameras, personal photography and the reconfiguration of spatial experience. *The Information Society*, 26(4), 266–275.

Dorfles, G., & Pinotti, A. (2009). *Comunicazione visiva*. Milano: Atlas.

Echtner, C. M., & Ritchie, J. R. B. (2003). The meaning and measurement of destination image. *The Journal of Tourism Studies*, 14(1), 37–48.

Frías, D. M., Rodríguez, M. A., Castañeda, J. A., Sabiote, C. M., & Buhalis, D. (2012). The formation of a tourist destination's image via information sources: the moderating effect of culture. *International Journal of Tourism Research*, 14(5), 437–450.

Gallarza, M. G., Saura, I. G., & Garcìa, H. C. (2002). Destination image. Towards a conceptual framework. *Annals of Tourism Research*, 29(1), 56–78.

Gartner, W. C. (1993). Image formation process. *Journal of Travel & Tourism Marketing*, 2(2/3), 191–215.

Govers, R., & Go, F. M. (2005). Projected destination image online: website content analysis of pictures and text. *Information Technology & Tourism*, 7, 73–89.

Ipsos (2015). *Brand Milano. Il patrimonio simbolico della città. Dopo Expo 2015, aggiornamento dell'indagine quantitativa in Italia e all'estero.*

Jenkins, O. H. (1999). Understanding and measuring tourist destination images. *International Journal of Tourism Research*, 1(1), 1–15.

Kim, S. H., Hooland, S., & Han, H. S. (2013). A structural model for examining how destination image, perceived value, and service quality affect destination loyalty: a case study of Orlando. *International Journal of Tourism Research*, 15(4), 313–328.

Krippendorff, K. (2004). *Content analysis. An introduction to its methodology.* Thousand Oaks, CA: Sage Publications.

Latorre-Martínez, M. P, & Iñiguez-Berrozpe, T. (2014). Image-focused social media for a market analysis of tourism consumption. *International Journal of Technology Management*, 64(1), 17–30.

Lo, I. S., McKerker, B., Lo, A., Cheung, C. & Law, R. (2011). Tourism and online photography. *Tourism Management*, 32(4), 725–731.

Manhas, P. S., Manrai, L. A., & Manrai, A. K. (2016). Role of tourist destination development in building its brand image: a conceptual model. *Journal of Economics, Finance and Administrative Science*, 21(40), 25–29.

McCartney, G. (2008). Does one culture all think the same? An investigation of destination image perceptions from several origins. *Tourism Review*, 63(4), 13–26.

Morgan, N., Pritchard, A., & Pride R. (2004). *Destination branding: creating the unique destination proposition.* Oxford: Elsevier.

Neuendorf, K. A. (2002). *The content analysis guidebook.* Thousand Oaks, CA: Sage Publications.

Nov, O., & Ye, C. (2010). Why do people tag? Motivations for photo tagging. *Communication of the ACM, 53*(7), 128–131.

Phillips, W. M. J., & Jang, S. C. (2010). Destination image differences between visitors and non-visitors: the case of New York City. *International Journal of Tourism Research, 12*(5), 642–645.

San Martìn, H., & Rodrìguez del Bosque, I. A. (2008). Exploring the cognitive-affective nature of destination image and the role of psychological factors in its formation. *Tourism Management, 29*(2), 263–277.

Serna, A., Gerrikagoitia, J. K., & Alzue, A. (2014). Toward a better understanding of the cognitive destination image of Euskadi-Basque country based on the analysis of UGC. *Information and Communication Technologies in Tourism, 5,* 395–407.

Stepaniuk, K. (2015). The relation between destination image and social media user engagement – theoretical approach. *Procedia. Social and Behavioral Sciences, 213,* 616–621.

Stepchenkova, S., & Zhan, F. (2013). Visual destination images of Peru: comparative content analysis of DMO and user-generated photography. *Tourism Management, 36*(1), 590–601.

World Tourism Organization (UNWTO) (2007). *A practical guide to tourism destination management.* Madrid: World Tourism Organization.

Xiang, Z., & Gretzel, U. (2010). Role of social media in online travel information search. *Tourism Management, 31*(2), 179–188.

6 Developing a "customer-based place brand equity – destination branding" instrument

Sunny Bose, Sanjit Kumar Roy, and Bang Nguyen

Learning outcomes

At the end of this chapter, readers should be able to:

1 Understand the basic ideas of place branding
2 Comprehend the notion of destination branding
3 Make the connection to customer-based brand equity (CBBE)
4 Conceptualize customer-based place brand equity (CBPBE)
5 Analyze the example of West Bengal as a tourism destination brand
6 Evaluate the scale development process

Research background

The study sets out to develop an instrument to measure customer-based place brand equity (CBPBE) from the destination branding perspective. The region of West Bengal in eastern India is considered as the "place brand" for the study. Responses through questionnaire surveys are collected from various tourist destinations in West Bengal. Exploratory factor analysis (EFA) and confirmatory factor analysis (CFA) on 239 and 226 respondents respectively suggest a 12-item scale with four dimensions namely, Brand Awareness, Brand Image, Perceived Quality, and Brand Loyalty. The instrument is labeled CBPBE-DB (customer-based place brand equity-destination branding). Subsequently, the limitations of the study are discussed and the future research options pertaining to the study are deliberated.

Main body

Today, places are competing against each other. The traditional battle for the customers' wallets is no longer limited to business entities. Contemporary times are witnessing geographies compete among each other for investments, and trading and business opportunities. Nations and regions are competing for exports, tourists (domestic and international), investments (FDIs and domestic), immigrants and students. This rivalry among geographic entities has led to the gradual development of a new stream of marketing – place branding (Anholt, 2010). Place branding incorporates the traditional and non-traditional approaches of branding strategies with particular focus on promotion, development, and enhancement of salability of a particular place or region toward its prospective customers from the perspectives of exports, tourism, investments, and immigration. Branding theory views customer-based brand equity (CBBE) as a psychological construct that measures perceived value endowed by the "brand" to a customer. This view insists that marketing managers should promote the brand in a manner that the target customers perceive higher utility over the brand's competing alternatives. Given this premise and as mentioned earlier that a "place" can and is considered a brand; therefore, just like a product or service, CBBE can be applied to places.

It must be mentioned that today, destination branding is the most popular perspective of place branding (Bose, 2014). Destination branding focuses the place as a tourist destination and thus a destination "brand." The result of being a "brand" enables tourist places to command price premiums. For example, cities like Venice or regions like Tuscany (Italy) and Santorini (Greece) command a price premium from the tourists especially honeymooners (www.usnews.com). Thus, premising on branding theory it can be said that a destination brand commands brand equity among its target customers. In this regard, it may be said that CBBE for tourism destinations (Gartner & Ruzzier, 2011) is perhaps the oldest and most popular perspective of measuring a place's brand equity (Bose, 2014).

However, it must be mentioned that one of the biggest challenges of CBBE measurement for tourism destinations is the lack of uniform and globally generalizable measures due to the uniqueness of destination, for example, a destination like Delhi is popular for its history and culture and has very limited natural/physical attractions). In such a case, one cannot measure the brand equity of Delhi on the basis of a set of items that measure natural beauty like mountains/sea beaches. Thus, a dearth of generalizable instruments to measure a destination's brand equity has resulted in complex brand equity measurement instruments or instruments that are a fit for a particular type of destination. Given this background, the study develops a small, simplistic and generalizable instrument that measures brand equity for a tourism destination.

Literature review and construct definition

Place branding

Hanna and Rowley (2011) developed a strategic place-brand management (SPBM) model. They conclude that SPBM encompasses brand evaluation or the feedback about the brand image; stakeholder engagement and management; infrastructure; brand identity which is the brand essence; brand architecture; brand articulation or the process of expressing the brand; brand communication; brand experience during the consumer's engagement(s) with the place brand; and Word of Mouth among consumers about the brand experience(s). Of these, infrastructure is the existence and accessibility of tangible (functional) and intangible (experiential) place attributes, brand architecture is designing and/or management of the place brand portfolios and the sub-brands, and brand communications are the focus on the communication of the brand identity. Here, it must be mentioned that some of these attributes suggest being inter-related and are extensions of other mentioned attributes.

Destination branding

Destination branding at its very basic level implies branding of a tourism destination or a place. Branding has been defined as

> The process involved in creating a unique name and image for a product in the consumers' mind, mainly through advertising campaigns with a consistent theme. Branding aims to establish a significant and differentiated presence in the market that attracts and retains loyal customers.
>
> (www.businessdictionary.com)

Now, destination branding serves the purpose of creating unique images that a potential tourist can associate with a particular place or tourism destination. Ekinci (2003) opines that destination branding involves the creation of a strong emotional attachment between the prospective tourist and the destination or the place through the creation of those unique images. Successful destination branding involves the establishment of a relationship between the tourist and the destination by satisfying the former's emotional (for example, picturesque and fun) and basic (for example, eating and shopping) needs. Ritchie and Ritchie (1998, p. 17) define a destination brand as

> A Destination Brand is a name, symbol, logo, word mark or other graphic that both identifies and differentiates the destination; furthermore, it conveys the promise of a memorable travel experience that is uniquely associated with the destination; it also serves to consolidate and reinforce the recollection of pleasurable memories of the destination experience.

Thus, it can be said that destination branding involves the creation of distinctive emotional associations and/or images between the place and the tourist through opportunities and experiences provided to the later by the place. Therefore, the essence of destination branding is the creation of a destination image.

Tourism destination image (TDI) or destination image has seen voluminous research conducted in the domain of tourism research and tourism marketing. Destination has been described as a location visited by a tourist that can be a country (Chon, 1991; Echtner & Ritchie, 1993), region (Ahmed, 1991; Fakeye & Crompton, 1991), or even a city (Dadgostar & Isotalo, 1996; Oppermann, 1996). Therefore, destination image is the image(s) that an individual has about a particular destination given the beliefs, ideas he/she has about the destination. Baloglu and McCleary (1999, p. 870) defined destination image as "an attitudinal construct consisting of an individual's mental representation of knowledge (beliefs), feelings, and global impression about an object or destination." TDI is defined as the effect of ideas, beliefs, and impressions of an individual about a destination (Kotler et al., 1993).

Destination branding, tourism destination image (TDI) and place branding

Place branding in the form of nation branding has gained the most importance from the standpoint of tourism marketing and destination branding. In their paper, Blain et al. (2005) suggest a comprehensive definition of "destination branding": (1) creation of a name, logo, symbol, wordmark, or other graphic to make the destination identifiable and differentiable; (2) send cues of memorable travel experience that is unique to the destination; (3) create and strengthen the emotional connection between the visitor and the destination; and (4) reduce consumer search costs and perceived risk. In this context, nation branding activities taken up by different countries have been under study in recent times; some of these studies are made in the context of Spain (Gilmore, 2002), African countries (Wanjiru, 2006), Singapore (Henderson, 2007), New Zealand (Morgan et al., 2002), Dubai (Balakrishnan, 2008) and Slovenia (Konecnik & Go, 2008).

Customer-based brand equity (CBBE) and customer-based place brand equity (CBPBE)

CBBE may be described as a set of all assets and liabilities that can be attached to a brand (name and/or symbol) and, in turn, gives additional value to the customer consuming the product or service (Aaker, 2012). This "value-added" that the product or service provides results in price premium and/or customer loyalty toward the brand (Aaker, 2012; Keller, 1993; Pitta & Katsanis, 1995). Aaker (2012) opines that CBBE primarily has four components, which are: (a) brand awareness, (b) brand, (c) perceived, and (d) brand loyalty.

Bose et al. (2018) had operationalized CBPBE based on CBBE and had described CBPBE as the CBBE of a place (brand).

Research objectives

The objective of the study is to develop a place brand equity measure considering the place as a tourism destination. There are extant destination brand equity instruments (Boo et al., 2009; Gartner & Ruzzier, 2011). However, one of the major flaws of these scales is the context specificity of the particular destination that has been considered for the study. This study ventures into developing a place brand equity instrument from a destination branding perspective that is much more generalizable.

The methodologies applied relate to the purpose of the study and follow the instrument development procedure as suggested by Churchill (1979) and Ping (2004). The first stage of the study applies exploratory research techniques to identify dimensions of place brand equity with particular reference to West Bengal. On the collected data, statistical techniques are applied, and reliability and validity tests are subsequently conducted to adapt and/or develop reliable instruments that measure CBPBE-DB.

Model conceptualization and scale development process

West Bengal as the destination

The state (place) offers various kinds of tourism opportunities to prospective and actual travelers. The northern parts of the state, "Darjeeling" and other nearby hill stations are major tourist destinations as they provide access to the Himalayas. Moreover, "Darjeeling" is famous across the world for its tea. Therefore, such places provide huge opportunities for leisure and adventure tourism. The southernmost parts of West Bengal are covered with the mangrove deltas of Sunderbans and are collectively considered as a biodiversity hotspot of the world and have been declared a World Heritage site by UNESCO. The place is also the breeding ground of the famous Bengal tiger. In addition, there are other places that can be promoted for adventure tourism, history, culture tourism, etc. (refer to Table 6.1).

However, West Bengal is not considered as the topmost tourist destination in India with the state lying in the eighth position among all states in the number or domestic tourists and overall sixth in the number of international tourists (Ministry of Tourism, 2017), irrespective of tremendous potential in tourism. Therefore, the state (place) acts as a good reference point for this study as its brand equity is neither very high nor very low.

Exploratory research

Exploratory research started with a review of the literature to identify items that measure place brand equity or that can be adapted for measuring place brand equity. For this purpose, Yoo and Donthu (2001) scale that measures CBBE from the aspects of multidimensional brand equity and overall brand equity (OBE) is considered as the fundamental approach to

Table 6.1 Attributes of brand equity for West Bengal

Theme	Attribute
Product	Nature
	• Different natural environments • Himalayas to Sunderbans (mangrove deltas) History and culture Sports and adventures
	• Adventure tourism opportunities • Jungle safaris
Infrastructure	Connectivity with major airports and railway stations
	• Infrastructure not well developed Hotels and accommodation
	• Star category hotels and resorts outside Kolkata • Quality of private properties in less popular destinations • Most of the government properties are in shambles
Communication	Governmental initiatives
	• Limited in comparison to those of more popular regions • Lacks proper planning and coordination More proactive participation in tourism expos Tour operators and travel agencies need to inform prospects

the CBPBE instrument(s). Subsequently, literature is reviewed to identify attributes that can measure CBPBE from the aforesaid perspective. Destination branding literature contains an existing scale that measures CBBE from a tourism perspective. The customer-based brand equity for tourism destination (CBBETD) scale as utilized by Gartner and Ruzzier (2011) is applied in this study. The CBBETD is a 23-item instrument that measures place brand equity as tourist destination through the dimensions of brand awareness, brand image, perceived quality, and brand loyalty. However, in "West Bengal" context some of the items of the instrument are redundant whereas some other items might require to be added. Therefore, the instrument was adapted to suit the purpose of the study.

In-depth interviews

For the purpose of the study, two depth interviews (DIs) are conducted with senior managers of two reputed travel agencies in Kolkata with the focus on inferring about attributes of CBBETD, in general, and West Bengal, in particular. The DIs on travel trade executives are run with a motive of uncovering any other aspects of brand equity that are not mentioned in the CBBETD scale. As the CBBETD is adapted for the purpose of the study, the DIs are conducted to make necessary modifications in the set of attributes that will finally be tested and adapted into the instrument that measures CBPBE from the perspective of destination branding. Table 6.2 refers to the thematic analysis of the DIs.

Table 6.2 Attributes of place brand equity from the perspective of destination branding

Theme	Attribute
Product	Nature and natural environment
	Sports and adventure
	History and culture
	Lifestyle and shopping
Infrastructure	Hotel and accommodation
	Transportation
	Communication
Viability	Affordability
	Proximity (time required for traveling)
Communication	Promotion by local government and/or concerned authority
	Promotion by a tour operator
	Existing reputation

One inference that is made from the interviews with travel trade executives is that the brand equity for a destination varies among prospective customers based on its proximity to the later. That is to say that the brand equity of a destination would get affected differently by the fact whether the prospective tourist sees that destination as a short trip or a full holiday. This gets affected by the distance that the destination has from the tourist's location and how expensive the entire tour would get in the perception of the tourist. In this context, one executive opines that:

> Brand equity for a tourist destination is not absolute, it depends largely on the customer's perception about the entire journey including the proximity and time taken to reach there (destination) and the level of expense he perceives. Therefore, for a tourist from Kolkata the brand equity of Thailand including Pattaya is quite different from that of Indonesia and Bali. If not anything, the basic fact that you do not have direct flight to Indonesia from Kolkata makes the country more difficult to reach and thus more exotic and desirable as a destination brand. Moreover, because of a direct flight one can reach Bangkok and back within short time and thus, it's a casual destination brand, whereas the time taken and the greater cost makes Jakarta and Bali a destination for special occasions or once in lifetime journey.

Pilot tests

The initial questionnaire is developed from the items identified in the literature and DIs. The first set of questionnaires suggests 17 items for CB-PBE from the perspective of destination branding. These questionnaires are then scrutinized by two academicians from marketing and one academician from international business from a reputed business school in Kolkata and two senior executives from two local chambers of commerce.

The scrutiny of the aforesaid questionnaire results in the deletion of one item from the destination branding questionnaire. Based on their feedback, the questionnaires are modified and sent to 12 doctoral research scholars and one faculty of marketing in a university in southern India for the review of the language of the questionnaires and any additional feedback on the items selected. The final questionnaire has 16 items. The pilot surveys are then conducted on the questionnaire. The surveys are conducted on 118 (age between 23 and 52 years) respondents across the Indian states West Bengal, Andhra Pradesh and Delhi and include businessmen, executives and MBA students of two reputed business schools in India. The pilot survey data suggest good overall reliability. The Cronbach α value for the questionnaire was 0.85 suggesting that the questionnaires have strong internal consistencies and are reliable for measuring CBPBE from the perspectives of destination branding.

Sample collection for exploratory factor analysis (EFA) and confirmatory factor analysis (CFA)

The sample is collected using a seven-point Likert scale from major tourist destinations in West Bengal that belong to either the northern or southern part of the state. A total of 265 responses are collected, of which 26 responses are found to be unusable relating to various reasons like double-marking, incomplete responses, or biased responses. The final sample consists of 239 respondents of which 146 (61%) are males and 97 (39%) are female respondents (refer to Table 6.3).

Table 6.3 Sample for measuring CBPBE from the perspective of destination branding

Number of respondents based on geography

Siliguri	Darjeeling	Shantiniketan	Sunderbans	Kolkata
41	55	28	43	72

Number of respondents based on nationality

Indians (West Bengal)	Indians (Other states)	Foreigners (Bangladesh)	Foreigners (Others)
78	102	36	23

Number of respondents based on occupation

Service	Business	Professional	Student	Others
64	41	42	53	39

Table 6.4 Sample for measuring CBPBE from the perspective of destination branding

Number of respondents based on location

Siliguri	Darjeeling	Shantiniketan	Sunderbans	Kolkata
37	44	31	42	72

Number of respondents based on nationality

Indians (West Bengal)	Indians (Other states)	Foreigners (Bangladesh)	Foreigners (Others)
80	72	49	25

Number of respondents based on occupation

Service	Business	Professional	Student	Others
66	40	36	53	31

For running the CFA for CBPBE relating to destination branding, 242 responses are collected from the five tourist destinations in West Bengal used as the sample frame for the EFA. Personal administration of the surveys leads to only 16 (7.08%) responses being unusable. The categorizations of the 226 usable responses are given in Table 6.4.

Instrument to Measure CBPBE from the perspective of destination branding

Based on the questionnaire developed that measures CBPBE for a place and sample collected EFA is run with varimax rotation. The KMO value of 0.75 suggests that the sample is adequate for EFA. The analysis suggests 12-item and four-factor solution (refer to Table 6.5) with total variance explained of 65% which acceptable (Hair et al., 2010).

The high factor loadings (between 0.66 and 0.91) suggest that the items provide strong contributions to their respective factors. The Cronbach α of .85 for the factor structure suggests a reliable model. Intuitively, the structure suggests a model that directly related to the CBBE dimensions proposed by Aaker (2012). The first two items (DB01 and DB02) relate to brand awareness, DB05 to DB08 relate to brand image, DB11 to DB14 measure perceived quality of the brand and lastly DB15 and DB16 measure the level of brand loyalty for the brand. The model is also in concordance with the CBBETD scale used by Gartner and Ruzzier (2011) and is reflective of the similar factor structure. The structure

Table 6.5 Exploratory factor analysis for CBPBE from the perspective of destination branding

Dimension	Measurement items	Code	Factor loadings
Brand Awareness	The place is a good tourism destination	DB01	0.692
	The place provides opportunities for different kinds of tourism	DB02	0.660
Brand image	The place stands for historical attractions	DB05	0.856
	The place stands for cultural attractions	DB06	0.911
	The place stands for lovely towns and cities	DB07	0.914
	The place stands for a good lifestyle	DB08	0.855
Perceived quality	The place provides high-quality accommodation	DB11	0.788
	The place has high-quality infrastructure	DB12	0.848
	The place stands for easy accessibility	DB13	0.666
	The place provides high level of personal safety	DB14	0.719
Brand loyalty	The place is one of my preferred destination for visit(s)	DB15	0.840
	I would recommend the place a destination for visit(s)	DB16	0.847

Table 6.6 Scale reliability and validity (CFA) – CBPBE from the perspective of destination branding

	Construct reliability	AVE	Squared inter-group correlations			
			Brand awareness	Brand image	Perceived quality	Brand loyalty
Brand awareness	0.83	0.7130	1	0.0004	0.1857	0.3612
Brand image	0.81	0.5187		1	0.0228	0.0056
Perceived quality	0.80	0.5073			1	0.5069
Brand loyalty	0.88	0.7832				1

supports the literature about the effects of destination branding practices and touristic images, and thus place brand equity from the perspective of destination branding.

CFA is run on the new sample of 226 responses (refer to Table 6.6). The estimation of the confirmatory model is made using maximum likelihood estimation with Amos 16 (refer to Figure 6.1). The final model suggests acceptable fit (X^2/DF = 2.48, p = 0.00; GFI = 0.92; AGFI = 0.86). The baseline comparisons (CFI = 0.94; NFI = 0.90) also suggest acceptable model fit (Hair et al., 2010). RMSEA that measures the badness of fit is 0.08. The RMSEA is a touch on the higher side but is within the acceptable range of 0.05 to 0.08 (Jöreskog, 1993; Hair et al., 2010).

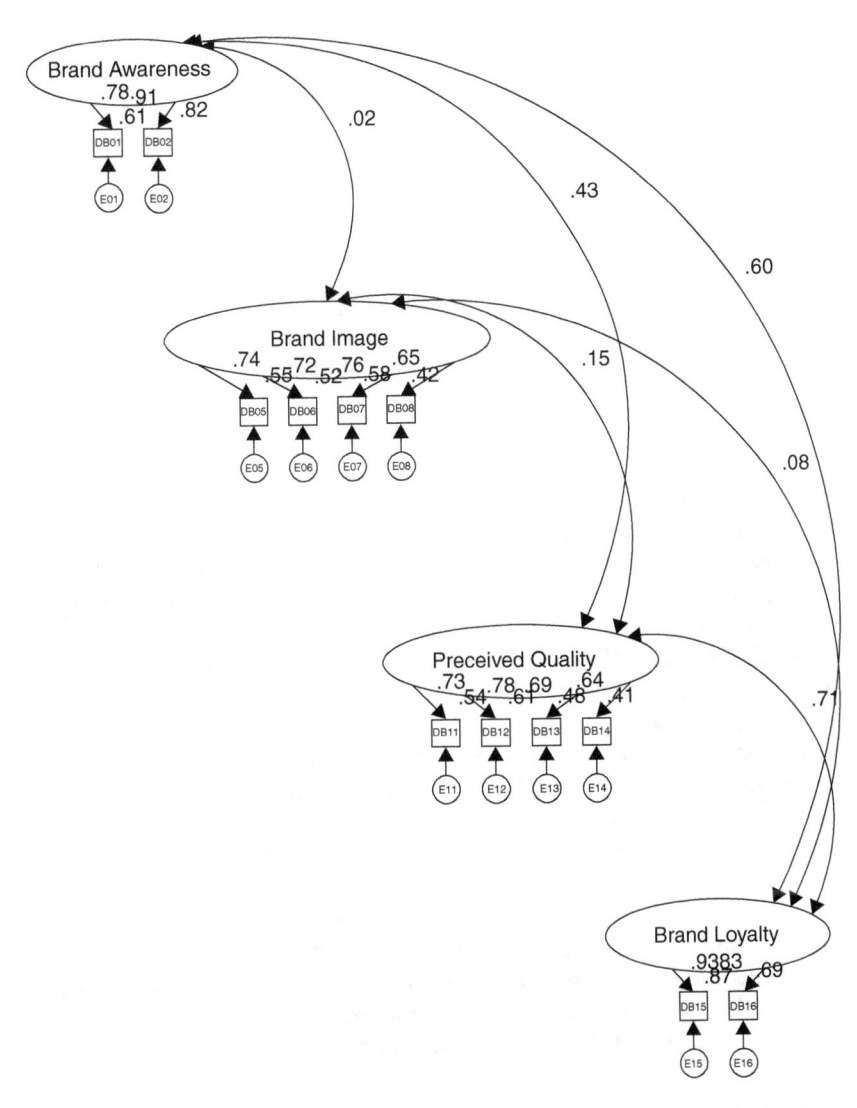

Figure 6.1 CFA model for CBPBE from the perspective of destination branding.

The validation of an instrument requires the test of the validities, namely convergent validity, discriminant validity, and nomological validity. Table 6.6 suggests that all the factor loadings are significant and the average variance extracted (AVE) for each of the dimensions is >0.5. Therefore, the scale fulfills the convergent validity criterion laid by Fornell and Larcker (1981). Moreover, the coefficient α for each of the dimensions lies between 0.80 and 0.88, suggesting good internal consistency. The squared inter-factor correlation (SIC) (refer to Table 6.6) values lie between 0.00 and 0.51 and are less than AVEs.

Table 6.7 Relationships between all the antecedents of CBPBE and overall brand equity (OBE)

	Adjusted R^2	Beta coefficient	t-value	Significance level
Brand awareness	.51	0.16	3.18	.002
Brand image		0.20	4.31	.000
Perceived quality		0.59	11.68	.000

Table 6.8 Relationship between overall brand equity (OBE) and brand Loyalty

	Adjusted R^2	Beta coefficient	t-value	Significance level
Brand equity	.37	0.61	11.52	.000

Thus, discriminant validity criterion holds. This suggests that the latent dimensions are unique in measuring CBPBE.

A measure is said to be nomologically valid if it correlates moderately with theoretically related constructs in the accepted direction. For testing the nomological validity of the instrument, the relationships between the CBBE dimensions' OBE are tested. Literature suggests that brand awareness, brand image, and perceived quality have a positive relationship with brand equity (Aaker, 2012; Keller, 1993). Brand equity, in turn, has a positive influence on brand loyalty (Aaker, 2012; Pitta & Katsanis, 1995). Responses are collected about the OBE for the region (on a scale of 1 to 7, where 1 stands for the lowest brand equity score and 7 for the highest) by using the CFA questionnaire. Then, multiple regression is run using factor scores for each of the dimensions: namely brand awareness, brand image, and perceived quality taken together on overall place brand equity (refer to Table 6.7). Subsequently, the relationship between brand equity and brand loyalty is tested. Regression equation based on factor scores suggests that OBE positively affects brand loyalty (refer to Table 6.8).

Therefore, the scale has nomological validity.

Discussion

As mentioned earlier, the instrument is an adaption of the CBBETD instrument to suit the current study. However, the present study adds a new measure in the form of "ease of accessibility" (DB13) as a component of brand equity for a destination. The overall CBPBE instrument suggests an acceptable fit. However, while testing the discriminant validities the difference between the AVEs and the square inter-group correlations (SICs) are found to be very small. This might happen due to the scale specifications. The original CBBETD instrument has 23 items in all, whereas for the CB-PBE measure only 15 of those measures are considered. Moreover, after the initial EFA, the number of items got reduced to 12 that include the above-mentioned new measure (DB13). These weak differences between the AVEs and SICs might rise due to the over-simplification of the CBPBE instrument. In addition, CFA is data sensitive. Hair et al. (2010) mentioned that a minimum of 200 responses can prove to generate reliable CFA results. In this case, the number of responses used for the CFA was only 226. Therefore, the smaller sample size might have resulted in weak discriminant validity. However, the instrument passed all the other validity and reliability measures, and even the above-mentioned discriminant validity criterion, though weak, was also met. Therefore, this instrument that measures CBPBE from the perspective of destination branding is psychographically robust and can be used to measure CBBE for a place in the context of destination branding. Summarizing, the CBBETD instrument is successfully adapted to measure CBPBE from the perspective of destination branding given the present research focuses on West Bengal as the place.

Contributions and limitations

Contributions

The primary contribution of the study is the adaptation and in another way development of new instrument (CBPBE-DB) that can measure place brand equity for a tourism destination; this instrument is smaller and more generalizable than other destination brand equity scales (Boo et al., 2009, Gartner & Ruzzier, 2011). This instrument, therefore, is expected to be easier to operationalize by both theorists and practitioners. Second, the instrument brings in a new item that enhances place brand equity of a destination "The place stands for easy accessibility" which previous instruments failed to capture. This item would no doubt affect prospective tourists' choice of selecting a destination for visitation. Lastly, the adaptation of CBBETD scale (Gartner & Ruzzier, 2011) acts as a test of the generalizability of that instrument.

Limitations

The exploratory studies could generate only 12 items in the final instruments. This leaves a great opportunity to improve and purify the scales further by finding out new measures of place brand equity. The structuring of the instruments is based upon the CBBE dimensions suggested by Aaker (2012) and Keller (1993) as the researchers felt it to be the best approach to develop a scale for place brand equity from the perspective of investments, given the serious dearth of literature that studies this relationship. An alternative approach to this process might yield quite different measures. Lastly, the greater sample size could have been used, which, in turn, might have strengthened the discriminant validity.

Future research directions

The aforementioned limitations need to be reviewed by future researchers to make this instrument more robust. However, other than these studies there are plenty of opportunities to use this instrument for CBPBE-related studies that are more inter-disciplinary in nature. First, this instrument can directly be operationalized with the place brand equity instrument developed by Bose et al. (2016) pertaining to the investment attractiveness of a place. Such a study can entail the impact of destination branding on inward investments from the CBPBE point of view. Similar studies from the perspectives of public diplomacy (Bose et al., 2018) and country of origin effects (Parameswaran & Pisharodi, 1994) may be undertaken. Another stream of studies could be testing the instrument across different geographical destinations and among varied respondents (for example, first-time visitors or return visitors) to check for its generalizability. This scale can also be used to study the impact of the destination's brand equity on its actual inward tourist inflow in terms of real numbers and revenue. This can enable authorities to make critical strategic decisions about the performance of the "place" brand as a tourist destination.

Conclusion

The study set out to develop a CBPBE instrument from a destination branding perspective. For this purpose, West Bengal is chosen as the "place" brand. CBBETD (Gartner & Ruzzier, 2011) instrument is used as the base instrument, and Yoo and Donthu (2001) CBBE scale is used for the scale structure. Using Churchill (1979) scale development paradigm, a 12-item instrument relating to four dimensions is developed and validated. These dimensions principally relate to the four CBBE dimensions by Aaker (2012): namely, brand awareness, brand image, perceived quality, and brand loyalty. This scale is a relatively smaller scale than the CBBETD and is understood to be easier to administer than CBBETD. However, certain limitations in the scale development process are observed. Future research may be undertaken to answer those limitations. In the end, future research options relating to this instrument are elicited.

Key construct definitions

CBBE – It may be described as a set of all assets and liabilities that can be attached to a brand (name and/or symbol) and, in turn, gives additional value to the customer consuming the product or service (Aaker, 2012).

CBPBE – It can be operationally defined as the CBBE of "place" brand

Destination branding – Destination branding at a very basic level implies branding of a place as a tourism destination.

Place branding – It incorporates the traditional and non-traditional approaches of branding strategies with a particular focus on promotion, development, and enhancement of salability of a particular place or region toward its prospective customers.

References

Aaker, D. A. (2012). *Building strong brands*. London: Simon and Schuster.

Ahmed, Z. U. (1991). The influence of the components of a state's tourist image on product positioning strategy. *Tourism Management*, 12(4), 331–340.

Anholt, S. (2010). Definitions of place branding – Working towards a resolution. *Place Branding and Public Diplomacy*, 6(1), 1–10.

Balakrishnan, M. S. (2008). Dubai–A star in the east: A case study in strategic destination branding. *Journal of Place Management and Development*, 1(1), 62–91.

Baloglu, S., & McCleary, K. W. (1999). A model of destination image formation. *Annals of Tourism Research*, 26(4), 868–897.

Blain, C., Levy, S. E., & Ritchie, J. B. (2005). Destination branding: Insights and practices from destination management organizations. *Journal of Travel Research*, 43(4), 328–338.

Boo, S., Busser, J., & Baloglu, S. (2009). A model of customer-based brand equity and its application to multiple destinations. *Tourism Management*, 30(2), 219–231.

Bose, S. (2014). Branding West Bengal antecedents and consequences of place branding strategies with respect to destination branding public diplomacy and regional identity. Doctoral dissertation, ICFAI University, Dehradun.

Bose, S., Roy, S. K., Alwi, S. F. S., & Nguyen, B. (2018). Measuring customer based place brand equity (CBPBE) from a public diplomacy perspective: Evidence from West Bengal. *Journal of Business Research*. doi:10.1016/j.jbusres.2018.01.059

Bose, S., Roy, S. K., & Tiwari, A. K. (2016). Measuring customer-based place brand equity (CBPBE): An investment attractiveness perspective. *Journal of Strategic Marketing*, 24(7), 617–634.

Chon, K. S. (1991). Tourism destination image modification process: Marketing implications. *Tourism Management*, 12(1), 68–72.

Churchill Jr, G. A. (1979). A paradigm for developing better measures of marketing constructs. *Journal of Marketing Research*, 16(1), 64–73.

Dadgostar, B., & Isotalo, R. M. (1996). Content of city destination image for near-home tourists. *Journal of Hospitality & Leisure Marketing*, 3(2), 25–34.

Echtner, C. M., & Ritchie, J. B. (1993). The measurement of destination image: An empirical assessment. *Journal of Travel Research*, 31(4), 3–13.

Ekinci, Y. (2003). From destination image to destination branding: An emerging area of research. *E-review of Tourism Research*, 1(2), 21–24.

Fakeye, P. C., & Crompton, J. L. (1991). Image differences between prospective, first-time, and repeat visitors to the Lower Rio Grande Valley. *Journal of Travel Research*, 30(2), 10–16.

Fornell, C., & Larcker, D. F. (1981). Evaluating structural equation models with unobservable variables and measurement error. *Journal of Marketing Research*, 18(1), 39–50.

Gartner, W. C., & Ruzzier, M. K. (2011). Tourism destination brand equity dimensions: Renewal versus repeat market. *Journal of Travel Research*, 50(5), 471–481.

Gilmore, F. (2002). A country – Can it be repositioned? Spain – The success story of country branding. *Journal of Brand Management*, 9(4), 281–293.

Hair, J. F., Black, W. C., Babin, B. J., Anderson, R. E., & Tatham, R. L. (2010). *Multivariate data analysis*. Upper Saddle River: Pearson Education.

Hanna, S., & Rowley, J. (2011). Towards a strategic place brand-management model. *Journal of Marketing Management*, 27(5–6), 458–476.

Henderson, J. C. (2007). Uniquely Singapore? A case study in destination branding. *Journal of Vacation Marketing*, 13(3), 261–274.

Jöreskog, K. G. (1993). *Testing structural equation models* (Vol. 154, p. 294). Newbury Park: Sage Focus Editions.

Keller, K. L. (1993). Conceptualizing, measuring, and managing customer-based brand equity. *Journal of Marketing*, 57(1), 1–22.

Konecnik, M., & Go, F. (2008). Tourism destination brand identity: The case of Slovenia. *Journal of Brand Management*, 15(3), 177–189.

Kotler, P., Haider, D. H., & Rein, I. (1993). *Marketing places: Attracting investment. Industry, and tourism to cities, states, and nations.* New York: The Free Press.

Ministry of Tourism, Government of India (2017). *India tourism statistics 2017.* Government of India. Available at: http://tourism.gov.in/sites/default/files/Other/INDIA%20TOURISM%20STATISTICS%202017.pdf [accessed 2 August 2018].

Morgan, N., Pritchard, A., & Piggott, R. (2002). New Zealand, 100% pure. The creation of a powerful niche destination brand. *Journal of Brand Management*, 9(4), 335–354.

Oppermann, M. (1996). Convention destination images: analysis of association meeting planners' perceptions. *Tourism Management*, 17(3), 175–182.

Parameswaran, R., & Pisharodi, R. M. (1994). Facets of country of origin image: An empirical assessment. *Journal of Advertising*, 23(1), 43–56.

Ping Jr, R. A. (2004). On assuring valid measures for theoretical models using survey data. *Journal of Business Research*, 57(2), 125–141.

Pitta, D. A., & Katsanis, L. P. (1995). Understanding brand equity for successful brand extension. *Journal of Consumer Marketing*, 12(4), 51–64.

Ritchie, J. B., & Ritchie, R. J. (1998, September). The branding of tourism destinations: Past achievements and future challenges. In *Proceedings of the 1998 Annual Congress of the International Association of Scientific Experts in Tourism, Destination Marketing: Scopes and Limitations* (pp. 89–116). Marrakech: International Association of Scientific Experts in Tourism.

Wanjiru, E. (2006). Branding African countries: A prospect for the future. *Place Branding*, 2(1), 84–95.

Yoo, B., & Donthu N. (2001). Developing and validating a multidimensional customer-based brand equity scale. *Journal of Business Research*, 52(1), 1–14.

Part III
Place branding
A customer-based view

7 A land for all season

The effect of travelers' orientation on awareness, satisfaction, place image, and travelers' loyalty

Pantea Foroudi, Kayhan Tajeddini, and Reza Marvi

Learning outcomes

At the end of this chapter, readers should be able to:

1 What is traveler orientation?
2 The importance of travelers' orientation.
3 The role of travelers' orientation on the awareness, place image, satisfaction, travelers' loyalty.
4 The moderating role of digital marketing in the travelers' orientation in the relationship of awareness, place image, satisfaction, and loyalty.
5 What is the moderating role of gender in the relationship of awareness, place image, satisfaction, and travelers' loyalty?

Introduction

This research investigates the impact of customer/travelers' orientation on awareness, place image, travelers' satisfaction, and travelers' loyalty. By collecting data from 397 travelers in Thailand, this research analyzes the impact of customer/travelers' orientation on travelers' awareness, place image, travelers' satisfaction, and place loyalty by the moderating role of digital marketing. The results show that travelers' orientation impacts positively on the travelers' awareness, place image, travelers' satisfaction, and travelers' loyalty. Moreover, the results show that while awareness and traveler satisfaction positively influence the place image and travelers' loyalty, respectively, place image has no influence on the travelers' satisfaction. The research yields useful guidance for the hospitality manager to apply more efficient loyalty programs. The outcomes add new insight into the loyalty process with the moderating role of digital marketing. The findings suggest that through travelers' orientation tourism managers can establish and enhance travelers' loyalty.

Research background

Travelers' orientation is a widely accepted construct for firm/place survival, which each tourist company adapts to maintain the strong association with travelers and to satisfy their needs. Travelers' orientation is the main effective plan that allows organizations to continually improve their offerings to their users (Lukas & Maignan, 1996; Narver & Slater, 1990; Zhu et al., 2017). It is a critical factor in the success of customer relationship management (King & Burgess, 2008) which has a positive influence on marketing planning capabilities (Morgan et al., 2009), helps to upsurge perceived service/product quality in order to improve their performance (Kim et al., 2006; Sin et al., 2005), and ultimately raises traveler loyalty. Hillebrand et al. (2011) conceptualized travelers' orientation as the level that a tourism firm tries to achieve in order to identify and accommodate its travelers' needs.

What distinguishes hotels' travelers' orientation that has an enormous impact on the traveler-hotel relationship? What is the essence of the relationships that create awareness, place image, satisfaction and travelers' loyalty? How does digital media impact the relationships? How and when are such associations likely to happen? A wide extent of research, ranging from travelers' orientation (Tajeddini et al., 2017), digital media (Cheng & Foley, 2018), awareness (Foroudi, 2018), place image (Kim et al., 2018), satisfaction (Wang et al., 2018), and place loyalty (Kim et al., 2018), tried to answer to such questions.

This paper contributes to the growing study on consumer/visitor/guest associations within the hotel industry. Furthermore, based on the theory of social identity (Brewer, 1991), it attempts to provide a proper understanding of which visitors are likely to recognize and feel loyal to the hotel/place. It will also present a traveler view about the online tourist relationship and examine whether online marketing is a useful tool for this relationship. This study aims to provide some contribution to the hotel industries, specifically to Thailand. With the data from various sources, hotel managers can use this research to implement their strategies and to understand the attitude of participants toward their marketing.

To date, the concept of travelers' orientation has been studied in Europe and the US, and there are a limited number of researchers studying the effectiveness of travelers' orientation and its necessary consequences in the hotel industry (Kasim et al., 2018; Tang, 2014). Also, based on the authors' knowledge, although Thailand is one of the world's most famous destinations (WTTC, 2018), there is a limited study.

The following sections draw on an existing study to discuss the nature of travelers' orientation and articulate our travelers' level conceptual framework, which provides a more profound understanding regarding the important consequences of such adjustment in the marketplace. Then, method, methodology, and analysis are discussed. Later, theoretical significance, implications, and limitation are explained.

Theoretical framework and hypothesis development

Travelers' loyalty

Travelers' loyalty is defined as a situation where visitors/tourists visit the same place/brand/hotel repeatedly. The services/products can be the same or various, but the main point is the visitors are loyal to the brand, not a product or services (Moisescu, 2006). Authors (Khoshsima et al., 2013) defined brand/place loyalty as when consumers have a good attitude with the place and also tend to visit the place in the future. Travellers' loyalty refers to the state of visitors who always choose one hotel brand over a long period, although there are a variety of brands (Haryanto et al., 2016; Jacoby & Kyner, 1973; Touzani & Temessek, 2009).

In the world of competition, hotels survive mainly because of existing customers and attracting new customers. Therefore, they have to persuade customers to repurchase items with them. A customer loyalty program is, consequently, very special as it could encourage customers and increase the number of visits. The hotel can attempt to build customer loyalty in two ways. First, the hotel should use the right strategies to find loyal customers. This can depend on the consistency of purchase. In this way, the hotel tends to get potential customers and reach the market share, and a customer loyalty program will protect these target customers from competitors. Another way is to look for new customers. Doing it this way, however, the company/place has to invest much more money than in trying to keep existing customers/visitors.

According to Kumar and Shah (2004), although it is very hard to maintain travelers' loyalty, it is worth doing so because businesses could get sustainable benefits from loyal customers. For example, it is found that existing customers tend to be less price sensitive than new customers (Godey et al., 2016). Besides, loyal customers might forgive the hotel more easily if they are not satisfied with something (Bruwer et al., 2014). Additionally, regular visitors/customers will make more and more transactions if they still have a good relationship with the place. Another benefit the hotel/company will get from loyal customers is the power of word-of-mouth (Hemsley-Brown & Alnawas, 2016). To illustrate, these loyal customers will recommend the brand to their friends and family (Yen & Tang, 2019) or post their positive attitude toward the brand on social media (Kim et al., 2016), which may attract many new customers. Besides, the loyal customers tend to believe and trust the brand, so that they will buy different types of products from the brand (Hwang et al., 2019).

Some advantages they could get are (a) practical benefits – these benefits, such as saving money, are a great motivation for customers to be loyal. The company can offer many such promotions, like cash back and coupons to customers (Mimouni-Chaabane & Volle, 2010). Previous studies (Mimouni-Chaabane & Volle, 2010; Sheth & Parvatiyar, 1995) stated that the obstruction that makes customers feel that it is inconvenient to be loyal to the brand is that they do not have enough experience with firms. With the practical benefits, consumers might see the value of a loyalty program, so it will help customers get more used to the brand (Berry, 1995; Bolton et al., 2000; Mimouni-Chaabane & Volle, 2010). This helps customers search and find products more easily.

Therefore, the connection feels convenient and customers believe that using a certain company can save time. For instance, with a service desk exclusively for the loyalty program, loyal customers do not need to wait so long and can make an exclusive reservation. (b) Hedonic benefits – customers will get updated news of products, promotions or events (Arnold & Reynolds, 2003; Baumgartner & Steenkamp, 1996; Mimouni-Chaabane & Volle, 2010). Some hotels will also provide activities for customers to join (Mimouni-Chaabane & Volle, 2010; Tauber, 1972). The loyalty program tends to affect customers concerning their experience, such as collecting points (Mimouni-Chaabane & Volle, 2010). (c) Symbolic benefits – loyal customers might feel unique or privileged if the brand which they are loyal to tends to provide many opportunities to them before other customers who are not members or loyal to the brand (Beatty et al., 1996; Gwinner et al., 1998; Mimouni-Chaabane & Volle, 2010). They can also receive offers that are different from those offered to ordinary customers (Mimouni-Chaabane & Volle, 2010). This program has a social benefit for the brand (Mimouni-Chaabane & Volle, 2010). Customers will feel privileged and feel that the brand is a part of them (Mimouni-Chaabane & Volle, 2010; Muniz & O'guinn, 2001).

Traveler orientation

Travellers' orientation is when companies first pay attention to travelers' needs and attempt to satisfy them (Lee & Hwang, 2016). According to Taleghani et al. (2013) in the past, businesses considered their profits only from selling as many products or services as possible. However, companies now focus on selling satisfaction and loyalty, as they offer what is "value" for the customers. Travellers' orientation comprises three concepts. First, companies should know and understand the travelers' needs from the past and into the future (Kao et al., 2016). Second, the information about the travelers' needs should be comprehensive and useful for the production team (Seilov, 2015). Third, the knowledge about tourists should be analyzed by various departments to create a better way to develop products (Tang, 2014). With these features, travelers could be attracted and would select the companies that could fulfil their demands (Li & Huang, 2017). Therefore, it can be summarized that travelers' orientation could impact the effectiveness of market orientation (Lee et al., 2015; Ruizalba et al., 2014).

According to Narver and Slater (1990), travelers' orientation leads to a seller realizing and understanding the travelers' needs and situation. Sellers should know their customers with regard to political, social, economic, and environmental concerns. These factors must be discussed and forecasted to summarize the present position and future trend. McEachern and Warnaby (2005) stated that travelers' orientation is an element of market orientation that attempts to have a customer as the company's focus or at the center of their attention (Asikhia, 2010). Travellers' orientation is also defined as the activities and efforts of companies with the purpose of meeting a customer's expectation and fulfilling a customer's wants (Mehrabi et al., 2012).

Also, companies should focus on the competitor's situation, including the skills or things they do that are right or weak, and the abilities and strategies they have currently and may have in the future. This information also helps tourist's companies to know the market trend, what is new and what is next in the market, and how to compete with the new strategies of the competitors. In other words, if the competitor's potentials and trends are analyzed correctly, and companies could manage the current and future situation correctly, they may become or stay at the very first position in the market (Narver & Slater, 1990). It means that competitor orientation affects the market orientation, as the companies know the market situations and could create the strategies that tend to increase and keep customers in the long term (Maydeu-Olivares & Lado, 2003). According to O'Cass and Ngo (2009), market orientation may not work if there is no involvement from various sections of the company to share information and opinions from their views or positions. Therefore, every department has to sit together and help each other to find the strategies or solutions that are most effective and can reach the goal of market orientation, which is to generate new customers and to retain the existing ones.

Travellers' orientation, awareness, and place image

Awareness is defined as the ability of consumers to recognize or differentiate the hotel that is in their mind (Keller, 1993; Moisescu, 2009), or the familiarity of the hotel (Malik et al., 2013), which finally makes them prefer that hotel. Tourisms Company's performance is related to awareness. According to Tuominen et al. (2009) and Yin Wong and Merriles (2008), company performance will be enhanced if the business has well-planned strategies including market orientation. It could be summarized that robust market orientation strategies can have a positive impact on awareness (Ewing & Napoli, 2005; Tuominen et al., 2009). As discussed earlier, hotels, which are customer oriented, tend to have good performances because they sell products based on actual customers' needs. When companies have a good performance, they tend to be reliable.

It could lead to good images of the companies and hotels (Tuominen et al., 2009). Also, organizations which are customer oriented tend to have good performance because they can sell products based on actual customer needs. When companies have a good performance, they tend to be reliable which could lead to good images of the companies (Tuominen et al., 2009). Thus, based on what has been discussed, these hypotheses are proposed,

H1: *The more favorable the hotel travelers' orientation, the more awareness is created among travelers.*

H2: *The more favorable the hotel travelers' orientation, the more favorable attitude travelers have towards the place's image.*

Travellers' orientation, traveler satisfaction, and traveler loyalty

Travellers' orientation could affect travelers' satisfaction (Alhelalat et al., 2017) and travelers' loyalty (Lo et al., 2017). The first reason is that, with strong market orientation, companies which have a customer-focused strategy could respond to tourists needs (Chow et al., 2015) by offering what they want. Second, due to the competitor orientation, the hotels tend to be aware of their competitors in many respects, including the quality of the products, services, and price (Herrero et al., 2018). This intense competition does benefit customers. For example, customers could pay less to get a particular product. Concerning hotels, companies are supposed to look after their staff with regard to developing their proficiency including their cross-functional skills, offering good welfare and benefits, and providing a good work environment and conditions to make sure they are ready to deal with all situations. According to Krepapa et al. (2003), the concept of value creation is linked to marketing orientation and customer satisfaction. To illustrate, customers tend to view companies which provide products or services to them from different positions and environments. Therefore, the business needs to understand the perception of the customers and create value in its products to fulfil customer expectations, which will undoubtedly lead to customer satisfaction.

Currently, the stiff competitive market tends to cause many companies to be more focused on offering products and services to loyal customers (Kotler, 1984; Maydeu-Olivares & Lado, 2003) as it is harder and more expensive to attract new customers. Moreover, maintaining regular guests can also affect the sustainable competitive advantage of organizations (O'Cass & Sok, 2015). To build and keep loyalty among the customers, market orientation should be applied. Deshpandé et al. (1993) and Maydeu-Olivares and Lado (2003) stated that the concept of market orientation is based on the profit which comes from customer satisfaction and relationship with the brand. When the companies have a strong market orientation, focusing on what customers want, understanding strengths and weaknesses of the competitors, and knowing the situations in the organization, they tend to succeed in customer loyalty, which leads to good performance (Herrero et al., 2018). Kohli and Jaworski (1990) and Maydeu-Olivares and Lado (2003) agreed that there is a relationship between market orientation and customer loyalty. An intensive market orientation could positively impact customer satisfaction, while customer satisfaction could make customers loyal to the brand. Moreover, the number of customers repurchasing with market-oriented firms is higher. Therefore, it can be summarized that market orientation could be a factor that builds customer loyalty (Dick & Basu, 1994; Kamakura et al., 2002; Loveman, 1998; Maydeu-Olivares & Lado, 2003).

H3: *The more favorable the hotel travelers' orientation, the more satisfied the travelers are.*
H4: *The more desirable the hotel travelers' orientation, the more loyal the travelers are.*

Travellers' orientation, digital marketing, awareness, and place image

Travellers' orientation influences the structure of social media as a company wants to learn more about their customers and to make them feel more comfortable with the online experience (Dolan & Goodman, 2017). According to Habibi et al. (2015) travelers' orientation, which is a part of the market adjustment, affects digital marketing in the way that the programmer tries to design the website to fulfil the company's and customer's wants. Lewrick et al. (2011) stated that competitor orientation is another factor that has a significant impact on digital marketing development. According to Antioco and Lindgreen (2003), internet marketing is designed partly because of employee convenience, to gather as much data as possible and to access available information 24/7. Digital marketing is also considered a useful and low-cost tool for employees to communicate with other employees and customers.

Raoofi (2012) stated that the stronger market orientation strategy the company implements, the more potential they have to win over competitors. The company will have a sufficient market orientation if it selects digital marketing as its marketing tool to cover marketing activities, with the aim to achieve travelers' orientation, competitor orientation, and inter-functional orientation. Digital marketing could increase the effectiveness of market orientation and company performance because it is an innovation that helps the company to generate the data faster and more accurately. According to Zaman et al. (2012), digital marketing is essential to the market orientation as it could support companies to update the market situation and customer preference. Therefore, it is easier for an organization to analyze the customers' needs. Online marketing is also used to update the competitors' information so that the company could compete with its rivals. Besides, companies also apply digital marketing to ensure the competencies of the staff and support them to work efficiently.

Digital marketing is defined as a kind of marketing which uses technologies such as email, mobile phones, and social media to create a relationship with customers and to carry out actions that increase customer awareness by fulfilling the customer's wants (Chaffey & Chadwick, 2012; Khan & Siddiqui, 2013) for the purpose of making a profit and enhancing customer loyalty (Mustafi et al., 2011).

According to Carlsson (2010), digital marketing, especially social media, is valuable because it can create a relationship and awareness among consumers. There are various activities on social media that companies use to promote their brands. For instance, the company website represents the company's identity and provides information about corporate philosophy, which may include vision, mission, and goal so that customers can understand and easily take part in the business's activities (Zhang et al., 2016). Another example is Facebook and YouTube. Both are mostly used to create a viral campaign and post videos or photos to attract consumers with the purpose to create awareness among new clients and refresh existing customers. Nowadays, it is mandatory for a company to have a digital marketing strategy to create place awareness, as there are more and more internet users who are customers of the company. Hotels can advertise their brands online, send information to customers to convince them to choose their brands, and make them recognize the brand names and products all the time by keeping updated and existing in the online world.

According to Francoeur (2004), social media is used to represent the brand and connect with global customers rather than to compete with competitors. Therefore, it is essential for companies to take this into consideration when using digital marketing to communicate with the brands and customers as it could impact the brand images. Francoeur (2004) stated that a brand image would be strong or weak depending partly on how the organization manages its online content. Social media is also designed for customers to share their opinions and create strong word-of-mouth (Hur et al., 2017). To illustrate, customers will recommend the brand to others, which brings an excellent image to the brand. However, the company should also consider the content and proper strategies before using social media. For example, the information that the hotels want to share should be correct and interesting for the audience. The hotels also have to balance between organization information and consumer's opinions because there might even be some negative feedback which could be spread quickly and severely impact brand image.

H5: Digital marketing strengthens the relationships between travelers' orientation and awareness (H5a), and place image (H5b)

Travellers' orientation, digital marketing, satisfaction, and loyalty

The term satisfaction is used when the customers personally judge the brands by means of the expected and experienced products and services (Oliver, 1997; Sondoh et al., 2007) which could be high or low, depending on the level of the customer's fulfilment and expectation (Kotler & Keller, 2009). Brand/place loyalty is explained when customers select to buy particular products or services from the same brand over and over again (Moisescu, 2006), or the situation where customers have a strong potential to be engaged with the brand and promise to purchase products at any time (Khoshsima et al., 2013). Brand loyalty is considered a biased reaction because customers prefer to buy products or services from the selected brand, instead of any other brand (Touzani & Temessek, 2009).

It can be seen that the number of retailers using digital marketing, namely social media, is increasing. Apart from creating awareness and selling products, they also use digital marketing to fulfil consumer needs such as answering questions and providing areas for customer feedbacks, to increase satisfaction which could lead to positive word-of-mouth (Caner & Banu, 2015; Zhang & Daugherty, 2009), and high customer loyalty (Caner & Banu, 2015; Devaraj et al., 2002). According to Caner and Banu (2015) and Liang and Lai (2002), digital marketing could support the company to increase customer satisfaction. For instance, a well-designed website can attract attention from consumers and reflect the quality of the brand, which could impress the customer since it is the first touching point. Besides, the search engine function on the website could also satisfy the customers (Caner & Banu, 2015; Otim & Grover, 2006).

Moreover, customers like to use digital marketing as it is convenient and takes less time (Caner & Banu, 2015; Torkzadeh & Dhillon, 2002). To illustrate, the customers might feel more comfortable to use online services, taking time to research the facilities and product details including pictures of the products (Oliver, 1999). Online shopping also provides 24/7 service, which means customers can see the information about a service or make a transaction whenever they want (Hung et al., 2014). According to Caner and Banu (2015), customer satisfaction with online experience and the brand depends on many factors, such as attitude and computer skills.

Online marketing is a potential tool to create brand loyalty as it could help companies achieve customers' expectations more easily by integrating market orientation and customer relationship. A company can get in touch with their customers at all times. It could survey what customers want. Moreover, the company can still update information, particularly any special offers to the customers. Therefore, the clients might feel privileged, keep in touch with the company, and remain loyal to the organization (Pratminingsih et al., 2013). Erdogmus and Cicek (2012) also stated that companies should use digital marketing to build loyalty among customers as there are some studies showing that social media users tend to communicate about the brands, suggest the brands to others, or buy the brand items more often if they feel more engaged with the brand online marketing tools, especially the social media. According to Shankar et al. (2002), the company could use digital marketing to build customer loyalty in two ways. First, the company might use digital marketing to find existing customers who might potentially become loyal, for example, the customers who regularly make contact with the brand, and invite them to join the loyalty program. Another way is by the use of digital marketing to attract new customers.

H6: *Digital marketing strengthens the relationships between travelers' orientation and satisfaction (H6a), and place loyalty (H6b).*

Awareness, image, satisfaction, and loyalty

Awareness is a necessary part of building a place image as the more tourists remember the brand, the more they can get attached and related themselves to the brand. Awareness differs according to gender (Westwood et al., 2000). Although women and men are not different in the process of remembering a brand, they are different in what they recall from a brand (Valkenburg & Buijzen, 2005). Place image is an interpretation that tourists have about the place (Keller, 1993), which may not represent where the place is, in reality (Aaker, 1991).

H7: *The more awareness is raised among the hotel's travelers, the more favorable the attitude they have towards the place/hotel's image.*
H7a: *The effects of the hotel traveler's awareness and the place image are stronger for female travelers than for male travelers.*

According to Ranjbarian et al. (2012), a good place image could positively affect customer satisfaction. To illustrate, customers always have their attitude toward the place in their mind and then set their expectation. As the image is a mental picture based on different dimensions, gender plays a vital role in influencing the perception of a hotel both in male and female travelers (Beerli & Martín, 2004). Besides, the masculine and feminine image of a place can have an impact on the relationship between image and satisfaction (Grohmann, 2009). If their hope is aligned with their experience, the positive perception can influence customer behavior, and customers will be satisfied with the brand (Chen & Chen, 2010). However, if not, customers will develop dissatisfaction and negative brand attitude instead.

H8: The more favorable the place/hotel's image, the more satisfied the travelers are.

H8a: The effects of the hotel guest's image and satisfaction are stronger for female travelers than for male travelers.

Previous studies have shown that customer satisfaction impacts loyalty in many ways (Anderson & Sullivan, 1993; Bloemer & De Ruyter, 1998; Chiou et al., 2005; Sondoh et al., 2007; Vinhas Da Silva & Faridah Syed Alwi, 2006; Yang & Peterson, 2004). First, Bennett and Rundle-Thiele (2004) stated that when customers are satisfied with the brand (products and service), they might recommend the brand to friends, families, or others. Second, they tend to repurchase or use the brand again. Third, there is less possibility that customers will change to another brand. There is some evidence proving that customer satisfaction has strongly affected customer loyalty in many aspects, such as repurchasing (Kandampully & Suhartanto, 2000; Sondoh et al., 2007), recommendation (Kandampully & Suhartanto, 2000; Nguyen & LeBlanc, 1998; Sondoh et al., 2007), and returning to the store again (Bloemer & De Ruyter, 1998; Sondoh et al., 2007). The result of satisfaction is significant and influences loyalty. For instance, the excellent experience of previous purchases may affect the future purchase (Jones & Suh, 2000; Pritchard et al., 1999; Russell-Bennett et al., 2007). Gender difference can have an impact on the relationship between satisfaction and loyalty. Different researches (e.g., Chang & Chen, 2008; Ha et al., 2007; Hong & Tam, 2006) suggest that what makes women satisfied is different from what makes men satisfied. Consequently, gender difference can have an impact on the relationship between satisfaction and gender (Figure 7.1).

H9: The more satisfied the travelers are towards the hotel, the more loyalty travelers have in the hotel.

H9a: The effect of the hotel travelers' satisfaction and loyalty is stronger for female travelers than for male travelers.

Methods and measurement

A research survey was developed based on 46 item measurements. The first section contained five questions regarding the participants' demographics and background (frequency of visit, gender, age, employment, and degree). The next section includes six constructs where the participants were requested to specify on a seven-point Likert-type scale,

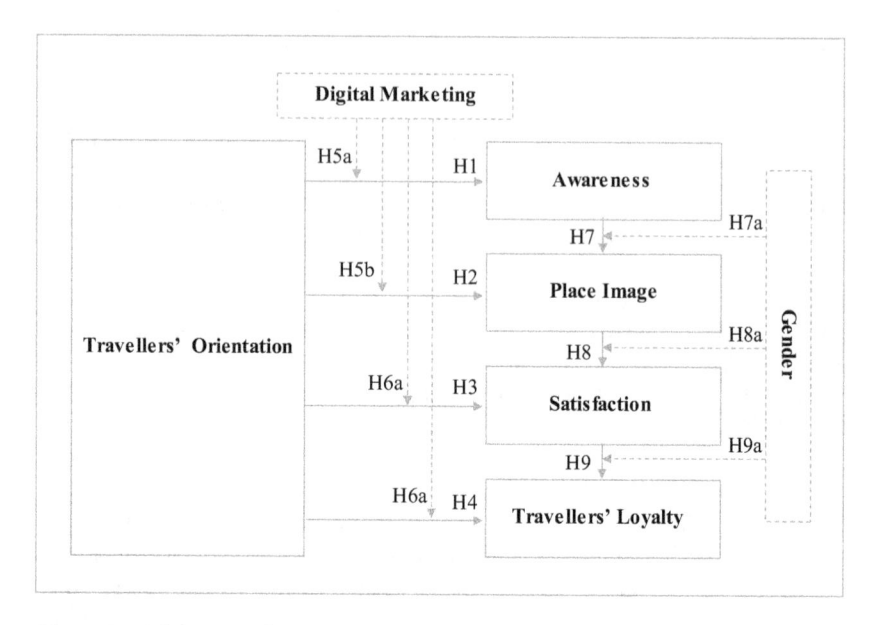

Figure 7.1 The research conceptual model.

ranging from (1) strongly disagree to (7) strongly agree. It offers satisfactory properties, which are concerned with the underlying distribution of replies to the hotel industry in Thailand. Travellers' orientation was investigated with nine validated items based on previous studies (Kumar et al., 1998; Lado et al., 1998; Tomaskova, 2009) and digital marketing with ten items (Khan & Siddiqui, 2013; Sarwar et al., 2013). Awareness (Aaker, 1991; Buil et al., 2013; Cornwell et al., 2011; Yoo & Donthu, 2001) and place image (Foroudi et al., 2014, 2017) scales were measured based on the items from earlier studies. Satisfaction was examined via five items recommended by Sondoh et al. (2007). Loyalty (Christodoulides et al., 2015; Ekinci et al., 2011; Yoo & Donthu, 2002) was adopted according to the context (Table 7.1).

Data collection

The research hypotheses were tested with a sample of hotel travelers from Thailand. The current research was conducted employing a non-random sampling (namely, convenience sampling technique) to remove the possible bias regarding the generalizability and validity of the measurement scales (Bell & Bryman, 2007). In total, 650 questionnaires were printed and distributed to the hotels' participants, and 397 usable surveys were returned and assessed. In addition to improving upsurge, the sample size and to ensure that the sample involved the most well-informed

Table 7.1 Constructs, codes, item measurement, and references

Code	Construct and items	Factor analysis	Mean	Std. Dev.	Reference
Travellers' orientation					Cronbach @.916
MCUS1	I think the Hotel/Place regularly analyses factors, which influence purchase behavior of customers/visitors	.705	5.4408	1.28497	Tomaskova (2009)
MCUS2	I think the Hotel/Place determines why potential customers/visitors/travelers have not bought the product yet				
MCUS3	I think the Hotel/Place systematically and frequently measures customers/visitors/travellers' satisfaction	.796	5.4987	1.22809	Lado et al. (1998)
MCUS4	I think the Hotel/Place systematically evaluates the impact of the environment on the customers/visitors/travelers				
MCUS5	I think the Hotel/Place periodically analyses the customers/visitors/travellers' current and future needs	.801	5.4106	1.34472	
MCUS6	I think the Hotel/Place periodically measures the customers/visitors/travellers' image of the product/service	.789	5.3728	1.36221	
MCUS7	I think the Hotel/Place develops monitoring of the changes in preferences of its customers/visitors/travellers' system				
MCUS8	I think the Hotel/Place creates services that offer value for me	.840	5.6297	1.17052	Kumar et al. (1998)
MCUS9	I think the Hotel/Place has customers/visitors/travelers satisfaction as a primary objective	.794	5.4962	1.13178	
Digital marketing					Cronbach @.917
DM1	I think the Hotel/Place social media accelerates revenue growth	.715	5.5668	1.24467	Khan and Siddiqui (2013)
DM2	I think the Hotel/Place social media has low investment				
DM3	I think the Hotel/Place social media provides customers/visitors/travellers' participation.	.820	5.8791	1.21460	

(Continued)

Code	Construct and items	Factor analysis	Mean	Std. Dev.	Reference
DM4	I think the Hotel/Place social media generates immediate response from customers/visitors/travelers	.838	5.7028	1.26024	
DM5	I think the Hotel/Place social media attracts attention very quickly				
DM6	I think the Hotel/Place social media is much more measurable				
DM7	I think I get information about certain product/services through social networking sites				Sarwar et al. (2013)
DM8	I think the information I get from the sites persuades me to buy the product/service	.755	5.3929	1.29753	
DM9	I am satisfied with the service/product that I ordered through the social network				
DM10	I agree that social networks influence people nowadays in buying products/services	.838	5.5743	1.26037	
Awareness					Cronbach @.962
AW1	I am interested in this Hotel/Place	.828	5.6877	1.26058	Aaker (1991), Cornwell et al. (2011)
AW2	I know what this Hotel/Place looks like				
AW3	Compared to other people, I know more about this Hotel/Place				
AW4	This Hotel/Place is a brand of hotel industries I am very familiar with	.921	5.8816	1.27469	Buil et al. (2013)
AW5	When I think of hotel industries, this Hotel/Place is one of the brands that come to mind	.912	5.8892	1.27041	
AW6	Some characteristics of this Hotel/Place come to my mind quickly				
AW7	I can quickly recognize the symbol or logo of this Hotel/Place	.899	5.8589	1.26940	Yoo and Donthu (2001)
Place image					Cronbach @.925
IM1	I like this Hotel/Place	.827	5.4257	1.16889	Foroudi et al. (2014, 2017), Foroudi (2018)

IM2	I like this Hotel/Place compared to other hotels	.847	5.3199	1.32228	
IM3	I think other customers/visitors/travelers like this Hotel/Place as well				
IM4	The Hotel/Place's logo communicates about the Hotel to its customers/visitors/travelers				
IM5	The Hotel/Place's logo enhances the Hotel's image	.901	5.4232	1.15569	
IM6	I think this Hotel/Place helps me feel accepted				
IM7	I think this Hotel/Place improves the way I am perceived by others				
IM8	I think this Hotel/Place prevents me from looking cheap				
IM9	I think the usage of this Hotel/Place is more effective to my needs than other brands				
Satisfaction					Cronbach @.940
SAT1	I think that I did the right thing when I used this Hotel/Place	.879	5.0403	1.32703	Sondoh et al. (2007)
SAT2	I believe that using this Hotel/Place is usually a very satisfying experience	.874	5.0630	1.27270	
SAT3	I am very satisfied with my decision to use this Hotel/Place	.881	5.0655	1.33361	
SAT4	My choice to use this Hotel/Place has been a wise one	.908	5.0655	1.32029	
SAT5	This Hotel/Place does a good job of satisfying my needs				
Travellers' loyalty					Cronbach @.909
LOY1	Compared to other hotels that have similar features, I am willing to pay a premium (higher) price for this Hotel/Place				Christodoulides et al. (2015)
LOY2	Even if another hotel has the same features as this Hotel, I would prefer to use this Hotel/Place	.764	5.2972	1.32662	Yoo and Donthu (2002)
LOY3	I prefer to book this Hotel/Place compare to others	.828	5.3929	1.24793	
LOY4	I consider myself to be loyal to this Hotel/Place				
LOY5	This Hotel/Place would be my first choice of hotel industries	.838	5.2191	1.38164	
LOY6	I think I am more likely to return to this Hotel/Place in the future	.804	5.1562	1.44976	Ekinci et al. (2011)

informants, non-probability "snowballing" was employed as a distribution technique by requesting the initial participants to recommend other guests who could provide additional information (Goodman 2011). Table 7.2 illustrates a summary of the demographic characteristics. The majority of the respondents have visited the hotel brand more than two times (37.3%). In total, 56.4% of the participants were male; the respondents were between 30 and 39, 20 and 29, and 40 and 49 years old (28.0%, 20.4%, 19.6%, respectively). Also, 35.3% were students; 12.1% were lawyers, dentists, or architects; and 10.1% were retired. A high proportion was holding a postgraduate degree or above (57.4%).

The preliminary measurement items were subjected to a series of reliability and factor investigations as initial examinations of their performance within the sample. We followed a two-stage procedure, suggested by Anderson and Gerbing (1988). Exploratory factor analyses (EFA) were run to identify inter-relationships between the factors and to explain such factors regarding their common underlying factors (Hair et al., 2006) which contribute to six theoretically recognized constructs and demonstrates which the item measurements fit within the theoretical factor structures. According to Tabachnick and Fidell (2007), the Kaiser-Meyer-Olkin measure of sampling appropriateness (.905 > .6) recommends the association among items as statistically acceptable and suitable for EFA to convey a parsimonious set of factors. Cronbach's

Table 7.2 Demographic profile (N = 397)

	Frequency	Percent		Frequency	Percent
Visit			Employment		
Once	107	27.0	Business person	4	1.0
Twice	142	35.8	Lawyer, dentist or architect, etc.	48	12.1
More than two times	148	37.3	Office/clerical staffs	39	9.8
			Worker	24	6.0
Gender					
Female	173	43.6	Civil servant	24	6.0
Male	224	56.4	Craftsman	32	8.1
			Student	140	35.3
Age					
19 years old or less	31	7.8	Homemaker	38	9.6
20 to 29 years	81	20.4	Retired	40	10.1
30 to 39 years	111	28.0	Unemployed	8	2.0
40 to 49 years	78	19.6			
			Degree		
50 to 59 years	48	12.1	High school	55	13.9
60 years old or more	48	12.1	Undergraduate	114	28.7
			Postgraduate and above	228	57.4

α measured the consistency of each element with its appropriate items and confirmed that the items in each factor (.916 to .962) were internally consistent (Nunnally, 1978). The descriptive information for the research constructs is illustrated in Table 7.2.

Confirmatory factor analysis (CFA) was used as a most appropriate method which allows a stricter valuation of the study's construct uni-dimensionality and measures discriminant validity (Tabachnick & Fidell, 2007). Based on suggestions of previous studies (Dillon and & Goldstein, 1984; Fornell & Larcker, 1981), each factor was compared to the square of each off diagonal-value in the Phi-matrix for the elements, and the findings demonstrate average variance extracted (AVE) for each factor ranged from .642 to .865, and the items suggest a distinctive underlying concept. AVE (a good rule of thumb of .5 or higher) specifies satisfactory convergent validity (Table 7.3).

Following the measurement model step, we examined the structural model fit via goodness-of-fit by employing Windows AMOS 24.0 to test the model and inspect hypotheses. The root mean squared approximation of error (RMSEA) provides adequate distinctive data to estimate the research model (.064 < .08 indicates acceptable fit) (Byrne, 2001; Garver & Mentzer, 1999; Hair et al., 2006). Comparative fit index (CFI) is an incremental index that assesses the fit of a model with the null baseline model (.962 > .08 indicates good fit). Normed fit index (NFI) tests the proportion by which a model is enhanced concerning fit compared to the base model, which is not controlled for degrees-of-freedom (.940 > .08 indicates good fit) (Hair et al., 2006). Tucker-Lewis index (TLI) compares the χ^2 value of the model with that of the independent model which takes degrees-of-freedom for the model into consideration (.955 > .08 indicates good fit). Relative fit index (RFI) and incremental fit index were .929 and .962, respectively, higher than the suggested threshold of .90 and each criterion of fit, so specified that the projected measurement model's fit was acceptable (Byrne, 2001; Hair et al., 2006; Tabachnick & Fidell, 2007).

According to the standardized parameter assessments for the research hypothesized association among the constructs, the results show that the more favorable the hotel travelers' orientation, the more awareness is

Table 7.3 Construct relationships and discriminant validity

	CR	AVE	MSV	Image	Cusorient	Awareness	Satisfaction	Loyalty
Image	.927	.763	.095	.873				
Travellers' orientation	.915	.641	.287	.304	.801			
Awareness	.962	.865	.138	.264	.372	.930		
Satisfaction	.934	.779	.222	.169	.349	.250	.882	
Loyalty	.915	.730	.287	.308	.536	.346	.471	.854

created among customers, so hypothesis 1 was fully accepted (β = .421, t = 7.065). Furthermore, to the hypothesized effects, directed by the hotel consumer's perception, the relationship between travelers' orientation and hotel's image (H2) was fully accepted (β = .236, t = 4.283). Hypotheses 3 and 4 illustrate the significant relationship between hotel's travelers' orientation and satisfaction (H3: β = .430, t = 5.833) and loyalty (H4: β = .507, t = 8.007). Hypothesis 5a demonstrates that digital marketing strengthens the positive association between travelers' orientation and awareness. However, digital marketing dampens the positive relationship between travelers' orientation and image (H5b) and satisfaction (H6a) and loyalty (H6b). Hypothesis 7 examines the relationship between awareness and image and the results illustrate the significant relationships. Hypothesis 7 was supported fully (β = .147, t = 3.105). The results of hypothesis 7a show that the effect of hotel guest's awareness and the image is stronger among female guests (β = .166, t = 2.466) than among male guests (β = .129, t = 1.947, p = .052).

Hypothesis 8 (image $\rightarrow$ satisfaction) was not confirmed for the hypothesized associations between image and satisfaction. The result is statistically different from 0 at the .05 significance level, and this may not be effective concerning a participant's perception (β = .094, t = 1.305, p = .192). Interestingly, the result of hypothesis 8a illustrates that the effect of hotel guest's image and satisfaction is stronger among female guests (β = .224, t = 1.958, p = .050, partially accepted) than among male guests (β = .023, t = .253, p = .800). It can be a challenge for the global hotel industry to upsurge their consumers' satisfaction with the products and services. The hypothesized examination demonstrates that the more satisfied the guests are toward the hotel, the more loyalty guests have to the hotel (H9a: β = .290, t = 6.202), and, therefore, hypothesis 9 was accepted. However, the effect of hotel guest's satisfaction and loyalty (H9a) was confirmed from female (β = .212, t = 3.185) and male guests (β = .331, t = 5.438) (Tables 7.4 and 7.5).

Table 7.4 Results of hypothesis testing

Standardized regression paths			Estimate	S.E	C.R	p	Hypothesis
H1	Travellers' orientation	$\rightarrow$ Awareness	.421	.060	7.065	***	Supported
H2	Travellers' orientation	$\rightarrow$ Image	.236	.055	4.283	***	Supported
H3	Travellers' orientation	$\rightarrow$ Satisfaction	.430	.074	5.833	***	Supported
H4	Travellers' orientation	$\rightarrow$ Loyalty	.507	.063	8.007	***	Supported
H7	Awareness	$\rightarrow$ Image	.147	.047	3.105	.002	Supported
H8	Image	$\rightarrow$ Satisfaction	.094	.072	1.305	.192	Not-Supported
H9	Satisfaction	$\rightarrow$ Loyalty	.290	.047	6.202	***	Supported

Standardized regression paths			Estimate	S.E	C.R	p	Hypothesis
Moderator (Gender)							
H7a Awareness	→	Image					
		Female	.166	.067	2.466	.014	Supported
		Male	.129	.066	1.947	.052	Not-Supported
H8a Image	→	Satisfaction					
		Female	.224	.114	1.958	.050	Partially supported
		Male	.023	.091	.253	.800	Not-supported
H9a Satisfaction	→	Loyalty					
		Female	.212	.067	3.185	.001	Supported
		Male	.331	.061	5.438	***	Supported

*** $p < .001$
Notes: Path = Relationship between independent variable on dependent variable; β = Standardised regression coefficient; S.E. = Standard error; p = Level of significance.

Table 7.5 Results of moderation impacts (digital marketing)

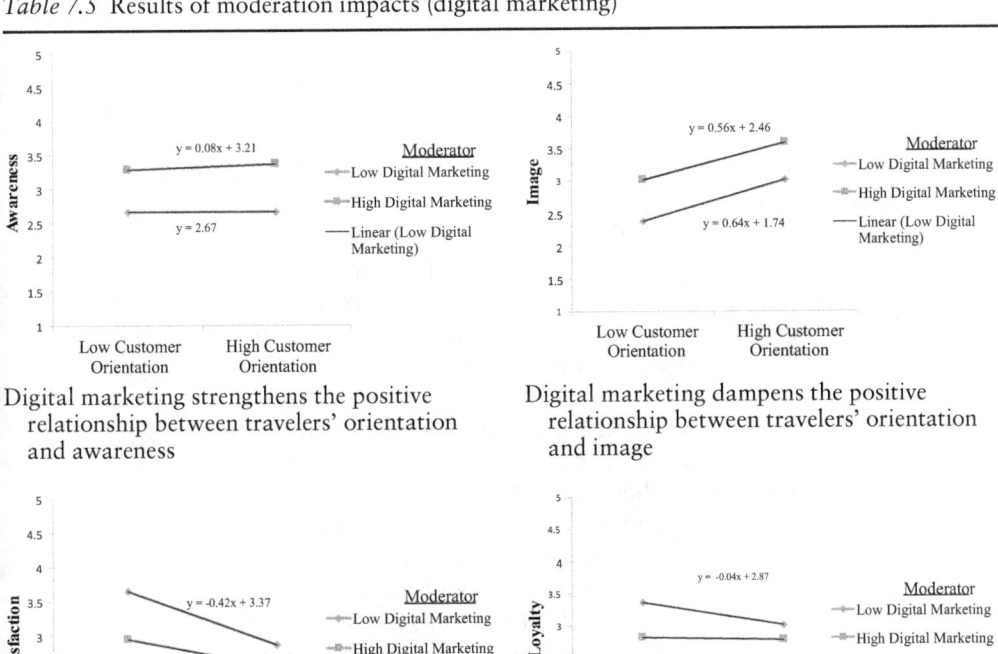

Digital marketing strengthens the positive relationship between travelers' orientation and awareness

Digital marketing dampens the positive relationship between travelers' orientation and image

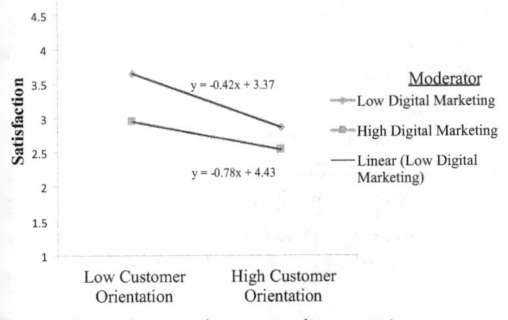
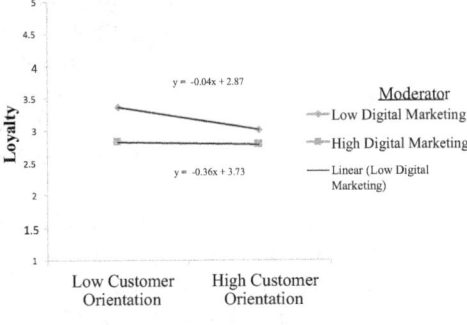

Digital marketing dampens the negative relationship between travelers' orientation and satisfaction

Digital marketing dampens the negative relationship between travelers' orientation and loyalty

Discussion

In the current era, due to the sweeping changes in the micro/macro environment, tourism managers have to cope with wide ranges of difficulties as travelers' and customers' needs are becoming more challenging than before (Kastenholz et al., 2012; Ritchie et al., 2000). Consequently, with such drastic changes, knowing the factors which can have an impact on loyalty is becoming more crucial than before.

Making a customer loyal is one of the essential worries for all of the tourism businesses (Han et al., 2017). Consideration such as this highlights the importance of the question of what distinguishes the hotels' travelers' orientation that has struck association-gold from the other hotels? What is the nature of the relationships that create awareness, image, satisfaction, and loyalty? How do digital media impact the relationships? When and why are such associations likely to occur? To answer such questions, there have been wide ranges of scholars to respond to such a crucial issue. Different researchers and travelers' managers tried to come up with the answers, so they can find the most prudent and effective strategy for such enormous changes in the hotel and tourism industry. Based on the above discussion, the prime aim of this research is to analyze an integrated model by investigating the impact of travelers' orientation toward loyalty, which, in turn, has an effect on awareness, image, satisfaction, and ultimately loyalty.

This study offers valuable insight into the demand part of the hotel industry in Thailand. The results show that travelers' orientation has an impact on awareness. This finding is consistent with the previous research studies (Chandon et al., 2016; Lui et al., 2018), suggesting that orientation has a positive impact on awareness. This outcome informs tourism managers on the importance of the travelers' orientation regarding being more aware of their business. In this regard, as companies try more to accommodate their customers' needs, customers become more aware of the market (Chow et al., 2015).

Travellers' orientation was found to have an impact on image. It was found that being customer oriented for hotels can give them a better image among travelers who use them. Previous studies in the tourism sector (e.g., Dolan & Goodman, 2017; Lin et al., 2018; Thomas-Francois et al., 2017) suggest that travelers' orientation can be built on a tourism firm's image. A traveler-orientated hotel can distinguish and accommodate their travelers' needs. Doing so can result in the hotel's having a customer-orientated image. Hotel managers should pay attention to having such an image which can bring many sustainable benefits to their hotels (Tassiello et al., 2018).

As expected, travelers' orientation was also found to be effective on satisfaction. Previous research studies suggest that when a firm can identify and accommodate their customers' needs, they can make their travelers and customers more satisfied (Yolal et al., 2016). The findings of this research support the outcomes of Dhar (2015), Lui et al. (2018), and Youn et al. (2018) that travelers' orientation has a positive impact on satisfaction. This finding helps tourism managers to understand the importance of travelers' orientation and its considerable impact on the travelers' satisfaction. As hotels become more customer orientated, they can meet their travelers' needs, and this can have an impact on their satisfaction and also their future visit intention.

Travellers' orientation was also found to be effective on loyalty. As previous scholars have suggested, knowing and being able to satisfy travelers' needs can result in making a traveler more loyal (Kohli & Jaworski, 1990; Maydeu-Olivares & Lado, 2003). As loyal travelers are a good and sustainable source of income (Molina-Azorín et al., 2015), the hotel managers should try to make their customers loyal by knowing their needs and trying to accommodate them. Furthermore, as Lai and Hitchcock (2017) suggested, owing to the importance of loyal travelers, they should be provided with superior service.

Digital marketing can have an impact on the relationship between travelers' orientation and awareness (H5a), place image (H5b), satisfaction (H5c), and finally loyalty (H6a). As hotels use social media to interact with their travelers (Hudson et al., 2015), this can have an impact on how much they can promote themselves as consumer orientated, and it can also affect the relationship between travelers' orientation and awareness, and image of a hotel. This interaction with travelers can help hotels and hotel managers to understand their travelers' needs (Filieri et al., 2015) resulting in making visitors more satisfied. Besides, as social media shows hotels should have more consistent interaction with their travelers and visitors, travelers can perceive how customer orientated a hotel is, which can make a visitor more loyal (Erdogmus & Cicek, 2012). As discussed above, because nowadays travelers use social and online platforms to have access to the service/products of a firm, it is vital for every hotel to handle its social media efficiently and adequately.

Awareness was found to have a positive impact on the place image. This result supports the previous research studies (Barreda et al., 2016; Esch et al., 2006; Nicolau & Sharma, 2018). In other words, awareness can boost image (H7). Also, the results suggest that being a woman can positively influence the relationship between awareness and place image (H7a). As a female traveler's perception is different from a male's (Guimarães & Silva, 2016), and women pay more attention to details (Brosnan & De Waal, 2003), they remember the brand differently as compared to the men, and this can result in the relationship between awareness and image. Hotel managers can apply this idea in their advertising campaigns and plans to impact on both male and female visitors. Also, hotel managers can try to provide a superior service for their female travelers, resulting in having a better and better hotel image.

The place image was found to have no impact on the satisfaction of travelers. Contrary to previous research studies (e.g., Bloemer & De Ruyter, 1998; Kim et al., 2013) this study did not support the relationship between place image and satisfaction. As travelers have an image of services and products of a place, their satisfaction forms on their previous images (H8). However, due to the advancements in technology and new peer-peer accommodation sites such as Airbnb, a hotel's images have changed, resulting in the visitor's satisfaction. Furthermore, as the perceptions of men and women are different, due to their cognitive and emotional differences (Aslan, 2016), this gender difference can strengthen or weaken the relationship between image and satisfaction. However, this effect is partially supported in women and was not supported in men. As the image perception is different in women and men, women tend to remember what they experience in a hotel more easily, and this can result in how satisfied they are. This result can add invaluable insight to hotel managers about forming the image of their male and female travelers. As this image is distinctive in male and female tourists, their satisfaction with the received services/products is different (H8a).

Ultimately, consistent with previous research studies (Gao & Lai, 2015; Han & Hyun, 2018), satisfaction was found to have an impact on loyalty (H9). Furthermore, gender was found to have an impact on the relationship between satisfaction and loyalty. This result supports the study of Tran et al. (2018). As females find exclusion harder as compared to males (Hwang & Mattila, 2018), they show more signs of being loyal to a hotel. Thus, hotel managers can apply this notion to have more loyal female visitors (H9a).

Future research directions

This research has been conducted to examine the effectiveness of travelers' orientation, digital media, and customer relationship in the hotel industry in Thailand. First, the hotels for selection should be more varied in terms of the hotel grades, international or local brand, and locations so that the data are more available for comparison and to see whether or not the types of hotel, the locations, and the estimated amount of investment affect the effectiveness of digital marketing. Second, the sampling should be expanded. The number of participants should be increased, and the respondents should come from varied backgrounds as, currently, most are Thai, with similar age, education, and salary. There might be additional questions asking about their occupations as well. The suggestion is provided to make the results of future research more reliable. Finally, the questionnaire might offer open questions for the participants to provide their opinion regarding the constructs to evaluate the feeling or attitude of the customers that could not be assessed by the questions provided.

For future research, this study might be one of the information backgrounds that the researcher can use and develop. The topic of future research in hotel industries might be expanded to various types of hotels and locations, such as in Southeast Asia or even in Asia and comparing with other continents like Europe, as the characteristics of companies and customers from a different culture may affect the attitude of each construct. Also, future research might focus on the five-star hotels or the local hotels. Another choice is that the investigation may be conducted with the case study in other industries. Besides, researchers may compare the effectiveness of digital and traditional marketing toward the market orientation and customer relationship. Apart from types of business, research methodology should also be considered. Quantitative research might be conducted as well as qualitative research. There should be more analysis of the factors that may affect the constructs, such as gender, work background, and age. Sampling may be more varied regarding gender, age, education, and income for a different perspective. It is true that there are so many constructs to evaluate, but the questionnaire should be shorter. Otherwise, the respondents may lose their attention to the survey.

Regarding limitations, there are only a few choices of hotel industries in Thailand. Next, the respondents should be chosen from various backgrounds, and lastly, the questionnaire should provide open questions for multiple answers for a better comparison. For future research, the research can be expanded to the hotel industry in Asia or to another industry. There might be a comparison between digital and traditional marketing toward market orientation and customer relationship as well.

Conclusion

The increase in tourism competition and the hotel industry is becoming a challenge for many hotels. Due to such an increase in the competition, many hotels are trying to make their travelers more loyal using the tools they have, such as social media. Having a loyal visitor is directly associated with the profit increase and future hotel success. As customers are becoming interested in sharing experiences (Ha & Lee, 2018), making visitors loyal using social media is becoming more critical than ever. The first and the most important contribution of the study is analyzing the consequences of customer orientation by the moderating role of social media. This research tries to suggest that customer orientation and other essential attributes of a hotel can result in loyalty.

Theoretical contribution

Since digital marketing plays an essential role in the marketing world, its effectiveness should, therefore, be studied and evaluated to ensure the value of the investment in this kind of marketing and to further understand the expectation and satisfaction of customers toward digital marketing. The research framework has been proposed to make a clear relationship among constructs and to develop the hypotheses for further measurement. This research has contributed the knowledge of the relationship among digital marketing, market orientation, and customer relationship, which includes place awareness, brand image, customer satisfaction, and brand loyalty. In total, 13 hypotheses cover all aspects of the relationship. This research proposes that digital marketing itself affects market orientation, place awareness, brand image, customer satisfaction, and travelers' loyalty. Focusing on market orientation, it is found that market orientation is not only impacted by digital marketing, it also could be an antecedent of digital marketing and other constructs as well. Concerning the customer relationship, the research shows the association among elements. To illustrate, the level of awareness impacts on the level of a place image. Place image affects customer satisfaction, and customer satisfaction influences the degree of brand loyalty.

It might be concluded that the relationships among variables are related and linked to one another. In explanation, the greater awareness the customers have, the better place image customers perceive, and the stronger the brand image is, the more customers are satisfied and loyal to the brand. In other words, if the company fails to provide an excellent digital marketing and market orientation, including travelers' orientation, competitor orientation, and inter-functional coordination, there might be a lack of place awareness, negative place image, lower customer satisfaction, and a lower level of brand loyalty.

Managerial implications

The current study provides managerial implications to the companies that are investing in travelers' orientation and using digital marketing, to influence their customer relationship. This research also helps businesses to understand better the whole picture of how they can increase the efficiency of digital marketing and market orientation. They will learn more about how to raise awareness, place image, customer satisfaction, and brand loyalty, which might be considered as one of the goals of the service industry, including hotels. Regarding the effectiveness of digital marketing, the result shows that digital marketing is significant among all elements, i.e., market orientation which includes travelers' orientation, competitor orientation, and inter-functional coordination, place awareness, place image, customer satisfaction, and brand loyalty.

Moreover, travelers' orientation is also an essential factor to increase the potential of digital marketing and the level of place awareness, place image, customer satisfaction, and brand loyalty. In other words, if businesses have a strong digital marketing and market orientation, their relationships with customers tend to be positive. Regarding customer relationship, it is found that the higher the awareness is, the better image customers have toward the place. Moreover, place image has a potential impact on customer satisfaction, and customer satisfaction effectively increases brand loyalty. Therefore, it could be summarized that the data collected from the questionnaire are aligned with the literature review. The company could trust and might invest in digital marketing and travelers' orientation, which are the factors of a successful customer relationship.

Key construct definitions

Travellers' orientation: this refers to the time when companies first pay attention to travelers' needs and attempt to satisfy them (Lee & Hwang, 2016).

Awareness: this is defined as the ability of consumers to recognize or differentiate the hotel that is in their mind (Keller, 1993; Moisescu, 2009), or the familiarity of the hotel about the place (Malik et al., 2013).

Place image: place image refers to the tourist interpretation about the place (Keller, 1993; Korchia, 2015).

Satisfaction: the term satisfaction is used when the customers personally judge the brands by means of the expected and experienced products and services (Oliver, 1997; Sondoh et al., 2007).

Loyalty: loyalty is explained when customers select to buy particular products or services from the same brand over and over again (Moisescu, 2006).

Acknowledgment

The authors would like to thank Pornteera Ngampongvanich for helping them to conduct this study.

References

Aaker, D. (1991). *Managing brand equity. Capitalizing on the value of a brand name.* New York: Free Press.

Alhelalat, J. A., Ma'moun, A. H., & Twaissi, N. M. (2017). The impact of personal and functional aspects of restaurant employee service behaviour on customer satisfaction. *International Journal of Hospitality Management*, 66(Sep), 46–53.

Anderson, E. W., & Sullivan, M. W. (1993). The antecedents and consequences of customer satisfaction for firms. *Marketing Science*, 12(2), 125–143.

Anderson, J. C., & Gerbing, D. W. (1988). Structural equation modelling in practice: A review and recommended the two-step approach. *Psychological Bulletin*, 103(3), 411–420.

Antioco, M., & Lindgreen, A. (2003). Relationship marketing in the Internet age (Doctoral dissertation, MA thesis, Catholic University of Louvain, Belgium).

Arnold, M. J., & Reynolds, K. E. (2003). Hedonic shopping motivations. *Journal of Retailing*, 79(2), 77–95.

Asikhia, O. (2010). Tourists orientation and firm performance among Nigerian small and medium scale businesses. *International Journal of Marketing Studies*, 2(1), 197–212.

Aslan, A. (2016). An exploratory study on the sexual intimacy of male hotel workers and female foreign tourists. *International Journal of Hospitality Management*, 58(Sep), 107–116.

Barreda, A. A., Bilgihan, A., Nusair, K., & Okumus, F. (2016). Online branding: Development of hotel branding through interactivity theory. *Tourism Management*, 57(Dec), 180–192.

Baumgartner, H., & Steenkamp, J. B. E. (1996). Exploratory consumer buying behaviour: Conceptualization and measurement. *International Journal of Research in Marketing*, 13(2), 121–137.

Beatty, S. E., Mayer, M., Coleman, J. E., Reynolds, K. E., & Lee, J. (1996). Customer-sales associate direct relationships. *Journal of Retailing*, 72(3), 223–247.

Beerli, A., & Martín, J. D. (2004). Tourists' characteristics and the perceived image of tourist destinations: A quantitative analysis – A case study of Lanzarote, Spain. *Tourism Management*, 25(5), 623–636.

Bell, E., & Bryman, A. (2007). The ethics of management research: An exploratory content analysis. *British Journal of Management*, 18(1), 63–77.

Bennett, R., & Rundle-Thiele, S. (2004). Customer satisfaction should not be the only goal. *Journal of Services Marketing*, 18(7), 514–523.

Berry, L. L. (1995). Relationship marketing of services – Growing interest, emerging perspectives. *Journal of the Academy of Marketing Science*, 23(4), 236–245.

Bloemer, J., & De Ruyter, K. (1998). On the relationship between store image, store satisfaction and store loyalty. *European Journal of Marketing*, 32(5/6), 499–513.

Bolton, R. N., Kannan, P. K., & Bramlett, M. D. (2000). Implications of loyalty program membership and service experiences for customer retention and value. *Journal of the Academy of Marketing Science*, 28(1), 95–108.

Brewer, M. B. (1991). The social self: On being the same and different at the same time. *Personality and Social Psychology Bulletin*, 17(5), 475–482.

Brosnan, S. F., & De Waal, F. B. (2003). Monkeys reject unequal pay. *Nature*, 425(6955), 297–299.

Bruwer, J., Buller, C., Saliba, A. J., & Li, E. (2014). Country-of-origin (COO) brand loyalty and related consumer behaviour in the Japanese wine market. *International Journal of Wine Business Research*, 26(2), 97–119.

Buil, I., Martínez, E., & de Chernatony, L. (2013). The influence of brand equity on consumer responses. *Journal of Consumer Marketing*, 30(1), 62–74.

Byrne, B. M. (2001). Structural equation modelling with AMOS, EQS, and LISREL: Comparative approaches to testing for the factorial validity of a measuring instrument. *International Journal of Testing*, 1(1), 55–86.

Caner, D., & Banu, D. (2015). Key factors of online customer satisfaction. *International Journal of Academic Research in Business and Social Sciences*, 5(7), 97–111.

Carlsson, J. (2010). An assessment of social media business models and strategic implications for future implementation. Diploma in Advanced Strategy University of Oxford (Saïd) Business School.

Chaffey, D., & Chadwick, F. (2012). *Digital marketing: Strategy, implementation and practice.* 5th ed. Harlow: Pearson.

Chandon, J. L., Laurent, G., & Valette-Florence, P. (2016). Pursuing the concept of luxury: Introduction to the JBR special issue on "luxury marketing from tradition to innovation". *Journal of Business Research*, 69(1), 299–303.

Chang, H. H., & Chen, S. W. (2008). The impact of customer interface quality, satisfaction and switching costs on e-loyalty: Internet experience as a moderator. *Computers in Human Behavior*, 24(6), 2927–2944.

Chen, C. F., & Chen, F. S. (2010). Experience quality, perceived value, satisfaction and behavioural intentions for heritage tourists. *Tourism Management*, 31(1), 29–35.

Cheng, M., & Foley, C. (2018). The sharing economy and digital discrimination: The case of Airbnb. *International Journal of Hospitality Management*, 70(Mar), 95–98.

Chiou, J. S., Huang, C. Y., & Lee, H. H. (2005). The antecedents of music piracy attitudes and intentions. *Journal of Business Ethics*, 57(2), 161–174.

Chow, C. W., Lai, J. Y., & Loi, R. (2015). The motivation of travel agents' customer service behaviour and organisational citizenship behaviour: The role of leader-member exchange and internal marketing orientation. *Tourism Management*, 48(Jun), 362–369.

Christodoulides, G., Cadogan, J., & Veloutsou, C. (2015). Consumer-based brand equity measurement: Lessons learned from an international study. *International Marketing Review*, 32(3/4), 307–328.

Cornwell, B., Johnston, W., & Nickell, D. (2011). Sponsorship-linked marketing: A set of research propositions. *Journal of Business and Industrial Marketing*, 26(8), 577–589.

Deshpandé, R., Farley, J. U., & Webster Jr, F. E. (1993). Corporate culture, tourist's orientation, and innovativeness in Japanese firms: A quadrat analysis. *The Journal of Marketing*, 1(Jan), 23–37.

Devaraj, S., Fan, M., & Kohli, R. (2002). Antecedents of B2C channel satisfaction and preference: Validating e-commerce metrics. *Information Systems Research*, 13(3), 316–333.

Dhar, R. L. (2015). Service quality and the training of employees: The mediating role of organisational commitment. *Tourism Management*, 46(Feb), 419–430.

Dick, A. S., & Basu, K. (1994). Customer loyalty: Toward an integrated conceptual framework. *Journal of the Academy of Marketing Science*, 22(2), 99–113.

Dillon, W. R., & Goldstein, M. (1984). Multivariate analysis methods and applications (No. 519.535 D5).Dolan, R., & Goodman, S. (2017). Succeeding on social media: Exploring communication strategies for wine marketing. *Journal of Hospitality and Tourism Management*, 33(Dec), 23–30.

Ekinci, Y., Nam, J., & Whyatt, G. (2011). Brand equity, brand loyalty and consumer satisfaction. *Annals of Tourism Research*, 38(3), 1009–1030.

Erdogmus, I., & Cicek, M. (2012). The impact of social media marketing on brand loyalty. *Procedia-Social and Behavioral Sciences*, 58(Oct), 1353–1360.

Esch, F. R., Langner, T., Schmitt, B. H., & Geus, P. (2006). Are brands forever? How brand knowledge and relationships affect current and future purchases. *Journal of Product & Brand Management*, 15(2), 98–105.

Ewing, M. T., & Napoli, J. (2005). Developing and validating a multidimensional nonprofit brand orientation scale. *Journal of Business Research*, 58(6), 841–853.

Filieri, R., Alguezaui, S., & McLeay, F. (2015). Why do travellers trust TripAdvisor? Antecedents of trust towards consumer-generated media and its influence on recommendation adoption and word of mouth. *Tourism Management*, 51(Dec), 174–185.

Fornell, C., & Larcker, D. F. (1981). Structural equation models with unobservable variables and measurement error: Algebra and statistics. *Journal of Marketing Research*, 1(Feb), 382–388.

Foroudi, P. (2018). Influence of brand signature, place awareness, brand attitude, brand reputation on the hotel industry's brand performance. *International Journal of Hospitality Management*, 8(Oct), 1–15.

Foroudi, P., Dinnie, K., Kitchen, P. J., Melewar, T. C., & Foroudi, M. M. (2017). IMC antecedents and the consequences of planned brand identity in higher education. *European Journal of Marketing*, 51(3), 528–550.

Foroudi, P., Melewar, T. C., & Gupta, S. (2014). Linking corporate logo, corporate image, and reputation: An examination of consumer perceptions in the commercial setting. *Journal of Business Research*, 67(11), 2269–2281.

Francoeur, B. (2004). Brand image and Walt Disney: A qualitative analysis of "magical gatherings". *Journal of Undergraduate Research*, 4(1), 1–8.

Gao, B. W., & Lai, I. K. W. (2015). The effects of transaction-specific satisfactions and integrated satisfaction on customer loyalty. *International Journal of Hospitality Management*, 44(Jan), 38–47.

Garver, M. S., & Mentzer, J. T. (1999). Logistics research methods: Employing structural equation modelling to test for construct validity. *Journal of Business Logistics*, 20(1), 33–57.

Godey, B., Manthiou, A., Pederzoli, D., Rokka, J., Aiello, G., Donvito, R., & Singh, R. (2016). Social media marketing efforts of luxury brands: Influence on brand equity and consumer behaviour. *Journal of Business Research*, 69(12), 5833–5841.

Goodman, L. A. (2011). Comment: On respondent-driven sampling and snowball sampling in hard-to-reach populations and snowball sampling not in hard-to-reach populations. *Sociological Methodology*, 41(1), 347–353.

Grohmann, B. (2009). Gender dimensions of brand personality. *Journal of Marketing Research*, 46(1), 105–119.

Guimarães, C. R. F. F., & Silva, J. R. (2016). Pay gap by gender in the tourism industry of Brazil. *Tourism Management*, 52(Feb), 440–450.

Gwinner, K. P., Gremler, D. D., & Bitner, M. J. (1998). Relational benefits in services industries: The customer's perspective. *Journal of the Academy of Marketing Science*, 26(2), 101–114.

Ha, E. Y., & Lee, H. (2018). Projecting service quality: The effects of social media reviews on service perception. *International Journal of Hospitality Management*, 69(Jan), 132–141.

Ha, I., Yoon, Y., & Choi, M. (2007). Determinants of adoption of mobile games under mobile broadband wireless access environment. *Information & Management*, 44(3), 276–286.

Habibi, F., Hamilton, C., Valos, M., & Callaghan, M. (2015). E-marketing orientation and social media implementation in B2B marketing. *European Business Review*, 27(6), 638–655.

Hair, J. F., Black, W. C., Babin, B. J., Anderson, R. E., & Tatham, R. L. (2006). *Multivariate data analysis* (Vol. 6(3), pp. 289–300). Upper Saddle River: Pearson Prentice Hall.

Han, H., & Hyun, S. S. (2018). Role of motivations for luxury cruise travelling, satisfaction, and involvement in building traveller loyalty. *International Journal of Hospitality Management*, 70(Mar), 75–84.

Han, H., Meng, B., & Kim, W. (2017). Bike-traveling as a growing phenomenon: Role of attributes, value, satisfaction, desire, and gender in developing loyalty. *Tourism Management*, 59(Apr), 91–103.

Haryanto, J. O., Moutinho, L., & Coelho, A. (2016). Is brand loyalty really present in the children's market? A comparative study from Indonesia, Portugal, and Brazil. *Journal of Business Research*, 69(10), 4020–4032.

Hemsley-Brown, J., & Alnawas, I. (2016). Service quality and brand loyalty: The mediation effect of brand passion, brand affection and self-brand connection. *International Journal of Contemporary Hospitality Management*, 28(12), 2771–2794.

Herrero, A., San Martín, H., & Collado, J. (2018). Market orientation and SNS adoption for marketing purposes in hospitality microenterprises. *Journal of Hospitality and Tourism Management*, 34(Mar), 30–40.

Hillebrand, B., Nijholt, J. J., & Nijssen, E. J. (2011). Exploring CRM effectiveness: An institutional theory perspective. *Journal of the Academy of Marketing Science*, 39(4), 592–608.

Hong, S.-J., & Tam, K. Y. (2006). Understanding the adoption of multipurpose information appliances: The case of mobile data services. *Information Systems Research*, 17(2), 162–179.

Hudson, S., Roth, M. S., Madden, T. J., & Hudson, R. (2015). The effects of social media on emotions, brand relationship quality, and word of mouth: An empirical study of music festival attendees. *Tourism Management*, 47(4), 68–76.

Hung, S. Y., Chen, C. C., & Huang, N. H. (2014). An integrative approach to understanding customer satisfaction with e-service of online stores. *Journal of Electronic Commerce Research*, 15(1), 40–57.

Hur, K., Kim, T. T., Karatepe, O. M., & Lee, G. (2017). An exploration of the factors influencing social media continuance usage and information sharing intentions among Korean travellers. *Tourism Management*, 63(Dec), 170–178,

Hwang, E., Baloglu, S., & Tanford, S. (2019). Building loyalty through reward programs: The influence of perceptions of fairness and brand attachment. *International Journal of Hospitality Management*, 76(Jan), 19–28.

Hwang, Y., & Mattila, A. S. (2018). Feeling left out and losing control: The interactive effect of social exclusion and gender on brand attitude. *International Journal of Hospitality Management*, 3(Aug), 1–8.

Jacoby, J., & Kyner, D. B. (1973). Brand loyalty vs repeat purchasing behaviour. *Journal of Marketing Research*, 1(Feb), 1–9.

Jones, M. A., & Suh, J. (2000). Transaction-specific satisfaction and overall satisfaction: An empirical analysis. *Journal of Services Marketing*, 14(2), 147–159.

Kamakura, W. A., Mittal, V., De Rosa, F., & Mazzon, J. A. (2002). Assessing the service-profit chain. *Marketing Science*, 21(3), 294–317.

Kandampully, J., & Suhartanto, D. (2000). Customer loyalty in the hotel industry: The role of customer satisfaction and image. *International Journal of Contemporary Hospitality Management*, 12(6), 346–351.

Kao, C. Y., Tsaur, S. H., & Wu, T. C. E. (2016). Organizational culture on customer delight in the hospitality industry. *International Journal of Hospitality Management*, 56(Jul), 98–108.

Kasim, A., Ekinci, Y., Altinay, L., & Hussain, K. (2018). Impact of market orientation, organisational learning and market conditions on small and medium-sized hospitality enterprises. *Journal of Hospitality Marketing & Management*, 5(Mar) 1–21.

Kastenholz, E., Carneiro, M. J., Marques, C. P., & Lima, J. (2012). Understanding and managing the rural tourism experience – The case of a historical village in Portugal. *Tourism Management Perspectives*, 4(Oct), 207–214.

Keller, K. L. (1993). Conceptualizing, measuring, and managing customer-based brand equity. *The Journal of Marketing*, 1(Jan), 1–22.

Khan, F., & Siddiqui, K. (2013). The importance of digital marketing: An exploratory study to find the perception and effectiveness of digital marketing amongst the marketing professionals in Pakistan. *Journal of Information Systems & Operations Management*, 7(2), 12–19.

Khoshsima, S., Kiani, A., Safari, A., Amari, S., Shifte, M., & Vaseei, M. (2013). The impact of brand credibility on customer loyalty. *International Journal of Business and Behavioural Sciences*, 3(5), 24–34.

Kim, H. J., Park, J., Kim, M., & Ryu, K. (2013). Does perceived restaurant food healthiness matter? Its influence on value, satisfaction and revisit intentions in restaurant operations in South Korea. *International Journal of Hospital Management*, 1(Jul), 397–405.

Kim, S., Ham, S., Moon, H., Chua, B. L., & Han, H. (2018). Experience, brand prestige, perceived value (functional, hedonic, social, and financial), and loyalty among GROCERANT customers. *International Journal of Hospitality Management*, 14(Jul), 15–22.

Kim, W. G., Lee, Y-K., & Yoo, Y.-J. (2006). Predictors of relationship quality and relationship outcomes in luxury restaurants. *Journal of Hospitality and Tourism Research*, 3(2), 43–69.

Kim, W. G., Li, J. J., & Brymer, R. A. (2016). The impact of social media reviews on restaurant performance: The moderating role of excellence certificate. *International Journal of Hospitality Management*, 55(May), 41–51.

King, S. F., & Burgess, T. F. (2008). Understanding success and failure in customer relationship management. *Industrial Marketing Management*, 37(4), 421–431.

Kohli, A. K., & Jaworski, B. J. (1990). Market orientation: The construct, research propositions, and managerial implications. *The Journal of Marketing*, 54(2), 1–18.

Kotler, P. (1984). *Marketing essentials.* Englewood Cliffs: Prentice Hall.

Kotler, P., & Keller, K. L. (2009). *Dirección de marketing.* Pearson educación.

Krepapa, A., Berthon, P., Webb, D., & Pitt, L. (2003). Mind the gap: An analysis of service provider versus customer perceptions of market orientation and the impact on satisfaction. *European Journal of Marketing*, 37(1/2), 197–218.

Kumar, K., Subramanian, R., & Yauger, C. (1998). Examining the market orientation-performance relationship: A context-specific study. *Journal of Management*, 24(2), 201–233.

Kumar, V., & Shah, D. (2004). Building and sustaining profitable customer loyalty for the 21st century. *Journal of Retailing*, 80(4), 317–329.

Lado, N., Maydeu-Olivares, A., & Rivera, J. (1998). Measuring market orientation in several populations: A structural equations model. *European Journal of Marketing*, 32(1/2), 23–39.

Lai, I. K. W., & Hitchcock, M. (2017). Local reactions to mass tourism and community tourism development in Macau. *Journal of Sustainable Tourism*, 25(4), 451–470.

Lee, J. J., & Hwang, J. (2016). An emotional labour perspective on the relationship between tourist's orientation and job satisfaction. *International Journal of Hospitality Management*, 54(Apr), 139–150.

Lee, Y. K., Kim, S. H., Seo, M. K., & Hight, S. K. (2015). Market orientation and business performance: Evidence from the franchising industry. *International Journal of Hospitality Management*, 44(Jan), 28–37.

Lewrick, M., Omar, M., & Williams, R. (2011). Market orientation and innovators' success: An exploration of the influence of customer and competitor orientation. *Journal of Technology Management & Innovation*, 6(3), 48–62.

Li, Y., & Huang, S. S. (2017). Hospitality service climate, employee service orientation, career aspiration and performance: A moderated mediation model. *International Journal of Hospitality Management*, 67(Oct), 24–32.

Liang, T. P., & Lai, H. J. (2002). Effect of store design on consumer purchases: An empirical study of online bookstores. *Information & Management*, 39(6), 431–444.

Lin, Y. H., Ryan, C., Wise, N., & Low, L. W. (2018). A content analysis of airline mission statements: Changing trends and contemporary components. *Tourism Management Perspectives*, 28(Oct), 156–165.

Lo, A. S., Im, H. H., Chen, Y., & Qu, H. (2017). Building brand relationship quality among hotel loyalty program members. *International Journal of Contemporary Hospitality Management*, 29(1), 458–488.

Loveman, G. W. (1998). Employee satisfaction, customer loyalty, and financial performance: An empirical examination of the service profit chain in retail banking. *Journal of Service Research*, 1(1), 18–31.

Lui, T. W., Bartosiak, M., Piccoli, G., & Sadhya, V. (2018). Online review response strategy and its effects on competitive performance. *Tourism Management*, 67(31), 180–190.

Lukas, B. A., & Maignan, I. (1996). Striving for quality: The key role of internal and external customers. *Journal of Market-Focused Management*, 1(2), 175–187.

Malik, M. E., Ghafoor, M. M., Hafiz, K. I., Riaz, U., Hassan, N. U., Mustafa, M., & Shahbaz, S. (2013). Importance of awareness and brand loyalty in assessing purchase intentions of a consumer. *International Journal of Business and Social Science*, 4(5), 1–5.

Maydeu-Olivares, A., & Lado, N. (2003). Market orientation and business economic performance: A mediated model. *International Journal of Service Industry Management*. 14(3), 284–309.

McEachern, M., & Warnaby, G. G. (2005). Improving tourist's orientation within the fresh meat supply chain: A focus on assurance schemes. *Journal of Marketing Management*, 21(1–2), 89–115.

Mehrabi, J., Noorbakhash, K., Shoja, M., & Karim, M. (2012). Impact of tourists orientation and sales orientation on sales' performance in international market of Bilehsavar County. *International Journal of Business and Social Science*, 3(17), 216–222.

Mimouni-Chaabane, A., & Volle, P. (2010). Perceived benefits of loyalty programs: Scale development and implications for relational strategies. *Journal of Business Research*, 63(1), 32–37.

Moisescu, O. I. (2006). A conceptual analysis of brand loyalty as a core dimension of brand equity. *Proceedings of the International Conference on Competitiveness and Stability in the Knowledge-Based Economy*, 24(3), 1128–1136.

Moisescu, O. I. (2009). The importance of awareness in consumers' buying decision and perceived risk assessment. *Journal of Management & Marketing*, 7(2), 103–110.

Molina-Azorín, J. F., Tarí, J. J., Pereira-Moliner, J., López-Gamero, M. D., & Pertusa-Ortega, E. M. (2015). The effects of quality and environmental management on competitive advantage: A mixed methods study in the hotel industry. *Tourism Management*, 50(Oct), 41–54.

Morgan, N. A., Vorhies, D. W., & Mason, C. H. (2009). Market orientation, marketing capabilities and firm performance. *Strategic Management Journal*, 30(8), 909–920.

Muniz, A. M., & O'guinn, T. C. (2001). Brand community. *Journal of Consumer Research*, 27(4), 412–432.

Mustafi, S., Jost, L., & Nguyen, T. (2011). The relationship between online and offline marketing.

Narver, J. C., & Slater, S. F. (1990). The effect of a market orientation on business profitability. *Journal of Marketing*, 54(4), 20–35.

Nguyen, N., & LeBlanc, G. (1998). The mediating role of corporate image on customers' retention decisions: An investigation in financial services. *International Journal of Bank Marketing*, 16(2), 52–65.

Nicolau, J. L., & Sharma, A. (2018). A generalisation of the FIFA World Cup effect. *Tourism Management*, 66(30), 315–317.

Nunnally, J. (1978). *Psychometric methods*. New York: McGraw-Hill.

O'Cass, A., & Ngo, L. (2009). Achieving customer satisfaction via market orientation, brand orientation, and customer empowerment: Evidence from Australia.

O'Cass, A., & Sok, P. (2015). An exploratory study into managing value creation in tourism service firms: Understanding value creation phases at the intersection of the tourism service firm and their customers. *Tourism Management*, 51(Dec), 186–200.

Oliver, C. (1997). Sustainable competitive advantage: Combining institutional and resource-based views. *Strategic Management Journal*, 18(9), 697–713.

Oliver, R. L. (1999). Whence consumer loyalty? *The Journal of Marketing*, 1(Jan), 33–44.

Otim, S., & Grover, V. (2006). An empirical study on web-based services and customer loyalty. *European Journal of Information Systems*, 15(6), 527–541.

Pratminingsih, S., Lipuringtyas, C., & Rimenta, T. (2013). Factors influencing customer loyalty toward online shopping. *International Journal of Trade, Economics and Finance*, 4(3), 104–110.

Pritchard, M. P., Havitz, M. E., & Howard, D. R. (1999). Analyzing the commitment-loyalty link in service contexts. *Journal of the Academy of Marketing Science*, 27(3), 333–348.

Ranjbarian, B., Sanayei, A., Kaboli, M., & Hadadian, A. (2012). An analysis of brand image, perceived quality, customer satisfaction and re-purchase intention in Iranian department stores. *International Journal of Business and Management*, 7(6), 40–48.

Raoofi, M. (2012). Moderating role of e-marketing on the consequences of market orientation in Iranian firms. *Management and Marketing*, 10(2), 301–316.

Ritchie, J. R., Crouch, G. I., & Hudson, S. (2000). Assessing the role of consumers in the measurement of destination competitiveness and sustainability. *Tourism Analysis*, 5(2–3), 69–76.

Ruizalba, J. L., Bermúdez-González, G., Rodríguez-Molina, M. A., & Blanca, M. J. (2014). Internal market orientation: An empirical research in hotel sector. *International Journal of Hospitality Management*, 38(1), 11–19.

Russell-Bennett, R., McColl-Kennedy, J., & Coote, L. (2007). Involvement, satisfaction, and brand loyalty in a small business services setting. *Journal of Business Research*, 60(12), 1253–1260.

Sarwar, A., Haque, A., & Yasmin, F. (2013). The usage of social network as a marketing tool: Malaysian Muslim consumers' perspective. *International Journal of Academic Research in Economics and Management Sciences*, 2(1), 93–102.

Seilov, G. A. (2015). Does the adoption of customer and competitor orientations make small hospitality businesses more entrepreneurial? Evidence from Kazakhstan. *International Journal of Contemporary Hospitality Management*, 27(1), 71–86.

Shankar, V., Smith, K., & Rangaswamy, A. (2002). Customer satisfaction and loyalty in online and offline environments. *International Journal of Research in Marketing*, 20(2), 153–175.

Sheth, J. N., & Parvatiyar, A. (1995). The evolution of relationship marketing. *International Business Review*, 4(4), 397–418.

Sin, L. Y., Alan, C. B., Heung, V. C., & Yim, F. H. (2005). An analysis of the relationship between market orientation and business performance in the hotel industry. *International Journal of Hospitality Management*, 24(4), 555–577.

Sondoh Jr, S., Omar, M., Wahid, N., Ismail, I., & Harun, A. (2007). The effect of brand image on overall satisfaction and loyalty intention in the context of colour cosmetic. *Asian Academy of Management Journal*, 12(1), 83–107.

Tabachnick, B. G., & Fidell, L. S. (2007). *Using multivariate statistics*. Boston: Allyn & Bacon/Pearson Education.

Tajeddini, K., Altinay, L., & Ratten, V. (2017). Service innovativeness and the structuring of organisations: The moderating roles of learning orientation and inter-functional coordination. *International Journal of Hospitality Management*, 65(1), 100–114.

Taleghani, M., Gilaninia, S., & Talab, S. (2013). Market orientation and business performance. *Singapore Journal of Business Economics and Management Studies*, 1(11), 13–17.

Tang, T. W. (2014). Becoming an ambidextrous hotel: The role of tourist's orientation. *International Journal of Hospitality Management*, 39(May), 1–10.

Tassiello, V., Viglia, G., & Mattila, A. S. (2018). How handwriting reduces negative online ratings. *Annals of Tourism Research*, 3(June), 1–9.

Tauber, E. M. (1972). Why do people shop? *The Journal of Marketing*, 36(4), 46–49.

Thomas-Francois, K., von Massow, M., & Joppe, M. (2017). Service-oriented, sustainable, local food value chain – A case study. *Annals of Tourism Research*, 65(Jul), 83–96.

Tomaskova, I. (2009). The current methods of measurement of market orientation. *European Research Studies*, 12(3), 135–150.

Torkzadeh, G., & Dhillon, G. (2002). Measuring factors that influence the success of Internet commerce. *Information Systems Research*, 13(2), 187–204.

Touzani, M., & Temessek, A. (2009). Brand Loyalty: Impact of Cognitive and Affective Variables. *The Annals of Dunarea de Jos University of Galati Fascicle*, 1(1), 227–242.

Tran, L. T. T., Pham, L. M. T., & Le, L. T. (2018). E-satisfaction and continuance intention: The moderator role of online ratings. *International Journal of Hospitality Management*, 5(7), 1–12.

Tuominen, S., Laukkanen, T., & Reijonen, H. (2009, November). Market orientation, brand orientation and brand performance in SMEs: Related constructs. In *Proceedings of the Australian and New Zealand Marketing Academy Conference, Melbourne, Australia*.

Valkenburg, P. M., & Buijzen, M. (2005). Identifying determinants of young children's place awareness: Television, parents, and peers. *Journal of Applied Developmental Psychology*, 26(4), 456–468.

Vinhas Da Silva, R., & Faridah Syed Alwi, S. (2006). Cognitive, affective attributes and conative, behavioural responses in retail, corporate branding. *Journal of Product & Brand Management*, 15(5), 293–305.

Wang, Y. C., Qu, H., & Yang, J. (2018). The formation of sub-brand love and corporate brand love in hotel brand portfolios. *International Journal of Hospitality Management*, 15(3), 1–10.

Westwood, S., Pritchard, A., & Morgan, N. J. (2000). Gender-blind marketing: Business women's perceptions of airline services. *Tourism Management*, 21(4), 353–362.

WTTC (2019). Travel & tourism economic impact 2015: Thailand, https://www.wttc.org/errors/404 (Assessed 1 June 2019).

Yang, Z., & Peterson, R. T. (2004). Customer perceived value, satisfaction, and loyalty: The role of switching costs. *Psychology & Marketing*, 21(10), 799–822.

Yen, C. L. A., & Tang, C. H. H. (2019). The effects of hotel attribute performance on electronic word-of-mouth (eWOM) behaviours. *International Journal of Hospitality Management*, 76(Jan), 9–18.

Yin Wong, H., & Merrilees, B. (2008). The performance benefits of being brand-orientated. *Journal of Product & Brand Management*, 17(6), 372–383.

Yolal, M., Gursoy, D., Uysal, M., Kim, H. L., & Karacaoğlu, S. (2016). Impacts of festivals and events on residents' well-being. *Annals of Tourism Research*, 61(Nov), 1–18.

Yoo, B., & Donthu, N. (2001). Developing and validating a multidimensional consumer-based brand equity scale. *Journal of Business Research*, 52(1), 1–14.

Yoo, B., & Donthu, N. (2002). Testing cross-cultural invariance of the brand equity creation process. *Journal of Product and Brand Management*, 11(6), 380–398.

Youn, H., Lee, K., & Lee, S. (2018). Effects of corporate social responsibility on employees in the casino industry. *Tourism Management*, 68(Oct), 328–335.

Zaman, K., Javaid, N., Arshad, A., & Bibi, S. (2012). Impact of internal marketing on market orientation and business performance. *International Journal of Business and Social Science*, 3(12), 76–87.

Zhang, J., & Daugherty, T. (2009). Third-person effect and social networking: Implications for online marketing and word-of-mouth communication. *American Journal of Business*, 24(2), 53–64.

Zhang, Z., Zhang, Z., & Yang, Y. (2016). The power of expert identity: How website-recognised expert reviews influence travellers' online rating behaviour. *Tourism Management*, 55(Aug), 15–24.

Zhu, H., Lyu, Y., Deng, X., & Ye, Y. (2017). Workplace ostracism and proactive customer service performance: A conservation of resources perspective. *International Journal of Hospitality Management*, 64(Jul), 62–72.

8 Exploring the nation brand perception of Ghana

Samuel Marfo, Ogechi Adeola, Awele Achi, and Robert Ebo Hinson

Learning outcomes

At the end of this chapter, readers should be able to:

1 Discuss the concept of nation branding
2 Discuss the benefits and importance of nation branding
3 Describe the four dominant perspectives of nation branding
4 Discuss Brand Ghana and the importance of developing a nation branding strategy
5 Highlight key themes that can aid in enhancing a nation's brand image and perception.

Introduction

This study documented current perceptions of Ghana's image in order to compile evidence that will support recommendations for the development and implementation of a strong nation branding strategy. The study employed a qualitative approach grounded in primary data gleaned from focus group discussions and in-depth personal interviews. The study offers new perspectives on the meaning of nation branding. Our findings confirmed that the negative image perceptions generally inhibiting Africa's capacity to attract either foreign business or direct investment can be corrected by adopting principles of nation branding that would re-define Ghana as an attractive country for investment by Ghanaians or foreign interests. This study provides recommendations for establishing and implementing a holistic and promising nation branding policy where the inputs of key stakeholders would ensure internal buy-in and support.

Research background

The brand management domain is experiencing a paradigm shift that has swayed the focus of scholars and practitioners from product branding to corporate branding (Aaker, 1996; Ward & Lee, 2000) and even more recently to nation branding (Browning, 2015; Dinnie, 2008; Hakala & Lemmetyinen, 2011; Rojas-Méndez, Murphy & Papadopoulos, 2013).

Some scholars have argued that the notion of nation branding should be perceived as being similar to product or corporate branding (Olins, 1999; Papadopoulos & Heslop, 2002).

Several factors contribute to this heightened attention to nation branding. First is the increasing level of fierce rivalry between nations (Weidner, 2011) in a bid to draw foreign direct investment (FDI) (Papadopoulos, 2004), bolster their tourism industries (Loo & Davies, 2006; Papadopoulos, 2004), attract international students (Martens & Starke, 2008), and expand their product exports (Loo & Davies, 2006; Papadopoulos, 2004).

Second, there is a changing perception that countries are competing brands (Anholt, 2002) that require unrelenting efforts of governments to establish, build up, and coordinate their branding efforts (Rawson, 2007) while also reinforcing their self-esteem and identity (Browning, 2015).

Third, scholars and practitioners acknowledge that foreign policy goes beyond the interaction among nations (Browning, 2015) and that managing a nation brand is more complex than managing corporate brands (Dinnie, 2008). The challenges associated with nation branding are daunting, specifically as they deal with the attraction of tourists, investors, and talents (Aronczyk, 2008).

Nation branding involves the adoption of names, logos, and other branding tools by a country to establish and develop a distinct identity (Pappu & Quester, 2010). Nation branding can only be successful when it is regarded as a critical element of a country's national policy (Anholt, 2008). Studies such as Rojas-Méndez, Murphy, and Papadopoulos (2013) and Fan (2006) reported cases where nation branding efforts failed to catch the attention of target audiences due to the adoption of inapposite communication strategies or a lack of fit between nation branding strategies and nations' features. Examples of successful nation branding were found to be China (Barr, 2012) and Singapore (Song, 2011). Nation brand managers must have a holistic picture of the essentials required to carve out an effective nation branding strategy that will position a nation favorably in the minds of the target audience(s).

It is safe to assume that countries engage in nation branding with the aim of attracting investments and enhancing their images (Anholt, 2007). Developing nations, having recognized this crucial aim of nation branding (Herstein, 2012), are faced with the complexities of meeting that challenge (Hanna & Rowley, 2011). The review of extant literature has shown that Africa has been identified as having a weak brand, and Ghana is no exception (Osei & Gbadamosi, 2011; Wanjiru, 2006). Calls from the developed world encourage third world nations to adopt branding as a means of improving their competitiveness and shore up the economic development gap that exists between them (Akotia, 2010; Anholt, 2003).

Studies focusing on nation branding in Ghana (Akotia, 2010; Akotia, Spio & Frempong, 2010) have looked closely at the contributions of management and the role of citizens to the development of the nation's brand. It appears that a fundamental issue yet to be addressed is the perception the world has of Ghana's nation brand and how people resonate with the brand. An examination of Ghana's image and perceived benefits will provide insight into fundamental branding issues that are relevant to every nation (Osei & Gbadamosi, 2011; Pappu & Quester, 2010).

To create and firmly establish a nation branding strategy, a country must dedicate resources to learning how it is perceived among its target market. Thus, our research attempts to conceptualize the image perception of Ghana as a brand. In addition, we seek to examine the current brand equity status of Ghana and at the same time explore the inherent benefits Ghana could derive from nation branding. Specifically, our study hopes to provide answers to the following questions: (1) How is Ghana's brand image perceived currently by her people? (2) What is the present status of brand Ghana equity? and (3) What are the possible benefits Ghana could obtain from nation branding?

In the following section, we discuss the dominant perspectives of nation branding. We identify several issues surrounding nation branding before discussing the Ghana Brand Office project. The following section provides a case of presenting the nation brand perception of Ghana. The final sections offer a summary, draw general conclusions, and provide directions for future research.

Literature review

Nation branding

The concept of nation branding has garnered considerable attention in mainstream literature in recent years (Anholt, 2007; Fan, 2010; Zeineddine, 2017); however, scholars seem to disagree on a universal definition, with most concluding that nation branding must be proved on the domestic front before being tested abroad (Simonin, 2008). A review of extant literature reveals four dominant perspectives of nation branding: identity, strategic, political, and outcome.

Identity perspective

An identity perspective exists among nations that are making constant efforts to project a good image for themselves (Dinnie, Melewar, Seidenfuss, & Musa, 2010; Fan, 2006, 2010; Gudjonsson, 2005; Hurn, 2016; Olins, 2002). A mantra of this perspective was put forward by Anholt: "The reputations of countries are rather like the brand images of companies and products, and equally important" (2007, p. xi).

An identity perspective argues that the gains of nation branding are more appreciated in marketing (Papadopoulos & Heslop, 2002) because they can invariably explicate the nexus between brand identity (marketing) and national identity (politics and culture) (Skinner & Kubacki, 2007) and nations being perceived as brands through branding efforts (O'Shaughnessy & O'Shaughnessy, 2000). Nation branding entails using a holistic approach when building that brand (Skinner & Kubacki, 2007), defined by Fan as "a process by which a nation's images can be created, monitored, evaluated and proactively managed in order to improve or enhance the country's reputation among a target international audience" (2009, p. 6).

Strategic perspective

This perspective of nation branding has been drawn from the works of authors who have approached the concept from a strategic management standpoint (Anholt, 1998, 2002, 2008; Aronczyk, 2013; Dinnie, 2008; Kaneva, 2011; Warnaby & Medway, 2013). The purpose of nation branding is to strategically improve the reputation and image of a nation through aligning, remodeling, and modernizing a nation's realities to achieve the desired image (Anholt, 2008). This perspective is a way of looking at nation branding as a means to leverage branding principles to gain a competitive advantage.

Political perspective

A number of scholars have written about nation branding from the angle of politics and diplomacy (El-Nawawy, 2006; Eshuis & Klijn, 2012; Hughes, 2007; Kunczik, 1997; Papadopoulos, Hamzaoui-Essoussi & El Banna, 2016; Szondi, 2010; Van Ham, 2001, 2008; Varga, 2013; Volcic & Andrejevic, 2011; Wang, 2007; Zhang, 2007; Zaharna, 2008; Zeineddine, 2017). This perspective views nation branding as a kind of propaganda (political tool) (Kaneva, 2011) used by nations to place themselves in an advantageous position in the international arena (Van Ham, 2003; Wang, 2006). Nation branding becomes a tool for developing relations among nations (Zeineddeine, 2017) and a key determinant of how they are perceived by the rest of the globe (Gilboa, 2001). This perspective also explicates nation branding as a paradigm shift in the political arena culminating in a movement from geopolitics and power era to an era of influence and reputation (Van Ham, 2001).

Outcome perspective

This perspective is derived from the assertions by some authors about what nation branding can do for a nation economically, socially, or

Table 8.1 Classification of authors and their views on nation branding

Areas of Focus	Contributors
Identity perspective	Anholt (2003), Dinnie, Melewar, Seidenfuss and Musa (2010), Fan (2006, 2009, 2010), Hurn (2016), Gudjonsson (2005) and Olins (2002)
Strategic perspective	Anholt (2008, 2002, 1998), Aronczyk (2013), Dinnie (2008), Kaneva (2011), and Warnaby and Medway (2013)
Political perspective	El-Nawawy (2006), Eshuis and Klijn (2012), Hughes (2007), Kunczik (1997), Varga (2013), Volcic and Andrejevic (2011), Van Ham (2001, 2008), Wang (2007), Zaharna (2008), Zeineddine (2017), and Zhang (2007)
Outcome perspective	Alam, Almotairi and Gaadar (2013), Frig and Sorsa (2018), Huang (2011), Kalamova and Konrad (2010), Kam and Tse (2018), Mamuti & Özgüner (2014), Matiza and Oni (2013), Pamment and Cassinger (2018), Papadopoulos, Hamzaoui-Essoussi & El Banna (2016), and Silvanto, Ryan and McNulty (2015)

Source: Developed by the authors.

politically (Alam, Almotairi & Gaadar, 2013; Frig & Sorsa, 2018; Huang, 2011; Kalamova & Konrad, 2010; Kam & Tse, 2018; Mamuti & Özgüner, 2014; Matiza & Oni, 2013; Pamment & Cassinger, 2017; Papadopoulos, Hamzaoui-Essoussi & El Banna, 2016; Silvanto, Ryan & McNulty, 2015). The outcome perspective of nation branding rests on the belief that it could lead to certain consequences such as foreign direct investment, attracting internationally mobile skilled professionals, business sustainability, social participation, and transnational consumption. According to Anholt (1998, 2002), the attractiveness of nation branding lies in its strategic values and the gains derived from its successful implementation. Table 8.1 presents a summary of scholars' descriptions of nation branding based on the four dominant perspectives derived from extant literature.

The image and identity of nations

Despite the presence or absence of branding, every nation possesses an image (Fan, 2010; Papadopoulos & Heslop, 2002). Branding propagates that image and advances it into an ideal image meant to attract a targeted audience (Fan, 2006; Rainisto, 2003). A nation's brand image is at the receiving end of the communication continuum, i.e., the way it is perceived by a prospective or current, local or international, consumer. Kotler and Gertner define a country's image as "the sum of beliefs and impressions people hold about places [as] images represent a simplification of a large number of associations and pieces of information connected with a place" (2002, p. 250).

A country's image is influenced by several factors – their music, people, history, physical, and natural features (Kotler & Gertner, 2002). The media and entertainment sectors define people's views, particularly negatively held perceptions. These views can have an impact on purchasing decisions, investment, and tourist visits (Kotler & Gertner, 2002). Hence, we define a nation's image as individuals' deeply held opinions of a nation's tangible and intangible offerings and activities. It follows that a nation's brand must reflect the reality on the ground so that individuals who make important decisions based on the image are not misguided.

Fan (2006) argues for the presence of a nexus between countries building strong brands and those which are themselves strong brands. National brands could be good for developing economies such as Ghana, as branding can facilitate and develop market access for offerings from nations in such economies (Abimbola, 2006). All nations have distinctive images, and, through branding, attempts are made to mold, modify, or influence the shaping of these images. Nations and their corporations and institutions need to ensure that their national image accurately reflects their products and culture (Jaffe & Nebenzahl, 2006). Freire (2009) explains that the natives of a country are also important in the image-building process of a nation: they can be more influential than beautiful landscapes and should be incorporated into the overall marketing plan.

The competitive nature of a nation depends on the creation of a compelling identity in a way that is like commercial organizations. A nation's identity is what a country believes it is or wants to be and should be framed in a manner that will attract the attention of the target demographic, emphasize reality, and resonate with both the local and international community through a sustained marketing program aimed at driving investments, tourism, and diplomacy (Simonin, 2008).

A solid nation identity hinges upon communicating the core values of a nation in a way that leads to outcomes that encourage nation brand building (Jaworski & Fosher, 2003). Anholt (2003) described situations where exports, corporations, and nation branding intersect and employ country-of-origin tactics to bolster the economies of emerging markets. Kapferer (2004) posits three questions, the answers to which are highly essential to developing a national identity: *What is the meaning and vision? How is that meaning and vision different from others? What are the nation's core values?*

Pappu and Quester (2010) observed that maintaining a brand's core values in every aspect of the branding process is crucial. Keller and Lehmann (2006) suggest that a perceived similarity between a nation's citizens and her projected identity is imperative for building a citizen-nation brand relationship. Because a place brand is fueled by her people's identity, engaging them will assist in the development of a nation brand

(Campelo, Aitken, Thyne & Gnoth, 2014). This manifests as co-creation, where citizens are engaged and empowered to aid in defining elements that should be used in describing the nation, in this case, Ghana.

A nation can build a persuasive, positive image, and a competitive identity when it exploits inherent core values and a vision that distinguishes it from other nations. Currently, it has dawned on governments to search for novel perspectives on strategy and identity to enhance their nations' competitiveness in the global market (Anholt, 2007). Our research regards nation branding as a strategic, systemized, methodical process employed to create and reinforce a nation's image and identity.

A nation as a brand

The concept of a nation as a brand has drawn the attention of both academic scholars and professionals (Fan, 2006; Harengel & Gbadamosi, 2014; Olins, 2002; O'Shaughnessy & O'Shaughnessy, 2000). The extent to which branding can be applied to nations and its distinction from product branding is a hotbed debate in brand management literature (Hakala & Lemmetyinen, 2011). Every country is associated with a distinct name and image in the minds of its own citizens and people around the world; hence, nations are brands. Fan (2010) argues that a nation brand is an aggregate of the opinions and perceptions held by people about a country based on her culture, food, location, history, and language. This follows the views of Dinnie (2009) who describes a nation brand as special and multi-faceted elements that define the cultural differences among countries.

Stereotypes based on negative and destructive views vis-à-vis favorable aspects may be a starting point for developing and reinforcing a nation brand (Hakala & Lemmetyinen, 2011). Scholars have suggested that artefacts which include movies, music, and products can be used to strategically affect perceptual stereotypes and propagate the nation (De Mooij, 2010; Dinnie, 2009). Gnoth (2002) advances the idea that nation brands arouse emotions because they constitute the relations formed between a nation and its people. Hence, the question: *What attributes do people associate with the name "Ghana"?*

Creating a nation brand requires identifying the nation's core and translating into an attractive and emotionally beneficial identity. As it is in most branding situations, the "product," in this case, Ghana, should be examined and discerned from the point of view of the "end users" (e.g., investors, corporations, media, and visitors), because they represent key elements in brand building (Aaker & Joachimsthaler, 2000). Successful nation brands metamorphose into positive perceptions that encourage investors, drive tourism, and boost exports (Fetscherin, 2010).

A pragmatic model for appraising customers' opinions and perceptions of investment, culture, export, heritage, and immigration of a country is the Nation Brand Hexagon developed by Anholt (2007). When countries find that perceptions are biased due to the presence of imprecise and counterfactual information, they must do everything possible to correct such bias. Stakeholders must be motivated to take actions that will positively project the country's image.

The reputation and image of a nation are crucial elements of her competitiveness and total brand equity (Jaffe & Nebenzahl, 2006; Loo & Davies, 2006). It follows that stakeholders' behavioral patterns determine a nation's reputation, which is the outcome of all stakeholders' views of a nation's image (Martensen & Grønholdt, 2005). The 2002 Kotler and Gertner study found that the branded products with "made in Germany" or "made in Japan" were perceived as high-quality products. How, then, are products bearing "made in Ghana" labels regarded? Brand equity leads to value-added activities to a nation's citizenry and simultaneously builds a competitive edge (Delgado-Ballaster & Munuera-Aleman, 2005). It is imperative for Ghana to consciously develop a preemptive nation branding campaign with the purpose of attracting investors and driving exports while building the nation's brand equity.

It must be acknowledged that extant literature has highlighted factors such as poverty, food insecurity, corruption, and under-development as having a negative effect among developing countries, impeding successful nation branding and hampering Africa's marketability potential (see Kuyvenhoven, 2008; Letiche, 2010; Maiello, 2009; Osei & Gbadamosi, 2011). It is safe to assume that this effect has been a barrier to FDI into several African nations (Bezuidenhout, 2009), given the negative image the continent has built over the years (Osei & Gbadamosi, 2011). The key obstacle is the daunting challenge separating Ghana from the overall negative image of "brand" Africa.

Using Ghana as a case study, we examined the components and impact of nation brand perception. Data was drawn from in-depth interviews conducted and focus group discussions with a total of 26 participants. The participants comprised of Brand Ghana Office officials and the University of Ghana Business School Marketing Department graduate students. Questions asked and/or discussed were categorized as follows:

1   The perception of Ghana's brand image
2   The current brand equity of Ghana
3   The benefits of nation branding to Ghana.

Participants' perceptions shared in focus group discussions included Ghana's brand as being resilient, creative, intellectual, courteous, and flexible. A respondent in an in-depth interview described Ghana's current brand image as having a rich cultural heritage, stable political environment, and a reputation for being hospitable. A respondent from the Brand Ghana Office added that while there is no database to document Ghanaian consumer activity, there is evidence that the trend toward "Friday Wear" – casual attire worn in a business environment – is beginning to feature popular Ghanaian brands that incorporate traditional African motifs.

However, a majority of the focus group discussion participants agreed that Ghana needed to improve its image as an international brand. When asked which dimension of Ghana's brand could offer a competitive advantage in the international marketplace, respondents listed tourism, reliable governance policies, local artisans, and sports as being attractive brands, particularly among their peers in sub-Saharan African countries.

Participants were asked to describe ways that Ghana could attract investment, especially FDIs. One participant stated in an in-depth interview that Ghana's image must be reshaped to rid the country of its current negative perception of corruption among government officials, a high inflation rate, ongoing energy crises, and depreciation of the cedi (Ghana's currency), all of which, coupled with the negative image of brand Africa, make it difficult for Ghana to attract FDI. Some within the focus group discussions argued that the depreciating currency and insecurity may well hinder investments, while others were convinced that Ghana is perceived on the international scene as being politically stable and is thus capable of attracting investors into the country.

Asked to identify their perceived strengths of Brand Ghana, a majority of the participants named football (having one of the best teams in Africa), peace, political stability, cultural heritage, and mineral and agricultural resources as the country's notable strengths. Participants' perceived weaknesses included a continuous rise in crime, insecurity, poverty, corruption, ineffective disease control, and a disorganized government that lacks focus in the face of disruptive change and acts against its own best interests. Based on the responses, it was established that, on the whole, Ghana's brand negatively influences investment in the country.

Participants were asked to consider their personal perceptions of Ghana's brand and how Ghana could promote a more positive image to the outside world. Virtually all the participants pointed out that the media and Ghanaians themselves play a vital role in projecting an image of Ghana as an attractive, stable, and welcoming location. One participant in an in-depth interview felt that Ghana's brand equity lies in its cultural heritage and traditions; a view also held by participants in focus group discussions. One focus group participant identified Ghana's natural resources and potential as a tourism destination as its claim to brand equity. Most of the participants in the focus group clearly attributed Ghana's brand equity to its governance (political stability and peace), friendliness, culture, and tourism.

Finally, regarding the benefits of nation branding, during an in-depth interview a respondent emphasized that creating a brand image for Ghana would serve as a bedrock for attracting investments, increasing exports, enhancing superior citizen value, and positioning Ghana as a tourist welcoming oasis of hospitality, stability, and opportunity. Participants in the focus groups were of the view that a positive brand image of Ghana could increase job creation, improve export opportunities, inspire hope and confidence in the citizens, and attract foreign tourists. It can be inferred from the analysis of the interviews that branding the Ghanaian nation is an appropriate technique for redefining Ghana's image to derive needed benefits.

Recommendations

The following recommendations are provided in light of the findings of this study:

First, the government of Ghana, through the Brand Ghana Office, should develop and implement a strategic nation branding policy targeted at tackling and transforming any negative images of the nation.

Second, the Ghanaian Ministry of Tourism, Ministry of Trade, and other key stakeholders should conceive of an inclusive multi-stakeholder long-term strategic plan that can raise the profile of Ghana, establish a conducive environment for investors, and encourage brand image enhancement activities.

Third, brand ambassadors who are enthusiastic about participating in the nation's branding efforts should be identified and given the tools to communicate the Ghana brand values to targeted audiences.

Finally, Ghanaians must become involved in the branding efforts of the country through stakeholder consultations to gain internal buy-in and support. When stakeholders in a nation become invested in the image and reputation of their country, the result will be positive brand recognition outside her shores.

Future research directions

The authors have presented four dominant perspectives to the meaning of nation branding: identity, strategic, political, and outcome. In addition, the study has been able to explicate Ghana's nation branding efforts and highlight key themes that can aid in measuring and advancing a nation's brand image, while also learning more about how the Ghana brand character is perceived by its own citizens. This study helps to fill an information gap about Ghana's image and how it is perceived, and aids in assessing the consistency of Ghana's projected brand image to discover if there is a lacuna between the perceived image and the projected image.

There were two notable limitations to this study: the small sample size and population. Because the study was limited to a small sample size, the findings cannot be generalized. It is, therefore, recommended that future research should utilize a larger sample that includes respondents from various backgrounds in order to allow for effective generalization of the findings. Because the respondents were all indigenous Ghanaians, future studies should consider replicating the study by focusing on stakeholders from other countries.

Conclusion

This paper examined the work of the Brand Ghana Office with the aim of providing an in-depth look at the need for nation branding of Ghana. This objective was addressed through the exploration of the current image of Ghana, the status of Ghana's brand equity, and the benefits Ghana could derive from nation branding.

The value of nation branding is gradually being understood as a pre-requisite for developing countries like Ghana as they build and re-define their national identities in a bid to bridge the prevailing economic gap with developed nations. The findings from this study show that Ghana's nation branding efforts require thoughtful consideration of the present perceptions of stakeholders and development of an inclusive, multi-stakeholder, long-term strategic plan to raise Ghana's profile, establish a conducive environment for investors, encourage brand image enhancement activities, and communicate the Ghana brand values to targeted audiences.

This research drew conclusions from its study of the benefits of nation branding, a phenomenon that can be assumed to have contributed to Ghana's turnaround into an investment, tourism, export, and talent attraction destination. The current gap between the projected brand identity and the brand image as perceived by non-Ghanaians can be bridged. Effective nation branding can reshape Ghana's image and achieve the desired benefit – to improve Ghana's international competitiveness and thereby her overall economy.

Key construct definitions

Branding: This is a strategic process usually carried out by an organization to craft an identity or create an image for an organization, products, and services in the minds of consumers. This is mainly achieved through the use of promotions and advertisements with a consistent theme. Branding allows for easy identification of a company's products and/or services from its competitors.

Brand image: This refers to the overall impression or perception of a product/service in the minds of consumers, which is formed over time.

Brand equity: This is a term used to describe the value of a brand, which is determined by the perceptions formed and experiences consumers have had with the brand. When the consumer positively perceives a brand, it connotes positive brand equity. The same is true when a consumer has a negative perception of the brand, forming negative brand equity.

Nation branding: This is the application of corporate branding concepts to a country in order to boost her global reputation. It involves combining key features that make a country unique, memorable, and competitive in the hearts of citizens and non-citizens.

Perception: This refers to people's opinion/belief regarding a particular concept/entity. It is the impressions formed of the subject matter or concept.

References

Aaker, D. A. (1996). Measuring brand equity across products and markets. *California Management Review, 38*(3), 102–120.

Aaker, D. A. & Joachimsthaler, E. (2000). *Brand leadership: The next level of the brand revolution.* New York: The Free Press.

Abimbola, T. (2006). Market access for developing economies: Branding in Africa. *Place Branding, 2*(2), 108–117.

Akotia, M. (2010). *Understanding nation branding.* Retrieved from www.ghanaweb.com. Accessed 15 December 2017.

Akotia, M., Spio, A. E. & Frimpong, K. (2010). *Exploring a behavioural approach to country brand management.* Retrieved from www.ghanaweb.com/Ghana HomePage/NewsArchive/artikel.php?ID=194922. Accessed 22 January 2018.

Alam, A., Almotairi, M. & Gaadar, K. (2013). Nation branding: An effective tool to enhance fore going direct investment (FDI) in Pakistan. *Research Journal of International Studies, 25*, 134–141.

Anholt, S. (1998). Nation-brands of the twenty-first century. *Journal of Brand Management, 5*(6), 395–406.

Anholt, S. (2002). Nation branding: A continuing theme. *Journal of Brand Management, 10*(1), 59–60.

Anholt, S. (2003). *Brand new justice: The upside of global branding.* Oxford: Butterworth-Heinemann.

Anholt, S. (2007). Competitive identity: The new brand management for nations, cities and regions. *Journal of Brand Management, 14*(6), 474–485.

Anholt, S. (2008). Place branding: Is it marketing, or isn't it?. *Place Branding and Public Diplomacy, 4*(1), 1–6.

Aronczyk, M. (2008). 'Living the brand': Nationality, globality, and the identity strategies of nation branding consultants. *International Journal of Communication, 2*, 25–37.

Barr, M. (2012). Nation branding as nation building: China's image campaign. *East Asia, 29*(1), 81–94.

Bezuidenhout, H. (2009). A regional perspective on aid and FDI in southern Africa. *International Advances in Economic Research, 15*(3), 310–321.

Browning, C. S. (2015). Nation branding, national self-esteem, and the constitution of subjectivity in late modernity. *Foreign Policy Analysis, 11*(2), 95–214.

Campelo, A., Aitken, R., Thyne, M. & Gnoth, J. (2014). Sense of place: The importance for destination branding. *Journal of Travel Research, 53*(2), 154–166.

De Mooij, M. (2010). *Consumer behavior and culture: Consequences for global marketing and advertising.* Thousand Oaks: Sage.

Delgado-Ballaster, E. & Munuera-Alemán, J. L. (2005). Does brand trust matter to brand equity?. *Journal of Product & Brand Management, 14*(3), 187–196.

Dinnie, K. (2008). *Nation branding: Concepts, issues, practice* (6th ed.). Oxford: Butterworth-Heineman.

Dinnie, K. (2009). Repositioning the Korea brand to a global audience: Challenges, pitfalls, and current strategy. *Korean Economic Institute of America academic paper series.* Retrieved from www.keia.org/sites/default/files/publications/APS-Dinnie_Final.pdf. Accessed 18 April 2018.

Dinnie, K., Melewar, T. C., Seidenfuss, K. U. & Musa, G. (2010). Nation branding and integrated marketing communications: An ASEAN perspective. *International Marketing Review, 27*(4), 388–403.

El-Nawawy, M. (2006). U.S. public diplomacy in the Arab world: The news credibility of Radio Sawa and Television Alhurra in five countries. *Global Media and Communication, 2*(2), 183–203.

Eshuis, J. & Klijn, E. H. (2012). *Branding in governance and public management.* London: Routledge.

Fan, Y. (2006). Branding the nation: What is being branded?. *Journal of vacation marketing, 12*(1), 5–14.

Fan, Y. (2010). Branding the nation: Towards a better understanding. *Place Branding and Public Diplomacy, 6*(2), 97–103.

Fetscherin, M. (2010). The determinants and measurement of a country brand: The country brand strength index. *International Marketing Review, 27*(4), 466–479.

Freire, J. R. (2009). 'Local People' a critical dimension for place brands. *Journal of Brand Management, 16*(7), 420–438.

Frig, M. & Sorsa, V. P. (2018). Nation branding as sustainability governance: A comparative case analysis. *Business & Society,* 1–30. doi:10.1177/0007650318758322

Ghana Tourism Authority (2009). Road map. Retrieved from www.gta.com.gh. Accessed 17 April 2018.

Gilboa, E. (2001). Diplomacy in the media age: Three models of uses and effects. *Diplomacy & Statecraft, 12*(2), 1–28.

Gnoth, J. (2002). Leveraging export brands through a tourism destination brand. *Journal of Brand Management, 9*(4), 262–280.

Gudjonsson, H. (2005). Nation branding. *Place Branding, 1*(3), 283–298.

Hakala, U. & Lemmetyinen, A. (2011). Co-creating a nation brand 'bottom up'. *Tourism Review, 66*(3), 14–24.

Hanna, S. & Rowley, J. (2011). Towards a strategic place brand-management model. *Journal of Marketing Management, 27*(5–6), 458–476.

Harengel, P. & Gbadamosi, A. (2014). 'Launching' a new nation: The unfolding brand of South Sudan. *Place Branding and Public Diplomacy, 10*(1), 35–54.

Herstein, R. (2012). Thin line between country, city, and region branding. *Journal of Vacation Marketing, 18*(2), 147–155.

Huang, S. (2011). Nation-branding and transnational consumption: Japanmania and the Korean wave in Taiwan. *Media, Culture & Society, 33*(1), 3–18.

Hughes, K. P. (2007). 'Waging peace': A new paradigm for public diplomacy. *Mediterranean Quarterly, 18*(2), 18–36.

Hurn, B. J. (2016). The role of cultural diplomacy in nation branding. *Industrial and Commercial Training, 48*(2), 80–85.

Jaffe, E. D. & Nebenzahl, I. D. (2006). *National image and competitive advantage: The theory and practice of place branding* (2nd ed.). Copenhagen: Copenhagen Business School Press.

Jaworski, P. S. & Fosher, D. (2003). National brand identity & its effect on corporate brands: The national brand effect (NBE). *Multinational Business Review, 11*(2), 99–113.

Kalamova, M. M. & Konrad, K. A. (2010). Nation brands and foreign direct investment. *Kyklos, 63*(3), 400–431.

Kam, O. Y. & Tse, C. B. (2018). The trend of foreign direct investment movement: Did unintended nation brand of legal-families play an instrumental role?. *Journal of Business Research*, 1–18. doi:10.1016/j.jbusres.2018.01.008

Kaneva, N. (2011). Nation branding: Toward an agenda for critical research. *International journal of communication, 5*, 117–141.

Kapferer, J. N. (2004). *The new strategic brand management: Creating and sustaining brand equity long term.* London: Kogan Page.

Keller, K. L. (2003). Understanding brands, branding and brand equity. *Interactive Marketing, 5*(1), 7–20.

Keller, K. L. & Lehmann, D. R. (2006). Brands and branding: Research findings and future priorities. *Marketing Science, 25*(6), 740–759.

Kotler, P. & Gertner, D. (2002). Country as brand, product, and beyond: A place marketing and brand management perspective. *Journal of Brand Management, 9*(4), 249–261.

Kunczik, M. (1997). *Images of nations and international public relations.* Mahwah: Lawrence Erlbaum.

Kuyvenhoven, A. (2008). Africa, agriculture, aid. *NJAS-Wageningen Journal of Life Sciences, 55*(2), 93–112.

Letiche, J. M. (2010). Transforming sub-Saharan Africa. *Journal of Policy Modeling, 32*(2), 163–175.

Loo, T. & Davies, G. (2006). Branding China: The ultimate challenge in reputation management?. *Corporate Reputation Review, 9*(3), 198–210.

Maiello, M. (2009). The business of Africa. *Forbes Magazine, 5*(1), 121–126.

Mamuti, A. & Özgüner, D. (2014). Nation branding as a means of attracting FDI: The case of Bosnia and Herzegovina. *International Journal of Business and Globalisation, 13*(2), 197–208.

Martens, K. & Starke, P. (2008). Small country, big business?. New Zealand as education exporter. *Comparative Education, 44*(1), 3–19.

Martensen, A & Gronholdt, L. (2005). Analyzing customer satisfaction data: A comparison of regression and artificial neural networks. *International Journal of Market Research, 47*(2), 121–130.

Matiza, T. & Oni, O. A. (2013). Nation branding as a strategic marketing approach to foreign direct investment promotion: The case of Zimbabwe. *Mediterranean Journal of Social Sciences, 4*(13), 475–488.

Olins, W. (1999). *Trading identities: Why countries and companies are taking on each other's' roles.* London: Foreign Policy Centre.

Olins, W. (2002). Branding the nation – The historical context. *Journal of Brand Management, 9*(4), 241–248.

Osei, C. & Gbadamosi, A. (2011). Re-branding Africa. *Marketing Intelligence & Planning, 29*(3), 284–304.

O'Shaughnessy, J. & O'Shaughnessy, N. J. (2000). Treating the nation as a brand: Some neglected issues. *Journal of Macromarketing, 20*(1), 56–64.

Pamment, J. & Cassinger, C. (2017). Nation branding and the social imaginary of participation: An exploratory study of the Swedish Number campaign. *European Journal of Cultural Studies, 1*, 1–14.

Papadopoulos, N. (2004). Place branding: Evolution, meaning and implications. *Place Branding, 1*(1), 36–49.Papadopoulos, N., Hamzaoui-Essoussi, L. & El Banna, A. (2016). Nation branding for foreign direct investment: An integrative review and directions for research and strategy. *Journal of Product & Brand Management, 25*(7), 615–628.

Papadopoulos, N. & Heslop, L. (2002). Country equity and country branding: Problems and prospects. *Journal of brand management, 9*(4), 294–314.

Pappu, R. & Quester, P. (2010). Country equity: Conceptualization and empirical evidence. *International Business Review, 19*(3), 276–291.

Rainisto, S. K. (2003). Success factors of place marketing: A study of place marketing relationships. *Journal of Advertising Research, 40*(6), 101–105.

Rawson, E. A. G. (2007). Perceptions of the United States of America: Exploring the political brand of a nation. *Place Branding and Public Diplomacy, 3*(3), 213–221.

Rojas-Méndez, J. I., Murphy, S. A. & Papadopoulos, N. (2013). The US brand personality: A Sino perspective. *Journal of Business Research, 66*(8), 1028–1034.

Silvanto, S., Ryan, J. & McNulty, Y. (2015). An empirical study of nation branding for attracting internationally mobile skilled professionals. *Career Development International, 20*(3), 238–258.

Simonin, B. L. (2008). Nation branding and public diplomacy: Challenges and opportunities. *Fletcher Forum of World Affairs, 32*(3), 19–34.

Skinner, H. & Kubacki, K. (2007). Unravelling the complex relationship between nationhood, national and cultural identity, and place branding. *Place Branding and Public Diplomacy, 3*(4), 305–316.

Song, K. B. (2011). *Brand Singapore: How nation branding built Asia's leading global city.* Singapore: Marshall Cavendish International Asia Pte Ltd.

Szondi, G. (2010). From image management to relationship building: A public relations approach to nation branding. *Place Branding and Public Diplomacy, 6*(4), 333–343.

Van Ham, P. (2001). The rise of the brand state: The postmodern politics of image and reputation. *Foreign Affairs, 8*(5), 2–6.

Van Ham, P. (2008). Place branding: The state of the art. *The Annals of the American Academy of Political and Social Science, 616*(1), 126–149.

Varga, S. (2013). The politics of nation branding: Collective identity and public sphere in the neoliberal state. *Philosophy & Social Criticism, 39*(8), 825–845.

Volcic, Z. & Andrejevic, M. (2011). Nation branding in the era of commercial nationalism. *International Journal of Communication, 5*, 598–618.

Wang, J. (2006). Managing national reputation and international relations in the global era: Public diplomacy revisited. *Public Relations Review, 32*(2), 91–96.

Wang, J. (2007). Telling the American story to the world: The purpose of U.S. public diplomacy in historical perspective. *Public Relations Review, 33*(1), 21–30.

Wanjiru, E. (2006). Branding African countries: A prospect for the future. *Place Branding, 2*(1), 84–95.

Ward, M. R. & Lee, M. J. (2000). Internet shopping, consumer search and product branding. *Journal of Product & Brand Management, 9*(1), 6–20.

Warnaby, G. & Medway, D. (2013). What about the 'place' in place marketing?. *Marketing Theory, 13*(3), 345–363.

Weidner, J. R. (2011). *Nation branding, technologies of the self, and the political subject of the nation-state.* Presented at the Annual Meeting of the International Studies Association, Montreal, Canada from March 16–19, 2011.

Zaharna, R. S. (2008). Mapping out a spectrum of public diplomacy initiatives: Information and relational communication networks. In N. Snow & P. Taylor (eds.) *Routledge handbook of public diplomacy.* New York: Routledge.

Zeineddine, C. (2017). Employing nation branding in the Middle East – United Arab Emirates (UAE) and Qatar. *Management & Marketing, 12*(2), 208–221.

Zhang, J. (2007). Beyond anti-terrorism: Metaphors as message strategy of post-September 11 U.S public diplomacy. *Public Relations Review, 33*(1), 31–39.

9 Whispering experience

Configuring the symmetrical and asymmetrical paths to travelers' satisfaction and passion

Pantea Foroudi, Reza Marvi, and Alireza Nazarian

Learning outcomes

At the end of this chapter, readers should be able to:

1 Understand the impact of visual and non-visual content and trust-worthiness on travelers' experience.
2 Recognize the impact of travelers' experience on loyalty, reputation, satisfaction, and passion.
3 Explain the role that the demographics of travelers (age, education, occupation, and age) play in such associations, and suggests a conceptual research framework along with research tenets.

Introduction

This research investigates the impact of visual and non-visual content and trustworthiness on travelers' experience. It also conceptualizes and operationalizes travelers' experience of loyalty, reputation, satisfaction, and passion. We show the role that the travelers' demographics (age, education, occupation, and age) play in such associations, and suggest a conceptual research framework along with research tenets. This research suggests a conceptual model and item measurement and makes a managerial contribution to the understanding of website designers and tourism managers and supports the significance of travelers' experience of sharing an economy website, which needs to be more interactive to increase their reputation and customers' loyalty, satisfaction and passion.

Research background

New experiences can aid people in experiencing a new journey. As for the changing market environment, perhaps the only way to have a sustainable competitive advantage is by providing a unique experience for customers/travelers (Edelman and Singer, 2015). Through these experiences, customers build a relationship with an online retailer (Voorhees et al., 2014). It is also through these experiences that customers judge the asset quality of an online retailer (Lemon and Verhoef, 2016). Recent researchers have defined customer experience as a "customer's journey with a firm over time during the purchase cycle across multiple touchpoints" (Lemon and Verhoef, 2016, p. 6) to fully understand how service retailers can forge and develop relationships with tourists, scholars have concentrated on how to enhance customer experience (Gustafsson et al., 2015; Ostrom et al., 2015). This study focuses on the antecedents and consequences of customer experience through both intellectual and affective experience in the peer-to-peer tourism context.

After the global financial crisis began in 2008, consumers started searching for another form of finding and using products and services. A new economic model called the *sharing economy* or *collaborative consumption* emerged by combining technology with the ambition to be more efficient (Botsman and Rogers, 2011). Sharing programs, in which people actively share their possessions, have grown ever since (Powanga and Powanga, 2008). The burgeoning usage of the sharing economy among travelers has made researchers ask questions about why people are getting involved in this new form of consumption and what the critical motives for doing so might be. Besides, it seems that programs like Airbnb, in which travelers can choose to stay at a local house in exchange for a specified fee, are also becoming popular. New technology and consumer awareness have eliminated the barriers to sharing and, as a result, make it more comfortable on a larger scale.

What differentiates the sharing economy e-retailers that have struck relationship-gold, from the rest? What is the primary influencing construct that impacts on travelers' experience in online retailing? What and how can travelers' experience influence travelers toward e-tailors? What makes e-retailer start to become a passion of one of these firms? When and why are such relationships most likely to occur? A large body of study, in domains ranging from customer experience (Lemon and Verhoef, 2016), loyalty (Russo et al., 2016), reputation (Baka, 2016), satisfaction (Han and Hyun, 2015), and passion (Aro et al., 2018) has tried to understand and explain how online retailers build relationships with their traveler customers and turn them into being passionate about them. In line with the dramatic growth of interest in services from practitioners and academics in today's global economy, the main aim of this research is to inspect the notion of travelers' experience with a focus on the peer-to-peer industry in the UK as there is increasing competition and developing online retailers' platforms such as Airbnb.

This study draws upon the theory of complexity, and it attempts to find a deep understanding of travelers' experience as part of peer-to-peer accommodation and its antecedents and consequences. Also, this research contributes to the fast-growing research on the peer-to-peer relationship by suggesting that the nature of experience is one of the most crucial elements of this sustainable and meaningful relationship between tourism and managers and policy-makers. Furthermore, there is a shortage of studies on why people choose peer-to-peer websites instead of their local travel agencies, and why this is becoming a new trend worldwide. To answer these research objectives, this study focuses on the deployment of visual and non-visual content (photo/color/design/layout/appearance, information, reviews/comments, and price) and trustworthiness (trust, benevolence, and privacy/security) in the sharing economy. The e-retail environment can influence travelers' experience (affective and intellectual) which can result in reputation, satisfaction, loyalty, and passion.

Theoretical background and conceptual model

Researchers consider customer experience as one of the essential tools for forging tourist relationships (Hsiao et al., 2015; Özgener and İraz, 2006). Tourist experience is the interaction that tourists have with an online retailer, product, or service (Grewal et al., 2009). Different types of contact with an e-retailer can have different impacts on travelers' assessment of whether they should form a relationship, such as loyalty, with the online e-retailer or not (Ou and Verhoef, 2017). Creating a relationship with an online retailer is the result of experience. In other words, users who were satisfied and delighted with their decision usually end up developing a relationship with an online retailer (Shukla et al., 2016).

Tourists can experience an e-retailer both intellectually and affectively. Affective experience refers to the feelings that tourists experience concerning an online retailer (Martin et al., 2015). Affective experience usually has an impact on satisfaction (Martin et al., 2015) and on constructs that are related to the feelings of the tourist. On the other hand, intellectual experience refers to how much a tourist considers an online retailer helpful in times of need and how much of their problems can be solved through the online retailer (Dennis et al., 2014).

Customer experience in the current era depends on different factors, for instance, the capability of an online retailer to use and employ technology (Foroudi et al., 2014). Trustworthiness was also found useful in customer experience (So et al., 2017). Besides, the visual and non-visual content of a retail website was found to be helpful as well (Dedeke, 2016). In return, travelers' experience affects reputation (Foroudi, Jin et al., 2016); satisfaction (Radojevic et al., 2015); loyalty (So et al., 2017); and, ultimately, passion (Eide et al., 2017).

This research examines effective and intellectual experiences. Also, it aims to identify the relationship that experience can create for an online retailer for different needs of tourists. So far, there hasn't been a study regarding the effect of visual and non-visual content on customer experience, trustworthiness, and the influence of experience on satisfaction, reputation, passion, or loyalty by considering demographically complex customer segmentation according to their age, education, gender, and occupation. Figure 9.1 presents the foundational complex model utilized here

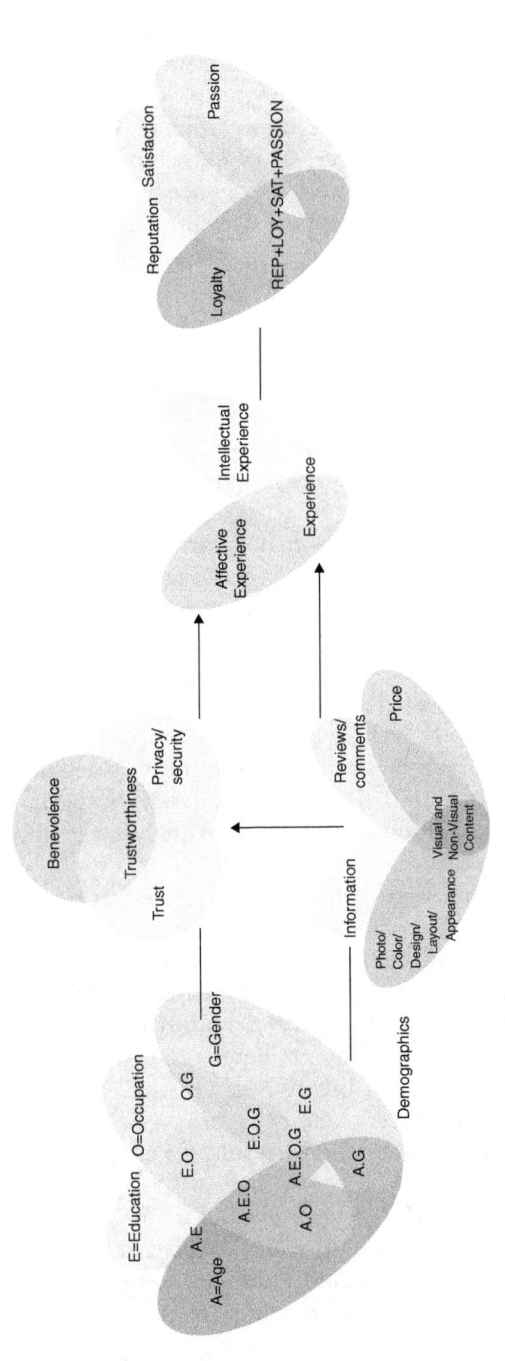

Figure 9.1 Modeling multiple realities.

Research hypotheses

By using demographic factors to identify different market segments the characteristics of different tourist segments may be studied (Kumar et al., 2017). The demographic configuration of tourists that leads to being able to bring about higher trustworthiness, satisfaction, reputation, loyalty, and passion which derives from the customers' experience and may be classified as (1) effective experience and (2) intellectual experience. Reputation is about the past actions of an online retailer in the form of respect. Thus, the reputation that an online retailer builds with its customers depends on how it responds to these different demographic segments (Fombrun and Shanley, 1990). Complexity theory suggests the happening of causal irregularity (asymmetry) (Woodside, 2014), which uses the presence and absence of causation between constructs. For example, a high level of tourist experience with a booking website can be a source of loyalty, reputation, satisfaction, and passion. Previous studies, like Adner and Kapoor (2010), have shown how demographic attributes such as social relationships and economic features can have an impact on travelers' loyalty in a contractual service setting.

Dennis et al. (2014) showed the effect of age as a moderator of customer-based reputation and loyalty, using data from the retail setting of fast food restaurants in France, the United Kingdom, and the United States of America based on the cultural differences between countries. It also showed the influence of elements such as gender and age on the customers' experiences in the service encounter. Besides, Nguyen et al. (2016) showed that demographics are important for elegant dining. Moreover, Foroudi, Gupta et al. (2016) also revealed that demographics are useful regarding loyalty. Although these studies analyze the influence of attributes such as age, gender, education, and occupation in a wide range of ways, they have not been able to show their effect on trustworthiness, reputation, satisfaction, and passion.

On the other hand, demographic attributes such as age, gender, and the occupation can have an impact on the reception of visual/non-visual content; however, there has not been a study to analyze this phenomenon. Ultimately, demographic attributes can affect the trustworthiness of an online retailer. According to Moin et al. (2017), different tourists with different ages, genders, and occupations can have different understandings of trustworthiness. As a result, we propose that:

T1a: A combination of demographic factors (including age, education, occupation, and gender) predicts loyalty, reputation, satisfaction, and passion. No single best configuration of factors leads to loyalty, reputation, satisfaction, and passion favorability, but there are multiple, equally effective configurations of these causal factors.
T1b: A combination of demographic factors (including age, education, occupation, and gender) predicts visual and non-visual content. No

single best configuration of factors leads to visual and non-visual content favorability, but there are multiple, equally effective configurations of these causal factors.

T1c: *A combination of demographic factors (including age, education, occupation, and gender) predicts trustworthiness. No single best configuration of factors leads to trustworthiness favorability, but there are multiple, equally effective configurations of these causal factors.*

Visual and non-visual content and trustworthiness

One of the most valuable assets for any online retailer is their trustworthiness in the perception of their customers (Strader and Ramaswami, 2002) which is the ultimate determinant of online purchase intention for tourists (Kim and Peterson, 2017). It is the central notion of forming long-lasting relationships in the online retailing industry context (Mukherjee and Nath, 2007). Romani (2006) revealed that prices of online e-retailers have a direct impact on customer trust in a firm (Romani, 2006). Also, prices can affect customers' judgement of the trustworthiness of an online retailer. Trifts and Häubl (2003) suggest that providing information about competitors' prices can have an impact on trustworthiness for the customer in a particular retailer. Furthermore, the more customers trust a website, the fairer they perceive the advertised prices (Lien et al., 2015).

The majority of researchers have focused on the effect of online customers' reviews on online consumers' behavior (e.g., Chu and Kamal, 2008; Lee et al., 2008; Lee and Youn, 2009). Online reviews have a profound impact on online tourists' decisions about whether to choose an online retailer or not, although some studies argue that not all travelers might find online reviews trustworthy (Zhou et al., 2014). Other scholars have found that online reviews and comments provided by customers can have a profound impact on the perceived trustworthiness of an online retailer (Cantallops and Salvi, 2014; Ziegele and Weber, 2015) and have an impact on the customer purchase decision.

In less than two decades, the Internet has turned in to the main source of information for travelers and customers (Cahyanto et al., 2016). However, the trustworthiness of the information provided on the Internet is still under the shadow of doubt (Pan and Chiou, 2011; Utz et al., 2012). As these days many travelers try to obtain more information for their trip on the Internet, it is vital for an online retailer to be considered trustworthy (Filieri et al., 2015). Besides, benevolence is another critical factor regarding the information provided. The customer should believe that the collected data is objective, and it is not just for the benefit of an online retailer (Belanger et al., 2002). As discussed, information is one of the main contributing factors to trust for an e-retailer.

Websites have become a competitive tool for promoting products and services for every online retailer (Alcántara-Pilar et al., 2018). The design of a website is an attribute that travelers who are seeking information pay attention to very much (Baloglu and Pekcan, 2006) and consider good design to be essential. Visual content, like the quality of the images and firm logo, on a particular website, can have an impact on customer trust (Kuo et al., 2015). Herrero et al. (2015) suggest that the textual and visual content provided can shape other perceptions and contribute to the source's credibility. Cyr et al. (2010) conducted a study on how colors used in an online retailer website can have an impact on trust. Another study conducted by Wang et al. (2007) suggested that website design can have an impact on customer trust in a particular online e-retailer. Hence, we propose that:

T2: A combination of visual and non-visual factors (including photos/ color/design/layout/appearance, information, reviews/comments, and price) predicts trustworthiness. No single best configuration of visual and non-visual factors leads to trustworthiness, but there are multiple, equally effective configurations of these causal factors.

Non-visual/visual content and experience

Past experience can shape future online travelers' behavior. Tourists' experience can aid online retailers to develop a relationship with their customers which can be sustainable for them (Foroudi et al., 2017). Besides, the customer evaluates a product/service based on their experience. Tourists' experience may be analyzed into two constructs, affective experience and intellectual experience, and these mainly shape tourists' behavior in an online context (Tynan and McKechnie, 2009). Travellers can gain experience through firms' touchpoints, which can range from images to reviews and comments written and provided on the website (Straker and Wrigley, 2018).

These touchpoints create an impression of an e-retailer's website both intellectually and affectively (Gentile et al., 2007). The travelers are involved in the intellectual and effective process of obtaining information from a website which creates an impression in a traveler's mind. As a result, travelers can recall a well-designed webpage better and with more ease (Bai et al., 2008). Just like hotel employees who can deliver a good impression to the guests, a well-designed retail website can convey a favorable impression about the e-retailer to the potential customers (Bilgihan et al., 2014). In other words, every firm tries to make a superior experience for its customers in the quest for sustainable competitive advantage (Melero et al., 2016).

T3: A combination of visual and non-visual factors (including photos/ color/design/layout/appearance, information, reviews/comments, and price) predicts experience. No single best configuration of factors leads to experience favorability, but there are multiple, equally effective configurations of these causal factors.

Trustworthiness and experience

The most important thing for travelers' trust in an e-retailer is privacy. Parasuraman and Zinkhan (2002) state that what customers/travellers want from an e-retailer are features such as easy navigation and privacy. Also, new travelers who are trying to work with a website seek some kind of pledge that their privacy is guaranteed (Kim and Benbasat, 2003). What's more, an earlier study by Hoffman et al. (1999) suggests that customers do not purchase anything without believing that their privacy is guaranteed.

Benevolence is conceptualized as e-retailers being interested in the wellbeing of the travelers without necessarily expecting to sell them anything (Rubio et al., 2017). While there are many important features to bear in mind for developing and establishing an e-retail website, the most important one is benevolence (Hwang and Kim, 2007). A fast response to travelers' and customers' needs is an essential way for e-retailers to show how benevolent they are (Gummerus et al., 2004). Besides, acting helpfully in times of need can show how benevolently online e-retailers behave toward their customers. All these attributes will either have a positive or negative impact on the traveler's experience. As travelers pay more attention to their prior experiences with an e-retailer, these attributes are considered vital for any successful firm in the market (Vázquez-Casielles et al., 2010).

Trust is assumed to be more critical in an e-retail context due to higher risk compared to traditional retailers (Toufaily et al., 2013). Trust has been regarded as a significant factor for forging relationships with travelers and customers. In other words, trust has been seen as a substantial part of successful electronic commerce (Deng et al., 2010). When customers realize they can trust their e-retailers, they begin to regard the online retailer as a satisfactory choice (Kamran-Disfani et al., 2017; Stathopoulou and Balabanis, 2016). Besides, when travelers trust in an e-retailer, they start to experience positive feelings toward their choice and become happy with their decision (Agnihotri et al., 2017; Inoue et al., 2017).

T4: A combination of factors including, trust, privacy, benevolence predicts experience. No single best configuration of elements leads to experience favorability, but there are multiple, equally effective configurations of these causal factors.

Experience and reputation

Customer experience is an essential factor in forming customer relationships (Nysveen et al., 2013). The customer can experience in two main ways, effectively and intellectually. Affective experience refers to all different subjective experience which relates to the feelings of customers (Dennis et al., 2014; Foroudi, Gupta et al., 2016; Yuksel et al., 2010). Affective experience can influence reputation, loyalty, satisfaction, and passion about an e-retailer (Bennett et al., 2005; Horppu et al., 2008; Iglesias et al., 2011; Karjaluoto et al., 2016). Intellectual experience suggests that customers are intermeshed in purposeful activity in search of information and deciding to purchase or not to purchase a particular product/service (Frow and Payne, 2007). What's more, the cognitive experience is considered to be relevant to how satisfied customers are with their choice of using an online retailer (Pullman and Gross, 2004).

Travellers forge an attachment to an e-retailer first through their cognitive experience followed by liking or disliking them (Yuksel et al., 2010). Travelers' experience can have a positive influence on loyalty, satisfaction, and reputation (Horppu et al., 2008). While some studies suggest that satisfaction is mainly as the result of a cognitive experience (Ali et al., 2016; Zhong et al., 2017), other studies believe it a consequence of an affective experience (Altunel and Erkut, 2015; del Bosque and San Martín, 2008). Experience both intellectual and affective has a capacity of affecting the reputation of an online retailer (Foroudi, Gupta et al., 2016). Reputation is conceptualized as the customer apprehension of service quality associated with e-retailer names (Sengupta et al., 2015). Finally, customers can be passionate about an e-retailer. Passion refers to the degree of enthusiasm of tourists' relationships, and it expresses positive and negative feelings toward a brand (Batra et al., 2012). Although affective experience can have a positive influence on passion, the intellectual experience might not have much impact on passion (Ho et al., 2011). Figure 9.1, on the other hand, shows that dissatisfaction occurs due to cognitive experience (judgment), and passion is mainly due to affective experienced (Carroll and Ahuvia, 2006). As discussed here, we propose:

T5: *A combination of experience factors including affective and intellectual experience predicts loyalty, reputation, satisfaction, and passion. No single best configuration of factors leads to loyalty, reputation, satisfaction, and passion favorability, but there are multiple, equally effective configurations of these causal factors.*

Methodology

To understand the influence of tourists' demographic attributes (age, education, occupation, and gender) on the relationships between the constructs and to identify configurations that can explain travelers' experiences in a peer-to-peer context, we adopted fuzzy set-theoretic analysis to investigate the causal effect of visual and non-visual content, trustworthiness, and travelers' experiences on loyalty, reputation, satisfaction, and passion (Ragin, 2009). According to Woodside (2014), the main advantage of using fuzzy set-theory is the notion of equifinality, and its capability to deal with causal-asymmetry. Fuzzy set-theory "provides a theoretical underpinning for the persistence of a variety of design choices that can all lead to the desired outcome" (Fiss, 2011, p. 394). Given the multi-faceted and varying conditions of loyalty, reputation, satisfaction, and passion, the current research uses this method rather than the traditional regression-/correlation-based approach.

Complexity theory integrates the principle of equifinality (Foroudi, Gupta et al., 2016; Woodside, 2014) to develop a clear reflection of nonlinearity between the links under analysis in a competitive market and under uncertainty. The uses of exploratory factor analysis and confirmatory factor analysis (CFA) confirm the reliability and validity of the research scales. In addition, CFA and fuzzy set qualitative comparative analysis (fsQCA) are also employed to analyze the data (Ageeva et al., 2018; Foroudi, Gupta et al., 2016; Foroudi et al., 2018; Woodside, 2014).

Data collection

A mixed-methodology was used, beginning with interviews to gain a better understanding of the relationships between the research constructs. Then, a questionnaire was distributed among travellers/users of peer-to-peer websites for scale purification and hypotheses testing. The question of why travelers use sharing economy platforms remains elusive. To answer this question, many scholars have highlighted the importance of price reduction in such services (Tussyadiah, 2015). Other scholars have paid more attention to the functional attributes of such services (Adner, 2002).

On the other hand, other scholars have found that travelers book their trips through services like Airbnb to have authentic experience (Yannopoulou et al., 2013). As such, the perception of the travelers' experience could not be assessed without referencing specific companies and asking for consumer feedback. Hence, a particular company is referenced in the evaluation questionnaires (Elsbach and Bhattacharya, 2001) for assessing the company.

Measures

We used 41 items related to the identified scales from previous studies (Foroudi et al., 2014) that had been found to be psychometrically valid (Churchill, 1979; Hair et al., 2006). Seven-point Likert-type scales ranging from strongly disagree (1), to strongly agree (7) were adopted. The visual content section had five items (Photo, Color, Design, Layout, Appearance, and Information) (Foroudi, Gupta et al., 2016; Foroudi et al., 2014). The non-visual content was measured by four items (Information, Reviews/Comments, and Price) (Cyr, 2008, 2013; Kim and Stoel, 2004; Tarafdar and Zhang, 2005, 2008). Trustworthiness was measured by three sub-constructs (Trust,

Benevolence, and Privacy/Security) (Nusair and Hua, 2010; Tarafdar and Zhang, 2005, 2008; Wolfinbarger and Gilly, 2003). Furthermore, experience was measured by two sub-constructs (affective experience, intellectual experience). Loyalty was measured through four items (Kolar and Zabkar, 2010), reputation by six items, satisfaction by three items, and passion by three items (Albert and Valette-Florence, 2010). Table 9.1 shows the measurement items of the theoretical constructs and their sources.

Table 9.1 Measurement items of the theoretical constructs

Constructs and items	References
Visual content	
Photo/color/design/layout/appearance	
Color	Foroudi et al. (2014); Foroudi, Gupta et al. (2016)
Design	
Photo	
Layout	
Appearance	
Non-visual content	
Information	Cyr (2008), Kim and Stoel (2004), Tarafdar and Zhang (2005, 2008)
Reviews	
Comments	
Prices	
Trustworthiness	
Trust	
X is trustworthy	Nusair and Hua (2010)
X can be trusted	
X can be counted on	
Benevolence	
X is sincere	Choi et al. (2016)
X is helpful	
X is goodwill	
Privacy/security	
In X using a credit card is safe	Wolfinbarger and Gilly (2003); Tarafdar and Zhang (2005, 2008)
In X online payment is risk free	
In X privacy is guaranteed online	
In X consumers' personal information is kept safe	
Experience	
Affective experience	
My decision to use X made me happy	Dennis et al. (2014); Foroudi, Gupta et al. (2016); Yuksel et al. (2010)
My decision to use X was a right decision	
My decision to use X made me satisfied	

Constructs and items	References
Intellectual Experience	
I can find what I am looking for in X	Dennis et al. (2014); Foroudi, Gupta et al. (2016)
I find X helpful	
I find X as a solution for searching accommodation for tourists	
I can decide better with X	
Loyalty	
I will use X again	Kolar and Zabkar (2010)
I will recommend X to my friends and relatives	
I will visit X again in the future	
Reputation	
X service is famous	Foroudi et al. (2014)
X customer treatment is favorable	
X vision is favorable	
X is responsible for society and environment	
X leadership is favorable	
Satisfaction	
My decision to use X was wise	Chu and Lu (2007)
My decision to purchase from X was a right decision	
My decision to use X met my needs	
Passion	
I think about X during the day	Albert and Valette-Florence (2010)
I feel lonely when I am no longer with X	
I have some obsessive thoughts about X	

Conclusion and theoretical and managerial implications

Because of the changes that are occurring in the micro and macro-environment (political, demographic), the tourism industry is facing new challenges that no one could have predicted. As a result, the question of what makes a tourist choose an online retailer and not to select another type has remained ambiguous. Making a tourist experience a unique experience is vital for all firms in the industry. Scholars and tourism managers need to find the most effective and best strategy within such sweeping and fast changes. In light of the preceding discussion, the first aim of this research was to find an integrated model including antecedents and consequences of experience.

This study provides invaluable and profound insights regarding the demand side of e-retailers performing in the peer-to-peer context. The results reveal that non-visual and visual content positively impacts on tourists' perception of trustworthiness. This result adds knowledge about non-visual and visual content. Furthermore, due to the growth and widely increasing usage of the Internet, it is necessary for managers to consider the tools used in creating and enhancing customers' perception of trustworthiness through visual and non-visual content.

Our findings also reveal that non-visual and visual content (design, color, logo) are the key contributing factors for experience. This result is consistent with the previous research in the marketing literature, which shows that visual/non-visual content can influence customer experience (Lemon and Verhoef, 2016; Stein and Ramaseshan, 2016; Visinescu et al., 2015). However, as there has been no study analyzing the relationship using the fsQCA methodology, this outcome can shed light on the relationship between visual/non-visual content and experience and increase our understanding of the relationship. Also because of the importance of the relationship and the necessity of content, either visual or non-visual, managers and brand managers should carefully monitor their website contents. Trustworthiness was found to have an impact on the experience.

As the customers come to realize they can trust their chosen online retailer, they start to share information, and as a result, they can have a better experience in return (Ert et al., 2016). There has been a wide range of studies analyzing the relationship between experience and trust (e.g., Cai et al., 2018; Filieri et al., 2015; Keeling et al., 2010); however, there have been limited studies regarding the link between trustworthiness and experience (e.g., Gupta et al., 2019). Our findings on this relationship add valuable knowledge to the current literature about the relationship between trustworthiness and experience. Besides, managers can provide a better experience for their customers by enhancing their trust. For example, they can provide a platform for users' to share their experiences on the website resulting in a higher level of trust among their customers.

Ultimately, experience was found to be useful for building reputation, loyalty, satisfaction, and passion. Through their experience customers judge an online retailer and start to understand how good an e-retailer is (Caruana and Ewing, 2010; Huang and Hsu, 2010; Rajaobelina, 2017). As Foroudi, Gupta et al. (2016) mentioned having a unique experience is the first reason that tourists and travelers use such online retailers instead of traditional ones. This result highlights the importance of experience as one of the strongest antecedents of having a better reputation, satisfaction, love, and loyalty for firms. In this regard, scholars understand the relationship between the experience gained in firm touchpoints and its impact on the reputation, loyalty, satisfaction, and love of a firm. As having a unique experience is the main reason why people choose to use online peer-to-peer accommodation platforms and customers decide whether to forge a relationship with an e-retailer based on their experience, policy-makers, and tourist managers should pay attention to the experience they can provide for their customers.

Future research directions

We propose future researchers should use our model, collect data, and employ the item measurements which we have introduced in this study. Especially, we recommend that researchers focus on cities with diverse tourists. Second, a future study could consider tourists who use peer-to-peer accommodation website. Finally, an individual assessment can vary; it might be that different cultural backgrounds may be related to the various evaluations of the experience. In another viewpoint, different cultures might praise or criticize different forms of experience. As a result, future studies should be expanded to develop the conceptual model by adding cultural variables as well.

Conclusions

Peer-to-peer accommodation websites are becoming the next phenomena of the twenty-first century as they are changing the way travelers choose and book their ideal destinations. Tourists are increasingly trusting online retailers rather than their local travel agency who they might have known for years. The main contribution of this research is to increase understanding of the traveler's perception of these emerging peer-to-peer accommodation websites and how experience can impact on the relationship customers forge with their chosen e-retailers.

Key construct definitions

Visual Content: visual content is the images which are used to convey information to the customers (Foroudi et al., 2014).

Non-Visual Content: it is the content which is not considered image or image related. Non-visual content mainly refers to Information, Reviews/Comments, and Price (Cyr, 2008, 2013; Kim and Stoel 2004; Tarafdar and Zhang 2005, 2008).

Trustworthiness: it is the firm's ability to be considered as honest and truthful (Jiang et al., 2016).

Trust: it is the customer belief in a firm's goodness (Eisingerich and Bell, 2008).

Benevolence: when customer believes the service is sincere, helpful and thoughtful (Choei et al., 2016).

Experience: it is the customer's reaction to a set of interactions between themselves and firms, products/services (Gentile et al., 2007; Frow and Payne, 2007; Lemon and Verhoef, 2016).

Affective Experience: it is conceptualized as the emotional (Foroudi et al., 2016) and pleasurable (Foroudi, Gupta et al., 2016) customer experiences when interacting with a firm.

Intellectual Experience: it is helpful for problem solving, finding information (Foroudi, Gupta et al., 2016) and experience values which appeal to customers.

Loyalty: customers' interests in continuing their relationship with a particular firm or service/product (Foroudi et al., 2018).

Reputation: it is a collective compound of all prior transactions over the life of the entity, a historical notion, and requires consistency of an entity's actions over a prolonged time (Herbig and Milewicz, 1993, p. 18).

Satisfaction: it is the customers' evaluation of their experience with a company (Fornell, 1992).

Passion: it is an intense feeling of consumers towards a particular firm (Albert et al., 2013).

Privacy/Security: privacy is the customer point of view that is not available to the firm or any other third parties (Wirtz and Lwin, 2009).

References

Adner, R. (2002). When are technologies disruptive?. A demand-based view of the emergence of competition. *Strategic Management Journal, 23*(8), 667–688.

Adner, R., & Kapoor, R. (2010). Value creation in innovation ecosystems: How the structure of technological interdependence affects firm performance in new technology generations. *Strategic Management Journal, 31*(3), 306–333.

Ageeva, E., Melewar, T. C., Foroudi, P., Dennis, C., and Jin, Z. (2018). Examining the influence of corporate website favorability on corporate image and corporate reputation: Findings from fsQCA. *Journal of Business Research, 89*(August), 287–304.

Agnihotri, R., Trainor, K. J., Itani, O. S., and Rodriguez, M. (2017). Examining the role of sales-based CRM technology and social media use on post-sale service behaviors in India. *Journal of Business Research, 81*, 144–154.

Albert, N., Merunka, D., and Valette-Florence, P. (2013). Brand passion: Antecedents and consequences. *Journal of Business Research, 66*(7), 904–909.

Albert, N., and Valette-Florence, P. (2010). Measuring the love feeling for a brand using interpersonal love items. *Journal of Marketing development and Competitiveness, 5*(1), 57–63.

Alcántara-Pilar, J. M., Blanco-Encomienda, F. J., Rodríguez-López, M. E., and Del Barrio-García, S. (2018). Enhancing consumer attitudes toward a website as a contributing factor in business success. *Tourism and Management Studies, 14*(1), 108–116.

Ali, F., Amin, M., and Cobanoglu, C. (2016). An integrated model of service experience, emotions, satisfaction, and price acceptance: An empirical analysis in the Chinese hospitality industry. *Journal of Hospitality Marketing and Management, 25*(4), 449–475.

Altunel, M. C., and Erkut, B. (2015). Cultural tourism in Istanbul: The mediation effect of tourist experience and satisfaction on the relationship between involvement and recommendation intention. *Journal of Destination Marketing and Management, 4*(4), 213–221.

Aro, K., Suomi, K., and Saraniemi, S. (2018). Antecedents and consequences of destination brand love – A case study from Finnish Lapland. *Tourism Management, 67*, 71–81.

Bai, B., Law, R., and Wen, I. (2008). The impact of website quality on customer satisfaction and purchase intentions: Evidence from Chinese online visitors. *International Journal of Hospitality Management*, 27(3), 391–402.

Baka, V. (2016). The becoming of user-generated reviews: Looking at the past to understand the future of managing reputation in the travel sector. *Tourism Management*, 53, 148–162.

Baloglu, S., and Pekcan, Y. A. (2006). The website design and Internet site marketing practices of upscale and luxury hotels in Turkey. *Tourism Management*, 27(1), 171–176.

Belanger, F., Hiller, J. S., and Smith, W. J. (2002). Trustworthiness in electronic commerce: The role of privacy, security, and site attributes. *The Journal of Strategic Information Systems*, 11(3–4), 245–270.

Bennett, R., Härtel, C. E., and McColl-Kennedy, J. R. (2005). Experience as a moderator of involvement and satisfaction on brand loyalty in a business-to-business setting 02-314R. *Industrial Marketing Management*, 34(1), 97–107.

Bilgihan, A., Okumus, F., Nusair, K., and Bujisic, M. (2014). Online experiences: Flow theory, measuring online customer experience in e-commerce and managerial implications for the lodging industry. *Information Technology and Tourism*, 14(1), 49–71.

Botsman, R., and Rogers, R. (2011). *What's mine is yours: How collaborative consumption is changing the way we live*. London: Collins.

Cahyanto, I., Pennington-Gray, L., Thapa, B., Srinivasan, S., Villegas, J., Matyas, C., and Kiousis, S. (2016). Predicting information seeking regarding hurricane evacuation in the destination. *Tourism Management*, 52, 264–275.

Cai, R. R., Lu, L., and Gursoy, D. (2018). Effect of disruptive customer behaviors on others' overall service experience: An appraisal theory perspective. *Tourism Management*, 69, 330–344.

Cantallops, A. S., and Salvi, F. (2014). New consumer behavior: A review of research on eWOM and hotels. *International Journal of Hospitality Management*, 36, 41–51.

Carroll, B. A., and Ahuvia, A. C. (2006). Some antecedents and outcomes of brand love. *Marketing Letters*, 17(2), 79–89.

Caruana, A., and Ewing, M. T. (2010). How corporate reputation, quality, and value influence online loyalty. *Journal of Business Research*, 63(9), 1103–1110.

Choi, M., Law, R., & Heo, C. Y. (2016). Shopping destinations and trust–tourist attitudes: Scale development and validation. *Tourism Management*, 54, 490–501.

Chu, S. C., and Kamal, S. (2008). The effect of perceived blogger credibility and argument quality on message elaboration and brand attitudes: An exploratory study. *Journal of Interactive Advertising*, 8(2), 26–37.

Churchill Jr, G. A. (1979). A paradigm for developing better measures of marketing constructs. *Journal of Marketing Research*, 16(1), 64–73.

Cyr, D., Head, M., and Larios, H. (2010). Colour appeal in website design within and across cultures: A multi-method evaluation. *International Journal of Human-Computer Studies*, 68(1-2), 1–21.

Cyr, D. (2008). Modeling web site design across cultures: Relationships to trust, satisfaction, and e-loyalty. *Journal of Management Information Systems*, 24(4), 47–72.

Dedeke, A. N. (2016). Travel web-site design: Information task-fit, service quality and purchase intention. *Tourism Management*, *54*, 541–554.

del Bosque, I. R., and San Martín, H. (2008). Tourist satisfaction a cognitive-affective model. *Annals of Tourism Research*, *35*(2), 551–573.

Deng, Z., Lu, Y., Wei, K. K., and Zhang, J. (2010). Understanding customer satisfaction and loyalty: An empirical study of mobile instant messages in China. *International Journal of Information Management*, *30*(4), 289–300.

Dennis, C., Brakus, J. J., Gupta, S., and Alamanos, E. (2014). The effect of digital signage on shoppers' behavior: The role of the evoked experience. *Journal of Business Research*, *67*(11), 2250–2257.

Edelman, D. C., and Singer, M. (2015). Competing on customer journeys. *Harvard Business Review*, *93*(11), 88–100.

Eide, D., Fuglsang, L., and Sundbo, J. (2017). Management challenges with the maintenance of tourism experience concept innovations: Toward a new research agenda. *Tourism Management*, *63*, 452–463.

Eisingerich, A. B., and Bell, S. J. (2008). Perceived service quality and customer trust: Does enhancing customers' service knowledge matter?. *Journal of Service Research*, *10*(3), 256–268.

Elsbach, K. D., and Bhattacharya, C. B. (2001). Defining who you are by what you're not: Organizational disidentification and the National Rifle Association. *Organization Science*, *12*(4), 393–413.

Ert, E., Fleischer, A., and Magen, N. (2016). Trust and reputation in the sharing economy: The role of personal photos in Airbnb. *Tourism Management*, *55*, 62–73.

Filieri, R., Alguezaui, S., and McLeay, F. (2015). Why do travelers trust TripAdvisor?. Antecedents of trust towards consumer-generated media and its influence on recommendation adoption and word of mouth. *Tourism Management*, *51*, 174–185.

Fiss, P. C. (2011). Building better causal theories: A fuzzy set approach to typologies in organization research. *Academy of Management Journal*, *54*(2), 393–420.

Fombrun, C., and Shanley, M. (1990). What's in a name?. Reputation building and corporate strategy. *Academy of Management Journal*, *33*(2), 233–258.

Fornell, C. (1992). A national customer satisfaction barometer: The Swedish experience. *Journal of Marketing*, *56*(1), 6–21.

Foroudi, P., Dinnie, K., Kitchen, P. J., Melewar, T. C., and Foroudi, M. M. (2017). IMC antecedents and the consequences of planned brand identity in higher education. *European Journal of Marketing*, *51*(3), 528–550.

Foroudi, P., Gupta, S., Kitchen, P., Foroudi, M. M., and Nguyen, B. (2016). A framework of place branding, place image, and place reputation: Antecedents and moderators. *Qualitative Market Research: An International Journal*, *19*(2), 241–264.

Foroudi, P., Jin, Z., Gupta, S., Melewar, T. C., and Foroudi, M. M. (2016). Influence of innovation capability and customer experience on reputation and loyalty. *Journal of Business Research*, *69*(11), 4882–4889.

Foroudi, P., Jin, Z., Gupta, S., Foroudi, M. M., and Kitchen, P. J. (2018). Perceptional components of brand equity: Configuring the Symmetrical and Asymmetrical Paths to brand loyalty and brand purchase intention. *Journal of Business Research*, *89*, 462–474.

Foroudi, P., Melewar, T. C., and Gupta, S. (2014). Linking corporate logo, corporate image, and reputation: An examination of consumer perceptions in the financial setting. *Journal of Business Research*, 67(11), 2269–2281.

Frow, P., and Payne, A. (2007). Towards the 'perfect' customer experience. *Journal of Brand Management*, 15(2), 89–101.

Gavilan, D., Avello, M., and Martinez-Navarro, G. (2018). The influence of online ratings and reviews on hotel booking consideration. *Tourism Management*, 66, 53–61.

Gentile, C., Spiller, N., and Noci, G. (2007). How to sustain the customer experience: An overview of experience components that co-create value with the customer. *European Management Journal*, 25(5), 395–410.

Grewal, D., Levy, M., and Kumar, V. (2009). Customer experience management in retailing: An organizing framework. *Journal of Retailing*, 85(1), 1–14.

Gummerus, J., Liljander, V., Pura, M., and Van Riel, A. (2004). Customer loyalty to content-based web sites: The case of an online health-care service. *Journal of services Marketing*, 18(3), 175–186.

Gupta, A., Dash, S., and Mishra, A. (2019). All that glitters is not green: Creating trustworthy ecofriendly services at green hotels. *Tourism Management*, 70, 155–169.

Gustafsson, A., Aksoy, L., Brady, M. K., McColl-Kennedy, J. R., Sirianni, N. J., Witell, L., and Wuenderlich, N. V. (2015). Conducting service research that matters. *Journal of Services Marketing*, 29(6/7), 425–429.

Hair Jr, J. F., Black, W. C., Babin, B. J., Anderson, R. E., and Tatham, R. L. (2006). *Multivariate data analysis* (6th ed.). Upper Saddle River: Pearson Prentice Hall.

Han, H., and Hyun, S. S. (2015). Customer retention in the medical tourism industry: Impact of quality, satisfaction, trust, and price reasonableness. *Tourism Management*, 46, 20–29.

Herbig, P., and Milewicz, J. (1993). The relationship of reputation and credibility to brand success. *Journal of consumer marketing*, 10(3), 18–24.

Herrero, A., San Martín, H., and Hernández, J. M. (2015). How online search behavior is influenced by user-generated content on review websites and hotel interactive websites. *International Journal of Contemporary Hospitality Management*, 27(7), 1573–1597.

Ho, V. T., Wong, S. S., and Lee, C. H. (2011). A tale of passion: Linking job passion and cognitive engagement to employee work performance. *Journal of Management Studies*, 48(1), 26–47.

Hoffman, D. L., Novak, T. P., and Peralta, M. (1999). Building consumer trust online. *Communications of the ACM*, 42(4), 80–85.

Horppu, M., Kuivalainen, O., Tarkiainen, A., and. Ellonen, H. K. (2008). Online satisfaction, trust and loyalty and the impact of the offline parent brand. *Journal of Product and Brand Management*, 17(6), 403–413.

Hsiao, C., Lee, Y. H., and Chen, W. J. (2015). The effect of servant leadership on customer value co-creation: A cross-level analysis of key mediating roles. *Tourism Management*, 49, 45–57.

Huang, J., and Hsu, C. H. (2010). The impact of customer-to-customer interaction on cruise experience and vacation satisfaction. *Journal of Travel Research*, 49(1), 79–92.

Hwang, Y., and Kim, D. J. (2007). Customer self-service systems: The effects of perceived Web quality with service contents on enjoyment, anxiety, and e-trust. *Decision Support Systems, 43*(3), 746–760.

Iglesias, O., Singh, J. J., and Batista-Foguet, J. M. (2011). The role of brand experience and affective commitment in determining brand loyalty. *Journal of Brand Management, 18*(8), 570–582.

Inoue, Y., Funk, D. C., and McDonald, H. (2017). Predicting behavioral loyalty through corporate social responsibility: The mediating role of involvement and commitment. *Journal of Business Research, 75*, 46–56.

Jiang, X., Bao, Y., Xie, Y., and Gao, S. (2016). Partner trustworthiness, knowledge flow in strategic alliances, and firm competitiveness: A contingency perspective. *Journal of Business Research, 69*(2), 804–814.

Kamran-Disfani, O., Mantrala, M. K., Izquierdo-Yusta, A., and Martínez-Ruiz, M. P. (2017). The impact of retail store format on the satisfaction-loyalty link: An empirical investigation. *Journal of Business Research, 77*, 14–22.

Karjaluoto, H., Munnukka, J., and Kiuru, K. (2016). Brand love and positive word of mouth: The moderating effects of experience and price. *Journal of Product and Brand Management, 25*(6), 527–537.

Keeling, K., McGoldrick, P., and Beatty, S. (2010). Avatars as salespeople: Communication style, trust, and intentions. *Journal of Business Research, 63*(8), 793–800.

Kim, D., and Benbasat, I. (2003). Trust-related arguments in Internet stores: A framework for evaluation. *Journal of Electronic Commerce Research, 4*(2), 49–64.

Kim, S., and Stoel, L. (2004). Apparel retailers: Website quality dimensions and satisfaction. *Journal of Retailing and Consumer Services, 11*(2), 109–117.

Kim, Y., and Peterson, R. A. (2017). A meta-analysis of online trust relationships in E-commerce. *Journal of Interactive Marketing, 38*, 44–54.

Kolar, T., and Zabkar, V. (2010). A consumer-based model of authenticity: An oxymoron or the foundation of cultural heritage marketing?. *Tourism Management, 31*(5), 652–664.

Kumar, V., Anand, A., and Song, H. (2017). Future of retailer profitability: An organizing framework. *Journal of Retailing, 93*(1), 96–119.

Kuo, P. J., Zhang, L., and Cranage, D. A. (2015). What you get is not what you saw: Exploring the impacts of misleading hotel website photos. *International Journal of Contemporary Hospitality Management, 27*(6), 1301–1319.

Lee, J., Park, D. H., and Han, I. (2008). The effect of negative online consumer reviews on product attitude: An information processing view. *Electronic Commerce Research and Applications, 7*(3), 341–352.

Lee, M., and Youn, S. (2009). Electronic word of mouth (eWOM) How eWOM platforms influence consumer product judgement. International Journal of Advertising, 28(3), 473–499.

Lemon, K. N., and Verhoef, P. C. (2016). Understanding customer experience throughout the customer journey. *Journal of Marketing, 80*(6), 69–96.

Lien, C. H., Wen, M. J., Huang, L. C., and Wu, K. L. (2015). Online hotel booking: The effects of brand image, price, trust and value on purchase intentions. *Asia Pacific Management Review, 20*(4), 210–218.

Martin, J., Mortimer, G., and Andrews, L. (2015). Re-examining online customer experience to include purchase frequency and perceived risk. *Journal of Retailing and Consumer Services, 25*, 81–95.

Melero, I., Sese, F. J., and Verhoef, P. C. (2016). Recasting the customer experience in today's omni-channel environment 1/Redefiniendo la experiencia del cliente en el entorno omnicanal. *Universia Business Review*, 50, 18–37.

Moin, S. M. A., Devlin, J. F., and McKechnie, S. (2017). Trust in financial services: The influence of demographics and dispositional characteristics. *Journal of Financial Services Marketing*, 22(2), 64–76.

Mukherjee, A., and Nath, P. (2007). Role of electronic trust in online retailing: A re-examination of the commitment-trust theory. *European Journal of Marketing*, 41(9/10), 1173–1202.

Nguyen, B., Yu, X., Melewar, T. C., and Gupta, S. (2016). Critical brand innovation factors (CBIF): Understanding innovation and market performance in the Chinese high-tech service industry. *Journal of Business Research*, 69(7), 2471–2479.

Nusair, K., and Hua, N. (2010). Comparative assessment of structural equation modeling and multiple regression research methodologies: E-commerce context. *Tourism Management*, 31(3), 314–324.

Nysveen, H., Pedersen, P. E., and Skard, S. (2013). Brand experiences in service organizations: Exploring the individual effects of brand experience dimensions. *Journal of Brand Management*, 20(5), 404–423.

Ostrom, A. L., Parasuraman, A., Bowen, D. E., Patricio, L., and Voss, C. A. (2015). Service research priorities in a rapidly changing context. *Journal of Service Research*, 18(2), 127–159.

Ou, Y. C., and Verhoef, P. C. (2017). The impact of positive and negative emotions on loyalty intentions and their interactions with customer equity drivers. *Journal of Business Research*, 80, 106–115.

Özgener, Ş., and İraz, R. (2006). Customer relationship management in small–medium enterprises: The case of Turkish tourism industry. *Tourism Management*, 27(6), 1356–1363.

Pan, L. Y., and Chiou, J. S. (2011). How much can you trust online information?. Cues for perceived trustworthiness of consumer-generated online information. *Journal of Interactive Marketing*, 25(2), 67–74.

Parasuraman, A., and Zinkhan, G. M. (2002). Marketing to and serving customers through the Internet: An overview and research agenda. *Journal of the Academy of Marketing Science*, 30(4), 286–295.

Powanga, A., and Powanga, L. (2008). An economic analysis of a timeshare ownership. *Journal of Retail and Leisure Property*, 7(1), 69–83.

Pullman, M. E., and Gross, M. A. (2004). Ability of experience design elements to elicit emotions and loyalty behaviors. *Decision Sciences*, 35(3), 551–578.

Radojevic, T., Stanisic, N., and Stanic, N. (2015). Ensuring positive feedback: Factors that influence customer satisfaction in the contemporary hospitality industry. *Tourism Management*, 51, 13–21.

Ragin, C. C. (2009). *Redesigning social inquiry: Fuzzy sets and beyond*. Chicago: University of Chicago Press.

Rajaobelina, L. (2017). The impact of customer experience on relationship quality with travel agencies in a multichannel environment. *Journal of Travel Research*. doi:10.1177/0047287516688565.

Romani, S. (2006). Price misleading advertising: Effects on trustworthiness toward the source of information and willingness to buy. *Journal of Product and Brand Management*, 15(2), 130–138.

Rubio, N., Villaseñor, N., and Yagüe, M. J. (2017). Creation of consumer loyalty and trust in the retailer through store brands: The moderating effect of choice of store brand name. *Journal of Retailing and Consumer Services*, 34, 358–368.

Russo, I., Confente, I., Gligor, D. M., and Autry, C. W. (2016). To be or not to be (loyal): Is there a recipe for customer loyalty in the B2B context?. *Journal of Business Research*, 69(2), 888–896.

Sengupta, A. S., Balaji, M. S., and Krishnan, B. C. (2015). How customers cope with service failure?. A study of brand reputation and customer satisfaction. *Journal of Business Research*, 68(3), 665–674.

Shukla, P., Banerjee, M., and Singh, J. (2016). Customer commitment to luxury brands: Antecedents and consequences. *Journal of Business Research*, 69(1), 323–331.

So, K. K. F., King, C., Hudson, S., and Meng, F. (2017). The missing link in building customer brand identification: The role of brand attractiveness. *Tourism Management*, 59, 640–651.

Stathopoulou, A., and Balabanis, G. (2016). The effects of loyalty programs on customer satisfaction, trust, and loyalty toward high-and low-end fashion retailers. *Journal of Business Research*, 69(12), 5801–5808.

Stein, A., and Ramaseshan, B. (2016). Towards the identification of customer experience touch point elements. *Journal of Retailing and Consumer Services*, 30, 8–19.

Strader, T. J., and Ramaswami, S. N. (2002). The value of seller trustworthiness in C2C online markets. *Communications of the ACM*, 45(12), 45–49.

Straker, K., and Wrigley, C. (2018). Engaging passengers across digital channels: An international study of 100 airports. *Journal of Hospitality and Tourism Management*, 34, 82–92.

Tarafdar, M., and Zhang, J. (2005). Analyzing the influence of web site design parameters on web site usability. *Information Resources Management Journal*, 18(4), 62–80.

Tarafdar, M., and Zhang, J. (2008). Determinants of reach and loyalty—A study of website performance and implications for website design. *Journal of Computer Information Systems*, 48(2), 16–24.

Toufaily, E., Souiden, N., and Ladhari, R. (2013). Consumer trust toward retail websites: Comparison between pure click and click-and-brick retailers. *Journal of Retailing and Consumer Services*, 20(6), 538–548.

Trifts, V., and Häubl, G. (2003). Information availability and consumer preference: Can online retailers benefit from providing access to competitor price information?. *Journal of Consumer Psychology*, 13(1–2), 149–159.

Tussyadiah, I. P. (2015). An exploratory study on drivers and deterrents of collaborative consumption in travel. In I. Tussyadiah & A. Inversini (Eds.) *Information and communication technologies in tourism 2015* (pp. 817–830). Cham: Springer.

Tynan, C., and McKechnie, S. (2009). Experience marketing: A review and reassessment. *Journal of Marketing Management*, 25(5–6), 501–517.

Utz, S., Kerkhof, P., and Van Den Bos, J. (2012). Consumers rule: How consumer reviews influence perceived trustworthiness of online stores. *Electronic Commerce Research and Applications*, 11(1), 49–58.

Vázquez-Casielles, R., Suárez Álvarez, L., and Diaz Martin, A. M. (2010). Perceived justice of service recovery strategies: Impact on customer satisfaction and quality relationship. *Psychology and Marketing*, 27(5), 487–509.

Visinescu, L. L., Sidorova, A., Jones, M. C., and Prybutok, V. R. (2015). The influence of website dimensionality on customer experiences, perceptions and behavioral intentions: An exploration of 2D vs. 3D web design. *Information and Management*, *52*(1), 1–17.

Voorhees, C. M., Fombelle, P. W., Allen, A. M., Bone, S. A., and Aach, J. (2014). *Managing post-purchase moments of truth: Leveraging customer feedback to increase loyalty*. Marketing Science Institute Working Paper. Report (14-115).

Wang, K. C., Chou, S. H., Su, C. J., and Tsai, H. Y. (2007). More information, stronger effectiveness?. Different group package tour advertising components on web page. *Journal of Business Research*, *60*(4), 382–387.

Wirtz, J., & Lwin, M. O. (2009). Regulatory focus theory, trust, and privacy concern. *Journal of Service Research*, *12*(2), 190–207.

Wolfinbarger, M., and Gilly, M. C. (2003). eTailQ: Dimensionalizing, measuring and predicting Etail quality. *Journal of Retailing*, *79*(3), 183–198.

Woodside, A. G. (2014). Embrace• perform• model: Complexity theory, contrarian case analysis, and multiple realities. *Journal of Business Research*, *67*(12), 2495–2503.

Yannopoulou, N., Moufahim, M., and Bian, X. (2013). User-generated brands and social media: Couchsurfing and AirBnb. *Contemporary Management Research*, *9*(1), 85–90.

Yuksel, A., Yuksel, F., and Bilim, Y. (2010). Destination attachment: Effects on customer satisfaction and cognitive, affective and conative loyalty. *Tourism Management*, *31*(2), 274–284.

Zhong, Y. Y. S., Busser, J., and Baloglu, S. (2017). A model of memorable tourism experience: The effects on satisfaction, affective commitment, and storytelling. *Tourism Analysis*, *22*(2), 201–217.

Zhou, L., Ye, S., Pearce, P. L., and Wu, M. Y. (2014). Refreshing hotel satisfaction studies by reconfiguring customer review data. *International Journal of Hospitality Management*, *38*(April), 1–10.

Ziegele, M., and Weber, M. (2015). Example, please! Comparing the effects of single customer reviews and aggregate review scores on online shoppers' product evaluations. *Journal of Consumer Behaviour*, *14*(2), 103–114.

10 Towards the development of community commitment based on musical events in the Dominican Republic

Pantea Foroudi, Saheb Imani, Mohammad M. Foroudi, and Magdiel Y. Espinal R.

Learning outcomes

At the end of this chapter, readers should be able to:

1 Understand if a resident's sense of place identity impacts on their intention of supporting tourism' or 'of giving support to(wards) tourism'.
2 Recognize the relationship between participation in cultural music events and place identity.
3 Understand how the community commitment towards an event developed by residents could affect their support for tourism in the Dominican Republic.

Introduction

The purpose of this study is to (i) understand if residents' sense of place identity impacts on their intention of support towards tourism development projects, (ii) establish if there is a relationship between the participation in cultural music events and place identity, and (iii) investigate if the community commitment towards an event developed by residents affects their support for tourism in the Dominican Republic. To fulfill the research objectives, the data were collected through surveys of 200 Dominican residents and analyzed through Structural Equation Modelling (SEM) with application Smart PLS 3 software. Although all five hypotheses were accepted, this research found that the relationship between place identity and residents' perception with community commitment is not strong enough, which needs to be further researched. Based on the result, community commitment has a complementary partial mediating role in the proposed model. Besides, our result has shown that cultural music events play a positive and significant role in the link between residents' sense of place identity and community commitment as well as between community commitment and residents' intention to support tourism.

Research background

The concept of nation branding is becoming more important through the years as countries are more competitive in regards to their portrayal of the world for the attraction of tourists, investors, talent, export promotion and public diplomacy (Foroudi et al., 2016, 2017, 2018). As nations try to be distinctive in their offer, they must have their culture and arts at the core of their nation's brand strategies. Their spirit and values, their beliefs and traditions are part of the identity that must come through in their successful promotions. As culture is essential, music, as its representation, can play a decisive role in said promotions, but this element has been hardly studied in the field.

The tourism sector is one of the first in underdeveloped countries to adopt strategies that are incorporated later in the nation brand plans because a lot of its activities have the objective of attracting tourists and investors continuously for the industry to develop. Tourism events have a direct influence on the lives of residents and local communities, as they often create an area to involve residents in their making process (Herrero et al., 2012). As a result, residents have an important role in the activities held in their environment and make them an important target to include in tourism strategies.

Since locals interrelate with visitors, their support for the good development of touristic projects has been distinguished as a critical or pivotal factor (Sharma et al., 2008). Their involvement can alter the development of the event and create a pleasant, memorable experience for themselves as hosts and those who are visiting their community (Choi & Murray, 2010; Gursoy et al., 2002; Gursoy & Kendall, 2006; Potwarka & Banyai, 2016). To understand the reasons or elements that may affect residents' support towards tourism activities, such as cultural music events, it is imperative.

The Dominican Republic is a country in the Caribbean Sea that depends heavily on the tourism industry. In 2011, 4.7 million tourists visited the country, and in 2022, this number is predicted to surpass 10 million visitors (Bancentral.gov.do, 2018). As a famous tourist destination, the Dominican Republic has a set of touristic activities that help promote the island and its culture. Government bodies need to focus on the influences that make residents more involved and support the industry to grow.

Phenomena of residents' feelings, attitudes and subsequent support or opposition to tourist development have been paid much attention and a variety of studies are offered on this matter (Vargas-Sanchez et al., 2011). Still, most of them are based on the perceptions of consequences that the development of the industry has and how much residents back it up (Nunkoo & Gursoy, 2012; Vargas-Sanchez et al., 2011). Previous studies have examined residents' attitude and support towards tourism development applied the social exchange theory and found that residents ponder the potential benefits and costs that a specific activity will bring to them to support it (Lee, 2013; Nunkoo & Ramkissoon, 2012; Stylidis & Terzidou, 2014).

Even though the subject of what may influence residents' support for tourism has been studied, the integration of cultural music events to strengthen place identity has not been done or covered in previous researches, nor has the Dominican Republic featured in any of them. Scholars disagree with the supposition that the issues presented in the development of the tourism industry are the same from one place to the other (Foroudi et al., 2016). This uniqueness forces the destinations to investigate their own set of features and identify their distinctive factors which will be the motor for development in the local context (Twining-Ward & Butler, 2002).

That being said, most of the research done on the subject was conducted on communities from developed countries (Nepal, 2008; Ouyang et al., 2017; Sirakaya et al., 2002; Wang & Xu, 2015), however, a brief research has been done on small islands' developing economies (Andriotis, 2005), regardless of the belief that residents' support for projects and the development of the tourism industry is expected to be different in developed and underdeveloped parts of the world (Nunkoo & Gursoy, 2012). Small islands have unique factors that other parts of the world might not share such as susceptibility and delicate environment (Douglas, 2006). Consequently, the involvement of local communities in developing activities plays a key role (Lim & Cooper, 2009). Despite the numerous researches done in terms of tourism and residents' support, some of them might not be applicable in a small island country (Nunkoo & Gursoy, 2012). This research, by applying these concepts and models to the Dominican Republic, is trying to bridge that gap, testing a model of residents' support for tourism and applying it in an island economy.

We propose that residents' perception, cultural music events, and residents' place identity impact on community commitment and these relationships then have a direct effect on their community commitment, which results in their support for the development of the tourism industry. One theoretical contribution of this study is the use of identity theory, which has been underused as a framework in comparison with social exchange theory. By developing a model that uses both theories, this research adds to the small number of studies held in developing countries especially in a small island economy setting (Nunkoo & Gursoy, 2012).

Theoretical background and hypotheses

In terms of the residents' intention to support tourism, this research, like some others, is going to take the premise that residents' attitudes and support for tourism go hand in hand (Jackson & Inbarakan, 2006; MacKay & Campbell, 2004; Nunkoo & Ramkissoon, 2010), which means that the supporting or opposing of tourism development from residents is a behavioral intent. To do so, the premise that residents perform on their attitudes (Nunkoo & Gursoy, 2012) is also included in this study. As proposed by other research, these constructs were selected for being viewed as significant factors for the economy in small islands and are relevant to the field to study the community support for tourism (Douglas, 2006; Nunkoo & Gursoy, 2012; Petrzelka et al., 2006).

Therefore, to bridge the gap in the current literature regarding the integration of residents in cultural activities to further develop the tourism sector, this research proposes a model to establish a relationship between development and participation in cultural music events and residents' intention to support tourism. This research framework sets out from the resident's awareness and participation of several cultural music events celebrated in the Dominican Republic. It then analyzes if there is an important relationship between these events and a series of constructs such as place identity, community commitment and the residents' perceptions of benefits of the events, which ultimately will influence residents to further support tourism development activities. In Figure 10.1, a graphical representation of the conceptual framework is shown.

Several theories have been developed to study the behavior of individuals towards tourism. The Identity Theory suggests that there is a direct connection between identity and behavior. A positive place identity can occur when the environment or place have the resources a person

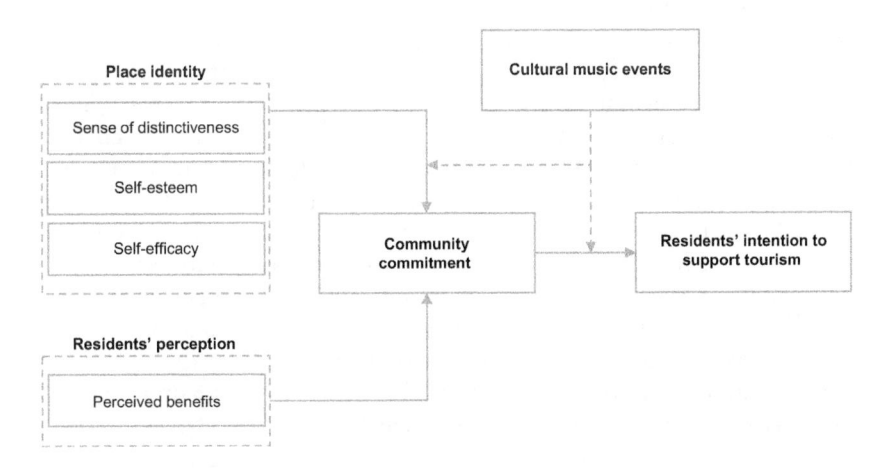

Figure 10.1 Research conceptual model.
Source: The researchers.

needs and prefers and has an impact on the behavior of that person (Shumaker & Taylor, 1983). According to Kitnuntaviwat and Tang (2008) and McCool and Martin (1994), place identity and community attachment may be a key factor in residents' attitudes and support for tourism. But the relationship between both constructs has not been established.

In this regard, drawing from the identity theory, the model proposed in this study takes the place identity as an influential force for community commitment. To analyze place identity, three sub-constructs are considered: a sense of distinctiveness, self-esteem, and self-efficacy. In the literature review, a fourth sub-construct is included under place identity, which is a sense of continuity. This construct was not taken as part of the construct in this study because the events in which this study is based are not organized in only one location in the Dominican Republic but several places through the island which are changed each year. However, this idea is ignored as only two of the events are done in the same place each year. When a person identifies themselves within an environment a series of behaviors towards it are triggered and, the more people participate in their local communities' activities, the more solid their place identity, and vice versa. Therefore, the first hypothesis is stated:

H1. Residents' place identity has a direct effect on residents' community commitment.

Another theory considered for the development of this research framework is the Social Exchange Theory. It suggests that the perception residents have of how much an event or activity will benefit and cost them is an important influencer of their support towards it (Gursoy et al., 2010). Following this declaration, research was done in the relationship concerning residents' perception of benefits and costs and its mediating effect between community attachment and on residents' support for tourism. A cost-benefit approach is taken in this study to assess, in a simple and uncomplicated manner, the perceived costs and benefits of the organization of cultural music events and its impact on residents' community commitment. According to this approach, the benefits are viewed as a positive and costs as a negative consequence of the event in the community (Stylidis et al., 2014). We can extrapolate this notion by saying that the more knowledge residents have of the cultural music events happening in their environment, the more information will be gathered to analyze its benefits and consequences, influencing later their behavior and commitment to said event. By following this notion, Hypothesis 2 was developed and expressed as follows:

H2. The perception of event benefits has a direct influence on residents' community commitment towards it.

Community attachment and commitment share a similar background in terms of the concept meaning but are applied in two different fields: community attachment refers to a person's link to certain objects or environments like a place or a brand (Foroudi et al., 2018), whereas community commitment can also be defined as a person's link but with an organization (Meyer & Allen, 1991). Within the literature, the construct of community attachment has is a direct influence on residents' support for tourism in some studies (Gursoy & Rutherford, 2004), while others deny it causes an impact at all (Choi & Murray, 2010; Gursoy et al., 2002). Since there is not a unified front regarding this relationship in the existing literature, this research will study if an impactful relationship exists between residents' community commitment towards an event and their support for tourism. For the development of this research, the community commitment is taken as the community attachment construct, taking the premise that the event in the questionnaire is playing the role of an organization. Therefore,

H3. Residents' community commitment to cultural music events has a positive impact on their intention to support tourism.

As a consequence, based on the relationships mentioned and described above, the mediating hypotheses for reads as follow:

H4. Residents' community commitment to cultural music events mediates the link between place identity and their intention to support tourism.
H5. Residents' community commitment to cultural music events mediates the link between residents' perception and their intention to support tourism.

According to the theoretical and empirical considerations, the above discussions and the study hypotheses, the proposed model depicts an operational model where cultural music events are a potential moderating variable to provide a compelling explanation for the mechanism in the link between place identity and residents' community commitment. In this regard, cultural events such as concerts have become a target for locals to bring income and development to their communities. One of the aims of organizing such cultural events is not only to attract tourists and support local talent but also to reinforce locals' sense of identity (Getz, 2008; Yolal & Uysal, 2009). Governments are focusing more and more on strategies that cultivate the sense of uniqueness and distinctiveness among locals. As a result, the tourism development strategies nowadays are focusing their resources more and more on the development of local communities, where the support of the residents is the one thing that can determine the success or lack thereof the project. In this sense, this research states its six hypotheses about the moderating role of participation of residents in cultural music events on the nexus between place identity and residents' community commitment. The assumption of this research is that the participation of residents in local cultural music events will help them feel more identified with their environment. Thus, Hypothesis 6 reads as follow:

H6. Cultural music events positively moderate the link between residents' place identity and community commitment.

Furthermore, tourism has a direct impact on the lives of individuals as leisure activities and events are increasing and transforming its view, giving importance to the targeting of local communities. In this sense, special events such as the creation of festivals and concerts usually celebrate a certain lifestyle or culture and retain the participation of both residents and tourists. Hence, cultural events such as concerts and festivals are usually held to revitalize local communities and residents by reinforcing the locals' sense of identity and improving their quality of life and attract visitors (Getz, 2008; Yolal & Uysal, 2009). This happens when the residents take on the image of the events and analyze them in terms of how much they identify with them and develop powerful feelings of attachment and passion towards them (Holmes, 2000; Sperling & Berman, 1994) through paying attention intentions and behaviors of residents to support tourism. Residents are more prone to accepting tourist and tourism development and support if they have an optimistic attitude towards the industry in general and this feeling is reinforced when positive benefits are personally experienced and improve residents' quality of life (Sharma & Gursoy, 2015) and their culture. Therefore, residents' supportive behaviors and the existence of cultural events such as festivals in the expansion of tourism projects are essential for the maintenance of the industry and one of the factors that enhance its success (Bourke & Luloff, 1996; Gursoy et al., 2010). Hence, the following moderation hypothesis was developed:

H7. Cultural music events positively moderate the link between community commitment and residents' intention to support tourism.

Research methodology

Data collection and measures

A survey was used to collect data. This study was carried out in the Dominican Republic. The criteria followed in this study to fill out the questionnaire were that the participants needed to be Dominican residents and above 18 years of age. Their participation was voluntary and anonymous. We received 200 usable data. To capture *residents' place identity*, nine items were employed, which will answer this variable with three sub-constructs: a sense of distinctiveness (three items), self-esteem (three items) and self-efficacy (three items). Items measuring *residents' perception* were taken from (Gursoy & Kendall, 2006; Kim, Gursoy and Lee, 2006; Nunkoo & Ramkisson, 2011) to evaluate the perceived benefits with six items. *Community commitment* was also measured with five items (Allen and Meyer, 1990; Garbarino and Johnson, 1999). The participants are asked about their *intention to support tourism* with seven items (Ajzen, 1991; Gursoy & Kendall, 2006; Nunkoo & Gursoy, 2012), and finally, the development of *cultural music events* with four items based on the "strongly disagree" (1) to "strongly agree" (5) (see Table 10.2).

The questionnaire was filled in by 200 Dominican residents (n = 200), from which 115 (57.5%) were female and 84 (42%) males. According to their age, 48% of the participants were between 25 and 34 years old and the second largest group goes to those who were between 18 and 24 years old (25%). Although more than 60% of the participants were between 18 and 34 years old, and the amount of surveyed individuals per age is not the same, the results presented within this survey are of most importance to managers, event planners, and governmental institutions. As the audience participates the most in this kind of events, their responses to the questions presented in the survey can shine a light on some matters concerning their involvement and support in them. In terms of their marital status, 118 of them are single (59%) and 63 (31.5%) are married. Most of the surveyed work in the private sector (52.5%) and their highest education level is a bachelor's degree (47.50%) and master's degree (39%). It can be implied that most of the participants belong to the middle-working class as their household monthly income is approximately from DOP$40,000 to DOP$90,000 or more (above 60%). To finalize the demographic section, this research was targeting the residents of the Dominican Republic to fill in the questionnaire. In this sense, 98% of the participants are Dominicans and the other 2% are divided between an Italian, a Puerto-Rican, an American and a Haitian, all residing in the Dominican Republic (Table 10.1).

To measure the different constructs stated in the framework, scaled items from previous studies were applied. Therefore, to study and observe the research hypothesis, all the data were analyzed through SPSS and SEM with application Smart PLS 3 software. All constructs were measured using stales found in previous studies, as explained in Table 10.2.

Table 10.1 The participants' profile

Demographic

		Frequency	Percent (%)			Frequency	Percent (%)
Gender	Male	84	42	Marital	Single	118	59
	Female	115	57.50	Status	Married	63	31.50
	Prefer not to say	1	0.50		Free Union	9	4.50
					Divorced	9	4.50
					Widower	1	0.50
Age (years)	18–24	50	25				
	25–34	96	48				
	35–44	25	12.50	Education	Primary School or below	1	0.50
	45–54	16	8		High School	23	11.50
	55–64	10	5		Bachelor's degree	95	47.50
	$\geq$65	3	1.50		Master	78	39
					PhD	3	1.50
Current	Private sector employee	105	52.50				
Occupation	Public sector employee	28	14	Nationality	Dominican	196	98
	Self-employed	26	13		Puerto-Rican	1	0.50
	Student	34	17		American	1	0.50
	Housewife	2	1		Italian	1	0.50
	Retired	3	1.50		Haitian	1	0.50
	Unemployed	2	1				
Household	DOP $14,999 or less	17	8.50	Sample (n = 200)			
Monthly	DOP $15,000–$39,999	38	19				
Income	DOP $40,000–$64,999	44	22				
DOP	DOP $65,000–$89,999	32	16				
	DOP $90,000 or more	69	35				

Table 10.2 The item measurements and main authors

Construct	Items	Source
Place identity	*Sense of distinctiveness* I think Dominican Republic is a country with very distinctive features Dominican Republic's attractiveness is very different from other countries I know The lifestyle in Dominican Republic is unique *Self-esteem* When someone praises Dominican Republic, it feels like a personal compliment to me If a story in the media criticized Dominican Republic, I feel embarrassed Living in Dominican Republic makes me feel very proud *Self-efficacy* More tourism development in Dominican Republic makes me feel more confident in changing occupations if I'm not satisfied with my current one More tourism development in Dominican Republic makes me feel more confident in finding my ideal job in this country (Dominican Republic) Tourism development in Dominican Republic makes me feel more confident and enjoy the lifestyle of my community	Stokburger-Sauer (2011) Wang and Xu (2015); Wang and Chen (2015)
Residents perceptions	*Perceived benefits* Improve Dominican Republic's image worldwide Foster pride among the Dominican community Increase business opportunities Will strengthen local community bond and cohesion Encourage the development of more cultural activities in my country Attract investment	Nunkoo and Ramkisson (2011), Gursoy and Kendall (2006), Kim, Gursoy and Lee (2006)

(*Continued*)

Construct	Items	Source
Community commitment	I feel proud when I attend these events	Garbarino and Johnson (1999), Allen and Meyer (1990)
	I feel these events are part of me	
	I care for the long-term success of these events	
	I'm a loyal patron of these events	
	I will continuously participate in these events	
Residents intention to support tourism	These events are one of the most important activities to helps our community	Ajzen (1991), Gursoy and Kendall (2006), Nunkoo and Gursoy (2012)
	I support new event facilities that will attract new visitors (Locals and tourists) to my community	
	I am happy and proud to see that tourists are interested with what my community has to offer	
	I believe that this type of events should be actively encouraged in my area	
	The offer of musical events should be extended in Dominican Republic	
	I participate in the promotion of these events	
	I support the development of community-based musical events	
Cultural music events	Heard DR Jazz festival	Developed by researchers
	Seen Prom DR Jazz festival	
	DR JAZZ FESTIVAL_SM	
	STOD GO DEFIESTA_WOM	

Analysis and results

The present study's goal is to explore the link between cultural music events, residents' place identity, community commitment, and their intention to support tourism. To evaluate the validity of these constructs, we used SEM with an emphasis on the method of partial least squares (PLS) (Henseler et al., 2014). The constructs' reliability and validity were tested to examine the measurement model, and then the structural model was tested (Aparicio et al., 2017).

Model fit

Tenenhaus et al. (2004) proposed the Goodness of Fit (GoF) index as a way of evaluating the PLS-SEM path model. GoF index is assessed based on the mean geometric value for the mean communality score (average variance extracted [AVE] values) and average R^2 value (Farooq et al., 2018) (for endogenous constructs). In this study, a GoF value of 0.498 was achieved, which reveals a good model fit (see Table 10.3).

Evaluation of the measurement model

As a preliminary check of the measurement model, a confirmatory factor analysis (CFA) was used for testing this model with all measured constructs being modeled as correlated first-order factors. As seen in Table 10.4, reliability and convergent validity of the elements were estimated by Cronbach's alpha coefficients, composite reliability, and AVE. All alpha

Table 10.3 Model fit assessment

Fit indicator	GoF
Value in study	$\sqrt{R^2 \times \overline{AVE}} = \sqrt{0.362 \times 0.687} = 0.498$
Suggest value	$GoF_{small} = 0.1$; $GoF_{medium} = 0.25$; $GoF_{large} = 0.36$
Reference	Wetzels et al. (2009)

GoF: Goodness of Fit.

Table 10.4 Results of the measurement model

Construct/ indicator	Items	Loading	VIF	AVE	CR	Rho_A	C-α	DV?
Place identity				0.523	0.765	0.735	0.716	Yes
Sense of	SD1	0.792	1.441	0.601	0.817			
distinctiveness	SD2	0.844	1.470					
	SD3	0.679	1.165					
Self-esteem	SES1	0.803	1.286	0.534	0.773			
	SES2	0.659	1.199					
	SES3	0.723	1.117					
Self-efficacy	SEF1	0.716	1.333	0.659	0.852			
	SEF2	0.885	1.876					
	SEF3	0.825	1.603					
Residents perception				1.0	1.0	0.867	0.856	Yes
Perceived	PB1	0.773	1.782	0.586	0.894			
benefits	PB2	0.793	2.266					
	PB3	0.749	1.765					
	PB4	0.864	2.620					
	PB5	0.802	2.139					
	PB6	0.632	1.556					
Community commitment				0.718	0.927	0.907	0.902	Yes
	CC1	0.825	2.035					
	CC2	0.867	2.721					

(Continued)

Construct/ indicator	Items	Loading	VIF	AVE	CR	Rho_A	C-α	DV?
	CC3	0.850	2.395					
	CC4	0.835	3.433					
	CC5	0.859	3.586					
Residents intention to support tourism				0.506	0.877	0.840	0.837	Yes
	RIST1	0.723	1.633					
	RIST2	0.761	2.025					
	RIST3	0.681	2.008					
	RIST4	0.818	2.602					
	RIST5	0.696	1.701					
	RIST6	0.611	1.484					
	RIST7	0.673	1.580					

VIF: Variance inflation factor; CR = Composite reliability; AVE = Average variance extracted; Rho_A: Dijkstra-Henseler's indicator; DV: Discriminant validity.

Table 10.5 Discriminant validity and the square root of AVE (in bold on diagonal)

Fornell-Larcker criterion

	1	2	3	4
1 Place identity	0.723			
2 Residents perception	0.483	1.0		
3 Community commitment	0.501	0.501	0.847	
4 Residents intention to support tourism	0.342	0.551	0.620	0.711

HTMT ratio

	1	2	3	4
1 Place identity				
2 Residents perception	0.605			
3 Community commitment	0.606	0.552		
4 Residents intention to support tourism	0.458	0.648	0.682	

Threshold of HTMT criterion: For conceptually similar constructs: HTMT < 0.90; for conceptually different constructs: HTMT < 0.85 (Hair et al., 2019).

coefficients exceeded the 0.70 thresholds suggested by Hair et al. (2011), and additionally, composite reliabilities ranged from 0.765 to 1.0 thus satisfying the acceptance level (Bagozzi & Yi, 1988) for the reliability of study constructs (see Table 10.4). Also, all the AVE values were above the suggested cut-off value of 0.50 (Hair et al., 2014). Indicator reliability was examined through the evaluation of factor loadings. Multidimensional data with lower than a 0.50-factor loading were eliminated because they were not considered to be within the acceptable range (Hair et al., 2014) and results indicating that all indicators were reliable. As for the composite reliabilities, they are well above the recommended 0.70 cut-off point (Bagozzi & Yi, 1988; Hair et al., 2014), indicating good internal consistency of all reflective constructs.

Finally, as shown in Table 10.5, two measures were used to evaluate the discriminant validity of the measurement model. First, Fornell and Larcker (1981) stated the square root of the AVEs (diagonal results) in the construct needs to be more than the shared correlation between the construct and other model constructs (off-diagonal components), and the second Heterotrait-Monotrait ration of correlations (HTMT) ratio, which Henseler et al. (2015) recommended as a modern means of analyzing the discriminant validity of constructs in the measurement models (Farooq et al., 2018). The HTMT is defined as the mean value of the item correlations across constructs relative to the (geometric) mean of the average associations for the items measuring the same construct (Hair et al., 2019, p. 9). We concluded that all the constructs show evidence of acceptable discrimination.

Therefore, if the measurement model assessments meet all the acceptable criteria, then researchers allow evaluating the structural model (Hair et al., 2017).

Testing the structural model

In this part, to test hypotheses about the link between place identity, residents' perception, community commitment, residents' intention to support tourism, and the mediating effect of community commitment on the association between place identity and residents' perception of residents' intention to support tourism. We evaluated the structural model for the general explanatory power of constructs using the R^2 value and predictive accuracy of the model by Q^2 value. Before assessing the structural relationships all constructs were tested for multicollinearity to make sure it does not bias the regression results. In this process, the latent variable scores of the predictor constructs in a partial regression are used to calculate the variance inflation factor (VIF) values (Hair et al., 2019). A maximum VIF value for each latent variable was computed resulting in a maximum VIF value of 1.305, which is below the cut-off point of 3, whereas according to the Hair et al. (2019), the VIF scores should be close to 3 and lower (see Table 10.6).

The bootstrap method with 1,000 subsamples using the Smart PLS 3.0 software is applied to test the direction, strength, and significance of the hypothesized path coefficients. To evaluate the quality of the model,

Table 10.6 Full collinearity VIFs of constructs values for common method bias

Construct	*VIFs*	
	CC	*Intention to support tourism*
Place identity	1.305	
Residents perception	1.305	
Community commitment (CC)		1.000

Threshold of VIFs: ≤ 3.

the coefficient of determination (R^2), which represents the amount of explained variance of each endogenous latent variable, was computed (Hair et al., 2017). Accordingly, the proportion of the total variance of each endogenous construct explained by the model is 34% for community commitment and 39% for residents' intention to support tourism. The R^2 ranges from 0 to 1, with higher values indicating a greater explanatory power. As a guideline, R^2 values of 0.75, 0.50 and 0.25 can be considered substantial, moderate and weak (Hair et al., 2019, p. 11). In addition, another means of measuring the model's predictive accuracy is Q^2 value (Geisser, 1974; Stone, 1974). As a result, Q^2 scores higher than 0.02, 0.15 and 0.35 demonstrate small, medium and large predictive relevance (Henseler et al., 2009). Hence, the predictive relevance of residents' intention to support tourism in this study is estimated at 0.169. Accordingly, it can be contended that the proposed model has strong predictive relevance $\left(Q^2_{\text{Medium}} = 0.169\right)$ for predicting variation in the endogenous construct.

A graphical demonstration of the model results (path coefficient and t-value) is shown in Figure 10.2. The impact of place identity on community commitment (H1: β = 0.338, t-value= 5.429, $p < 0.001$) is supported, which confirms the first hypothesis (H1), similarity the influence of residents' perception on community commitment (H2: β = 0.338, t-value= 4.912, $p < 0.001$), is supported, followed by residents' intention to support tourism (H3: β = 0.620, t-value= 12.823, $p < 0.001$) which can be significantly explained by community commitment. Therefore, H2 and H3 are confirmed. H4 and H5 were confirmed, indicating that community commitment could be a mediator on the link place identity and residents' perception with support tourism respectively (see Table 10.7 and Figure 10.2).

Table 10.7 Results of hypotheses tests

Relationships	β-value	t-value	p-value	Remarks
Direct effects (overall model)				
H1: PI → CC	0.338	5.429	0.000	Supported
H2: RP → CC	0.338	4.912	0.000	Supported
H3: CC → RIST	0.620	12.823	0.000	Supported
Specific indirect effects (mediation)				
H4: PI → CC → RIST	0.209	5.081	0.000	Supported
H5: RP → CC → RIST	0.209	4.025	0.000	Supported
Total effect				
PI → RIST	0.571	–	–	–
RP → RIST	0.765	–	–	–

Effect size: >0.350 large; >0.150 and ≤0.350 medium; >0.20 and ≤0.150 small (Chin, 1998).

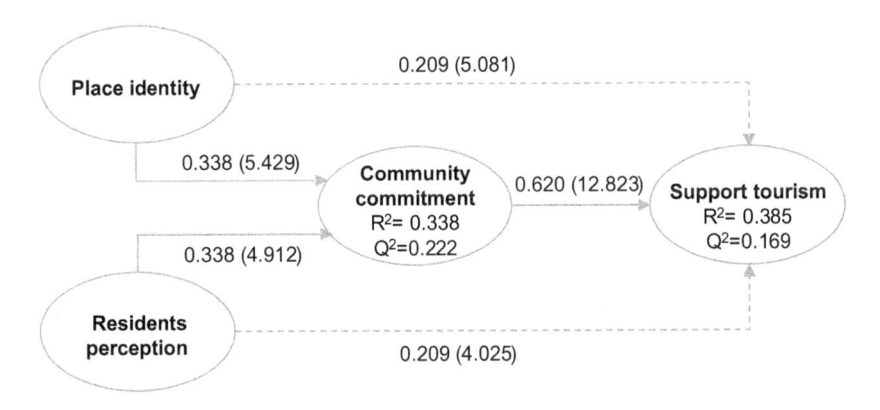

Figure 10.2 Results of the structural model analysis.

Table 10.8 Assessment VAF values to determining the kind of mediation

Hypothesis 4	Hypothesis 5
$PI \rightarrow CC \rightarrow RIST$ S.D (STDEV) = 0.041 $T-value = \left\|\dfrac{a \times b}{SD}\right\| = \dfrac{0.209}{0.041}$ $= 5.081$ $VAF = \dfrac{\text{Indirect effect}}{\text{Total effect}} = \dfrac{0.209}{0.571}$ $= 36.6\%$	$RP \rightarrow CC \rightarrow RIST$ S.D (STDEV) = 0.052 $T-value = \left\|\dfrac{a \times b}{SD}\right\| = \dfrac{0.209}{0.052}$ $= 4.25$ $VAF = \dfrac{\text{Indirect effect}}{\text{Total effect}} = \dfrac{0.209}{0.765}$ $= 27.32\%$

VAF < 20%	20% ≥ VAF ≤ 80%	VAF > 80%
No mediation (almost)	*Partial mediation*	*Full (perfect) mediation*

Post-hoc analysis

THE MEDIATION ANALYSES

In this section, we need to determine the strength (portion) of the mediation variable, which can use a variance accounted for (VAF) for determining the size of the indirect effect about the total effect (i.e., direct effect + indirect effect) (Hair et al., 2017). This assesses the ratio of indirect effect (i.e., a × b) on total effect (Prange & Pinho, 2017). Accordingly, to analyze and determine the mediating role of community commitment in the proposed model, we apply Hair et al. (2017) and Nitzl et al. (2016) phases in Table 10.8.

Always at least two types of mediation can occur (full and partial mediation) when the indirect effect (a × b) is significant. In this regard, because

VAF values in two paths are more significant than 20% but lower than 80%, partial mediation takes place. Hence, as the values of the indirect paths (a × b) and direct (c′) are both significant, and additionally the value of both paths (i.e., a × b × c′) is also positive (0.119, 0.160), finally, we conclude that community commitment acts as a *complementary partial mediation* in the relationship between place identity and residents' perception with residents' intention to support tourism, respectively.

The moderation analysis

For the moderation analyses, in the link between place identity and community commitment, when the moderator effect of the cultural music events is considered, our results indicate a positive and significant moderation by the cultural music events ($\beta = 0.161$, t-value = 2.100, $p < 0.05$), supporting H6. Also, in the relationship between community commitment and residents' intention to support tourism, when the moderator effect of the cultural music events is considered, our results indicate a positive and significant moderation by this variable ($\beta = 0.089$, t-value = 1.683, $p < 0.1$), supporting H7 (see Table 10.9).

Importance-performance map analysis

In the final step, to provide a better understanding of the most important constructs influencing residents' intention to support tourism, we analyzed the importance-performance map analysis (IPMA). IPMA is a very useful analytical tool in PLS-SEM; which graphically extends the standard path coefficient estimates in a more practical approach (Ringle &

Table 10.9 Results for the moderation model

Variables	Community commitment			Intention to support tourism		
	β	t	p	β	t	p
Main effect						
Place identity (PI)	0.307	4.773	0.000*			
Community commitment (CC)				0.551	9.312	0.000*
Moderator						
Music cultural events (MCE)	0.177	3.306	0.001*	0.139	2.396	0.017*
Interactive effects						
PI × MEC	0.161	2.100	0.036*			
CC × MEC				0.089	1.797	0.073**

* = $p < 0.05$; ** = $p < 0.1$.

Sarstedt, 2016). More precisely, IPMA presents a contrast of *importance* (i.e., the total effect of predecessor constructs in predicting a target construct) and *performance* (i.e., average latent variable scores). The goal of IPMA is to identify predecessors that have a relatively low performance but high importance for the target constructs. A one-unit point increase in the performance of predecessor construct will increase the performance of the target construct, by the total effect size (i.e., importance) of the same predecessor construct (Farooq et al., 2018, p. 176). As a result, conclusions can be drawn in two dimensions (i.e., both *importance* and *performance*), which is particularly important to prioritize managerial actions. Consequently, it is preferable to primarily focus on improving the performance of those constructs that exhibit high importance regarding their explanation of a specific target construct but, at the same time, have a relatively low performance (Hair et al., 2018).

According to the result in Figure 10.3 and Table 10.10, "community commitment" has the highest importance score (i.e., 0.620); if residents in the Dominican Republic increase their community commitment

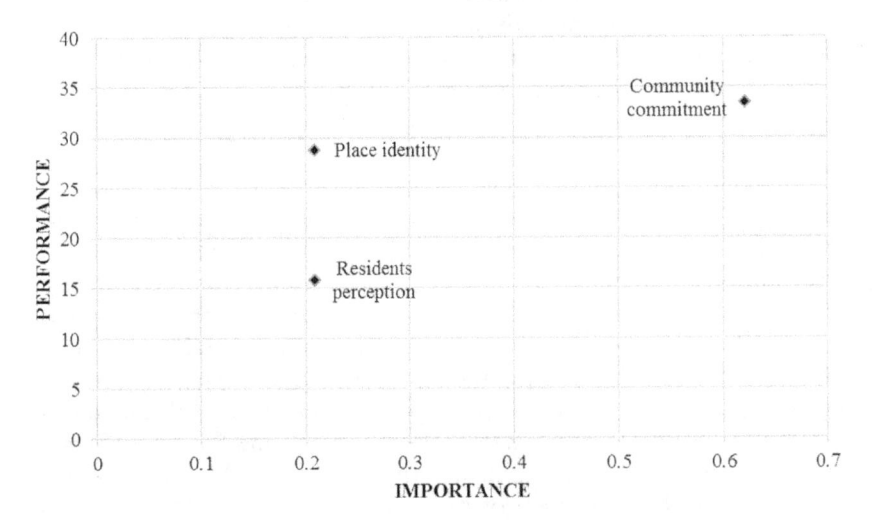

Figure 10.3 IPMA for resident's intention to support tourism.

Table 10.10 IPMAs for intention to support tourism

Constructs	Importance	Performance
Place identity	0.209	28.790
Residents perception	0.209	15.860
Community commitment	**0.620**	**33.437**
Average value	0.346	26.029

The bold values indicate the highest importance (total effect) and highest performance value.

performance by one-unit point; its overall residents' intention to support tourism will increase by 0.620. Moreover, our findings have revealed that there is the lowest performance in the Dominican Republic in residents' perceptions towards benefits and costs of tourism (i.e., 15.860 that lower than average value = 26.029), which means that there is a great room for improvement in this area. Also, IPMA depicted that "community commitment" has the highest performance score, that is, 33.437.

Discussion

This research aimed to deliver important facts and perspectives on the subject of music events and its inclusion in nation branding strategies. The principal input is related to how this topic, of cultural music event and their influence on residents' intention to support tourism, is being given a chance to bring to light some of the essential features of music and its involvement with culture and place identity used up. By conducting this study in a Third World Country, and an island of the Caribbean, in which the sense of uniqueness of the place needs to be emphasized in all communications to both tourists and locals, this study brings an essential contribution to the understanding of how residents can be included in current events and projects.

Theoretical implications

This chapter contributes to the expansion of the existing literature review concerning the inclusion of culture and music events and variables like place identity, community commitments and the effect on the residents' support for tourism that they can have. Starting from the proposed model and framework, in which all hypotheses were approved and supported, it proposes that from the participants on cultural music events, a stronger sense of place identity will be developed in residents and a subsequent relationship is created between this type of identity and the sense of community commitment. Another factor that surrounds this subject is the evaluations of the perception of benefits and costs that once again, as has been shown in previous studies, has a stronger impact on residents' community commitment. All these elements converge and work as the chain reaction initiated by the participation in the cultural music event and ending in the residents' support for tourism. The fact that the first and last relationship of the model is weaker than the others shows a path to further develop in other researches to broaden the knowledge.

Managerial implications

All the results found in this chapter can be applied to a variety of managerial scenarios in fields such as marketing, tourism development, and event planning. From a nation branding perspective, the music involved in the strategies to create and maintain a national brand has not been studied and there is a huge gap in the literature regarding this subject. In this manner, using existing events that are already part of the culture can be a good starting point in getting more involved with the community and applying the concepts of this research, as it highlights the benefits of this strategy. From tourism, the ideas worked with here are a path that must be taken to sustain projects in the sector. The importance of involving the community has always been remarked upon in the industry, but as the competence of nations evolves the key factors in developing are more internal than external. The identity of the country and its people should be at the heart of every strategy. But it is not only these two fields that can gain something out of this research as, just like these topics are getting more attention by governments, brands also are seeking increasingly their target community commitment growth to be a sustainable and successful brand.

Limitations and directions for future research

This study has several limitations and its development despite the achievement of its objectives. Beginning from the sample in which the questionnaire was given. A more inclusive and diverse sample may have given different results, which is why for future studies a new sampling technique should be applied and the results compared. In terms of the five events selected for the study, the application of this questionnaire while the events are being held might be a better way of distribution to get more detailed answers. A more in-depth method such as interviews can also add more insight o the information contained here, and that can be reflected as the limitation of depth in this research. Interviews with government officials who work in tourism and cultural development should be further researched and then compared with the results of this research to gain a full overview of the issue so that more paths to solutions can be identified. A final limitation to this research is the lack of documentation that the Dominican Republic has regarding the events and projects they held in regard to some projects of tourism and culture. As an example, how talks have begun about the construction of a national brand of the Dominican Republic, but not one piece of information can be found talking about the measures, projects developed for it or even the government institutions that are going to be involved in them.

Given the fact that all these limitations in this research exist, further studies have been suggested. The objective of this chapter was to provide the first insight into cultural music events and its implication on residents' support for tourism, but more research is needed regarding the elements that can be measured and studies to deepen the knowledge in this area.

Key terms and definitions – Definitions for the key constructs

Place identity – refers to 'what the place really is', as in marketing literature, corporate identity refers to 'what we really are' (actual identity) (Ageeva & Foroudi, 2019; Balmer et al., 2009, p. 7).

Sense of distinctiveness – refers to distinctive and unique features of the place (Wang et al., 2011).

Self-esteem – refers to the positive assessment of the self and the group to which the self belongs (Ellemers et al., 1999; Gu & Ryan, 2008; Twigger-Ross et al., 2003).

Community commitment – refers to a person's link with a company, place or event (Ageeva & Foroudi, 2019)

References

Ageeva, E., & Foroudi, P. (2019). Tourist's destination image through regional tourism: From supply and demand sides perspectives. *Journal of Business Research*, Just accepted.

Andriotis, K. (2005). Community groups' perceptions of and preferences for tourism development: Evidence from Crete. *Journal of Hospitality & Tourism Research*, 29(1), 67–90.

Aparicio, M., Bacao, F., & Oliveira, T. (2017). Grit in the path to e-learning success. *Computers in Human Behavior*, 66(Jan), 388–399.

Bagozzi, R.P., & Yi, Y. (1988). On the evaluation of structural equation models. *Journal of the Academy of Marketing Science*, 16(1), 74–94.

Balmer, J.M., Stuart, H., & Greyser, S. A. (2009). Aligning identity and strategy: Corporate branding at British Airways in the late 20th century. *California Management Review*, 51(3), 6–23.

Bancentral.gov.do (2018). www.bancentral.gov.do/ (Accessed by 10 April 2018).

Bourke, L., & Luloff, A. E. (1996). Rural tourism development: Are communities in southwest rural Pennsylvania ready to participate. In Harrison, L.C. & Husbands, W. (eds.) *Practising responsible tourism: International case studies in tourism planning, policy, and development* (pp. 277–295). Chichester: John Wiley & Sons.

Chin, W.W. (1998). The partial least squares approach to structural equation modeling. *Modern Methods for Business Research*, 295(2), 295–336.

Choi, H.C., & Murray, I. (2010). Resident attitudes toward sustainable community tourism. *Journal of Sustainable Tourism*, 18(4), 575–594.

Douglas, C.H. (2006). Small island states and territories: Sustainable development issues and strategies: Challenges for changing islands in a changing world. *Sustainable Development*, 14(Apr), 75–80.

Ellemers, N., Kortekaas, P., & Ouwerkerk, J. W. (1999). Self-categorisation, commitment to the group and group self-esteem as related but distinct aspects of social identity. *European Journal of Social Psychology*, 29(2–3), 371–389.

Farooq, M.S., Salam, M., Fayolle, A., Jaafar, N., & Ayupp, K. (2018). Impact of service quality on customer satisfaction in Malaysia airlines: A PLS-SEM approach. *Journal of Air Transport Management*, 67(Mar), 169–180.

Fornell, C.G., & Larcker, D.F. (1981). Evaluating structural equation models with unobservable variables and measurement error. *Journal of Marketing Research*, 18(1), 39–50.

Foroudi, P., Akarsu, T.N., Ageeva, E., Foroudi, M.M., Dennis, C., & Melewar, T. C. (2018). PROMISING THE DREAM: Changing destination image of London through the effect of website place. *Journal of Business Research*, 83, 97–110.

Foroudi, P., Gupta, S., Kitchen, P., Foroudi, M. M., & Nguyen, B. (2016). A framework of place branding, place image, and place reputation: Antecedents and moderators. *Qualitative Market Research: An International Journal*, 19(2), 241–264.

Foroudi, P., Hafeez, K., & Foroudi, M.M. (2017). Evaluating the impact of corporate logos towards corporate reputation: A case of Persia and Mexico. *Qualitative Market Research: An International Journal*, 20(2), 158–180.

Geisser, S. (1974). A predictive approach to the random effects model. *Biometrika*, 61(1), 101–107.

Getz, D. (2008). Event tourism: Definition, evolution, and research. *Tourism Management*, 29(3), 403–428.

Gu, H., & Ryan, C. (2008). Place attachment, identity and community impacts of tourism – The case of a Beijing hutong. *Tourism Management*, 29(Aug), 637–647.

Gursoy, D., Chi, C. G., & Dyer, P. (2010). Locals' attitudes toward mass and alternative tourism: The case of Sunshine Coast, Australia. *Journal of Travel Research*, 49(3), 381–394.

Gursoy, D., Jurowski, C., & Uysal, M. (2002). Resident attitudes: A structural modeling approach. *Annals of Tourism Research*, 29(1), 79–105.

Gursoy, D., & Kendall, K.W. (2006). Hosting mega events: Modeling locals' support. *Annals of Tourism Research*, 33(3), 603–623.

Gursoy, D., & Rutherford, D.G. (2004). Host attitudes toward tourism: An improved structural model. *Annals of Tourism Research*, 31(3), 495–516.

Hair, J.F., Black, W.C., Babin, B.J., & Anderson, R.E. (2014). *Multivariate data analysis*. Harlow: Pearson New International Edition, Pearson, USA.

Hair, J.F., Hult, G.T.M., Ringle, C.M., & Sarstedt, M. (2017). *A primer on partial least squares structural equation modeling PLS-SEM* (2nd ed.). Thousand Oaks, CA: Sage.

Hair, J.F., Ringle, C.M., & Sarstedt, M. (2011). PLS-SEM: Indeed a silver bullet. *Journal of Marketing Theory & Practice*, 19(2), 139–152.

Hair, J.F., Risher, J.J., Sarstedt, M., & Ringle, C.M. (2019). When to use and how to report the results of PLS-SEM. *European Business Review*, 31(1), 2–24.

Hair, J.F., Sarstedt, M., Ringle, C.M., & Gudergan, S.P. (2018). *Advanced issues in partial least squares structural equation modeling (PLS-SEM)*. Thousand Oaks, CA: Sage.

Henseler, J., Dijkstra, T.K., Sarstedt, M., Ringle, C.M., Diamantopoulos, A., Straub, D.W., & Calantone, R.J. (2014). Common beliefs and reality about

PLS: Comments on Rönkkö and Evermann (2013). *Organizational Research Methods*, 17(2), 182–209.

Henseler, J., Ringle, C.M., & Sarstedt, M. (2015). A new criterion for assessing discriminant validity in variance-based structural equation modeling. *Journal of the Academy of Marketing Science*, 43(1), 115–135.

Henseler, J., Ringle, C.M., & Sinkovics, R.R. (2009). The use of partial least squares path modeling in international marketing. In R.R. Sinkovics, & P.N. Ghauri (Eds.), *New challenges to international marketing (Advances in International Marketing)* (Vol. 20, pp. 277–319). Bingley (K): Emerald Group Publishing.

Herrero, L. C., Sanz, J. Á., Bedate, A., & del Barrio, M. J. (2012). Who pays more for a cultural festival, tourists or locals? A certainty analysis of a contingent valuation application. *International Journal of Tourism Research*, 14(5), 495–512.

Holmes, J. (2000). Attachment theory and psychoanalysis: A rapprochement. *British Journal of Psychotherapy*, 17(2), 157–172.

Jackson, M. S., & Inbakaran, R. J. (2006). Evaluating residents' attitudes and intentions to act towards tourism development in regional Victoria, Australia. *International Journal of Tourism Research*, 8(5), 355–366.

Kitnuntaviwat, V., & Tang, J.C. (2008). Residents' attitudes, perception and support for sustainable tourism development. *Tourism and Hospitality Planning & Development*, 5(1), 45–60.

Lee, T.H. (2013). Influence analysis of community resident support for sustainable tourism development. *Tourism Management*, 34(Feb), 37–46.

Lim, C.C., & Cooper, C. (2009). Beyond sustainability: Optimising island tourism development. *International Journal of Tourism Research*, 11(1), 89–103.

MacKay, K.J., & Campbell, J.M. (2004). An examination of residents' support for hunting as a tourism product. *Tourism Management*, 25(4), 443–452.

McCool, S.F., & Martin, S.R. (1994). Community attachment and attitudes toward tourism development. *Journal of Travel Research*, 32(3), 29–34.

Meyer, J.P., & Allen, N.J. (1991). A three-component conceptualization of organizational commitment. *Human Resource Management Review*, 1(1), 61–89.

Nepal, S. K. (2008). Residents' attitudes to tourism in central British Columbia, Canada. *Tourism Geographies*, 10(1), 42–65.

Nitzl, C., Roldan, J.L., & Cepeda, G. (2016). Mediation analysis in partial least squares path modeling: Helping researchers discuss more sophisticated models. *Industrial Management & Data Systems*, 116(9), 1849–1864.

Nunkoo, R., & Gursoy, D. (2012). Residents' support for tourism: An identity perspective. *Annals of Tourism Research*, 39(1), 243–268.

Nunkoo, R., & Ramkissoon, H. (2010). Small island urban tourism: A residents' perspective. *Current Issues in Tourism*, 13(1), 37–60.

Nunkoo, R., & Ramkissoon, H. (2012). Power, trust, social exchange and community support. *Annals of Tourism Research*, 39(2), 997–1023.

Ouyang, Z., Gursoy, D., & Sharma, B. (2017). Role of trust, emotions and event attachment on residents' attitudes toward tourism. *Tourism Management*, 63(Dec), 426–438.

Petrzelka, P., Krannich, R.S., & Brehm, J.M. (2006). Identification with resource-based occupations and desire for tourism: Are the two necessarily inconsistent? *Society and Natural Resources, 19*(8), 693–707.

Potwarka, L. R., & Banyai, M. (2016). Autonomous agents and destination image formation of an Olympic Host city: The case of Sochi 2014. *Journal of Hospitality Marketing & Management, 25*(2), 238–258.

Prange, C., & Pinho, J.C. (2017). How personal and organizational drivers impact on SME international performance: The mediating role of organizational innovation. *International Business Review, 26*(6), 1114–1123.

Ringle, C.M., & Sarstedt, M. (2016). Gain more insight from your PLS-SEM results: The importance-performance map analysis. *Industrial Management & Data Systems, 116*(9), 1865–1886.

Sharma, B., & Gursoy, D. (2015). An examination of changes in residents' perceptions of tourism impacts over time: The impact of residents' socio-demographic characteristics. *Asia Pacific Journal of Tourism Research, 20*(12), 1332–1352.

Sharma, B., Dyer, P., Carter, J., & Gursoy, D. (2008). Exploring residents' perceptions of the social impacts of tourism on the Sunshine Coast, Australia. *International Journal of Hospitality and Tourism Administration, 9*(3), 288–311.

Shumaker, S.A., & Taylor, R.B. (1983). Toward a clarification of people-place relationships: A model of attachment to place. *Environmental Psychology: Directions and Perspectives, 2*, 19–25.

Sirakaya, E., Teye, V., & Sönmez, S. (2002). Understanding residents' support for tourism development in the central region of Ghana. *Journal of Travel Research, 41*(1), 57–67.

Sperling, M.B., & Berman, W.H. (Eds.). (1994). *Attachment in adults: Clinical and developmental perspectives*. New York: Guilford Press.

Stone, M. (1974). Cross-validatory choice and assessment of statistical predictions. *Journal of the Royal Statistical Society, 36*(2), 111–147.

Stylidis, D., & Terzidou, M. (2014). Tourism and the economic crisis in Kavala, Greece. *Annals of Tourism Research, 44*, 210–226.

Stylidis, D., Biran, A., Sit, J., & Szivas, E.M. (2014). Residents' support for tourism development: The role of residents' place image and perceived tourism impacts. *Tourism Management, 45*, 260–274.

Tenenhaus, M., Amato, S., & Esposito Vinzi, V. (2004). A global goodness-of-fit index for PLS structural equation modelling. *Proceedings of the XLII SIS Scientific Meeting, 1*(Jun), 739–742.

Twigger-Ross, C.L., Bonaiuto, M., & Breakwell, G. (2003). Identity theories and environmental psychology. In M. Bonnes, T. Lee, & M. Bonaiuto (Eds.), *Psychological theories for environmental issues* (pp. 203–233). Aldershot: Ashgate.

Twining-Ward, L., & Butler, R. (2002). Implementing STD on a small island: Development and use of sustainable tourism development indicators in Samoa. *Journal of Sustainable Tourism, 10*(5), 363–387.

Vargas-Sanchez, A., Porras-Bueno, N., & de los Ángeles Plaza-Mejía, M. (2011). Explaining residents' attitudes to tourism: Is a universal model possible? *Annals of Tourism Research, 38*(2), 460–480.

Wang, S., & Xu, H. (2015). Influence of place-based senses of distinctiveness, continuity, self-esteem and self-efficacy on residents' attitudes toward tourism. *Tourism Management*, 47(Apr), 241–250.

Wetzels, M., Odekerken-Schröder, G., & Van Oppen, C. (2009). Using PLS path modeling for assessing hierarchical construct models: Guidelines and empirical illustration. *MIS Quarterly*, 33(1), 177–195.

Yolal, M., Çetinel, F., & Uysal, M. (2009, November). An examination of festival motivation and perceived benefits relationship: Eskişehir International Festival. *Journal of Convention & Event Tourism*, 10(4), 276–291.

Part IV

Destination brand management

11 Rethinking the nexus of TV series/movies and destination image

Changing perceptions through sensorial cues and authentic identity of a city

Tuğra Nazlı Akarsu, Pantea Foroudi, and T C Melewar

Learning outcomes

At the end of this chapter, readers should be able to:

1. Assess the opportunities for positive destination image formation
2. Identify opportunities arising from TV series/movies for destination-marketing organizations (DMOs) and policy-makers
3. Evaluate alternative strategic approaches for destination image formation by implementing TV series/movies, and authentic identity of a city
4. Identify different stages needed to create a positive destination image leading tourist and potential tourist on positive behavioral outcome.

Introduction

Considering film-induced industry has an undeniable effect on place branding, this chapter aims to give a wider perspective of the formation of destination image through visual media, TV serials and films, where it leads tourist to have positive behavioral outcomes and contribute to the phenomenon by adding new insights such as the authentic identity of a city and sensorial cues of TV serials/movies such as visual and audial cues. The proposed structure of the highlighted relations is developed through the scrutiny of the literature by the theoretical and exemplary cases from the practitioners. To establish the given concepts, this chapter aims to contribute to the knowledge on film-induced industry as well as add new perspectives to the debates on the potential inclusion of TV series and city-oriented films into tourism investments in destination-marketing organizations (DMOs) and policy-makers.

Background

The undeniable effect of films, TV serials, and visual media on tourism, especially on destination image are recognized and urged practitioners to recognize it as "film-induced tourism" (Kantarci et al., 2017; Koksal & Gjana, 2014). The inevitable influence of visual media, TV serials and films on the formation of positive destination image has been appreciated and advocated that "film-induced tourism is a specific pattern of tourism that attracts visitors to visit screened places during or after films or television productions" (Roesch, 2009, p. 6). Yet, the influence of TV series and films on behavioral outcomes such as actual visit or visit intention to the particular filmed destinations are prioritized (Beeton, 2010; Frost, 2006), including the positive perception regarding where the series has been filmed (Kim et al., 2007; Lee & Bai, 2016), pertinent literature has not been fully explored the wider connections regarding the antecedents and the consequences of attitude towards TV serials or films from a wider perspective (Connell, 2012).

According to Connell (2012), "… conceptualizing film tourism must go well beyond the basic premise that a tangential visual stimulus creates interest in visiting a particular destination as seen on the large or small screen" (p. 1012). For example, it has been advocated that combining the visual representation of a landscape with audial cues such as music can yield one to "express what is otherwise inexpressible" (Lefebvre, 2006, p. 12). Research on sensorial marketing asserting that using distinctive sensorial cues (i.e., visual, olfactory, taste, aural, and touch) can yield positive brand image perception on consumers, where it provides a competitive advantage to a brand against its competitors, especially in the retail context (Aziz et al., 2012). As such, research identifies the influence of music on consumer's product evaluation and positive behavioral intention (Grewal et al., 2003). Even though the value of stimulating consumers' senses has long been recognized in consumer behavior, despite the convenience of using TV series as changing potential tourists' perceptions by stimulating their audial or visual senses remained limited in the tourism discipline. As the key point of using media sources in the competitive tourism industry is influencing potential tourists' perceptions to lead them an actual visit, where "the key to robust perception is the combination and integration of multiple sources of sensory (i.e. taste, smell, touch, hearing, and sight) information" (Ernst & Bulthoff, 2004, p. 162).

The concept of "identity" is one more complexity, where it has been widely discussed and altered in the context of tourism (Dixon & Durheim, 2000; Foroudi et al., 2018). It has been argued that the film-induced industry is not just the facile desire to motivation or behavioral intention to visit the filmed place (Connell, 2012) but the tension of forming their sense of the place or a quest for an "authentic place identity", where authenticity. Authenticity often associated with the interpretation of the national identity as it is being projected by the identity of the place (Richardson & Fluker, 2007). Yet, the existence of "authentic identity" is not new and deeply embedded in the context of tourism as well as film-induced tourism; it can be worthwhile to understand the notion of authentic identity of a place in a broader context.

Changing perceptions through sensorial cues and the authentic identity of a city

This chapter, therefore, addresses different perspectives of destination image, motivation to travel, the familiarity of a destination through sensorial cues, and authentic identity of a city in TV series/movies. Therefore, this chapter aims to investigate the linkage between sensorial cues, attitude towards TV series/movies, the authentic identity of a city and its influence on consumers' attitudes, and consumers' behavioral outcomes. In doing so, the chapter contributes to the knowledge on film-induced tourism by adding sensorial cues and authentic identity of a city on consumers' attitude towards TV series, and their destination motivation, familiarity, and image formation as well as their satisfaction and intention to visit as behavioral outcomes and to the debates on the potential inclusion of TV series and city-oriented films into tourism investments in DMOs and policy-makers.

Why do sensorial cues and authentic identity matter?

It has been a known fact that the demand in tourism has shifted from 3S, *namely, sun, sand, and sea* to 4H, which is *habitat, heritage, history, and handicrafts* (Kruczek, 2014). With the changing trends in tourism, the tools of promoting the destinations as well as the features of the destinations have been transformed and had to be altered due to the changing demands. Since cinema is being considered as the "most important cultural form" (Shiel, & Fitzmaurice, (2003), p. 1), "tourism marketers must carefully review all aspects of movie/TV productions including target audience, storyline, and image of a location being featured in the program, since all these factors are interrelated" (Spears et al., 2012, p. 54).

The focus on audial and visual cues as well as the authentic identity of a place in film-induced tourism industry can be seen as crucial as the visual representations of the historical places, landscapes, the sightseeing can be named as the authentic identities of a city where seen in TV series/movies can enhance the familiarity of the destination, motivate potential tourists to travel the particular destination, influence the perception destination image, and subsequently lead potential tourists to have an actual visitation (Shakeela & Weaver, 2013), which is not yet fully recognized by the tourism industry. Considering the interrelatedness of film-induced industry/tourism with different disciplines such as geography, social sciences, media, and visual arts (Kucharska, 2014), it can be worthwhile to have a holistic approach to a worldwide phenomenon rather than a single approach.

Audial and visual cues of TV series/movies

Before visiting particular destinations, potential tourists are looking for a communication cue to see whether this particular destination that they intend to visit fits their travel desires (Ye & Tussyadiah, 2011). The importance of utilization visual cues has often been emphasized to change the perception of a particular destination and motivates tourists to visit the particular destination (Ye & Tussyadiah, 2011), as contented "photographic images organise our anticipation or daydreaming about the places we might gaze on" (Urry, 1990, p. 140). As a result of pictorial advertising research highlighted, visual stimuli affect attitudes towards products as visual stimuli enable them to recall pictorial advertising (Ye & Tussyadiah, 2011). When it comes to the tourism industry, it should be noted that the tourism industry has often associated with the visuality (Anderson, 1995), where visual stimuli "act as signifiers to stimulate the imagination and to communicate with tourists in a personal way" (Ye & Tussyadiah, 2011, p. 129). Since "film-induced tourism is a specific pattern of tourism that attracts visitors to visit screened places during or after films or television productions" (Roesch, 2009, p. 6) rather conveying visual stimuli through pictorial advertising, researchers urged destination managers to locate visual stimuli via TV programs (Tasci, 2009).

One of the leading tourism authorities in this field can be given as United Kingdom's *Visit Britain*, where United Kingdom attempted to associate the positive influence of the screen with their promotional campaigns by starting their "movie maps" (Zemla & Zadawski, 2014). The streaming effect of Visit Britain's initial attempt, in 2004, the USA started to associate screen with tourism with its prominent TV campaign "you have seen the movies, now visit the set" (Connell, 2012). To give prominent examples, *the Braveheart*, its filming locations as well as its music it provides a big leap to Scotland by the time the film was released (Shakeela & Weaver, 2013). Another success story was *the Lord of the Rings*, are a prominent examples of the importance of using visual stimuli into the films, which are known to make a great leap by attracting international tourists to New Zealand tourism, particularly the destinations where the movie was filmed (Jones & Smith, 2005; Shakeela & Weaver, 2013). According to Connell (2012), the practitioners' success stories are not limited with these cases where *Notting Hill* (Busby & Klug, 2001), *Downtown Abbey, Sense and Sensibility, Pride and Prejudice* (Sargent, 1998) are other prominent examples of how audial and visual cues can influence the destination image and behavioral outcome of potential tourists.

As literature highlighted (Gomez-Ramirez et al., 2009; Shams et al., 2002) communication cues can influence consumers' level and type of response to a product or information about a product. As such, visual stimuli conveying through TV series can influence the tourists' attitude towards TV series. Even though the importance of utilizing visual stimuli in typical forms of advertising (e.g., print media, radio, television, and the Internet) has been recognized, yet, despite of the being potential primary source of tourism industry, the importance of visual cues and their effect on tourists' attitude towards TV series/movies and as a consequence, positive image formation and behavioral outcome has been somehow overlooked in the tourism industry.

In order to utilize different communication tools to influence tourists' behavior, Kim and Kerstetter (2016) take the argument further by suggesting that DMOs need to understand the importance of stimulating multiple senses as "combinations can influence consumers' level and type of response to a product or information about a product (Gomez-Ramirez et al., 2009; Shams et al., 2002), draw upon memories, encourage emotional response and contribute to a feeling of being present (Dinh et al., 1999)" (p. 52). When it comes to the tourism industry, one should be recognizing the value of stimulating multiple senses of tourists; however, there is a little effort put on researching the impact of utilizing multiple senses to communicate with tourists (Kim & Kerstetter, 2016)

"Tourism is an industry based on imagery, its overriding concern is to construct … an imagery that entices the outsider to place himself or herself into that symbol defined space" where image is formed through the "construction of a mental representation of a destination on the basis of information cues delivered by the image formation agents and selected by a person" (Tasci & Gartner, 2007, p. 414). The perception about a destination matters more than the reality about the particular destination (Shakeela & Weaver, 2013). Movies and TV series are the most prominent tools than any other source of information (Cohen, 1986). Additionally, TV series/dramas have become an increasingly important mechanism for positive destination image formation as they are considered as soft power to increase the destination awareness and leads individuals to have a stronger attitude about the particular destination (Hudson & Ritchie, 2006; Koksal & Gjana, 2014; O'Connor & Kim, 2011).

Even though it has been established a long time ago that image is "the whole of all sensory perceptions and thought interrelationships associated with an entity by one individual" (Enis, 1967, p. 51), the literature is addressing a critical gap in terms of the importance of multisensory communication on destination image formation. The only exceptional study can be considered Lee et al.'s (2010) study, revealing that sensorial cues have a positive effect on individuals' mental image formation, where it leads an individual to have a stronger attitude about this particular destination. While communicating with tourists through visual images is one of the most critical tools for DMOs, it also enables DMOs "… to stimulate the imagination and to communicate with tourists in a personal way" (Ye & Tussyadiah, 2011, p. 129). Therefore, audial and visual cues in the TV series can dramatically influence tourists/potential tourists to have a positive destination where TV series have been filmed.

The authentic identity of a city

Authentic places can be defined with their way of being genuine and reliable, whereas authentic identities of place "are usually efforts to claim for, and impose on, a demarcated space a bounded, often simplistic, set of unchanging meanings that define an identity for a place, in turn, are constituted by it" (Stevenson, 2013, p. 42). With increasing knowledge, evolving technology, and being aware of shifting trends, it has been often noted that tourists became more informed and smarter, where they are seeking experienced, uniqueness as well as the authenticity (André, 2011; Ram et al., 2016). In the pertinent literature, identity has been frequently associated with authenticity, however, authentic place identity has been first acknowledged by where its importance has been highlighted to attract tourists. (Judd, 1995)

Even though the importance of the authentic identity of a place, as being an essential asset, where it "projects the true identity of the destination" (Richardson & Fluker, 2007, p. 82) and is a key trend in tourism for influencing on tourist motivation has been highlighted (European Travel Commission, 2006; Kolar & Zabkar, 2010; Ram et al., 2016) yet, previous research remains limited, merely as conceptual discussions. However, there are some important studies conducted in order to reveal the importance of authenticity on tourist behavior (Cohen, 1986; MacCannell, 1973), there is a need for a quest from scholars to understand the effective ways to deliver authenticity to motivate tourists and influence them to be familiar of a destination, where there is a fierce competition in the tourism industry (André, 2011; Kolar & Zabkar, 2010).

It is vital to comprehend that tourism differs from other fields where there is a need for a "'multi-sensual' understanding of place, and in this case, of narrative" (Waysdorf & Reijnders, 2017, p. 178). In this sense, delivering an emotional experience and leading tourists to have an attachment with this particular place, it becomes more and more important to deliver a narrative of the location to make tourists aware of a destination and create a connection towards the destination. Following this argument, it is worthwhile to mention that authentic identity is being considered as a focal concept for the positive image formation of a destination. Even though the term authentic identity has been defined in several ways depending upon the context that scholars have been empirically studied (MacCannell, 1973; Olsen, 2007; Urry, 1990), it has been associated with terms of "value" "a motivational force" and "a perception" (Cohen, 1986; Kolar & Zabkar, 2010).

How authentic identity of a city and sensorial cues can influence destination image formation? Istanbul, Turkey case

Rather than conceptualizing the importance of authentic identity and sensorial cues on destination image formation and tourist behavior here, it is worthwhile to explain the highlighted concepts on Istanbul, Turkey case where it is considered as an exemplary case in film-induced tourism and its potential effects on destination image formation and tourist behavior. Given the Istanbul case, the importance of visually representation authentic identity of a city has been coincidentally recognized by the tourism managers and destination marketers, when a Turkish TV series, Noor's finale has got 85 million views from the Middle East and Gulf region, the broadcasting company had forced by Middle Eastern tourists to turn the villa on the Bosphorus, where the TV series was filmed (Balli et al., 2013; Farah al-Sweel, 2008; Sobecki, 2010). Turkey's success of exporting its TV series to the Middle Eastern and Eastern Europe and contributing significant tourism revenue due to the success of ratings of Turkish TV series in other countries can be the most prominent example established over the last decade (Anadolu Agency, 2017; Balli et al., 2013). According to Turkish Exporters Assembly's (TIM) data, the export of Turkish TV series was substantially increased from $10.000 to $100 million from 2004 to 2012, where it is being expected to reach $1 billion by 2023, according to the head of Radio and Television Broadcast Society (Marketing Turkiye, 2017). With a big leap by not only the Middle East and Eastern Europe, but Turkish TV series has also reached a wide range of audience all over the world, where it has been exported to 80 countries with a value of $200 million in export (Deloitte, 2014)

The impact of TV series on actual visitation is striking: according to Skyscanner, a global search engine for travel research, there is a positive relationship between foreign TV series and flight searches to the destination seen on the TV series. It is not a surprise that when the series has been shot at touristic attractions, the relationship becomes even stronger (Deloitte, 2014). In the light of the applicability of this research, Deloitte (2014) revealed in their report "World's most colourful screen: TV series sector in Turkey", that compared to 2011, flight search to Turkey increased %100 from Kuwait, Qatar, Jordan, Yemen and Lebanon; and nearly increased %200 from Bahrain and Saudi Arabia, when the export of TV series to these particular regions reached to $60 million with more than 100 TV series (Oxford Business Group, 2012) What is surprising is that tourists coming to Gulf and Middle East region are willing to pay more to see the places where these TV series are shot when they come to Istanbul, according to Arab Travel Agencies and Tourism Development Association (ASATDER) (Anadolu Agency, 2017; Daily News, 2014).

This case may unveil a potential opportunity which has never been empirically studied by investigating the effect of visual and audial cues

216 Tuğra Nazlı Akarsu et al.

on the tourists' attitude towards TV series, its effect on motivation, familiarity and destination image, where authentic identity of the city as being moderator, which in turn lead tourist to have a satisfaction and intention to visit the particular destination as the behavioral outcome.

Theoretical background

Tourist motivation theory

The notion of travel motivation has its roots in different schools of thought such as psychology, anthropology, and sociology (Cohen, 1972; Crompton, 1979). Motivation refers to "a dynamic process of internal psychological factors (needs, wants, and goals) that generate an uncomfortable level of tension within an individual's minds and bodies" (Fodness, 1994, p. 2). To release the uncomfortable level of tension, individuals try to release the tension and satisfy their needs. Maslow's hierarchical theory of motivation can be considered as one of the most cited and frequently used to explain the tourist motivation in the tourism literature, as travel motivation is one of the most important psychological premises to explain tourist behavior (March & Woodside, 2005; Van Vuuren & Slabbert, 2011). Tourists seek to release mental and physical tension (Fodness, 1994; Van Vuuren & Slabbert, 2011).

One of the early works conducted by Crompton (1979) revealed the seven socio-psychological and cultural driven forces that motivate tourists to travel (Snepenger et al., 2006; Van Vuuren & Slabbert, 2011) which are "escape from an everyday environment, discovery and evaluation of oneself, relaxing or participation in recreational activities, gaining a certain level of prestige, for the purpose of regression, strengthening family ties and facilitating their level of social interaction" (Van Vuuren & Slabbert, 2011, p. 296).

In recent years, Jamal and Lee (2003) conducted a study to investigate the micro and macro factors that influence tourist motivations. According to Jamal and Lee (2003), macro factors are referring to the social forces that motivate tourist to travel, whereas micro factors refer to the internal forces such as the need to escape. The interesting outcome that this study has revealed that the "search for authenticity" has been identified as a micro factor that motivates a tourist to travel where it stems from the idea that "the modern world has left people with a sense of experiences that are phony and relationships that are disconnected" (Snepenger et al., 2006, p. 141). Even though there is an abundance of research conducted on travel motivation and tourist behavior, there is very few research on the antecedents and the motivational factors that motivate tourists to travel by using means-end theory (Snepenger et al., 2006; Van Vuuren & Slabbert, 2011). Hence, this chapter urges scholars to utilize tourist motivation theory to investigate the effects of visual and audial cues on attitudes towards TV series; the effect authentic identities of a city where seen in TV series on the relationship between attitudes towards TV series, the familiarity of the destination and motivation of tourists to travel the particular destination, influence the perception destination image and may lead potential tourists to have an actual visitation.

Motivation, familiarity, and destination image

Tourist motivation is an internal force originated from the tourist need that can construct their perceptions about the destination and lead to their specific behavior (Pratminingsih et al., 2014). It has been often noted that motivation plays an important part in grasping the tourist decision-making process (Jang & Feng, 2007; Nowacki, 2009; Pratminingsih et al., 2014). Tourist motivation deliberated to be the principal driver concerning the tourist behavior, where there is a strong link between the needs of the tourists and their motivations (Lee & Gross, 2010; Nowacki, 2009; Pratminingsih et al., 2014; Snepenger et al., 2006). Therefore, the motivation of the tourist is one of the key concepts for their traveling behavior. Destination familiarity in the tourism literature can be defined as the preliminary phase of destination knowledge consisted of the amount of information gathered by the tourists (Gursoy & Mccleary, 2004; Jani & Nguni, 2016).

Familiarity can be defined as the understanding or an ability to evaluate the quality of the product or a brand that can impact the perceptions that an individual holds about the company (Herrera & Blanco, 2011). Destination image is a concept that an individual grasp about a particular tourism destination consisted of the combination of feelings, perceptions, beliefs, and knowledge. It combines behavioral, affective and cognitive aspects as well as exhibits a multifaceted phenomenon (Foroudi et al., 2018; Pike & Ryan, 2004). Authors (Beerli & Martín, 2004; Chen & Tsai, 2007; Court & Lupton, 1997) suggested adopting the multi-attribute way to evaluate the image of the destination.

Satisfaction and intention to revisit

In the marketing literature, satisfaction refers to "the consumer's response to the evaluation of the perceived discrepancy between prior expectations and the actual performance of the product as perceived after its consumption" (Tse & Wilton, 1988, p. 204). Along with this definition, from tourism perspective satisfaction can refer to the responses of tourists to the evaluation of expectations from a particular destination and the actual pleasure and performance perceived from the destination (Foroudi et al., 2018). In the tourism literature, it has been acknowledged that satisfied tourists are more likely to have positive behavioral

intentions such as positive word of mouth, repeat visits or recommendation the destination others (Baker & Crompton, 2000; Yoon & Uysal,
2005). In the tourism literature, even though the repeat visitation, positive word of mouth, and recommendation has often established, the
research investing the influence of satisfaction on future behavioral intention has remained limited (Baker & Crompton, 2000; Cole & Illum,
2006)

According to Baker and Crompton (2000), "the primary motivation
among tourism providers for investing effort in evaluating and improving their quality of performance and seeking to enhance the level of
satisfaction, is that such improvements will result in increased visitation
and/or revenues" (p. 790). Therefore, it can be expected that the positive
destination image formed through TV series can increase potential tourist satisfaction, which can lead them to have an actual visit.

Future research directions

Drawing on the concept of "film-induced tourism" has become widely
established as a leading segment of tourism (Waysdorf & Reijnders,
2017) yet, the empirical evidence remained scarce regarding the utilization of authentic identity of a city as the destination and film-induced
tourism, where authentic identity seen in a TV series/movies can enhance the positive destination image formation, motivation to visit the
destination and familiarity of a destination, where it can help DMOs
to develop sustainable economic and social opportunities (Brass, 2005)
and reduce the problem of seasonality by promoting authentic identity
of a city in TV series (Hudson & Ritchie, 2006). As Moran (2006) highlighted the importance of the landscape as "sites of cinematic friction ...
form imaginary maps in the minds of viewers" (p. 225).

In spite of long recognition of film-induced tourism, to-date the literature remained limited in giving a holistic approach to the phenomenon where it is related to many different disciplines. When taking the
film-induced industry as a whole, one should take into account that as
much as the concepts are related with geography, social sciences, media
and visual arts, film-induced tourism is strongly related to stakeholders, policy-makers and governments. The current literature urges scholars to investigate the on-location and off-location film-induced tourism
(Zemla & Zawadzki, 2014) where the effects of two filmed places might
have different attributes on tourists' perceptions and behavioral outcomes. According to Roesch (2009), off-locations are the artificial locations where they build up for film purposes, whereas on-locations are
the authentic and natural environments appeared in the films. As this
distinct feature differences might be changed the authentic identity of a
place, it can be worthwhile to investigate more in-depth their effect on
tourists' perceptions. The idea can be tempting, since the current cases
of off-locations such as themed film parks where Universal Film Studios,

Warner Bros and Fox have, and deserted film sets such as Star Wars film set in Tunisian desert (Roesch, 2009) can attract tourists where they might have driven by different attributes or concepts.

Conclusion

This chapter aims to elaborate on how a long-term phenomenon, namely, as visual media, TV serials, and films are influenced the destination image formation, familiarity to the particular destination, motivation to travel and intention to visit. Even though the exemplary exists, there are several debates regarding whether it influences destination image, or visual media creates a disappointment on tourists about the displacement of the locations where the TV series are filmed and actual locations are two different places. This chapter put an effort to provide different cases to widen the concept of the film-induced industry to give a holistic approach to managers, DMOs and marketers.

Nonetheless, with portraying the authentic identity of a city, TV series are not only referring to the enhancing the positive perception of the destination image, but they also create a positive portrayal to the potential tourists and travelers, which lead them to be more familiar and motivate to visit the particular destination.

Key terms and definitions – Definitions for the key constructs

The authentic identity of a city: Authentic identity of a city projects the true identity of the destination, where it considered an essential asset of a place (Richardson & Fluker, 2007, p. 82).

Destination image: Destination image is a concept that an individual grasp about a particular tourism destination consisted of the combination of feelings, perceptions, beliefs, and knowledge. It combines behavioral, affective and cognitive aspects, as well as exhibits a multifaceted phenomenon (Foroudi et al., 2018; Pike & Ryan, 2004).

Tourist motivation theory: Motivation refers to "a dynamic process of internal psychological factors (needs, wants and goals) that generate an uncomfortable level of tension within individual's minds and bodies" (Fodness, 1994, p. 2). To release the uncomfortable level of tension, individuals try to release the tension and satisfy their needs. Maslow's hierarchical theory of motivation can be considered as one of the most cited and frequently used to explain the tourist motivation in the tourism literature, as travel motivation is one of the most important psychological premises to explain tourist behavior (March & Woodside, 2005; Van Vuuren & Slabbert, 2011).

Tourist motivation: Tourist motivation is an internal force originated from the tourist need that can construct their perceptions about the destination and lead to their specific behavior (Pratminingsih et al.,

2014). It has been often noted that motivation plays an important part in grasping the tourist decision-making process (Jang & Feng, 2007; Nowacki, 2009; Pratminingsih et al., 2014).

Tourist familiarity: Familiarity can be defined as the understanding or an ability to evaluate the quality of the product or a brand that can impact the perceptions that an individual holds about the company (Herrera & Blanco, 2011).

Satisfaction: Satisfaction refers to "the consumer's response to the evaluation of the perceived discrepancy between prior expectations and the actual performance of the product as perceived after its consumption" (Tse & Wilton, 1988, p. 204).

References

Anadolu Agency. (2017). *Turkish TV series inspire Arab tourists to vacation in Turkey*. Retrieved from: www.dailysabah.com/tourism/2017/07/06/turkish-tv-series-inspire-arab-tourists-to-vacation-in-turkey

Anderson, J. (1995). *Cognitive psychology and its implications* (4th ed.). New York: W. H. Freeman.

André, M. (2011). *Tourism and identity.* Paper presented at the Centre Maurits Coppieters, Brussels, 2011, Vol. 1, pp. 1–29.

Aziz, N., Kefallonitis E., & Barry F. (2012). Turkey as a destination brand: Perceptions of United States visitors. *American International Journal of Contemporary Research*, 2(9), 211–221.

Baker, D. A., & Crompton, J. L. (2000). Quality, satisfaction and behavioral intentions. *Annals of Tourism Research*, 27(3), 785–804.

Balli, F., Balli, H. O., & Cebeci, K. (2013). Impacts of exported Turkish soap operas and visa-free entry on inbound tourism to turkey. *Tourism Management*, 37, 186–192.

Beerli, A., & Martín, J. D. (2004). Factors influencing destination image. *Annals of Tourism Research*, 31(3), 657–681.

Beeton, S. (2010). The advance of film tourism. *Tourism and Hospitality Planning & Development*, 7(1), 1–6.

Brass, D. (2005). *The futures foundation: Changing lives.* Paper presented at the Futures Foundation: Changing Lives Conference, 7th December 2005.

Busby, G., & Klug, J. (2001). Movie-induced tourism: The challenge of measurement and other issues. *Journal of Vacation Marketing*, 7(4), 316–332.

Chen, C., & Tsai, D. (2007). How destination image and evaluative factors affect behavioral intentions? *Tourism Management*, 28(4), 1115–1122.

Cohen, E. (1972). Toward a sociology of international tourism. *Social Research*, 164–182.

Cohen, J. (1986). *Promotion of overseas tourism through media fiction.* Coral Gables, FL: Academy of Marketing Science, University of Miami.

Cole, S. T., & Illum, S. F. (2006). Examining the mediating role of festival visitors' satisfaction in the relationship between service quality and behavioral intentions. *Journal of Vacation Marketing*, 12(2), 160–173.

Connell, J. (2012). Film tourism: Evolution, progress and prospects. *Tourism Management*, 33(5), 1007–1029.

Court, B., & Lupton, R. A. (1997). Customer portfolio development: Modeling destination adopters, inactives, and rejecters. *Journal of Travel Research*, 36(1), 35–43.

Crompton, J. L. (1979). Motivations for pleasure vacation. *Annals of Tourism Research*, 6(4), 408–424.

Daily News. (2014). *Turkey world's second highest TV series exporter after US.* Retrieved from: http://www.hurriyetdailynews.com/turkey-worlds-second-highest-tv-series-exporter-after-us-73478

Deloitte. (2014). *World's most colorful screen TV series sector in Turkey.* Deloitte Turkey.

Dixon, J., & Durrheim, K. (2000). Displacing place-identity: A discursive approach to locating self and other. *British Journal of Social Psychology*, 39(1), 27–44.

Enis, B. M. (1967). An analytical approach to the concept of image. *California Management Review*, 9(4), 51–58.

Ernst, M. O., & Bulthoff, H. (2004). Merging the senses into a robust percept. *Trends in Cognitive Sciences*, 8(4), 162–169.

European Travel Commission. (2006). *Tourism trends for Europe.* London, UK: European Travel Commission. Retrieved from: www.hospitalitynet.org/file/152002793.pdf

Farah al-Sweel. (2008). *Turkish soap opera flop takes Arab world by storm.* Reuters. Retrieved from: https://uk.reuters.com/article/uk-saudi-soapopera/turkish-soap-opera-flop-takes-arab-world-by-storm-idUKL633715120080726

Fodness, D. (1994). Measuring tourist motivation. *Annals of Tourism Research*, 21(3), 555–581.

Foroudi, P., Akarsu, T. N., Ageeva, E., Foroudi, M. M., Dennis, C., & Melewar, T. C. (2018). PROMISING THE DREAM: Changing destination image of London through the effect of website place. *Journal of Business Research*, 83(February), 97–110.

Frost, W. (2006). Braveheart-ed Ned Kelly: Historic films, heritage tourism and destination image. *Tourism Management*, 27(2), 247–254.

Gomez-Ramirez, M., Kelly, S. P., Montesi, J. L., & Foxe, J. J. (2009). The effects of L-theanine on alpha-band oscillatory brain activity during a visuo-spatial attention task. *Brain Topography*, 22(1, June), 44–51.

Grewal, D., Baker, J., Levy, M., & Voss, G. B. (2003). The effects of wait expectations and store atmosphere evaluations on patronage intentions in service-intensive retail stores. *Journal of Retailing*, 79(4), 259–268.

Gursoy, D., & Mccleary, K. (2004). An integrative model of tourists' information search behavior. *Annals of Tourism Research*, 31, 353–373.

Herrera, C., & Blanco, C. (2011). Consequences of consumer trust in PDO food products: The role of familiarity. *Journal of Product & Brand Management*, 20(4), 282–296.

Hudson, S., & Ritchie, J. R. B. (2006). Promoting destinations via film tourism: An empirical identification of supporting marketing initiatives. *Journal of Travel Research*, 44(4), 387–396.

Jamal, T., & Lee, J. (2003). Integrating micro and macro approaches to tourist motivations: Toward an interdisciplinary theory. *Tourism Analysis*, 8(1) 47–59.

Jang, S. C., & Feng, R. M. (2007). Temporal destination revisit intention: The effects of novelty seeking and satisfaction. *Tourism Management*, 28(2), 580–590.

Jani, D., & Nguni, W. (2016). *Pre-trip vs. post-trip destination image variations: A case of inbound tourists to Tanzania (No. 64)*. Institut za turizam. Retrieved from https://hrcak.srce.hr/154830

Jones, D., & Smith, K. (2005). Middle-earth meets New Zealand: Authenticity and location in the making of the Lord of the Rings. *Journal of Management Studies*, 42(5), 923–945.

Judd, D. R. (1995). Promoting tourism in US cities. *Tourism Management*, 16(3), 175–187.

Kantarci, K., Başaran, M. A., & Özyurt, P. M. (2017). Understanding the impact of Turkish TV series on inbound tourists: A case of Saudi Arabia and Bulgaria. *Tourism Economics*, 23(3), 712–716.

Kim, J., & Kerstetter, D. L. (2016). Multisensory processing impacts on destination image and willingness to visit. *International Journal of Tourism Research*, 18(1), 52–61.

Kim, S. S., Agrusa, J., Lee, H., & Chon, K. (2007). Effects of Korean television dramas on the flow of Japanese tourists. *Tourism Management*, 28(5), 1340–1353.

Koksal, Y., & Gjana, N. I. (2014). Soap opera effect on product preferences in terms of country image: A case of Turkish TV serials in Albanian market. *Journal of Economic and Social Studies*, 5(1), 219–238.

Kolar, T., & Zabkar, V. (2010). A consumer-based model of authenticity: An oxymoron or the foundation of cultural heritage marketing? *Tourism Management*, 31(5), 652–664.

Kruczek, Z. (2014).Tour management and tourist guidance in Poland deregulation and new challenges. *Economic Problems of Tourism*, 4(28), 119–133.

Kucharska, S. (2014). Museum! Camera! Action!: Using film-induced tourism to promote museums and their resources. *The International Journal of the Inclusive Museum*, 6(4), 33–41.

Lee, H. C., & Gross, M. J. (2010). *Representations of Australia's tourism destination image: Regional differences in narration themes and topics by Korean travel agents in Australia*. Paper presented at the New Zealand Tourism and Hospitality Research Conference 2010. Retrieved from: https://trove.nla.gov.au/version/223359090

Lee, J., Hsu, L., Han, H., & Kim, Y. (2010). Understanding how consumers view green hotels: How a hotel's green image can influence behavioural intentions. *Journal of Sustainable Tourism*, 18(7), 901–914.

Lee, S., & Bai, B. (2016). Influence of popular culture on special interest tourists' destination image. *Tourism Management*, 52, 161–169.

Lefebvre, M. (2006). *Landscape and film*. New York: Routledge.

MacCannell, D. (1973). Staged authenticity: Arrangements of social space in tourist settings. *American Journal of Sociology*, 79(3), 589–603.

March, R., & Woodside, A. G. (2005). *Tourism behaviour: Travelers' decisions and actions* Wallingford: CABI.

Marketing Turkiye. (2017). *Türk dizileri ihracatın buz kırıcısı*. Retrieved from: www.marketingturkiye.com.tr/soylesiler/turk-dizileri-ihracatin-buz-kiricisi/

Moran, A. (2006). Migrancy, tourism, settlement and rural cinema. In C. F. Helfield, & G. Helfield (Eds.), *Representing the rural: Space, place and identity in films about the land* (pp. 224–239). Detroit, MI: Wayne State University Press.

Nowacki, M. M. (2009). Quality of visitor attractions, satisfaction, benefits and behavioural intentions of visitors: Verification of a model. *International Journal of Tourism Research*, 11(3), 297–309.

O'Connor, N., & Kim, S. (2011). A cross-cultural study of screen-tourist's profiles. *WW Hospitality Tourism Themes*, 3(2), 141–158.

Olsen, K. (2007). Staged authenticity: Grande idée? *Tourism Recreation Research*, 32(2), 83–85.

Oxford Business Group. (2012). *The report: Turkey 2012*. Oxford Business Group. Retrieved from: https://oxfordbusinessgroup.com/turkey-2012

Pike, S., & Ryan, C. (2004). Destination positioning analysis through a comparison of cognitive, affective, and conative perceptions. *Journal of Travel Research*, 42(4), 333–342.

Pratminingsih, S. A., Rudatin, C. L., & Rimenta, T. (2014). Roles of motivation and destination image in predicting tourist revisit intention: A case of Bandung–Indonesia. *International Journal of Innovation, Management and Technology*, 5(1), 19–24.

Ram, Y., Björk, P., & Weidenfeld, A. (2016). Authenticity and place attachment of major visitor attractions. *Tourism Management*, 2(February), 110–122.

Richardson, J. I., & Fluker, M. (2007). *Understanding and managing tourism*. Frenchs Forest, Australia: Pearson Education.

Roesch, S. (2009). *The experiences of film location tourists (aspects of tourism)*. Bristol, UK: Channel View Publications.

Sargent, A. (1998). The Darcy effect: Regional tourism and costume drama. *International Journal of Heritage Studies*, 4(3–4), 177–186.

Shakeela, A., & Weaver, D. (2013). Attitudes of potential inbound visitors to the Maldives towards an anti-tourist incident. In J. Fountain, & K. Moore (Eds.), *CAUTHE 2013: Tourism and Global Change: On the edge of something big* (pp. 741–752). Christchurch, New Zealand: Lincoln University.

Shams, L., Kamitani, Y., & Shimojo, S. (2002). Visual illusion induced by sound. *Cognitive Brain Research*, 14(1), 147–152.

Shiel, M., & Fitzmaurice, T. (2003). *Cinema and the city: Film and urban societies in a global context*. Hoboken, NJ: John Wiley & Sons.

Snepenger, D., King, J., Marshall, E., & Uysal, M. (2006). Modeling iso-ahola's motivation theory in the tourism context. *Journal of Travel Research*, 45(2), 140–149.

Sobecki, N. (2010). International: Turkish delight soap opera Noor brings tourist boom to Istanbul. *The Guardian*. Retrieved from: https://search.proquest.com/docview/743877266

Spears, D., Josiam, B. M., Kinley, T., & Pookulangara, S. (2012). Tourist see tourist do: The influence of hollywood movies and television on tourism motivation and activity behavior. *Chaplin School of Hospitality Management's Hospitality Review*, 30(1), 53–75.

Stevenson, D. (2013). *Cities of culture: A global perspective*. London, UK: Taylor & Francis.

Tasci, A. D. A. (2009). Social distance: The missing link in the loop of movies, destination image, and tourist behavior? *Journal of Travel Research*, 47(4), 494–507.

Tasci, A. D. A., & Gartner, W. C. (2007). Destination image and its functional relationships. *Journal of Travel Research*, 45(4), 413–425.

Tse, D. K., & Wilton, P. C. (1988). Models of consumer satisfaction formation: An extension. *Journal of Marketing Research*, 25(2), 204–212.

Urry, J. (1990). *The tourist gaze: Leisure and travel in contemporary societies.* London, UK: Sage Publications.

Van Vuuren, C., & Slabbert, E. (2011). Travel behaviour of tourists to a South African holiday resort. *African Journal for Physical Health Education, Recreation and Dance*, 17(1), 694–707.

Waysdorf, A., & Reijnders, S. (2017). The role of imagination in the film tourist experience: The case of Game of Thrones. *Journal of Audience and Reception Studies*, 14(1), 170–191.

Ye, H., & Tussyadiah, I. P. (2011). Destination visual image and expectation of experiences. *Journal of Travel & Tourism Marketing*, 28(2), 129–144.

Yoon, Y., & Uysal, M. (2005). An examination of the effects of motivation and satisfaction on destination loyalty: A structural model. *Tourism Management*, 26(1), 45–56.

Zemla, M., & Zawadzki, P. (2014). Film-induced tourism: Basic relations between films and tourism from tourism destinations perspective. *Economic Problems of Tourism*, 28(4), 200–220.

12 Toward a country-branding framework

A comparative analysis

Vittoria Marino and Giada Mainolfi

Learning outcomes

At the end of this chapter, readers should be able to:

1 Understand the basic steps of a country-branding process.
2 Understand the knowledge gaps relative to the implementation modalities of the country-branding process.
3 Use the methodological skills required for the qualitative research needed to set up a plan for country brand management.
4 Acquire awareness of the importance of country brand management for every country as concerns the management and promotion of their national image.
5 Identify strategic guidelines for establishing a synergic content-creation process for the visual identity of the country.

Introduction

Each country evokes images, sounds, colors, and moods, sometimes all enclosed in a name and an architecture of values that – combined together – can express an extraordinary communicative power. This issue is acquiring a peculiar relevance due to a competition between countries more and more played on intangible dimensions also linked to conveyed images, called to ensure the attractiveness of the territory to external resources. Consequently, countries need to define marketing tools capable of supporting the country's competitive positioning in a clear and distinctive way. Country brand strategies become an indispensable tool for the enhancement of the reputational capital of a nation. Following this perspective, it is therefore necessary to identify a systemic process capable of stigmatizing the different phases characterize the design of the visual identity. This chapter analyzes the process of country brand management through the emergence of an interpretative model, which resulted from a careful analysis of empirical research of the qualitative type. Research design has been structured on procedural phases (reconnaissance phase, exploratory phase and interpretative synthesis phase) that, starting from the identification of the conceptual categories, led to the emergence of a theoretical framework capable of reconstructing the complexity of the phenomenon under investigation. The holistic approach adopted for the framework proposal contributes to promoting greater social cohesion that can also favor cross-fertilizations between the different sectors composing the identity of the country.

Research background

Country-branding plays a fundamental role in promoting a country and capturing the interest of international stakeholders. Nations feel the need to differentiate themselves from each other with a clever management of their nation brand which can help the various publics to evaluate the strategies, actions and activities that have been implemented. This process can be carried out through the use of branding strategies and techniques (Go & Govers, 2010). However, nations face serious difficulties in activating a systemic and well thought out management process of their national reputation capital (Marino & Mainolfi, 2011). This condition may have been also due to the absence – in the academic field – of a common conceptual matrix and a theoretical model capable of conferring scientific dignity to this topic. This study aims to widen the knowledge on country-branding processes by providing an advancement of conceptual and theoretical issues aimed at filling the scientific gaps regarding to the adoption of a country-branding strategy. Following this perspective, the purpose of the study is to identify a normative country-branding framework through the comparison of the most significant international country-branding experiences. The complexity of the issue under investigation necessitated the adoption of a research design structured on procedural phases.

The research was structured in three different phases, each of which had a precisely defined goal: (1) the reconnaissance phase, (2) the exploratory phase, and (3) the interpretive synthesis phase. The reconnaissance phase comprised a broad and detailed survey of the major constructs used in the literature, highlighting the boundaries of conceptualizations at the basis of the speculative research. The exploratory research was aimed at obtaining a comprehensive mapping of the most important country-branding experiences carried out by nations on an international level. This step was carried out through the analysis of the official documentation available online from the institutional websites of each country. This activity led to the reconstruction of actions, solutions and images through which countries under investigation decided to communicate the values at the basis of their competitive identity. The third phase was characterized by an interpretive synthesis of the phenomenon, obtained by comparing the empirical results with theoretical assumptions. In order to guide the analysis of the collected data toward the construction of a scientifically valid process of country-branding, each phase has been defined with a specific research question (Table 12.1).

Table 12.1 Phases and research questions

Phases of the qualitative research on country-branding	Research questions	Objectives
Phase I Reconnaissance research	What does "country-branding" mean?	Explain the antecedents of a series of structures and verify the consequences
Phase II Explorative research	What are the empirical activities that lead to country-branding?	Explore the first stages of a theory in the start-up phase
Phase III Interpretative synthesis and presentation of the results	How does the country-branding process emerge?	Explain the processes and mechanisms on which the relations between the variables of the phenomenon are based

Source: Our elaboration.

Reconnaissance phase (theoretical reference framework)

The reconnaissance phase aims at analyzing the concept of "country-branding," paying attention to the antecedents at the basis of its formation and to the consequences shaped by this kind of process on national identity. Thus, the reconnaissance research allowed us to define the theoretical framework of the study through the analysis of the empirical activities leading to country-branding. Starting from the definition of the main concept, the exploratory research was aimed at understanding, describing and defining the basic features of the phenomenon. The analysis of national and international literature made it possible to identify the contiguous research areas of country-branding. These areas provided fertile ground for supporting new interdisciplinary perspectives from which to develop an integrated and systemic proposal of the concept of country brand management. The reconnaissance research identified four scientific ambits that can be considered starting points for insights into country-branding management.

The first research area can be found in country-of-origin studies (Bertoli & Resciniti, 2013; De Nisco, 2006; De Nisco et al., 2012; Papadopoulos & Heslop, 2002). The most important studies on country-of-origin focus on the influence exerted by country image on the purchasing behavior of foreign customers (Bilkey & Nes, 1982; Han & Terpstra, 1988). The results obtained by the different authors have in common the fact that the quality of a product is often (re)built on the basis of perceptions formulated by the public in relation to the main fields of action of the country of origin. This is the case of product-country images (PCI), the effects of which are analyzed on end-consumers, industrial customers and retailers (Papadopoulos, 2004; Papadopoulos et al., 1988). Several studies have highlighted the link between the country-of-origin effect and country-branding because it is believed that the "made in" effect and the country image are two aspects of the wider phenomenon of branding, which is the external expression of country-branding (Lee, 2009). Some studies also go even further to evaluate the role that a strategic approach in the promotion of the country image can exert on the global attractiveness of the nation (Kotler & Gertner, 2002). The studies aimed at investigating the role of the country-of-brand are characterized by limited empirical evidence and, in most cases, the analysis is conducted solely on the basis of successful cases. Although the literature has drawn up many different models of interpretation aimed at illustrating the management of the country image (Fan, 2008b), studies agree on recognizing the absolute hegemony of global competition among those countries where the national well-being is defined in terms of competitive advantages. Within this context, country-branding is considered a strategic tool capable of contributing to the attractiveness of the country system in terms of attracting investment, trade, tourism and human capital. However, past studies do not arrive at an interpretative model capable of expanding the focus of investigation, too often directed to the promotion of specific economic interests: for example, export performances or attracting investments.

The second contiguous research area is related to destination marketing studies. Findings from this field of study have shown that destination image, considered in its various constituent elements, can determine the choice of a tourist destination (Kavaratzis, 2005; Kotler et al., 1993). Studies on destination image date back to the early seventies, when Hunt (1975) published one of the most important works on the role of country image for tourism development. In 1998, the first theories of branding applied to destination marketing appeared. Subsequent contributions interpret the national brand as the visual presence of the country, and it is associated with the opinions and wishes of the international public. The lack of methodological soundness, the exclusive recourse to secondary sources and convenience samples, and the absence of a shared terminology are some of the problems that emerged in most of the works on place branding. Such a condition has compromised the achievement of significant progress in the conceptual and theoretical development of "country-branding."

The third strand of research includes studies aimed at verifying the impact of national image on the participation of nations in the global system of international relations. Studies on "public diplomacy" (Fan, 2008a) are included in the studies on public relations and international relations. The management of a favorable international opinion has always been a commitment of public diplomacy, as an institutional image of traditional diplomacy. Public diplomacy relies on the process of communication activated by the government toward foreign audiences in order to inform them about ideals of the country, its institutions, culture, and objectives of national policy (Szondi, 2008). Several studies have tried to stigmatize the similarities and differences between conceptualizations of public diplomacy and country-branding. Some scholars consider public diplomacy and country-branding as two distinct concepts, but related to each other (Gilboa, 2008; Szondi, 2008). Another interpretation, however, considers them as equal, ascertaining that country-branding is the extension of the concept of public diplomacy to the economic and managerial area (Kaneva, 2011, p. 124).

A final research area is on national identity, and it refers to the theories on the relationship between culture, communication and society. Studies in this area differ from other areas in that they are not orientated to the development of a theory of country-branding that may favor – even from a practical point of view – strategic management. The goal is to adopt a critical perspective of the relations between country brand strategies and the national culture and identity (Aronczyk, 2008; Volcic & Andrejevic, 2011). So far studies have revealed the critical limitations produced by the nation brand on the range of narratives of national identity, often molded for the sole benefit of foreign publics (Roy, 2007).

From the literature reconnaissance it is clear that the four main areas agree on the need for the adoption of proper management of the country brand by the governing body of the nation. One problem, however, is that despite the apparent agreement in thinking, there have been no significant reciprocal interactions between the different areas of study. This situation can be considered one of the causes of the failure to achieve a comprehensive understanding of country brand construct and therefore the absence of an interpretation matrix of the phenomenon. Taking this as a starting point, a contribution is needed to fill the knowledge gap concerning the mechanisms underlying the strategies related to the formation and long-term maintenance of a coherent identity of the country brand.

Explorative research (the methodological construct)

The reconnaissance phase analyzed the contribution of theoretical studies for a correct understanding and interpretation of the conceptual categories related to the phenomenon of country-branding. The exploratory research then intended to align the theoretical analysis to an empirical approach of the phenomenon, aimed at verifying the activities potentially related to the country-branding process through the observation of the most relevant international experiences. Given the complexity of the phenomenon under study, we hypothesized a plan of selected sampling.

In the specific, we proceeded with the identification of macro-regional clusters following the logic of the features/types of countries and according to the weight they carry, as far as economy, tradition, culture and history are concerned, in the system of international relations. In each group, by means of the logic of saturation, we then included those countries characterized by a significant activity in country-branding activities, especially in terms of international visibility. Particular importance was attached to the information content of institutional websites (government, government agencies for tourism sector, agencies for direct foreign investments, etc.) and the international press. Each group, therefore, contains only those countries for which it has been possible to reconstruct, thanks to the data available, a study and analysis of the documents, and a certain number of activities, statements, items, and operations carried out prior to the process of country-branding (Table 12.2).

In order to make our exploratory research more complete, we checked every national and institutional site, along with numerous blogs and journalistic portals, all divided into five main categories (politics, economy, tourism, events and information). The map of the countries we analyzed is the arrival point of a research performed along two main lines of study. The first was a thorough exploration of the numerous institutional and non-institutional websites run by government agencies, ministries, etc., as well as various private structures that supply staff and support for the specific countries (Table 12.3).

The second was an in-depth research into the leading scientific journals, consulted and classified according to the total number of articles published on place branding issues (Table 12.4). In many cases, the academic articles have been focused on the description of international experiences, therefore, contributing to the reconstruction of phases and processes related to country-branding strategies. The entire phase of data collection is based on the analysis of texts, images and audio-visual material aimed at creating an interpretive summary of the implemented activities. The desegregation of the contents and the

Table 12.2 Analysis of the territorial clusters

Territorial clusters	Countries
Europe	France, Spain, England, Germany, Italy, Greece
East Europe and the Balkans	Estonia, Poland, Hungary, Slovak Republic, Slovenia, Croatia, Serbia
BRIC	Brazil, Russia, India, China
CIVET	Colombia, Indonesia, Vietnam, Egypt, Turkey
Asia and the Middle East	Korea, Thailand, Taiwan, Singapore, Abu Dhabi, Dubai, Sharjah, Ras al Khaimah, United Emirate States, Japan
Australia and New Zealand	Australia
United States and Canada	USA, Canada
South America	Argentina, Chile, Mexico, Peru, Venezuela
Africa	Zimbabwe, Kenya, Nigeria, South Africa

Table 12.3 Analysis of the website categories

Type of website	Responsible body	Category
Institutional	Central governing authority	Politics
Institutional	Embassies	Politics
Institutional	Ministry of Commerce	Economy
Institutional	Ministry of Tourism	Economy
Institutional	Foreign investment agency	Economy
Institutional	National Board for Tourism	Tourism
Institutional	Associations for large event organization, e.g., Expo, FIFA World Cup, Olympics, etc.	Events
Private	National and foreign newspapers	Information
Private	Marketing and communication agency	Information
Private	International marketing agency	Information

Table 12.4 Classification of journals on place branding issues

Order	Journals	Number of articles consulted
1	*Place Branding and Public Diplomacy*	80
2	*Journal of Brand Management*	23
3	*Journal of Place Management and Development*	14
4	*Journal of Travel and Tourism Marketing*	5
5	*Journal of Business Research*	5
6	*Journal of Travel Research*	3
7	*Journal of Advertising Research*	3
8	*Journal of Product & Brand Management*	3
9	*Annals of Tourism Research*	2
10	*Corporate Reputation Review*	2
11	*European Journal of Marketing*	2
12	*Journal of Marketing Management*	2
13	*Journal of Public and International Affairs*	2
14	*Journal of Vacation Marketing*	2
15	*Australasian Marketing Journal*	1
16	*International Journal of Communication*	1
17	*International Journal of Culture, Tourism and Hospitality Research*	1
18	*Journal of Marketing*	1
19	*Management and Marketing*	1
20	*Urban Affairs Review*	1

comparison of the most significant experiences allowed us to identify a series of concepts and categories. In fact, the purpose of data collection was to provide an adequate representation of the phenomenon. The documents selected for the research underwent a textual analysis in order to identify main activities, assign meanings and methodology to their conduction, and finally reconstruct a map of international experiences of country-branding.

Interpretative synthesis (conceptual map)

Data collected during the exploratory phase were analyzed in the aim of reaching a first generalization of the most recurrent activities – performed on an international level – linked to the process of country-branding. At that point, it was used a deductive process from the reading of the documents and the reconstruction of notes and comments to highlight several actions that are recurrent in the description of the various international experiences. These activities take on the role of "concepts," still partly and poorly defined, but which permit an initial reconstruction of the decision-making processes undertaken by each country and, above all, a more precise definition of the emerging conceptual categories related to country-branding. Eight "concepts" emerged during the comparative analysis: (1) A group of technicians or experts, (2) A responsible authority, (3) A branding strategy to support the development of the country, (4) A strategy of destination branding, (5) The objective of country-branding, (6) The objective of destination branding, (7) The involvement of stakeholders, and (8) The values of the brand. Following this format, the countries were classified according to the presence or absence of a series of activities potentially related to each conceptual abstraction which led to the creation of a univocal and directional definition (Table 12.5).

The next step was to elaborate a further abstraction, considered necessary for the positioning of the "concepts" into categories capable of expressing the logical-deductive links and that could also encompass more of the previously defined elementary concepts. In this way, four conceptual categories emerged that are precise enough to isolate autonomous networks of relationships, even if inter-related. These relationships were analyzed by identifying the links between the categories and the type of relationship between them by developing the sub-categories based on the properties and dimensions of each category, and, finally, by creating a hierarchy, wherever possible, to allow the identification of the macro areas and their smaller categories. Data analysis made it possible to deduct a definition of the categories capable of covering the entire heterogeneous variety of the activities that emerged during the examination of documents.

The entire range of conceptual categories can, therefore, be summarized as follows: (1) *Working group*, which expresses the ability to attract and select the right professional and institutional talents and skills into the country-branding project; (2) *Strategic approach*, which synthesizes all the recognized activities and actions in order to strategically plan the development of the country through the implementation of country-branding; (3) *Mission*, which expresses, through the explicit declaration of its values and stakeholder engagement, the objectives pursued by the actions of country-branding; and (4) *Brand essence*, which includes the actions and activities related to a more precise definition of the brand name, the underlying project and the definition of its values (Table 12.6).

Table 12.5 The classification of countries according to the conceptual categories

Concept	Presence	Absence
Group of technicians or experts	Poland, Slovenia, Columbia, Australia, Mexico, South Africa	France, Spain, England, Germany, Italy, Greece, Estonia, Hungary, Slovac Republic, Croatia, Serbia, Brazil, Russia, India, China, Indonesia, Vietnam, Egypt, Turkey, Korea, Thailand, Taiwan, Singapore, Japan, Abu Dhabi, Dubai, Sharjah, USA, Canada, Argentina, Chile, Peru, Venezuela, Zimbabwe, Kenya, Nigeria
Responsible authority	France, Spain, England, Germany, Italy, Greece, Estonia, Hungary, Slovac Republic, Slovenia, Croatia, Serbia, Brazil, Russia, India, China, Columbia, Indonesia, Vietnam, Egypt, Turkey, Korea, Thailand, Taiwan, Singapore, Japan, Abu Dhabi, Dubai, Sharjah, USA, Canada, Australia, Argentina, Chile, Peru, Venezuela, Zimbabwe, Kenya, Nigeria, South Africa	–
Branding strategy in support of the development of the country	Germany, Estonia, Poland, Columbia, Dubai, Australia, Argentina, Chile, Mexico, Peru, South Africa	France, Spain, England, Italy, Greece, Hungary, Slovak Republic, Slovenia, Croatia, Serbia, Brazil, Russia, India, China, Indonesia, Vietnam, Egypt, Turkey, Korea, Thailand, Taiwan, Singapore, Japan, Abu Dhabi, Sharjah, USA, Canada, Venezuela, Zimbabwe, Kenya, Nigeria
Destination branding strategy	France Spain, England, Italy, Greece, Hungary, Slovak Republic, Slovenia, Croatia, Serbia, Brazil, Russia, India, China, Indonesia, Vietnam, Egypt, Turkey, Korea, Thailand, Taiwan, Singapore, Japan, Abu Dhabi, Sharjah, USA, Canada, Venezuela, Zimbabwe, Kenya, Nigeria	Estonia, Poland, Columbia, Dubai, Australia, Argentina, Chile, Mexico, Peru, South Africa

(*Continued*)

Concept	Presence	Absence
CBP objective	Germany, Estonia, Poland, Columbia, Dubai, Australia, Argentina, Chile, Mexico, Peru, South Africa	France, Spain, England, Italy, Greece, Hungary, Slovak Republic, Slovenia, Croatia, Serbia, Brazil, Russia, India, China, Indonesia, Vietnam, Egypt, Turkey, Korea, Thailand, Taiwan, Singapore, Japan, Abu Dhabi, Sharjah, USA, Canada, Venezuela, Zimbabwe, Kenya, Nigeria
Destination branding objective	France, Spain, England, Italy, Greece, Hungary, Slovak Republic, Slovenia, Croatia, Serbia, Brazil, Russia, India, China, Indonesia, Vietnam, Egypt, Turkey, Korea, Thailand, Taiwan, Singapore, Japan, Abu Dhabi, Sharjah, USA, Canada, Venezuela, Zimbabwe, Kenya, Nigeria	Estonia, Poland, Columbia, Dubai, Australia, Argentina, Chile, Mexico, Peru, South Africa
Stakeholder participation	France, Spain, England, Germany, Italy, Estonia, Brazil, Columbia, Korea, Thailand, Singapore, USA, Canada, Australia, Argentina, Chile, Mexico, Peru, Kenya, Nigeria, South Africa	Greece, Poland, Hungary, Slovak Republic, Slovenia, Croatia, Serbia, Russia, India, China, Indonesia, Vietnam, Egypt, Turkey, Taiwan, Japan, Abu Dhabi, Dubai, Sharjah, Venezuela, Zimbabwe
Brand values	France, Spain, England, Germany, Italy, Greece, Estonia, Poland, Hungary, Slovak Republic, Slovenia, Croatia, Serbia, Brazil, Russia, India, China, Columbia, Indonesia, Vietnam, Egypt, Turkey, Korea, Thailand, Taiwan, Singapore, Japan, Abu Dhabi, Dubai, Sharjah, USA, Canada, Australia, Argentina, Chile, Mexico, Peru, Venezuela, Zimbabwe, Kenya, Nigeria, South Africa	–

Source: Our elaboration.

Table 12.6 The definition of the conceptual categories

Concept	Category
Group of technicians or experts	Working group
Responsible authority	
Branding strategy in support of country development	Strategic approach of the process
Destination branding strategy	
Objective of the country-branding process	Mission of country brand
Objective of destination branding	
Engagement of stakeholders	
Brand values	Brand essence

These categories permit a continual expansion of their contents to include all the different branding activities that can be found in an emerging model for the analysis of the country-branding process aimed at the emergence of the competitive identity.

The proposal for a country-branding framework

The exploratory analysis of phenomena linked to country-branding has shown that many countries find it difficult to fully meet the requirements for a successful implementation of an integrated branding. Projects for a country brand have so far produced quite a varied and complex scenario in which the organs of government present varying degrees of awareness and accomplishment of the actions involved in nation branding. The investigation of this situation has allowed to isolate the most critical stages in the country-branding process, and the results were then integrated with the analysis of the world's best practices (South Africa and Australia), the only ones that can boast a strategic approach aimed at achieving a competitive global output. Too often we are in presence of country-branding projects that are not fully implemented, remaining in an embryonic stage because of the lack of interest or awareness of their potential economic, social and political impact. Moreover, where a greater focus on branding strategy was present, we find projects that are focused exclusively on the tourism sector, neglecting all the other national sectors. The privileged focus on tourism does not really justify the adoption of the term *country branding*, but is more specifically *destination branding*, that is, a strategy for the promotion of the national tourism industry. This situation, therefore, explains the presence of "concepts" devoted to a national tourism strategy within the proposed list (Table 12.6). It should be noted, however, that the whole process starts from the identification of a country vision, that is, the definition of a strategic approach for the management of country image that is capable of harmoniously and coherently integrating the specificities of each national sphere (social, economic, cultural, institutional and political), considered as strategic vectors.

If we then examine the individual categories, we can see how the working group and the strategic approach constitute a basis on which to implement the whole process of management of the country brand, and therefore, they can be considered the input for the process of country-branding. The definition of the mission and the brand essence, on the other hand, constitutes the scaffolding of the process, as they will shape the visual identity system of the country brand. The conceptual categories of mission and brand essence are useful in identifying the heart of construction process of the country brand (process) while the output of the process consists in defining the visual identity, aimed at achieving a competitive identity for the nation. For each phase of the framework (input, process, and output) we then identified the activities/actions to be implemented, managed and monitored in order to construct a country brand that is solid and consistent with the territorial identity of the country (Figure 12.1).

The antecedents of the country-branding process: the input phase

The first phase of the country-branding macro-process (input phase) is made up of two steps. The first is the constitution of the country brand team: namely, the *working group*, depositary of the strategic guidelines, which will assume the responsibility of the design, implementation and control of the entire process. The staff – as the result of a strong coalition

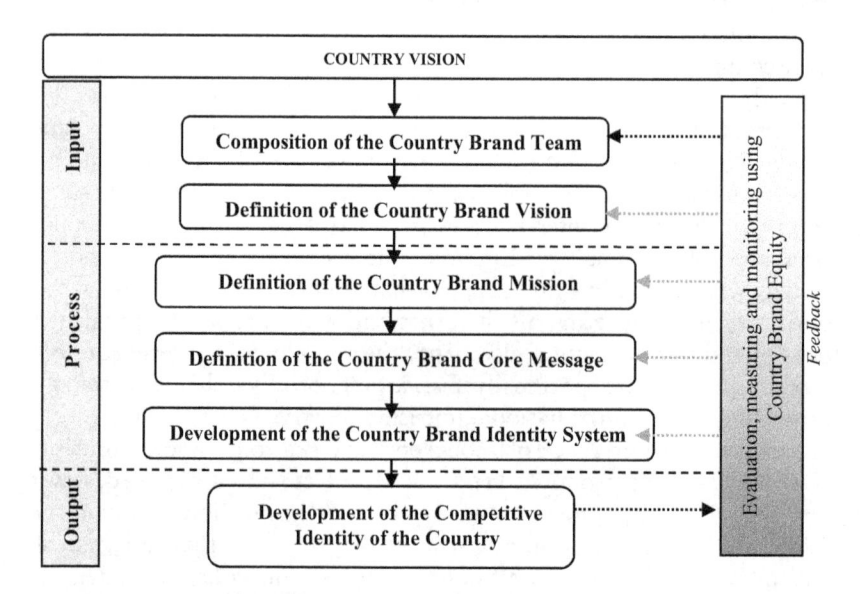

Figure 12.1 The country-branding framework.
Source: Our elaboration.

between the three main national areas (government, business and civil society) – will include experts, influential people and representatives of the national community, and act as a network hub that will be the central link for all communication activities regarding the country.

The second step is a period of evaluation, in which the country brand team must define the vision of the country-branding project. The identification of the guidelines of the entire country-branding project derives from the analysis of the current perceptions related to the three strategic vectors that inspired the philosophy of branding: the identity, the image and the reputation of the country. This phase is critical as it outlines the "core idea" of the whole project, materializing in the identification of the significant and distinctive features of the national identity. It is a phase in which the country investigates and dissects external and internal perceptions in relation to the essence of the national culture and identity.

The emergence of the country-branding process

The process of nation branding must move within the boundaries established by the vision identified by the organ of government concerning the most important national domains (economic, political-institutional, social and cultural). At this stage, the strategic analysis concerns the strategic positioning of the country in terms of external environment, internal resources and skills. This means conducting a kind of brand audit in order to identify the strengths and weaknesses of the brand, measured with respect to competition with other territories, and to influences exerted by target audiences, whose identification will have to be aligned with the emergence of the brand vision. Once the vision of the brand has been outlined, the team identifies the specific objective (goal statement) that will guide the country brand system (Lee, 2009). The emergence of the mission arises from an operation of specification of the strategic objectives set at national level. The country brand mission expresses the scope and the timing of the goals that the country brand team intends to achieve and that will direct the development of the whole strategy, summarized in two key elements: the core message and the country brand identity system that constitute the next steps of the process.

The purpose of the brand message is to deliver a new image of the country, capable of persuading the identity makers to modify the stereotypes that inhibit the full recognition of the real country identity. The most frequent errors, traced in several international experiences, regard the inability to agree on the criteria for determining what may, or may not, be appropriate and functional for the country image. The selection of the "core idea" of the project must be the result of an intensive collaboration between public and private actors, the expression of national interests involved in the activity of branding. The creation of a country brand team, as hypothesized in the framework, will facilitate the involvement of stakeholders in the phase of identification of the most representative values of national identity to be transferred to the core message.

Finding a country brand core message is the leitmotif for the communication plan chosen by the country to differentiate, symbolize and express itself in the eyes of the public of reference. In order to ensure maximum efficiency and effectiveness, it is essential to establish a visual identity system for the country brand (country brand identity system) thanks to which a transposition of the country core brand message is achieved in different communicational applications, in full respect of the strategy adopted in the mission phase. The identity system is built around all the main components of the brand that can be both tangible and intangible, functional or symbolic (De Chernatony & Riley, 1998). Specifically, the symbolic dimensions represent the immaterial plan that translates the levels of meaning of the brand (attributes, benefits, and values) in rhetorical elements to be narrated to the audience. The functional dimensions, on the other hand, constitute the visual presence of the brand of which the graphical representation of the name (country name) is the main component.

The definition of competitive identity: the output phase

The implementation of the country-branding process is the phase where all the strategies become operational in the marketplace through the identification of a number of sub-activities articulated on the basis of the structural characteristics of the various national sectors (economic, political, institutional, socio-cultural). The implementation phase is the most critical because it carries the overall responsibility for the success of the branding project. It is during this phase that the country brand faces its most decisive challenge: that of supporting the national development strategies geared to the competitiveness and prosperity of the country system. During this phase, it will be essential to have a unified and coordinated approach in the communication of national interests, one that will attract all the stakeholders, who are to be considered important partners bringing value, knowledge, resources, business skills and new opportunities for economic and social development.

Many country-branding strategies have failed precisely because of the lack of involvement of stakeholders and the failure to see the process of country-branding as a strategic moment in the implementation of a policy of branding that can satisfy the conditions of both internal and external efficiency. The country brand, therefore, is not only a graphic sign, but is a valuable asset that brings together all the intangible elements related to the history, economy, culture and society of a country, that is, its *genius loci*. These reflections testify to the complexity of the phenomenon that cannot be reduced simply to the creation of a brand but is in fact in the construction of a global branding strategy, which will ensure the perfect connubial between visual identity and national identity.

Process monitoring

From what has emerged so far, management of the country image can rely on the strategic tool of the country brand, capable of "customizing" the national identity for its representation outside the country. The interest of the governing body should not stop at the construction of the country-branding system. Like any process, once implemented, constant monitoring becomes imperative, ensuring compliance with the provisions made according to the strategic plan. So, alongside the three phases that characterize the framework for the country brand management (input, process, and output), we must consider another phase aimed at assessing the impact of the branding strategy on the perceptions of the identity makers. The monitoring phase also enables us to measure the effectiveness and efficiency of the marketing spending sustained by the country, through a constant feedback between the brand and the expected results, obtaining useful information on any actions that might be deemed necessary, such as adjustments or corrective reinforcements to realign performances (Mugobo & Ukpere, 2011).

Alongside the exemplary cases of country brands, such as Germany, Japan, France, where the representations of the country are so powerful and beneficial that they achieve a successful positioning in all areas of national interest, from the political to the socio-economic (Mainolfi, 2010), there are many other cases in which the country image, while positive, does not acquire persuasive force, and does not fully exploit the value of the brand. Similar reflections reveal the urgent need to include, in the analysis, a constant monitoring activity of the position acquired by the brand in relation to its target audiences. In fact, recent studies are focusing on the issue of measuring and assessing the value of the country brand, seen not only as a set of real and/or perceived assets, but also as a means by which the perceptions and opinions of identity makers can be used to promote national interests (Papadopoulos, 2004). Some scholars have extended the concept of brand equity to the nations, proposing the notion of country equity to designate the value of the country brand. The proposal of a theoretical model of country equity – capable of measuring the impact of the various components of the country image – could add a scientific interpretation to the current indices – of private derivation – used for the evaluation of country brands, thus filling the gaps in terms of equity measurement. The indices referred to are the Country Brand Index (CBI) and the Nation Brands Index (NBI). The first, developed by Future Brand Consultancy of the McCann-Erickson agency, is characterized by a framework of eight dimensions of analysis (attractions, authenticity, culture, ethics, geography, infrastructure, government, and economy), divided into two main groups (wants and needs). The focus of the framework is to evaluate the attractiveness of the country, regarded as a tourist destination. The Nation Brands Index (NBI), designed by Simon Anholt and GfK Roper agency, aims to monitor the reputation of nations around the world using six main dimensions (tourism, governance, exports, culture, immigration, investments and people) (Anholt, 2006; Mainolfi, 2010).

Future research directions

The present research could be further developed using primary data, obtained, for example, from in-depth interviews conducted with opinion leaders, strategist consultants, and managers involved in the implementation of country-branding projects. By using a quantitative approach, for example, thorough an online questionnaire to investigate citizen engagement. In fact, one of government's prerogatives is citizen participation and country-branding can be one of the main tools through which bringing citizen closer to Institutions. In addition, further progress in the research could be related to the application of the country-branding framework to a single or multiple case studies, giving empirical validity to the proposed model.

Conclusion

This research has contributed to a greater understanding of the country-branding phenomenon and its underlying processes, filling the gaps that emerged from a scientific survey of national and international literature on place branding. Not many studies, in fact, have analyzed the main contextual experiences of country-branding on an international level. Despite showing a very fragmented landscape, results obtained after the exploratory research made it possible to extrapolate the principal phases characterizing the country-branding process, thus expanding the knowledge of the structural and operational aspects.

By proposing an interpretative framework, it was possible to summarize the procedural steps of the country brand management capable of guiding and supporting the government bodies involved in the management and promotion of the country image. Reconstructing the whole framework of the phenomenon from a procedural viewpoint, the research showed the importance of sequencing in the process of country-branding, not haphazard operations, but a coherent pattern of creation and distribution of values of the country system for both national and international stakeholders. The country brand framework aims to be one of the first recognition map able to interpret the phenomenon and, above all, to make the necessary activities and their functional connections comprehensible.

In conclusion, findings offer a valuable decision support for those actors, institutional and otherwise, who intend to activate a construction process of the visual identity of their country. In addition, the systemic and holistic approach adopted for the drafting of the framework emphasizes the involvement of all stakeholders in defining the signposting values to be included in the branding project. Moreover, it contributes to promoting greater social cohesion. In fact, thanks to the adoption of such an approach, businesses and policy makers will be able to define sophisticated marketing strategies that improve the reputation and credibility of the national actors, who will be able to rely on country reputation, thanks to the promotion of the country brand.

Key construct definitions

Country image refers to the set of beliefs owned by external publics toward a specific country in a given time. The value of country image is measured through stereotypes related to country, created by the degree of economic and political maturity, historical events and relationships, culture and traditions, and the degree of technological and industrial expertise.

Country reputation is the result of a slow and complex process in which publics' opinions toward the country become sedimentary judgments. It is a dynamic phenomenon linked to the succession of country images perceived over a time span long enough to allow identity makers to form a weighted assessment of the country. Reputation can be interpreted as a global impression, i.e. the collective dimension of the expectations nurtured toward a country.

Country identity represents the collective self-perception of people inside a country. Identity is an international perception (self-image). However, country identity can impact on external perceptions as it affects the traits and attributes that a country may decide to emphasize for a nation branding strategy. Identity is something unique that is built around the beliefs, philosophy, nature of people, and ethical and cultural values of the nation.

References

Anholt, S. (2006). Public diplomacy and place branding: Where's the link? *Place Branding*, 2(4), 271–275.

Aronczyk, M. (2008). Living the brand: Nationality, globality and identity strategies of nation branding consultants. *International Journal of Communication*, 2, 41–65.

Bertoli, G., & Resciniti, R. (Eds.) (2013). *International Marketing and the Country of Origin Effect. The Global Impact of "Made in Italy"*. Cheltenham: Edward Elgar.

Bilkey, W.J., & Nes, E. (1982). Country-of-origin effects on product evaluations. *Journal of International Business Studies*, 13(1), 89–100.

De Chernatony, L., & Riley, F.D. (1998). Modeling the components of the brand. *European Journal of Marketing*, 32 (11–12), 1074–1090.

De Nisco, A. (2006). Country-of-origin e buyer behaviour: una meta-analisi della letteratura internazionale. *Mercati e Competitività*, 4, 81–102.

De Nisco, A., Elliot, S., Papadopoulos, N., Mainolfi, G., Marino, V., & Napolitano, M.R. (2012). Turismo internazionale ed effetto "made in". L'influenza dell'immagine Paese sulla soddisfazione turistica e le attitudini post-visita. *Mercati e Competitività*, 3, 131–151.

Fan, Y. (2008a). Soft power. The power of attraction or confusion. *Place Branding and Public Diplomacy*, 4(2), 147–158.

Fan, Y. (2008b). Key perspectives in nation image: A conceptual framework for nation branding. *Brunel Business School Research Papers Marketing*, 1(13), 1–16.

Gilboa, E. (2008). Searching for a theory of public diplomacy. *The Annals of the American Academy of Political and Social Science*, 615(55), 55–77.

Go, F.M., & Govers, R. (2010). *International Place Branding Yearbook 2010*. London: Palgrave Macmillan.

Han, C.M., & Terpstra, V. (1988). Country-of-origin effects for uni-national and bi-national products. *Journal of International Business Studies*, 19(2), 235–255.

Hunt, J.D. (1975). Image as a factor in tourism development. *Journal of Travel Research*, 13(3), 1–17.

Kaneva, N. (2011). Nation branding: Toward an agenda for critical research. *International Journal of Communication*, 5, 117–141.

Kavaratzis, M. (2005). Place branding: A review of trends and conceptual models. *The Marketing Review*, 5(4), 329–342.

Kotler, P., & Gertner, D. (2002). Country as brand, product and beyond: A place marketing and brand management perspective. *Journal of Brand Management*, 9(4–5), 249–261.

Kotler, P., Haider, D.H., & Rein, I.J. (1993). *Marketing Places: Attracting Investment, Industry and Tourism to Cities, States and Nations*. New York: Free Press.

Lee, K.M. (2009). *Nation branding and sustainable competitiveness of nations*. PhD. Thesis, University of Twente. Retrieved from doc.utwente.nl

Mainolfi, G. (2010). *Il modello della Country Reputation. Evidenze empiriche e implicazioni strategiche per le imprese del Made in Italy nel mercato cinese*. Torino: Giappichelli.

Marino, V., & Mainolfi, G. (2011). Il processo di country branding per la valorizzazione del capitale reputazionale. Un caso studio sul Paese Cina. *Esperienze d'impresa*, 2, 5–24.

Mugobo, V.V., & Ukpere, W.I. (2011). Is country branding a panacea or a poison? *African Journal of Business Management*, 5(20), 8248–8255.

Papadopoulos, N. (2004). Place branding: Evolution, meaning and implications. *Place Branding*, 1(1), 36–49.

Papadopoulos, N., & Heslop, L. (2002). Country equity and country branding: Problems and prospects. *Journal of Brand Management*, 9(4–5), 294–314.

Papadopoulos, N., Marshall, J.J., Heslop, L.A., Avlonitis, G., Bliemel, F., & Graby, F. (1988). Strategic implications of product and country images: A modeling approach. *Proceedings of the 41st* ESOMAR *Marketing Research Congress, Lisbon, 69–90.Roy, I.S. (2007). Worlds apart: Nation branding on the National Geographic channel. Media, Culture & Society, 29(4), 569–592.*

Szondi, G. (2008). Public diplomacy and nation branding: Conceptual similarities and differences. *Discussion Papers in Diplomacy*, Netherlands Institute of International Relations, 1–42. Retrieved from www.kamudiplomasisi.org

Volcic, Z., & Andrejevic, M. (2011). Nation branding in the era of commercial nationalism. *International Journal of Communication*, 5, 598–618.

13 Web communication for tourist destination. Analysis of tourism websites of the 28 Member States of the European Community

Tonino Pencarelli, Marco Cioppi, Simone Splendiani, and Mauro Dini

Learning outcomes

At the end of this chapter, readers should be able to:

1 Understand the relevance of the web in the tourist communication processes
2 Understand the importance of the website within the online strategies of tourist destinations
3 Obtain an evaluation grid useful for the study of tourist destination portals
4 Get an overview of the tourism promotion policies of all the member nations of the European Community
5 Study the strengths and weaknesses of tourism communication of European destinations through the websites

Introduction

The aim of this study is to analyze and assess the communication effectiveness of tourism websites in the 28 Member States of the European Community. In particular, the objective of the research is to verify how destination managers use the Internet to communicate the values, the unique characteristics, and the strengths that distinguish their nations and then, to persuade tourists to choose that nation as their holiday destination.

The study is based on an analysis of the main issues that influence brand destination policies implemented by the various nations through their tourism websites. A three-dimensional analysis model is proposed in order to offer a set of items able to guide researchers and scholars in the evaluation of websites but also destination managers or operators. These elements make it possible to bond with potential tourists and offer them an interactive experience that is essential to the image formation process of the destinations.

Research background

Over the past four decades, the tourism industry has been among those sectors most highly affected by the advent of computer technology. In particular, there was the introduction of the CRS (Computerized Reservation System) in the 1970s, the GDS (Global Distribution System) in the 1980s and the Internet Revolution in the second half of the 1990s (Buhalis, 2003). The first two technologies allowed entities to create, develop, and make the globally available basic tourism services through the intermediation of travel agencies which had exclusive access to computerized reservation systems. Thereafter, Internet technology extended this opportunity to the consumer by redefining the business system and increasing the options available in the distribution channel of tourism products.

In the last decade, the Internet Revolution has radically changed many industries while for the tourism sector, the advent of the online universe has brought with it a range of positive impacts (Xiang et al., 2014), such as more effective distribution channels (Berne et al., 2012; Carrol & Siguaw, 2003; Dale, 2003; O'Connor & Frew, 2004) and disintermediation phenomena (Buick, 2003; Garces et al., 2004; Tse, 2003; Vichi Martorell, 2004). At the same time, information and communication technologies (ICTs) have also dramatically changed the efficiency and effectiveness of tourism organizations, the way that business is conducted in the marketplace, as well as how consumers interact with organizations (Hays et al., 2013). In other words, the ICT advent generates a new paradigm-shift, by altering the structure of the entire industry and developing, at the same time, a whole range of opportunities and threats for all stakeholders (Buhalis, 1993; Standing et al., 2014).

In this context, the Internet and online services have become an essential part of making travel arrangements, both for finding information and booking (Buhalis, 2000) and for the marketing of tourism services[1] (Del Chiappa, 2013; Xiang et al., 2015). While ICTs can, in general, offer a range of tools to facilitate and improve the tourist's search process from information research, to destination/product consumption and post experience engagement (Buhalis & Law., 2008), the Internet, in particular, allows the tourist to better stay in touch with suppliers of travel services and with the infomediary before, during, and after the holiday. In addition, the Internet, and electronic media in general, may have the potential to strengthen the process of destination brand creation by facilitating interaction and cross-selling between complementary providers within a destination (Fernández-Cavia et al., 2014).

Defined as a collection of open source, interactive, and user-controlled online applications expanding the experience, knowledge, and market power of the users through the creation of informal users' networks (Constantinides & Fountain, 2008; Cooke & Buckley, 2008; Fortezza & Pencarelli, 2015), the new frontier of Web 2.0 allows people to get in touch with others. These can be tourists, friends, and other interested people (a "community") with whom they connect in order to share opinions, comments, photos, videos, and other emotions regarding the tourist experience, so that it becomes a crucial "place" they go to in the processes of buying a trip (Leung et al., 2013; Rodríguez-Molina et al., 2015).

In particular, through a Virtual Travel Community (VTC) tourists can obtain information, maintain connections, develop relationships, and make travel-related decisions (Elliot et al., 2013; Munar & Jacobsen, 2014; Stepchenkova et al., 2007). Considering that many tourists like to share their travel experiences with others, virtual travel communities have become one of their favorite places to post their travel diaries. Not only do travelers seem to be enthusiastic about meeting other tourists who present similar attitudes, interests, and ways of life (Wang et al., 2002); they also seem to place more trust in their peers than they do in marketing messages (Buhalis & Law, 2008). With regard to building relationships with tourists, ICTs allow both companies and tourist destinations to optimize one-to-one marketing policies, based on the increased use of knowledge relating to the consumer. In other words, web technologies can strongly accelerate the process of co-production and sharing of value,[2] as the Service Dominant Logic prospects (Lusch et al., 2007; Vargo & Lush, 2008).

With regard to branding, it is a concept that has been applied to different kinds of products and services over the past few decades. However, tourism destination branding is considered, by the literature, to be a more recent phenomenon[3] (Fyall et al., 2003). In other words, destination branding is becoming one of the most important topics among marketing professionals today (Campelo et al., 2013; Oliveira & Panyik, 2015) because more and more destinations,[4] from single cities to entire countries, are choosing to adopt branding strategies in order to differentiate themselves and to emotionally connect with potential tourists (Busacca, 2002; Morgan et al., 2005; Rodríguez-Molina et al., 2015).[5]

Through the web, destinations have the opportunity to revitalize their brands by widening their experiential content. The Internet "needs to be"—or can be—"a place where stories are told and dialogues are initiated, as well as information is discovered. This is where strong brand perceptions can be developed online" (Simmons, 2007). Furthermore, "boundaries between the brand and the experience in an online context are so blurred that in the eyes of consumers the brand is the experience and the experience is the brand" (Christodoulides et al., 2006).

For these reasons, a web presence has become a must for all Tourism Destinations to enhance their communication and branding policies (De Rosa et al., 2019; Jeong et al., 2011; Rodríguez-Molina et al., 2015; Splendiani, 2017). In particular, National Tourism Destinations have begun to understand that the relationship between the website and the tourist does not end with searching for information and planning the holiday, but should continue during the actual consumption phase and during the socialization phase of the tourist's post-consumption experience. In particular, with regard to the initial phase of the relationship between the user and a website, some authors (Tang & Jang, 2012) focus their attention on potential tourists' cognitive processes that take place when browsing the destination websites.

With this new awareness, many Destination Management Organizations (DMOs) have now begun to use Internet tools to promote the Destination, especially by creating websites that function as a virtual front office (Gregori & Bolzicco, 2009). As Li and Wang (2010) affirm, today "creating a website is no longer an option but a necessity for DMOs"[6] and that web space should not only provide information in a static manner, but should also try to anticipate the tourist experience and nourish the memory after travelers have returned home. Therefore, it becomes necessary to go beyond ownership of a web space and to adopt a systemic approach to the use of web technologies. This can be achieved through the adoption of a web-based Destination Management System, that is,

> a system that uses computer and communication technologies, especially the Internet and the World Wide Web, to fulfill the function of a DMO in its primary objective — the promotion of tourism businesses within geographically defined areas, most importantly by means of providing comprehensive tourism information and selections of tourism products to potential visitors.
> (Bronner & De Hoog, 2016; Buhalis & Laws, 2001; Wang, 2008)

In addition to being a vehicle for content on the Destination, destination websites may—if supported by the highest degree of interactivity—be able to establish a relationship of trust with persons visiting the site, according to a logic of relationship marketing. This is also thanks to the use of new Web 2.0 tools, which allow the sharing of experiences and opinions among tourists, recently defined as Electronic Word-of-Mouth (eWOM) because they allow the users themselves to generate content (User-Generated Content – UGC) (Del Chiappa, 2011; Osti, 2009). Designing a Destination website requires creativity, knowledge of the Internet, and recognition of the role of users in order to anticipate their needs and provide a platform upon which to interact with them. Based on these premises, in this work we ask the following research questions: how do European Destinations communicate with tourists via the Web? With what degree of success do they exploit the potential of the Internet?

Towards a three-dimensional model to analyze destination websites

With the abovementioned theoretical considerations in mind, many scholars have, in recent years, taken on the task of proposing a theoretical model that can help policy makers in the creation of Tourism Destination Websites without, however, achieving a generally recognized approach. This is likely due to the fact that every website is strongly affected by specific situations related to the objectives and target audience (Antonioli & Baggio, 2006; Franch, 2010; Han & Mills, 2006; Law et al., 2010; Morrison et al., 2004; Polizzi, 2010).

A general literature review on the topic shows that the success of a tourism website depends on the integrated application of the following four components/dimensions: (1) accurate and updated information, (2) constant and effective communication with consumers, (3) reliable electronic transactions, and (4) appropriate and sustainable services for building relationships with stakeholders (Bronner & De Hoog, 2016; Busacca, 2002; Casarin, 2007; Choi et al., 2007; Christodoulides et al., 2006; Han & Mills, 2006; Hoffman & Novak, 1996; Kotler et al., 1999; Luna-Navarez & Hyman, 2012; Novabos et al., 2015; Pencarelli et al., 2011, 2012; Porter, 2001; Prandelli & Verona, 2006; Simmons, 2007; Tierney, 2000; Wang & Russo, 2007).

These are important considerations for destination websites developed by public entities, as well. In fact, this type of website must first provide accurate and current information to tourists about the destination. The quality and effectiveness of such information which is becoming a strategic factor for Destinations because it can differentiate their offerings. Moreover, because Destinations are unique products, they need to communicate a large amount of different information (Sheldon, 1997). For this reason, a website represents a perfect medium to use in building effective communication channels with potential travelers. In particular, from a promotional perspective, it becomes fundamental to ensure that the internet search will lead to useful and positive information in order to create consumer awareness and interest as well as a favorable image of the destination in the traveler's perception. On the contrary, if a destination website does not provide the needed information, the potential traveler will be dissatisfied and will look to other websites or other destinations.

The relational component is probably the most difficult to implement because of the managerial and organizational implications that it determines. Since attracting new visitors is becoming increasingly more difficult and expensive, the most important and most complex goal becomes keeping existing users and converting visitors into customers. Following the literature analysis presented above, in order to assess tourism destination websites, we suggest a model that uses three dimensions of analysis.

Usability

By usability we mean the ability of tourism websites to offer easily accessible information, for example, through a series of keywords, used to foster a greater number of possible visits to the website and the presence of internal features that can simplify the search for information and navigating the website itself (such as the internal search engine, the site map, a language understood by as many people as possible, the user-friendly site design, etc.). Following Alcántara-Pilar et al. (2018) "usability can provide those elements that make the browsing experience more pleasurable and secure" (p. 27). The aim is to assess accessibility by checking internal functionality and tools that facilitate the retrieval of information.[7]

Content

With regard to the content dimension, the main objective is to evaluate the ability of websites to provide comprehensive and detailed information to the tourist targets through structured and precise content as well as the capacity to communicate in a suitable way in order to increase the perceived value of the tourist offer and its image. In particular, the communicative dimension must be able to highlight the distinctive elements of the tourism offer, helping the visitor easily identify the differentiating factors of the various offers on the market.

Relationship

The relational dimension refers to the ability of websites to manage interactions with users over time. This means not only transferring information to the user, but also developing useful knowledge of the demand in order to understand the characteristics and needs of the customer. The relational capacity of a website can be enhanced through three aspects: *personalization*, *customer care*, and *community*.

Personalization allows the delivery of content based on logged user profiles. In this way, the website recognizes and selects the most interesting information by eliminating irrelevant ones (Holland & Baker, 2001; Lee & Lehto, 2010). In particular, through the consumer's online profile, which includes personal data and preferences, the website can offer different and personalized information to specific market segments (Buhalis & Law, 2008).[8] Customer care has become more important in the digital world than the real one and is one of the main reasons for success or failure of online brands as well as a crucial component of perceived quality and trust (Christodoulides et al., 2006). This is due to the fact that consumers expect quick—if not instantaneous—answers to their problems regardless of the type of site they are visiting. If certain demands are not taken into account, the consumer most likely will not return to visit the website again (Breakenridge, 2001). Finally, to operate in the community perspective means creating the conditions to generate relationships among website users through the establishment of virtual communities, defined as "groups of people who share common interests and needs who come together online to share a sense of community with others, without the constraints of time and space" (Holland & Baker 2001), and through the integration with social networks.[9] Web 2.0 applications are able to generate, initiate, and circulate new and emerging sources of online information about users' experiences by allowing them to "post," "tag," "digg," or "blog" on the Net (Laroche et al., 2013; Xiang & Gretzel, 2010). Destinations have the opportunity to create web spaces where users can share information and stories about their holiday, arousing interest and anticipating the experience for those who have not yet visited the location (Han & Mills, 2006).

The three dimensions explained above are mutually connected. Each of the three dimensions is made up of a series of items used to measure the degree of effectiveness and functionality of the website.[10] In order to avoid subjective assessments of individual items, the model assigns them a score of one (1) if the item is in the website and a score of zero (0) if it is absent, except for two items (Table 13.1):

– U6 – Number of Foreign language options, to which we decided to apply 0.2 points for each foreign language in which the site is translated;
– R9 – Number of Social Network accounts/pages, to which we decided to apply 1 point for each Social Network account or page.

Table 13.1 List of items related to the three dimensions of the model

Dimension	Code	Description
Usability	U1	Internal search engine
	U2	Tag cloud
	U3	Sitemap
	U4	Responsive website
	U5	App
	U6	Number of language options
Content	C1	Information on "what to do"
	C2	Practical information for traveling (money, bureaucracy, health insurance, etc.)
	C3	Information on how to reach and move around the country (ports, airports, railways, taxis, buses, etc.)
	C4	Map of the place
	C5	Information on places to visit within the country
	C6	Information dedicated to specific targets (students/ seniors/families/people with pets, etc.)
	C7	FAQ – Frequently asked questions
	C8	Indication of UNESCO sites
	C9	Weather forecast
	C10	Upcoming events
	C11	Catalogues and brochures (available for download)
	C12	Photo gallery (within the website or through dedicated tools like Picasa or Instagram)

Dimension	Code	Description
	C13	Video gallery (within the website or through dedicated tools like YouTube)
	C14	Virtual tour
	C15	Live webcam
	C16	Press releases and news
	C17	Online booking (accommodation services or tourist packages)
	C18	Links to travel agencies or tour operator websites
	C19	Links to accommodation websites
	C20	Links to tourist attraction websites (museums, natural parks, etc.)
Relationship	R1	Phone number
	R2	E-mail address
	R3	Instant messaging (e.g. Skype)
	R4	Newsletter
	R5	Website registration
	R6	Blog
	R7	RSS
	R8	Space for sharing journey experiences
	R9	Number of Social Network accounts/pages

Based on these assessments, each dimension can earn the following total points:

- Usability: 5 (U1–U5) + maximum score achieved on U6;
- Content: 20;
- Relationship: 8 (R1–R8) + maximum score achieved on R9.

Results of the empirical analysis

The aim of the analysis is to test the three-dimensional model on the tourism websites of the 28 Member States of the European Community. The study was conducted in February of 2019. Table 13.2 shows the overall results achieved by each country.

Table 13.2 shows the scores obtained by each country, both in absolute and in percentage terms, sorted in descending order of the score achieved. The total obtainable score is equal to 47.8. On average, the 29 tourist websites obtained a total value of 28.2 (59.1%). More specifically, the scores for Malta and Finland are the farthest from the average: the first in a positive way, reaching a maximum higher than average score of 36.4 (76.2%), and the second in a negative way, with a lower than average score of 22.2 (46.9%).

Focusing on the dimensions themselves rather than the country, of the three, Content appears to achieve the best results on average with

Table 13.2 Ranking of the 29[a] websites analyzed

Country		Total			Usability			Content			Relationship		
		Points	%	Position	Points	%	Position	Points	%	Position	Points	%	Position
Malta	www.visitmalta.com	36.4	76.2	1	6.4	59.3	7	16.0	80.0	4	14.0	82.4	1
Holland	www.holland.com	34.6	72.4	2	9.6	88.9	1	16.0	80.0	2	9.0	52.9	11
Portugal	www.visitportugal.com	34.0	71.1	3	6	55.6	10	15.0	75.0	9	13.0	76.5	2
Denmark	www.visitdenmark.com	33.8	70.7	4	8.8	81.5	2	16.0	80.0	3	9.0	52.9	12
Hungary	www.gotohungary.com	32.6	68.2	5	7.6	70.4	5	15.0	75.0	7	10.0	58.8	7
Slovenia	www.slovenia.info	31.8	66.5	6	5.8	53.7	13	15.0	75.0	11	11.0	64.7	3
Germany	www.germany.travel	30.4	63.6	7	8.4	77.8	4	14.0	70.0	16	8.0	47.1	18
Belgium 2	www.valloniabelgioturismo.it	30.0	62.8	9	7	64.8	6	14.0	70.0	17	9.0	52.9	13
Belgium 1	www.visit-flanders.com	30.0	62.8	8	5	46.3	17	15.0	75.0	12	10.0	58.8	8
France	www.rendezvousenfrance.com	29.8	62.3	10	8.8	81.5	3	14.0	70.0	15	7.0	41.2	22
Poland	www.poland.travel	29.6	61.9	11	3.6	33.3	25	15.0	75.0	13	11.0	64.7	4
Croatia	www.croatia.hr	29.2	61.1	13	5.2	48.1	16	16.0	80.0	5	8.0	47.1	16
Britain	www.visitbritain.com	29.2	61.1	12	6.2	57.4	9	17.0	85.0	1	6.0	35.3	24
Ireland	www.ireland.com	29.0	60.7	15	5	46.3	18	13.0	65.0	21	11.0	64.7	5
Spain	www.spain.info	29.0	60.7	14	6	55.6	11	15.0	75.0	10	8.0	47.1	17
Cyprus	www.visitcyprus.com	28.0	58.6	16	4	37.0	23	14.0	70.0	19	10.0	58.8	9
Austria	www.austria.info	27.4	57.3	17	6.4	59.3	8	15.0	75.0	8	6.0	35.3	25
Czech Republic	www.czechtourism.com	27.0	56.5	18	6	55.6	12	13.0	65.0	20	8.0	47.1	19
Estonia	www.visitestonia.com	25.4	53.1	21	4.4	40.7	21	10.0	50.0	29	11.0	64.7	6
Slovakia	www.slovakia.travel	25.4	53.1	20	4.4	40.7	20	14.0	70.0	18	7.0	41.2	23
Greece	www.visitgreece.gr	25.4	53.1	19	2.4	22.2	28	13.0	65.0	23	10.0	58.8	10
Bulgaria	www.bulgariatravel.org	24.8	51.9	23	2.8	25.9	27	13.0	65.0	22	9.0	52.9	14
Lithuania	www.lithuania.travel	24.8	51.9	22	3.8	35.2	24	16.0	80.0	6	5.0	29.4	27
Luxembourg	www.visitluxembourg.lu	24.6	51.5	24	4.6	42.6	19	12.0	60.0	26	8.0	47.1	20
Italy	www.italia.it	24.4	51.0	25	4.4	40.7	22	12.0	60.0	27	8.0	47.1	21
Sweden	www.visitsweden.com	23.8	49.8	26	5.8	53.7	14	12.0	60.0	24	6.0	35.3	26
Romania	www.romania.travel	23.2	48.5	27	3.2	29.6	26	11.0	55.0	28	9.0	52.9	15
Latvia	www.latvia.travel	22.8	47.7	28	5.8	53.7	15	12.0	60.0	25	5.0	29.4	29
Finland	www.visitfinland.com	22.4	46.9	29	2.4	22.2	29	15.0	75.0	14	5.0	29.4	28
Max		47.8	100.0		10.8	100.0		20.0	100.0		17.0	100.0	
Average		28.2	59.1		5.5	51.0		14.1	70.3		8.7	50.9%	

a The total number of websites is 29 instead of 28, because Belgium has two different websites (one related to the Flanders and another for Wallonia).

14.1 (70.3%), while the other dimensions show weaker scores: Usability with 5.5 (51.0%) and Relationship with 8.7 (50.9%). The analysis can be deepened through comparison between sites of each dimension of the model: *Usability, Content, and Relationship.*

Usability

Focusing on usability, Table 13.2 shows the scores obtained by each website, both in absolute and percentage terms. The best performer in this dimension is Holland, with a score of 9.6 (88.9%), thanks to a huge number of foreign language options, followed by France and Denmark with 8.8 points (81.5%). The worst performances have been registered by Greece and Finland, both of them earning only 2.4 points (22.2%). Slightly above we find Bulgaria with 2.8 points (25.9%) (Figure 13.1).

Examining all the items related to usability, it emerges how all the tourist portals are equipped with an Internal Search Engine (U1). In the second place it is possible to find the responsive website—which means the ability to adapt the website's layout to different types of mobile devices (U4) —that reaches the percentage of 93.1, while the site map (U3) is present in most cases (69.0%). In 44.8% of cases is it possible to download a specific app (U5) and finally, the least used tool is the tag cloud

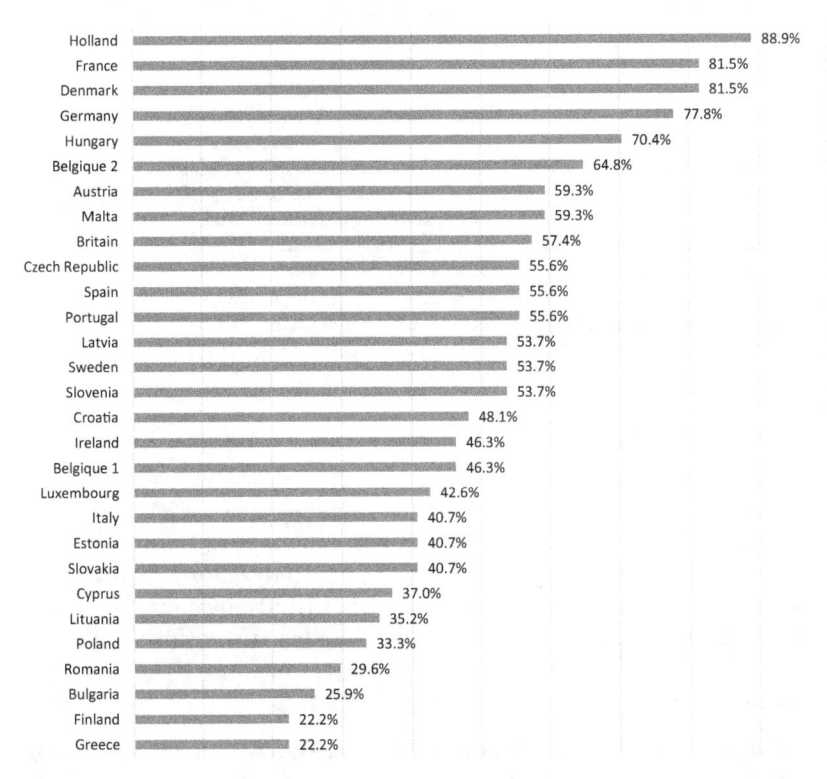

Figure 13.1 Percentage score of each website in relation to the usability dimension.

Table 13.3 Items frequencies in usability dimension

Frequency	%	Items
29	100	U1 – Internal search engine
27	93.1	U4 – Responsive website
20	69.0	U3 – Sitemap
13	44.8	U5 – App
1	3.4	U2 – Tag cloud

Britain — 85.0%
Lituania — 80.0%
Croatia — 80.0%
Denmark — 80.0%
Holland — 80.0%
Malta — 80.0%
Finland — 75.0%
Austria — 75.0%
Spain — 75.0%
Poland — 75.0%
Belgique 1 — 75.0%
Hungary — 75.0%
Slovenia — 75.0%
Portugal — 75.0%
Slovakia — 70.0%
Cyprus — 70.0%
France — 70.0%
Belgique 2 — 70.0%
Germany — 70.0%
Bulgaria — 65.0%
Greece — 65.0%
Czech Republic — 65.0%
Ireland — 65.0%
Latvia — 60.0%
Sweden — 60.0%
Italy — 60.0%
Luxembourg — 60.0%
Romania — 55.0%
Estonia — 50.0%

Figure 13.2 Percentage score of each website in relation to the content dimension.

(U2) —useful for quickly accessing information—that appears just in a single case. About the Number of Foreign Language options (U6), our findings show that, on average, the websites analyzed are available in Table 13.2 different foreign languages. Table 13.3 shows the frequency of appearance of each item related to the usability dimension.

Content

Looking at the content dimension, Table 13.2 shows an average score of 14.1 points (out of a maximum obtainable score of 20) which corresponds to 70.3%. The best performer is Britain with a score of 17 (85%), while at the second place—with a score of 16 (80%)—we can find Lithuania, Croatia, Denmark, Holland and Malta. At the bottom of the list Romania (points 11 and 55%) and Estonia (points 10 and 50%) (Figure 13.2).

In looking at the items related to content, it is possible to note that three of these are always present in the cases analyzed: namely, Information on "what to do" (C1), Information on how to reach and move around the country (C3), Information on places to visit within the country (C5) and Photo gallery (C12). At the bottom of the list are F.A.Q. (C7) with 20.7%, live Webcam (C15) with 6.9%, and Virtual tour (C14) with 3.4%. Table 13.4 shows the frequency of appearance of each item related to the content dimension.

Relationship

Table 13.2 also shows the results of the analysis connected to the relationship dimension. The maximum obtainable score is 17, and the mean

Table 13.4 Items frequencies in content dimension

Frequency	%	Items
29	100	C1 – Information on "what to do"; C3 – Information on how to reach and move around (ports, airports, railways, taxis, buses, etc.); C5 – Information on places to visit within the country; C12 – Photo gallery (within the website or through dedicated tools like Picasa or Instagram)
28	96.6	C2 – Practical information for traveling (money, bureaucracy, health insurance, etc.); C13 – Video gallery (within the website or through dedicated tools like YouTube)
27	93.1	C10 – Upcoming events
26	89.7	C4 – Map of the place
25	86.2	C19 – Links to accommodation websites
24	82.8	C20 – Links to tourist attraction websites (museums, natural parks, etc.)
23	79.3	C11 – Catalogues and brochures (available for download)
22	75.9	C8 – Indication of UNESCO sites; C16 – Press releases and news
19	65.5	C18 – Links to travel agencies or tour operator websites
14	48.3	C6 – Information dedicated to specific targets (students/ seniors/families/people with pets, etc.)
13	44.8	C9 – Weather forecast
12	41.4	C17 – Online booking (accommodation services or tourist packages)
6	20.7	C7 – FAQ – Frequently asked questions
2	6.9	C15 – Live webcam
1	3.4	C14 – Virtual tour

score achieved by the analyzed websites is 8.7 (50.9%). The best results are achieved by Malta with 14 points, corresponding to 82.4%. The worst, instead, are those of, Finland, Luxembourg and Latvia with five points (or 29.4%) (Figure 13.3).

From the analysis of the items tested for this dimension, our findings show that none of those provided by our model is present in all cases. The most used item is E-mail address (R2) with 96.6%, followed by

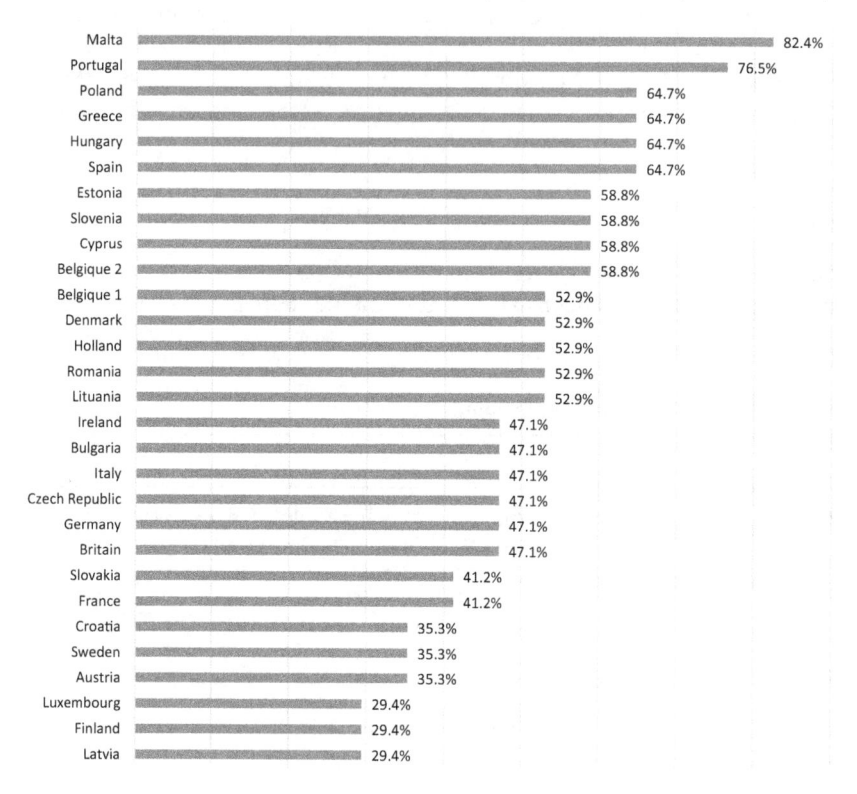

Figure 13.3 Percentage score of each website in relation to the relationship dimension.

Table 13.5 Items frequencies in relationship dimension

Frequency	%	Items
28	96.6	R2 – Email address
22	75.9	R1 – Phone number
21	72.4	R4 – Newsletter
10	34.5	R5 – Website registration
7	24.1	R7 – RSS
4	13.8	R6 – Blog; R8 – Space for sharing journey experiences
1	3.4	R3 – Instant messaging (e.g. Skype)

Phone number (R1) (75.9%) and Newsletter (R4) (72.4%). The least used tool is Instant messaging (R3), used only in one case (3.4%). Table 13.5 shows the frequency of appearance of each item related to the relationship dimension.

Finally, when looking at the Number of Social Network accounts (R9)—not included in Table 13.5—it emerges that the websites analyzed are connected to 5.3 different Social Networks, on average.

Future research directions

Future research on tourism communication must increasingly consider the Web not as an innovation but as a constant feature of tourism communication. The challenge will be to maximize value creation for tourists through web communication, thus overcoming the limiting approach that links tourism websites exclusively to tourists' searching-for-information phase.

Conclusions and limitations of research

As we also discussed in a previous study (Pencarelli et al., 2012), the analysis shows that the technological potential of tourism websites has not yet been fully exploited by the European countries analyzed. Overall, the websites analyzed exploit less than two thirds (59.10%) of the maximum score that can be reached based on our model (Table 13.2). In general, the evaluated countries seem to focus most of their attention on the need to give users a lot of information.

In fact, the content dimension is the one with the highest average score, showing something like almost 70% of the potential items being used. However, this dimension could be better exploited through greater use of multimedia tools, such as virtual tours and live webcams, but even more so via the ability to book tourist services online (C17), currently offered only in 41.4% of cases, and providing information dedicated to specific targets: for example, students/seniors/families/people with pets, etc. (C6), currently offered in 48.3% of cases (Table 13.3).

The relational capacity also shows considerable room for improvement. The untapped potential reaches almost 50%. Within this dimension, it is surprising that not all of the sites analyzed show their contact information, that is, e-mail address and phone number. Moreover, only in 34.5% of cases is there a registration page (R5) (Table 13.4). Finally, the usability with an amount of 51%. In this case, the data is affected by the number of foreign language options available, to which we have given 0.2 points for each of them. The presence of a case with a large number of foreign language options has profoundly affected the average.

The research must be considered a *work in progress*, primarily because of the rapidity with which technology provides tools potentially applicable to tourist communication via the websites.

The study allowed to realize an up-to-date survey model able to develop in-depth analyzes specifically focused on the effectiveness of online tourism communication.

Furthermore, the construction of this model has also made it possible to consider several elements that together can influence the effectiveness of the online communication as well as quantitatively measure the value of the online touristic communication of the European Community countries.

Managerially, the research implications are two-fold. First, the model represents a diagnostic tool for the tourist communication of the websites of the 28 Member States of the European Community. Indeed, it can be adopted as an operational management instrument allowing for acceleration of the identification of possible gaps in specific online communication areas, thus defining possible spheres of actions that can be achieved by mixing the different communication tools (managerial instrument). For instance, countries that identify their weakness in the social media area, can overcome this gap by better managing their social media participation, or they can strengthen their search engine presence, in the case that their weak point is related to the SEO campaigns.

Furthermore, the model developed presents margins of discretion which, on the one hand, represent a weakness, but on the other hand, allow a greater adaptability to the contexts of analysis. Such flexibility does not occur only in the choice of the item—the validity of which should be tested through user surveys—but also through the weight to be given to it, depending on the user target under consideration. For these reasons, the websites ranking of the European states that we have proposed in Table 13.2 has to be considered as a test of the proposed theoretical model and not as a final judgment about the online tourism communication policies developed by the EU member states. The study has three important limitations. The first is the basically static-approach of the three-dimensional model, which does not consider factors like website e-metrics or the functionality of the tools adopted (e.g., no assessment of whether the newsletter is actually delivered, if someone replies to an e-mail or a phone contact, etc.).

The second is the lack of a study on the overall tourist communication policies implemented by the EU member states, expressed in the tourism plans drawn up their respective national organizations. In other words, a more thorough and thoughtful evaluation of national tourism policies of communication should be included in the guidelines for tourism planning and destination management actions that each country has and is putting into place over time, this would require in-depth interviews with policy makers and the assumption of a longitudinal perspective, which is not covered in this research. This analysis should be preliminary geared to the study of digital tools that, in fact, support the overall strategic plan. The last limitation is the focus on only the official websites of the Member States which, although they are the main tools in terms of resources invested and liaison with the tourism policies, are only a small part of the universe of information available on the Web, and which influence a tourist's choice of destination.

Despite the declared limitations, the website analysis is a very useful tool for comparing the web communications approaches of European tourist destinations. The analysis offers a high degree of comparability between different approaches by using a shared model and also a wide territorial representation. Furthermore, the study highlights the main challenges policy-makers face regarding the introduction of new tools capable of enhancing the relationship with website users and tourists. These tools represent a substantial innovation in the communication approaches that requires not simply a huge financial investment, but rather, the understanding and the utilization of new languages and communication processes—especially for particular segments of tourists, like digital natives or frequent Internet navigators. In preparing the action plans for tourism communication, national governing bodies and national destination managers need to implement cultural and managerial innovation processes. This requires organizational changes aimed at using the growing potential of the Internet and ICTs, to open up new forms of unconventional marketing and communication. Social media marketing tools are also needed to increase the relational performance of web-based destination tourism marketing.

Key construct definitions

- Destination Management Organization (DMO): governing body of the tourist destination. It aims to integrate the policies of the different local actors in order to improve the tourist offer and to adopt shared marketing strategies. To this end, it promotes collaboration among tourism businesses, local authorities and non-profit organizations.
- Online communication: it concerns the communication policy developed through the web channels and tools. It does not refer to specific objectives or contents, but to approaches, techniques and languages born and grown in the context of the network.
- Tourist Destination Websites: web space that represents the basis for online communication strategies developed by DMOs. On the tourist demand side, it must be able to guarantee rich and updated contents, as well as the ability to be usable from a visual and technological point of view.

- Website usability: the website's ability to offer easily accessible information within a pleasant and quick navigation. To this end, various tools and approaches can be used, such as the internal search engine, the site map, the user-friendly site design, etc., as well as making the website accessible from mobile devices (responsive web design).
- Content management: activity aimed at providing complete and detailed information to tourist targets through structured and precise content, highlighting the distinctive features of the tourism offer. The contents must be interesting, fun, original, helpful, enjoyable, and updated.
- Online relationship marketing: a marketing approach aimed at creating and maintaining value relationships with customers. In the web context, the activity translates into the website's ability to manage interactions with users over time. This means not only transferring information to the users, but also developing a useful knowledge of the demand in order to understand the characteristics and needs of the customer.

Notes

1 Cf. Vicari (1983), Rispoli and Tamma (1996), Pencarelli (2010).
2 Cf. Micelli and Prandelli (2000); cf. Lee et al. (2006, p. 816), Cioppi (2009).
3 In particular, some authors (Pike, 2009) underline the importance of monitoring destination brand positions over time, whereas others (Blain et al., 2005) seek to more fully study and represent the complexity of the tourism product, which is a unique experience due to its heterogeneity, intangibility, and perishability (Sheldon, 1997; Wen, 2009) and the importance of tourism destinations' brand images (Fortezza & Pencarelli, 2015; Gallarza et al., 2002).
4 Traditionally, destinations were regarded as well-defined geographical areas, such as a country, an island, or a town (Buhalis, 2000; Davidson & Maitland, 1997), whereas today, they are regarded as a combination (or even as a brand) of all products, services, and ultimately, of experiences provided locally (Buhalis, 2000).
5 Breakenridge (2001, p. 72) defines e-branding or cyberbranding as

> an opportunity to create awareness of a brand online, develop name and logo recognition, communicate a brand message, drive traffic to a Web site, establish an identity with primary and secondary audiences, build a customer base online, increase sales over the Internet, and create a reputation so that as much as a mention of the brand elicits a feeling of a pleasurable experience.

6 Cf. Choi et al. (2007).
7 For Law and Ngai (2005), this ability includes five dimensions: language, layout and graphics, information architecture, user interface and navigation. Cf. Halliburton and Ziegfeld (2009), Choi et al. (2007), Alcántara-Pilar et al. (2018).
8 For example, Lastminute.com collects suitable information to personalize the weekly newsletter sent to consumers, identifying at the same time what parts

are read by potential tourists in order to personalize their offerings even further (Buhalis & Law, 2008). In other words, a successful website should take customers' interests into consideration, understand and capture their preferences and subsequently use this valuable information to provide personalized communication and services (Chung & Law, 2003; Doolin et al., 2002).

9 "A group of Internet-based applications that build on the ideological and technological foundations of Web 2.0 and that allow the creation and exchange of User Generated Content" (Kaplan & Haenlein, 2010).

10 On the destination website analysis an evaluation see: Alzua-Sorzabal et al. (2015), Del Vasto-Terrientes et al. (2015), Fernández-Cavia et al. (2014), Luna-Navarez and Hyman (2012). For a review on Website evaluation in tourism see Ip et al. (2010).

References

Alcántara-Pilar, J. M., Blanco-Encomienda, F. J., Armenski, T., & Del Barrio-Garcìa, S. (2018). The antecedent role of online satisfaction, perceived risk online, and perceived website usability on the affect towards travel destinations. *Journal of Destination Marketing & Management*, 9, 20–35.

Alzua-Sorzabal, A., Zurutuza, M., Rebón, F., & Gerrikagoitia, J. K. (2015). Obtaining the efficiency of tourism destination website based on data envelopment analysis. *Procedia – Social and Behavioral Sciences*, 175, 58–65.

Antonioli, C. M., & Baggio, R. (2006). *Internet & truism: tecnologie per competere*. Milano: Egea.

Berne, C., Garcia-Gonzalez, M., & Mugica, J. (2012). How ICT shifts the power balance of tourism distribution channels. *Tourism Management*, 33(1), 205–214.

Blain, C., Levy, S., & Ritchie, J. R. (2005). Destination branding: Insights and practices from destination management organizations. *Journal of Travel Research*, 43(4), 328–338.

Breakenridge, D. (2001). *Cyberbranding, brand building in the digital economy*. Upper Saddle River, NJ: Prentice Hall PTR.

Bronner, F., & De Hoog, R. (2016). Travel websites: Changing visits, evaluations and posts. *Annals of Tourism Research*, 57, 94–112.

Buhalis, D. (1993). RICIRMS as a strategic tool for small and medium tourism enterprises. *Tourism Management*, 14(5), 366–378.

Buhalis, D. (2000). Marketing the competitive destination of the future. *Tourism Management*, 21(1), 97–116.

Buhalis, D. (2003). *eTourism: Information technology for strategic tourism management*. Pearson Education.

Buhalis, D., & Laws E. (2001). *Tourism distribution channels: Patterns, practices and challenges*. London: Thomson.

Buhalis, D., & Law, R. (2008). Progress in information technology and tourism management: 20 years on and 10 years after the Internet – The state of eTourism research. *Tourism Management*, 29(4), 609–623.

Buick, I. (2003). Information technology in small Scottish hotels: Is it working?. *International Journal of Contemporary Hospitality Management*, 15(4), 243–247.

Busacca, B. (2002). *Le marche digitali, Strategie di sviluppo della brand equity*. Parma: Etas.

Campelo, A., Aitken, R., Thyne, M., & Gnoth, J. (2013). Sense of place: The importance for destination branding. *Journal of Travel Research*, 43(4), 328–338.

Carroll, B., & Siguaw, J. (2003). The evolution of electronic distribution: Effects on hotels and intermediaries. *The Cornell Hotel and Restaurant Administration Quarterly*, 44(4), 38–50.

Casarin, F. (2007). *Il marketing del prodotto turistico. Specificità e varietà.* Milano: Giappichelli.

Choi, S., Lehto, X. Y., & Oleary, J. T. (2007). What does the consumer want from a DMO website?. A study of US and Canadian tourists' perspectives. *International Journal of Tourism Research*, 9(2), 59–72.

Christodoulides, G., De Chernatony, L., Furrer, O., Shiu, E., & Abimbola, T. (2006). Conceptualising and measuring the equity of online brands. *Journal of Marketing Management*, 22(7–8), 799–825.

Chung, T., & Law, R. (2003). Developing a performance indicator for hotel websites. *International Journal of Hospitality Management*, 22(1), 119–125.

Cioppi, M. (2009). La comunicazione territoriale turistica in rete: un'analisi comparata dei siti delle regioni adriatiche. In Pencarelli, T. & Gregori, G.L. (Eds.), *Comunicazione e branding delle destinazioni turistiche. Una prospettiva managerial* (pp. 226–246). Milano: Franco Angeli.

Constantinides, E., & Fountain S. J. (2008). Web 2.0: Conceptual foundations and marketing issues. *Journal of Direct, Data and Digital Marketing Practice*, 9(3), 231–244.

Cooke, M., & Buckley, N. (2008). Web 2.0, social networks and the future of market research. *International Journal of Market Research*, 50(2), 267–292.

Dale, C. (2003). The competitive networks of tourism e-mediaries: New strategies, new advantages. *Journal of Vacation Marketing*, 9(2), 109–118.

Davidson, R., & Maitland, R. (1997). *Tourism destinations.* London: Hodder & Stoughton.

De Rosa, A. S., Bocci, E., & Dryjanska, L. (2019). Social representations of the European capitals and destination e-branding via multi-channel web communication. *Journal of Destination Marketing & Management*, 11, 150–165.

Del Chiappa, G. (2011). Trustworthiness of Travel 2.0 applications and their influence on tourist behaviour: An empirical investigation in Italy. In Law, R., Fuchis, M. & Ricci, F. (Eds.), *Information and communication technologies in tourism* (pp. 331–342). Vienna: Springer.

Del Chiappa, G. (2013). Internet versus travel agencies: The perception of different groups of Italian online buyers. *Journal of Vacation Marketing*, 19(1), 55–66.

Del Vasto-Terrientes, L., Fernández-Cavia, J., Huertas, A., Moreno, A., & Valls, A. (2015). Official tourist destination websites: Hierarchical analysis and assessment with ELECTRE-III-H. *Tourism Management Perspectives*, 15, 16–28.

Doolin, B., Burgess, L., & Cooper, J. (2002). Evaluating the use of the web for tourism marketing: A case study from New Zealand. *Tourism Management*, 23(5), 557–561.

Elliot, S., Li, G., & Choi, C. (2013). Understanding service quality in a virtual travel community environment. *Journal of Business Research*, 66(8), 1153–1160.

Fernández-Cavia, J., Rovira, C., Díaz-Luque, P., & Cavaller, V. (2014). Web Quality Index (WQI) for official tourist destination websites. Proposal for an assessment system. *Tourism Management Perspectives*, 9, 5–13.

Fortezza, F., & Pencarelli, T. (2015). Potentialities of Web 2.0 and new challenges for destinations: Insights from Italy. *Anatolia: An International Journal of Tourism and Hospitality Research*, 26(4), 563–573.

Franch, M. (2010). *Marketing delle destinazioni turistiche*. Milano: McGraw Hill.

Fyall, A., Callod, C., & Edwards, B. (2003). Relationship marketing: The challenge for destination. *Annals of Tourism Research*, 30(3), 644–659.

Gallarza, M., Saura, I., & Garcia, H. (2002). Destination image: Towards a conceptual framework. *Annals of Tourism Research*, 29(1), 56–78.

Garces, S. A., Gorgemans, S., Sánchez, A. M., & Perez, M. P. (2004). Implications of the Internet – An analysis of the Aragonese hospitality industry. *Tourism Management*, 25(5), 603–613.

Gregori, G. L., & Bolzicco, L. (2009). Gli strumenti operativi della comunicazione turistica territoriale. In: Pencarelli, T. & Gregori, G.L. (Eds.), *Comunicare le destinazioni balneari* (pp. 144–169). Milano: Franco Angeli.

Halliburton, C., & Ziegfeld, A. (2009). How do major European Companies communicate their corporate identity across countries?. An empirical investigation of corporate internet communications. *Journal of Marketing Management*, 25(9–10), 909–925.

Han, J. H., & Mills, J. E. (2006). Zero acquaintance benchmarking at travel destination websites: What is the first impression that national tourism organizations try to make?. *International Journal of Tourism Research*, 8(6), 405–430.

Hays, S., Page, S. J., & Buhalis, D. (2013). Social media as a destination marketing tool: Its use by national tourism organisations. *Current Issues in Tourism*, 16(3), 211–239.

Hoffman, D. L., & Novak, T. P. (1996). Marketing in hypermedia computer-mediated environments: Conceptual foundations. *Journal of Marketing*, 60(3), 50–68.

Holland, J., & Baker, S. M. (2001). Customer participation in creating site brand loyalty. *Journal of Interactive Marketing*, 15(4), 34–45.

Ip, C., Law, R., & Lee, H. (2010). A review of website evaluation studies in the tourism and hospitality fields from 1996 to 2009. *International Journal of Tourism Research*, 13(3), 234–265.

Jeong, C., Holland, S., Jun, S. H., & Gibson, H. (2011). Enhancing destination image through travel website information. *International Journal of Tourism Research*, 14(1), 16–27.

Kaplan, A. M., & Haenlein, M. (2010). Users of the world, unite! The challenges and opportunities of social media. *Business Horizons*, 53(1), 59–68.

Kotler, P., Bowen, J., & Makens, J. (1999). *Marketing for hospitality and tourism*. Upper Saddle River, NJ: Prentice-Hall.

Laroche, M., Habibi, M. R., & Richard, M. O. (2013). To be or not to be in social media: How brand loyalty is affected by social media?. *International Journal of Information Management*, 33(1), 76–82.

Law, R., & Ngai, C. (2005). Usability of travel websites: A case study of the perceptions of Hong Kong travelers. *Journal of Hospitality & Leisure Marketing*, 13(2), 19–31.

Law, R., Qi, S., & Buhalis, D. (2010). Progress in tourism management: A review of website evaluation in tourism research. *Tourism Management*, 31(3), 297–313.

Lee, G., Cai, L. A., & O'Leary, J. T. (2006). WWW. Branding. States. US: An analysis of brand-building elements in the US state tourism websites. *Tourism Management*, 27(5), 815–828.

Lee, J. K., & Lehto, X. (2010). E-personalization and online privacy features: The case with travel websites. *Journal of Management & Marketing Research*, 4, 1–14.

Leung, D., Law, R., Van Hoof, H., & Buhalis, D. (2013). Social media in tourism and hospitality: A literature review. *Journal of Travel & Tourism Marketing*, 30(1–2), 3–22.

Li, X., & Wang, Y. (2010). Evaluating the effectiveness of destination marketing organisations' websites: Evidence from China. *International Journal of Tourism Research*, 12(5), 536–549.

Luna-Navarez, C., & Hyman, M. R. (2012). Common practices in destination website design. *Journal of Destination Marketing & Management*, 1(1–2), 94–106.

Lusch, R. F., Vargo, S. L., & O'Brien, M. (2007). Competing through service: Insights from service-dominant logic. *Journal of Retailing*, 83(1), 5–18.

Micelli, S., & Prandelli, E. (2000). Net marketing. Ripensare il consumatore nel mondo della rete. *Economia & Management*, 4(4), 57–70.

Morgan, N., Pritchard, A., & Pride, R. (2005). *Destination branding: Creating the unique destination proposition*. Oxford: Elsevier.

Morrison, A. M., Taylor, J. S., & Douglas, A. (2004). Website evaluation in tourism and hospitality: The art is not yet stated. *Journal of Travel & Tourism Marketing*, 17(2/3), 233–251.

Munar, A. M., & Jacobsen, J. K. S. (2014). Motivations for sharing tourism experiences through social media. *Tourism Management*, 43, 46–54.

Novabos, C. R., Matias, A., & Mena, M. (2015). How good is this destination website: A user-centered evaluation of provincial tourism websites. *Procedia Manufacturing*, 3, 3478–3485.

O'Connor, P., & Frew, A. J. (2004). An evaluation methodology for hotel electronic channels of distribution. *International Journal of Hospitality Management*, 23(2), 179–199.

Oliveira, E., & Panyik, E. (2015). Content, context and co-creation: Digital challenges in destination branding with references to Portugal as a tourist destination. *Journal of Vacation Marketing*, 2(1), 53–74.

Osti, L. (2009). Creating UGC areas on official destination websites: Is there a recipe for success?. An insight through netnographic research. *Tourismos: An International Multidisciplinary Journal of Tourism*, 4(3), 99–112.

Pencarelli, T. (2010). *Marketing e Management del turismo*. Trieste: Edizioni Goliardiche.

Pencarelli, T., Cioppi, M., & Splendiani, S. (2011). Web communication nel Turismo: analisi dei portali turistici delle Regioni italiane, *Proceedings of the XXIII Congress of Sinergie Journal*, Milan, Italy.

Pencarelli, T., Cioppi, M., & Splendiani, S. (2012). Web communication of tourist destinations. Analysis of tourist websites of the 27 Member States of the European Community. In Morvillo A. (Ed.), *Proceedings of the 1st enlightening Tourism Conference 2012* (pp. 851–874). Naples: Enzo Albano Editore.

Pike, S. (2009). Destination brand positions of a competitive set of near-home destinations. *Tourism Management*, 30(6), 857–866.

Polizzi, G. (2010). *La comunicazione della destinazione turistica al tempo di Internet*. Milano: McGraw-Hill.

Porter, M. E. (2001). Strategy and the Internet. *Harvard Business Review*, 79(3), 62–78.

Prandelli, E., & Verona, G. (2006). *Marketing in rete: oltre internet verso il nuovo Marketing*. Milano: McGraw-Hill.

Rispoli, M., & Tamma, M. (1996). *Le imprese alberghiere nell'industria dei viaggi e del turismo*. Padova: Cedam.

Rodríguez-Molina, M. A., Frías-Jamilena, D. M., & Castañeda-García, J. A. (2015). The contribution of website design to the generation of tourist destination image: The moderating effect of involvement. *Tourism Management*, 47, 303–317.

Sheldon, P. J. (1997). *Tourism information technology*. New York: CAB International.

Simmons, G. J. (2007). I-branding: Developing the internet as a branding tool. *Marketing Intelligence & Planning*, 25(6), 544–562.

Splendiani, S. (2017). *Destination management e pianificazione turistica territorial. Casi e esperienze in Italia*. Milano: Franco Angeli.

Standing, C., Tang-Taye, J. P., & Boyer, M. (2014). The impact of the Internet in travel and tourism: A research review 2001–2010. *Journal of Travel & Tourism Marketing*, 31(1), 82–113.

Stepchenkova, S., Mills, J., & Jiang, H. (2007). Virtual travel communities: Self-reported experiences and satisfaction. In Sigala, M., Mich, L. & Murphy, J. (Eds.), *Information and communication technologies in tourism 2007* (pp. 163–174). New York: Springer-Verlag Wien.

Tang, L., & Jang, S. (2012). Investigating the routes of communication on destination websites. *Journal of Travel Research*, 51(1), 94–108.

Tierney, P. (2000). Internet-based evaluation of tourism web site effectiveness: Methodological issues and survey results. *Journal of Travel Research*, 39(2), 212–219.

Tse, A. C. B. (2003). Disintermediation of travel agents in the hotel industry. *International Journal of Hospitality Management*, 22(4), 453–460.

Vargo, S. L., & Lusch, R. F. (2008). Service dominant logic: Continuing the evolution. *Journal of the Academy of Marketing Science*, 36(1), 1–10.

Vicari, S. (1983). *Imprese di servizi e politiche di mercato. Le dimensioni del processo competitivo*. Milano: Giuffrè.

Vichi Martorell, G. À. (2004). The internet and tourism principals in the Balearic Islands. *Tourism and Hospitality Research*, 5(1), 25–44.

Wang, Y. (2008). Web-based destination marketing systems: Assessing the critical factors for management and implementation. *International Journal of Tourism Research*, 10(1), 55–70.

Wang, Y., & Russo, S. M. (2007). Conceptualizing and evaluating the functions of destination marketing systems. *Journal of Vacation Marketing*, 13(3), 187–203.

Wang, Y., Yu, Q., & Fesenmaier, D. R. (2002). Defining the virtual tourist community: Implications for tourism marketing. *Tourism Management*, 23(4), 407–417.

Wen, I. (2009). Factors affecting the online travel buying decision: A review. *International Journal of Contemporary Hospitality Management*, 21(6), 752–765.

Xiang, Z., & Gretzel, U. (2010). Role of social media in online travel information search. *Tourism Management*, 31(2), 179–188.

Xiang, Z., Magnini, V. P., & Fesenmaier, D. R. (2015). Information technology and consumer behavior in travel and tourism: Insights from travel planning using the internet. *Journal of Retailing and Consumer Services*, 22, 244–249.

Xiang, Z., Wang, D., O'Leary, J. T., & Fesenmaier, D. R. (2014). Adapting to the internet: Trends in travelers' use of the web for trip planning. *Journal of Travel Research*, 42(4), 357–371.

14 Examining the destination website

A case of Visit Tatarstan

Elena Ageeva and Pantea Foroudi

Learning outcomes

At the end of this chapter, readers should be able to:

1 Examine the factors that impact on the destination websites.
2 Develop a conceptual framework for the relationships among destination website, its antecedents and its consequences.
3 Examine the impact of destination website on destination image.
4 Examine the impact of destination identity on destination websites.
5 Examine the impact of destination culture on destination websites.

Introduction

This study adopts social identity and place identity theories to tackle two main questions: (1) what are the factors that impact on the destination website, and (2) what are the main influences of the destination website? The research addresses the study aims to close the gap in literature relating to the impact of destination website on the destination image, intention to revisit, intention to recommend. The researcher used a qualitative method to achieve the aims of the study. The favorable destination website is affected by the magnitude to which visitor favors destination identity and destination culture. Findings highlighted the importance of destination website in building positive destination image, intention to revisit and recommend. As well as satisfaction can influence on destination image. The importance of the findings for researchers and place managers is emphasized.

Research background

The online environment became dominant in our lives (Ageeva et al., 2018, 2019; Foroudi et al., 2018). To find out the information about the place/destination, people usually visit the destination website, social networks, and websites of the hotels, where the most popular considers are the destination website (Jimenez-Barreto and Campo-Martinez,

2018). Based on the ITB World Travel Trends Report 2017–2018 (IPK International, 2017), the key role is placed on the technology to personalize the experience in the place, to "tell their story". The destination website is a perfect place to tell the story about the destination and to influence the decision-making processes of the tourists (Choi et al., 2012; Foroudi et al., 2016, 2018; Jimenez-Barreto and Campo-Martinez, 2018). According to scholars (Choi et al., 2012; Jimenez-Barreto and Campo-Martinez, 2018) destination website represents the main source of information about the place.

As pointed out by Foroudi et al. (2018), there is an increase in the variety of choices that people faced each day to the choice of destination. In this rigid competition, destination websites can play a significant role in the people's decision-making process and result in improvement of the destination image (Foroudi et al., 2016, 2018). Recent scholars (Choi et al., 2012; Foroudi et al., 2016, 2018; Jimenez-Barreto and Campo-Martinez, 2018) highlighted the importance of the destination website phenomenon and emphasized that there should be more research conducted on its factors and main impacts.

Based on the discussion above, this study addresses two main questions: what are the factors that impact on the destination website, and what are the main influences of a destination website? To answer this research questions, this study adopted place identity (Rooney et al., 2010) and social identity (Tajfel and Turner, 1986) in order to give an explanation of the situations where consumers can form their ideas, sense of belonging, conceptions, and interpretations (Mael and Ashforth, 1992) in relation to a place and outcomes of such satisfaction (Foroudi et al., 2018).

In the next sections, the background of the study is presented relating to the destination website as the main phenomenon of the research. Next, the research methodology to study the research topic is outlined. Afterwards, the study is concluded with findings and discussion. Finally, the authors present the conclusion of the study with the research implications, potential future research suggestions, and limitations.

Tourists actively search for information about destinations by using search engines, social media, and asking their friends about it. If you google any destination, one of the first things that appear are popular hotels, destination websites, and social media links. Thus, for the destinations, it is paramount to communicate with the tourists efficiently by using easily accessible and interesting resources, such as website and social media accounts that are linked to the website. Tourists mainly consume information online and are eager to participate in the discussions (Oliveira and Panyik, 2015).

As scholars (Choi et al., 2012; Foroudi et al., 2016, 2018; Jimenez-Barreto and Campo-Martinez, 2018) highlighted, the destination website represents the key point of contact and the main source of information for tourists. It is the platform that is highly beneficial for destinations if done properly. A favorable destination website not only attracts more tourists but also improves the image of the destination and leads tourists to visit again and recommend to their friends (Foroudi et al., 2016, 2018). Providing and maintaining a high-quality favorable website enables impacting on consumers' fidelity and satisfaction (Bai et al., 2008; Jimenez-Barreto and Campo-Martinez, 2018).

Tourism literature emphasized the significance of a destination website (Foroudi et al., 2018; Jimenez-Barreto and Campo-Martinez, 2018; Luna-Nevarez and Hyman, 2012; Park and Gretzel, 2007). The same holds for the marketing literature (Ageeva et al., 2018, 2019; Foroudi et al., 2017; Melewar et al., 2017; Tang et al., 2012; Tsang et al., 2010). A website became the center of research in a number of scholarly work (Ageeva et al., 2018, 2019; Foroudi et al., 2017; Melewar et al., 2017) highlighting its crucial elements. Ageeva et al. (2019) conducted research in UK and Russia and established that crucial factors of favorable corporate websites in both countries are navigation, information, security, availability, perceived corporate social responsibility, and perceived corporate culture. Research of Ageeva et al. (2018) concluded from the research in Russia, that favorable corporate website should include usability, navigation, customer service, and information. Foroudi et al. (2018) conducted a study in London and found a positive place website to have the following elements: navigation, visual appeal, navigation, security, credibility, information, be convincing. Similarly, Cyr and Head (2013) found website included dimensions, such as information content, visual design, and navigation design. According to Tarafdar and Zhang (2008), the significant elements of the website include the organization of information and content, the usability of the website and its technical characteristics (availability, security, and access speed).

Thus, it is obvious that in the marketing literature, an increasing tendency is occurring towards creating a unique corporate website design for customers in order to gain a competitive advantage (Ageeva et al., 2018, 2019; Brown, 1998), improve integrated marketing communication strategies (Bellman and Rossiter, 2004), contribute to improving customer relationships and cost-saving (Downes and Mui, 1998), enable innovation (Mandeville et al., 1998) project the corporate identity of the company (Bravo et al., 2012), reputation management (Campbell and Beck, 2004), financial reporting (Marston, 2003), increase loyalty (Srinivasan et al., 2002), and satisfaction (Casalo et al., 2008; Santouridis et al., 2009).

A number of studies have explored website quality/dimensions/elements (Cyr, 2008; Santos, 2003; Tarafdar and Zhang, 2008), while others have looked at the adoption of technology, in particular, Internet banking (Alsajjan and Dennis, 2010; George and Kumar, 2014;

Kesharwani and Bisht, 2012; Santouridis et al., 2009; Yousafzai and Yani-de-Soriano, 2012). The work of Raman et al. (2008) combined both website service quality and Internet banking adoption. They proposed six key elements: (1) the degree of ease of use, (2) appearance, (3) reliability, (4) customization, (5) communication, and (6) incentive aspects that can evaluate consumer perceptions concerning the quality of e-services, and Internet banking adoption. A significant number of studies exist on information systems and websites that can help one identify the likely drivers of a favorable website. The big body of work recognizes a range of factors that impact in effective website performance, positive attitude towards website, trust, satisfaction, and loyalty. Furthermore, researchers have examined various website characteristics, namely, user satisfaction (Muylle et al., 2004), quality of the website and flexibility (Gefen and Straub, 2000), and the information content (Alba and Nee, 1997). The most important characteristics include the organization of information and content, the usability of the website and its technical characteristics (Tarafdar and Zhang, 2008).

Despite, destination websites received an increased attention (Fernandez-Cavia et al., 2014; Jimenez-Barreto and Campo-Martinez 2018), there is a gap in research of what factors influence destination website and how it can affect destination image, intention to revisit and recommend (Ageeva et al., 2018, 2019; Choi et al., 2012; Foroudi et al., 2016, 2018). Therefore, this study aims to clarify the phenomenon of the destination website, what are the main benefits, and outcomes of the favorable destination website.

Research methods

Ageeva et al. (2018, 2019) pointed out as there are limited studies on the website relating to Russia, a significant gap exists in this area. To address these gaps, this research aims to investigate the main elements of the destination website and the primary outcomes of the destination website. The context of this research is the Republic of Tatarstan in Russia. Tatarstan considers being one of the most attractive regions for investors in Russia (Glebova and Khamidulina, 2015; Forbes Rating, 2012) with tourism being one of the main priorities (tourism.tatarstan. ru, 2019). Tatarstan is a popular touristic destination in Russia not only for international tourism but is one of the most popular destinations among local Russian tourists (tourism.tatarstan.ru, 2019). The official destination website of Tatarstan is Visit-Tatarstan.com which is translated into seven languages.

The review of the literature resulted in the conclusion that there is still no clarity on what constitutes a favorable destination website and what is it main antecedents and consequences. Therefore, the qualitative method was adapted to a deeper understanding of the phenomenon of the favorable destination website. Qualitative research represents "a judgement sample of persons who can offer ideas and insights into the phenomenon". Authors emphasized (Foroudi et al., 2014, 2017, 2018), it is beneficial to conduct both focus groups and interviews with consumers to reach a more meaningful conclusion. Based on the phenomenon of the research, an interview and focus group guide was created that defined the destination website of Tatarstan (visit-tatarstan.com) as a subject of interest to encourage discussion. Following the recommendations, Foroudi et al. (2014, 2017) the qualitative research was conducted by adopting interviews and focus groups by using open-ended questions such as, "what are the factors that influence destination website? Following the suggestions of Foroudi et al. (2014, 2018), seven interviews were conducted with place brand managers and four focus groups (consisting of 27 participants in total) with tourists Interviews and focus groups were adopted to investigate feelings and attitude and beliefs relating to the study phenomenon (Foroudi et al., 2014).

Findings and discussion

The main aim of this qualitative research is to attain a greater understanding of destination website, its antecedents, and consequences. The importance of the destination website was highlighted by all the participants, in line with the previous literature reviewed. Practitioners and tourists emphasized that in the current competitive environment, it is paramount to stay true to the destination identity and culture and create a unified destination image that is revealed thought the building and maintenance of the favorable destination website. Based on the research results and prior literature, this study found destination identity and destination culture to be the main antecedents of the destination website. Additionally, it is concluded that destination website impacts positively on destination image, intention to revisit and recommend. Satisfaction was discovered to mediate between the destination website and destination image.

Destination website

The significance of examining destination website topic has been widely emphasized by scholars (Foroudi et al., 2016, 2018; Jimenez-Barreto and Campo-Martinez, 2018; Luna-Nevarez and Hyman, 2012; Park and Gretzel, 2007). However, there is no agreement on how the destination website is defined and what elements it consists of. Foroudi et al. (2018) used the term place website and defined it as "a primary vehicle of destination image formation process that plays a major role in the way that a destination portrays itself to internal and external audiences" (p. 104). The authors pointed out that a positive place website should have good navigation, information, be visually appealing, secure, credible, and convincing. Park and Gretzel (2007) noted that the successful destination website should include ease of use, responsiveness, fulfillment, security, personalization, visuals, information, trust, and interactivity.

Other authors (Dickinger and Stangl, 2013) stated that on the touristic website the major importance should be emphasized on usability, user-friendliness, enjoyment, design, confidence, content quality, navigation and availability. More recently, Jimenez-Barreto and Campo-Martinez (2018) and Loureiro (2015) in the assessment of destination website adopted the visual appearance, information, ease of use and interactivity.

In line with the literature, place managers commented about the Visit Tatarstan website:

> From the practitioner's perspective it can be seen that it includes personalised features such as 7 languages, beautiful and unique tourist's packages, which I never saw in any other website. You can see the creativity of the tourism team and the love for the region and it translate through the website.

Tourists similarly pointed out that

> Personally I have never been to Tatarstan, but by looking at the visual attracted website, with clear and interesting information, all necessary contacts details are there, I can go and explore the social media accounts that make me feel involved and entertained, it's easy to use and I feel that it adopted to different languages that gives it a personal feel to it.

Based on discussion above in the literature and from the qualitative findings from interviews with place managers and focus groups with tourists, destination website is defined as way for destination/place to communicate its uniqueness and authenticity by transmitting consistent images and messages about the nature of the destination in order to attain consumers positive view of the destination and to come back again to the destination (Ageeva et al., 2018, 2019; Foroudi et al., 2018). As presented in Figure 14.1, favorable destination website includes navigation, visual, information, usability, customer service, personalization and interactivity (Ageeva et al., 2018, 2019; Foroudi et al., 2018; Jimenez-Barreto and Campo-Martinez, 2018; Loureiro, 2015; Park and Gretzel, 2007).

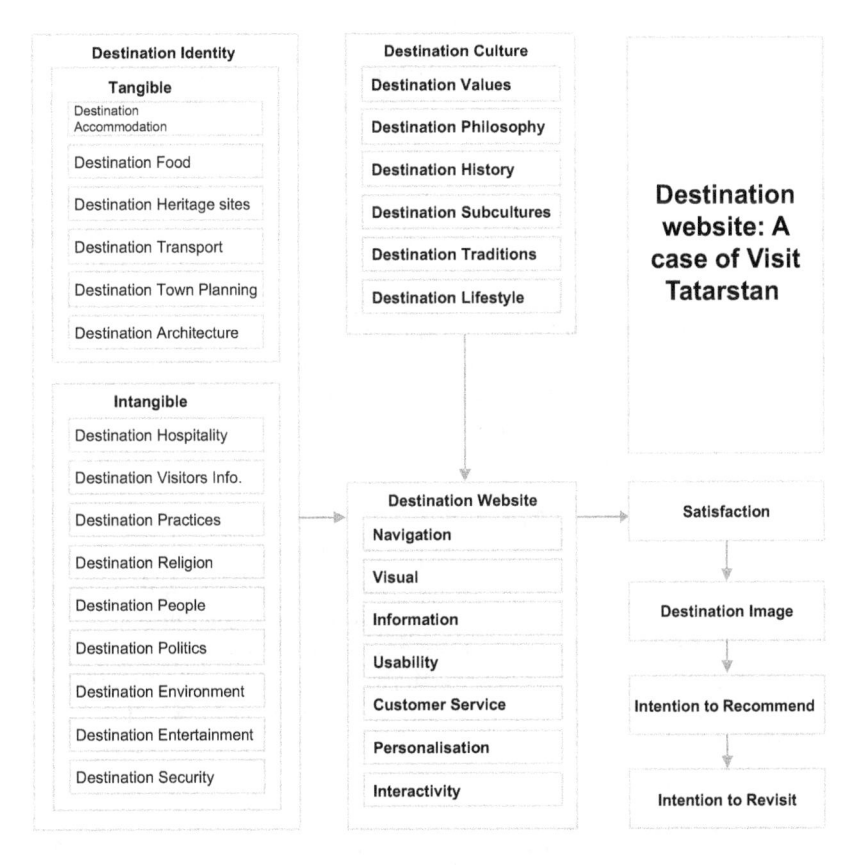

Figure 14.1 Destination website: a case of visit Tatarstan.

Destination identity, destination culture, and destination website

Based on the study findings, destination identity and destination culture represent the main factors that influence the destination website. According to Foroudi et al. (2018), the identity of the destination can have a positive impact on the website of the place. Identity of the place/destination defines as "what the place really is" (Foroudi et al., 2017, 2018), in a common way that Balmer et al. (2009) defined the corporate identity as "what we really are" (actual identity) (p. 7).

Finding from the interviews and focus groups presented the importance of the main themes and words in constructing the perception about destination identity. According to the analyzed qualitative data, the major themes of destination identity were tangible and intangible components. Tangible components included food, accommodation, heritage sites, transport, town planning, architecture, whereas intangible hospitality, visitors' information, practices, religion, people, politics, environment, entertainment, and security (Figure 14.1). The outcomes are consistent with the research related to the destinations (Govers and Go, 2009; Govers et al., 2007; Qu et al., 2011).

Additionally, participants highlighted destination culture as one of the main factors that influence the destination website. In marketing literature, Dowling (1986) defined the culture of the company as a company's "common beliefs, behavior, values", described as the "what" of a company. Ageeva et al. (2019) defined perceived corporate culture as "the consumers' perceptions about the corporate values, corporate philosophy, corporate mission, corporate principles, corporate history, founder of the company, country of origin and company's subculture running and resulting from the corporate identity" (p. 17). Based on the qualitative results, the main data themes were: destination values, destination philosophy, destination history, destination subcultures, destination traditions, and a destination lifestyle. In line with the marketing literature (Ageeva et al., 2019; Melewar, 2003) and qualitative findings, the destination culture is defined as people's perceptions about the destination values, destination philosophy, destination history, destination subcultures, destination traditions, and destination lifestyle extending and resulting from the identity of the destination.

Therefore, the qualitative results showed that participants expressed that for them it is paramount to project the positive identity of the destination and communicate its culture effectively through the website. For example,

> I've never visited Tatarstan before, but by looking at the Visit-Tatarstan.com I can feel that the place has a rich culture with its own unique values, beliefs, history, traditions. I would love to visit the place with the authentic feel.

Place brand experts noted that:

> I think that the website of the destination should include the essence of the destination i.e. identity of the destination and its culture. If the destination has a distinct authentic culture and clear about what it is about (its identity), it is a huge competitive advantage among other destinations. It should be projected in the website. For example, like here, on the visit-tatarstan.com I can see – identity; culture...

Based on the qualitative study and literature review destination identity and destination culture were found to represent the main antecedents of the destination website (Figure 14.1).

Destination website, satisfaction and destination image

A unified view of literature (Foroudi et al., 2016, 2018) and participants results that destination websites can positively affect destination image. An important component of the formation of a destination is considered to be a favorable website and it can impact the choice of the destination (Foroudi et al., 2016, 2018). Image is defined by Nguyen and LeBlanc (1998) as the subjective knowledge and attitude, and the composition of product features of the company, but only those that vary from the characteristics of the actual physical product (or service). According to Foroudi et al. (2014), "corporate image is the immediate mental picture an individual holds of the organisation" (p. 2271). Also, Zimmer and Golden (1988) described an image as the overall impression left in the minds of the consumers. Thus, consumers can create and change their impressions (corporate image) based on their perceptions about the website of the company (Bravo et al., 2009). In addition, Braddy et al. (2008) stated that a well-designed website has a significant positive impact on improving the perception of the viewers of the company as well as an increase in organizational attractiveness.

France et al. (2015) and Jimenez-Barreto and Campo-Martinez (2018) stated that consumers by actively sharing information, experiences, and thoughts on social media account of destination website effects the image improvement of the destination. According to Foroudi et al. (2018), to impact the tourists' decision-making process the destination website and image of the destination should be considered the key aims of a tourism destination strategy, where a website of destination is "one of the integral tools for the tourism industry to assist tourists by providing clear information overwhelmed by too much information about a destination" (p. 99). The tourism industry consists of the intangible services, thus images that are positioned on the destination website can become more significant than the reality (Foroudi et al., 2018; Govers et al., 2007). Image of the destination comprises the sum of feelings, knowledge, perceptions that an individual holds about the tourism destination (Govers et al., 2007). In this study, destination image defined as the immediate impression left in the minds of the consumers, which assists destinations to distinguish themselves (Foroudi et al., 2014, 2016, 2018).

The qualitative data presented the importance of the construction of a favorable destination images for the successful development of the place. The results showed that by developing a favorable destination website and bringing satisfaction, people can connect with the destination based on the emotional bond and it can assist in constructing a favorable destination image. As participants noted

"I believe Tatarstan is now aiming to modernize and package the tourism services in a new way by promoting its unique identity,

culture and Tatar lifestyle. Which combines the traditional uniqueness but at the same time adds modern twist. Communicating the
unique features of the place and its culture is best to do by using the
official tourism website. By looking at the carefully chosen images,
people can perceive the place positively"; "When I see the website,
I can say that in a way image of Tatarstan region is a view to the
future, what Tatarstan is trying to be based on what it has now and
what it is communicated".

This research emphasized that the power destination image should be
based on a clear and favorable destination website, which can result in
a positive image (Foroudi et al., 2018). As places can adopt the favorable place image to improve the tourism sector, business activities, and
overall investment climate for import and export (Aureli and Forlani,
2016), the favorable website of the company is an effective way to satisfy the consumers (Doll and Torkzadeh, 1988; Jayawardhena and Foley,
2000) in order to improve the image of the company in their minds. A
well-designed and -structured website signals to the audience that the
company is well managed and that it is a good company (Braddy et al.,
2008); therefore, a favorable corporate website leads to the consumers
being satisfied with the company and leads to an improvement in the
overall impression of the company.

Furthermore, satisfaction was found to influence the destination
image and mediate the relationship between destination website and
destination image. As respondents stated that "When I am looking on
the website, and when I am satisfied with the place, I feel more positive towards my overall impression of the destination". Previous literature highlighted the significance of tourism satisfaction (Foroudi et al.,
2018). As Foroudi et al. (2018) stated: "Satisfaction toward a tourist
destination can be defined as tourist's responses to the evaluation of
expectations from a particular destination and the actual pleasure and
performance perceived from the destination" (p. 104). Thus, the more
favorable tourists perceive the destination website the greater is there
satisfaction and the more likely they are to form the positive destination
image.

*Destination image, invention to revisit and
invention to recommend*

It is broadly highlighted by the previous studies that destination image
plays a key role in tourists' behaviors by influencing its decision-making
process (Chi and Qu, 2008; Foroudi et al., 2018; Lee and Lee, 2004;
Wang and Hsu, 2010). A favorable destination image can have a positive
impact on tourists and increased the intention to revisit (Chi and Qu,

2008; Choi et al., 2011; Foroudi et al., 2018; Ramkissoon et al., 2011; Wang and Hsu, 2010) and lead to the intention to recommend (Foroudi et al., 2018).

Intention to revisit is described as "tourists being willing to travel to other touring spots in a certain destination or in the same country" (Foroudi et al., 2018, p. 104). In the tourism sector, the intention to revisit is counted to be highly preferred by the governments, destination managers (Foroudi et al., 2018; Lau and McKercher, 2004) due to new visitors require higher costs. Prior literature emphasized that destination image can positively impact the intention to revisit (Foroudi et al., 2018). Similarly, respondents noted that "When I really liked the place and overall feeling of the destination it is positive, I want to come back to it again and again and bring friends and family".

Moreover, scholars highlighted that potential tourists depends greatly on the advice of previous tourists (Stylidis et al., 2017; Foroudi et al., 2018; Williams and Soutar, 2009; Zhang et al., 2014), where intention to revisit can impact on the intention to recommend (Foroudi et al., 2018). Intention to recommend is a significant indicator of tourists' loyalty and a source of information for the possible future tourists, that dramatically decreasing the perceived risk for the tourists (Foroudi et al., 2018). Moreover, the destination manager stated that "You can't get any better results as when advertisement of the destination is done on the people to people level. It is personal, it efficient and it just works!". Therefore, based on the qualitative results and literature, it is believed that when tourists have a positive image towards a particular destination, they are more likely to revisit the destination and recommend it to other people. Thus, the more positive is the destination image, the more it is their intention to revisit and intention to recommend.

Future research and study limitations

This research emphasized the notion of the destination website antecedents such as destination identity and culture and the destination image as the key outcome. Results pointed out the significance of destination website in building positive destination image, intention to revisit and recommend.

As with all studies, the current research has several limitations. The study limitations are directly linked to further research opportunities. The first limitation of this study relates to the research setting. This study was conducted in Russia (emerging market), thus, further study can adopt different research contexts to test further the research framework. Thus, researchers who are interested in the additional examination of the destination website can investigate the views of consumers from other countries. Though as the study was performed in Russia when conducted in other destinations findings can be different, therefore research can be performed in different places to expand the understanding of the phenomenon. Moreover, further study could comprise the validation of the research findings in particular in different cultural settings.

Second, in this study, the qualitative method was adopted to attain the aims of the research. Based on the study findings from the qualitative research the study framework was constructed, which could be further tested by using quantitative methods. Finally, it would be beneficial to perform the replicated study to attain better generalizability and validity for the relationships.

Conclusion

This research contributes to the understanding of the relationship between destination identity, destination culture, destination website, destination image, intention to revisit and intention to recommend (Foroudi et al., 2016, 2018; Kavaratzis and Hatch, 2013) and develops a destination website framework (Figure 14.1). Grasping the destination website and destination image and its impact on tourists' decision-making processes can assist governments and tourism managers to construct favorable destination images and increase the positive behavioral intentions of tourists (Chi and Qu, 2008; Foroudi et al., 2018; Lee and Lee, 2004; Wang and Hsu, 2010). Destinations are handling a rising competition that has "tremendous ramifications for the tourism industry and [is] therefore of considerable interest to practitioners and policy makers" (Ritchie and Crouch, 2000, p. 6).

Moreover, this study assists in closing the gap in the literature relating to emerging countries (Dinnie et al., 2010; Foroudi et al., 2016; Roth and Diamantopoulos, 2009). Additionally, this reach is important to the practitioners who aim to construct a favorable destination website and improve the perception of the destination. Finally, this study is of great importance to the government. The tourism sector is one of the main driving forces in economic growth by increasing rates of tourism income not only for a particular region but also for the entire country (Foroudi et al., 2018; Oh, 2000; Yoon and Uysal, 2005). Thus, the government would benefit from more research and guidelines in tourism development regarding destination website, destination image, intention to recommend, intention to revisit that will positively affect the economic growth of a country (Eusebio and Vieira, 2013; Foroudi et al., 2018). Furthermore, it is important to identify that this study has several limitations that must be overcome in future research projects. Firstly, the number of participants could be expanded. Secondly, the framework should be tested in other contexts. Finally, it would be beneficial for further studies to use a mixed methodology to test and improve the framework.

Key construct definitions

Destination identity represents "what the place really is" and consists of tangible and intangible components. Tangible components included food, accommodation, heritage sites, transport, town planning, architecture, whereas intangible hospitality, visitors' information, practices, religion, people, politics, environment, entertainment, and security (Balmer et al., 2009; Foroudi et al., 2017, 2018; Govers and Go, 2009; Govers et al., 2007; Qu et al., 2011)

Destination culture is defined as people's perceptions about the destination values, destination philosophy, destination history, destination subcultures, destination traditions, and destination lifestyle extending and resulting from the identity of the destination (Ageeva et al., 2019; Melewar, 2003).

Destination website is defined as way for destination/place to communicate its uniqueness and authenticity by transmitting consistent images and messages about the nature of the destination in order to attain consumers' positive view of the destination and to come back again to the destination (Ageeva et al., 2018, 2019; Foroudi et al., 2018).

Satisfaction towards a tourist destination is defined as the valuation of potential opportunities from a certain destination and the actual performance and pleasure observed from that destination (Bai et al., 2008; Casalo et al., 2008; Chi et al., 2008; Foroudi et al., 2018).

Destination image defined as the immediate impression left in the minds of the consumers, which assists destinations to distinguish themselves (Foroudi et al., 2014, 2016, 2018)

Intention to revisit represents the desire of tourists to visit the same particular destination again (Foroudi et al., 2016, 2018; Kavaratzis and Hatch, 2013).

Intention to recommend is defined as if the person recommended the destination to another person (Eusebio and Vieira, 2013; Foroudi et al., 2016; 2018; Kavaratzis and Hatch, 2013).

References

Ageeva, E., Melewar, T. C., Foroudi, P., and Dennis, C. (2019). Cues adopted by consumers in examining corporate website favorability: An empirical study of financial institutions in the UK and Russia. *Journal of Business Research*, 98(May), 15–32.

Ageeva, E., Melewar, T. C., Foroudi, P., Dennis, C., and Jin, Z. (2018). Examining the influence of corporate website favorability on corporate image and corporate reputation: Findings from fsQCA. *Journal of Business Research*, 89(August), 287–304.

Alba, R., and Nee, V. (1997). Rethinking assimilation theory for a new era of immigration. *International Migration Review*, 31(4), 826–874.

Alsajjan, B., and Dennis, C. (2010). Internet banking acceptance model: Cross-market examination. *Journal of Business Research*, 63(9), 957–963.

Aureli, S., and Forlani, F. (2016). The importance of brand architecture in business networks: The case of tourist network contracts in Italy. *Qualitative Market Research: An International Journal*, 19(2), 133–155.

Bai, B., Law, R., and Wen, I. (2008). The impact of website quality on customer satisfaction and purchase intentions: Evidence from Chinese online visitors. *International Journal of Hospitality Management*, 27(3), 391–402.

Balmer, J. M. T., Stuart, H. and Greyser, S. A. (2009). Aligning identity and strategy: Corporate branding at British Airways in the late 20th century. *California Management Review*, 51(3), 6–23.

Bellman, S., and Rossiter, J. R. (2004). The website schema. *Journal of Interactive Advertising*, 4(2), 38–48.

Braddy, P. W., Meade, A. W., and Kroustalis, C. M. (2008). Online recruiting: The effects of organisational familiarity, website usability, and website attractiveness on viewers' impressions of organisations. *Computers in Human Behaviour*, 24(6), 2992–3001.

Bravo, R., Matute, J., and Pina, J. M. (2012). Corporate social responsibility as a vehicle to reveal the corporate identity: A study focused on the websites of Spanish financial entities. *Journal of Business Ethics*, 107(2), 129–146.

Bravo, R., Montaner, T., and Pina, J. M. (2009). The role of bank image for customers versus non-customers. *International Journal of Bank Marketing*, 27(4), 315–334.

Brown, T. J. (1998). Corporate associations in marketing: Antecedents and consequences. *Corporate Reputation Review*, 1(3), 215–233.

Campbell, D. J., and Beck, A. C. (2004). Answering allegations: The use of the corporate website for issue-specific reputation management. *Business Ethics: A European Review*, 13(2/3), 100–116.

Casalo, L. V., Flavian, C., and Guinaliu, M. (2008). The role of satisfaction and website usability in developing customer loyalty and positive word-of-mouth in the e-banking services. *International Journal of Bank Marketing*, 26(6), 399–417.

Chi, C. G. Q., and Qu, H. (2008). Examining the structural relationships of destination image, tourist satisfaction and destination loyalty: An integrated approach. *Tourism Management*, 29(4), 624–636.

Choi, G. J., Tkachenko, T., and Sil, S. (2011). On the destination image of Korea by Russian tourists. *Tourism Management*, 32(1), 193–194.

Choi, S., Lehto, X. Y., Morrison, A. M. and Jang, S. S. (2012). Structure of travel planning processes and information use patterns. *Journal of Travel Research*, 51(1), 26–40.

Cyr, D. (2008). Modeling web site design across cultures: Relationships to trust, satisfaction, and e-loyalty. *Journal of Management Information Systems*, 24(4), 47–72.

Cyr, D., and Head, M. (2013). Website design in an international context: The role of gender in masculine versus feminine oriented countries. *Computers in Human Behaviour*, 29(4), 1358–1367.

Dickinger, A., and Stangl, B. (2013). Website performance and behavioral consequences: A formative measurement approach. *Journal of Business Research*, 66(6), 771–777.

Dinnie, K., Melewar, T. C., Seidenfuss, K. U., and Musa, G. (2010). Nation branding and integrated marketing communications: An ASEAN perspective. *International Marketing Review*, 27(4), 388–403.

Doll, W. J., and Torkzadeh, G. (1988). The measurement of end-user computing satisfaction. *MIS Quarterly*, 12(2), 259–274.

Dowling, G. R. (1986). Managing your corporate images. *Industrial Marketing Management*, 15(2), 109–115.

Downes, L., and Mui, C. (1998). The end of strategy. *Strategy and Leadership*, 26(5), 4–9.

Eusebio, C., and Vieira, A. L. (2013). Destination attributes' evaluation, satisfaction and behavioural intentions: A structural modelling approach. *International Journal of Tourism Research*, 15(1), 66–80.

Forbes Rating (2012). Top regions for business. Retrieved from www.forbes.ru/ (accessed October 20, 2018).

Foroudi, P., Akarsu, T. N., Ageeva, E., Foroudi, M. M., Dennis, C., and Melewar, T. C. (2018). PROMISING THE DREAM: Changing destination image of London through the effect of website place. *Journal of Business Research*, 83(February), 97–110.

Foroudi, P., Dinnie, K., Kitchen, P. J., Melewar, T. C., and Foroudi, M. M. (2017). IMC antecedents and the consequences of planned brand identity in higher education. European Journal of Marketing, 51(3), 528–550.

Foroudi, P., Jin, Z., Gupta, S., Melewar, T. C., and Foroudi, M. M. (2016). Influence of innovation capability and customer experience on reputation and loyalty. *Journal of Business Research*, 69(11), 4882–4889.

Foroudi, P., Melewar, T. C., and Gupta, S. (2014). Linking corporate logo, corporate image, and reputation: An examination of consumer perceptions in the financial setting. *Journal of Business Research*, 67(11), 2269–2281.

France, C., Merrilees, B., and Miller, D. (2015). Customer brand co-creation: A conceptual model. *Marketing Intelligence & Planning*, 33(6), 848–864.

Gefen, D., and Straub, D. W. (2000). The relative importance of perceived ease of use in IS adoption: A study of e-commerce adoption. *Journal of the Association for Information Systems*, 1(1), 8.

George, A., and Kumar, G. G. (2014). Impact of service quality dimensions in internet banking on customer satisfaction. *Decision*, 41(1), 73–85.

Glebova, I., and Khamidulina, A. (2015). An evaluation of entrepreneurial potential in the Republic of Tatarstan. *Procedia Economics and Finance*, 32(1), 345–351.

Govers, R. and Go, F. (2009). *Place branding: Virtual and physical identities, glocal, imagined and experienced*. London: Palgrave-Macmillan.

Govers, R., Go, F. M., and Kumar, K. (2007). Promoting tourism destination image. *Journal of Travel Research*, 46(1), 15–23.

IPK International (2017). ITB world travel trends report 2017–2018. Retrieved from www.itbkongress.de/media/itb/itb_dl_all/itb_presse_all/ITB_WTTR_A4_2018_interaktiv.pdf (accessed January 15, 2019).

Jayawardhena, C., and Foley, P. (2000). Changes in the banking sector-the case of Internet banking in the UK. *Internet Research*, 10(1), 19–31.

Jimenez-Barreto, J., and Campo-Martinez, S. (2018). Destination website quality, users' attitudes and the willingness to participate in online co-creation experiences. *European Journal of Management and Business Economics*, 27(1), 26–41.

Kavaratzis, M., and Hatch, M. J. (2013). The dynamics of place brands: An identity-based approach to place branding theory. *Marketing Theory*, 13(1), 69–86.

Kesharwani, A., and Bisht, S. (2012). The impact of trust and perceived risk on Internet banking adoption in India: an extension of technology acceptance model. *International Journal of Bank Marketing*, 30(4), 303–322.

Lau, A. L. S., and McKercher, B. (2004). Exploration versus acquisition: A comparison of first-time and repeat visitors. *Journal of Travel Research*, 42(3), 279–285.

Lee, B. K., and Lee, W. N. (2004). The effect of information-overload on consumer choice quality in an online environment. *Psychology and Marketing*, 21(3), 159–183.

Loureiro, S. M. C. (2015). The role of website quality on PAD, attitude and intentions to visit and recommend island destination. *International Journal of Tourism Research*, 17(6), 545–554.

Luna-Nevarez, C., and Hyman, M. R. (2012). Common practices in destination website design. *Journal of Destination Marketing & Management*, 1(1–2), 94–106.

Mael, F. A., and Ashforth, B. E. (1995). Loyal from day one: Biodata, organizational identification, and turnover among newcomers. *Personnel Psychology*, 48(2), 309–333.

Mandeville, J. B., Marota, J. J., Kosofsky, B. E., Keltner, J. R., Weissleder, R., Rosen, B. R., and Weisskoff, R. M. (1998). Dynamic functional imaging of relative cerebral blood volume during rat forepaw stimulation. *Magnetic Resonance in Medicine*, 39(4), 615–624.

Marston, C. (2003). Financial reporting on the Internet by leading Japanese companies. *Corporate Communications: An International Journal*, 8(1), 23–34.

Melewar, T. C. (2003). Determinants of the corporate identity construct: A review of the literature. *Journal of Marketing Communications*, 9(4), 195–220.

Melewar, T. C., Foroudi, P., Gupta, S., Kitchen, P. J., and Foroudi, M. M. (2017). Integrating identity, strategy and communications for trust, loyalty and commitment. *European Journal of Marketing*, 51(3), 572–604.

Muylle, S., Moenaert, R., and Despontin, M. (2004). The conceptualisation and empirical validation of web site user satisfaction. *Information and Management*, 41(5), 543–560.

Nguyen, N., and LeBlanc, G. (1998). The mediating role of corporate image on customers' retention decisions: An investigation in financial services. *International Journal of Bank Marketing*, 16(2), 52–65.

Oh, H. (2000). Diners' perceptions of quality, value, and satisfaction: A practical viewpoint. *Cornell Hotel and Restaurant Administration Quarterly*, 41(3), 58–66.

Oliveira, E., and Panyik, E. (2015). Content, context and co-creation: Digital challenges in destination branding with references to Portugal as a tourist destination. *Journal of Vacation Marketing*, 21(1), 53–74.

Park, Y. A., and Gretzel, U. (2007). Success factors for destination marketing web sites: A qualitative meta-analysis. *Journal of Travel Research*, 46(1), 46–63.

Qu, H., Kim, L. H., and Im, H. H. (2011). A model of destination branding: Integrating the concepts of the branding and destination image. *Tourism Management*, 32(3), 465–476.

Raman, M., Stephenaus, R., Alam, N., and Kuppusamy, M. (2008). Information technology in Malaysia: E-service quality and uptake of Internet banking. *Journal of Internet Banking and Commerce*, 13(2), 1–17.

Ramkissoon, H., Uysal, M., and Brown, K. (2011). Relationship between destination image and behavioural intentions of tourists to consume cultural attractions. *Journal of Hospitality Marketing and Management*, 20(5), 575–595.

Ritchie, J. R. B., and Crouch, G. I. (2000). The competitive destination: A sustainability perspective. *Tourism Management*, 21(1), 1–7.

Rooney, D., Paulsen, N., Callan, V. J., Brabant, M., Gallois, C., and Jones, E. (2010). A new role for place identity in managing organizational change. *Management Communication Quarterly*, 24(1), 44–73.

Roth, K. P. and Diamantopoulos, A. (2009). Advancing the country image construct. *Journal of Business Research*, 62(7), 726–740.

Santos, J. (2003). E-service quality: A model of virtual service quality dimensions. *Managing Service Quality: An International Journal*, 13(3), 233–246.

Santouridis, I., Trivellas, P., and Reklitis, P. (2009). Internet service quality and customer satisfaction: Examining Internet banking in Greece. *Total Quality Management*, 20(2), 223–239.

Srinivasan, S. S., Anderson, R., and Ponnavolu, K. (2002). Customer loyalty in e-commerce: An exploration of its antecedents and consequences. *Journal of Retailing*, 78(1), 41–50.

Stylidis, D., Shani, A., and Belhassen, Y. (2017). Testing an integrated destination image model across residents and tourists. *Tourism Management*, 58(February), 184–195.

Tajfel, H., and Turner, J. (1986). The social identity theory of intergroup behaviour: Worchel S. i Austin WG (ur.) Psychology of intergroup relations. *Chicago: Nelson Hall*, USA.

Tang, L. R., Jang, S. S., and Morrison, A. (2012). Dual-route communication of destination websites. *Tourism Management*, 33(1), 38–49.

Tarafdar, M., and Zhang, J. (2008). Determinants of reach and loyalty: A study of website performance and implications for website design. *Journal of Computer Information Systems*, 48(2), 16–24.

tourism.tatarstan.ru (2019). Retrieved from http://tourism.tatarstan.ru (accessed October 20, 2018).

Tsang, N. K., Lai, M. T., and Law, R. (2010). Measuring e-service quality for online travel agencies. *Journal of Travel & Tourism Marketing*, 27(3), 306–323.

Wang, C. Y., and Hsu, M. K. (2010). The relationships of destination image, satisfaction, and behavioral intentions: An integrated model. *Journal of Travel & Tourism Marketing*, 27(8), 829–843.

Williams, P., and Soutar, G. N. (2009). Value, satisfaction and behavioral intentions in an adventure tourism context. *Annals of Tourism Research*, 36(3), 413–438.

Yoon, Y., and Uysal, M. (2005). An examination of the effects of motivation and satisfaction on destination loyalty: A structural model. *Tourism Management*, 26(1), 45–56.

Yousafzai, S., and Yani-de-Soriano, M. (2012). Understanding customer-specific factors underpinning internet banking adoption. *International Journal of Bank Marketing*, 30(1), 60–81.

Zhang, H., Fu, X., Cai, L., and Lu, L. (2014). Destination image and tourist loyalty: A metaanalysis. *Tourism Management*, 40(February), 213–223.

Zimmer, M. R., and Golden, L. L. (1988). Impressions of retail stores: A content analysis of consume. *Journal of Retailing*, 64(3), 265.

15 Wine and food tourism and place identity

The strategic role of local networks

Magda Antonioli Corigliano and Cristina Mottironi

Learning outcomes

At the end of this chapter, readers should be able to

1 Identify wine and food tourism as a place specific activity
2 Understand the need of cooperation for the promotion of rural areas as tourism destinations
3 Define wine and food routes as economic local networks
4 Understand the objectives of wine and food routes, from destination marketing to territorial enhancement
5 Understand how wine and food routes can promote district economies

Introduction

Place identity is key to attract tourist demand. In the case of wine and food tourism, its role is particularly relevant. Typical wines and foods are deeply connected with the specific characteristics of their production area: its environment, micro-climate, culture and productive methods (Montanari, 1992). Tourism has a high potential in promoting this link in a persuasive way because tourists have a live experience of the productive environment (Antonioli Corigliano, 1996, 1999; Hjalager and Richards, 2002). In addition, tourism can improve the maintenance of the rural environment, the protection and renovation of cultural and social traditions and the diversification of the agricultural economy (Scarpato, 1999, 2003; Antonioli Corigliano and Mottironi, 2013). Tourism is thus a significant means of image transfer, consumer education, territorial enhancement and economic revitalization of rural and peripheral areas. However, the success of rural areas as tourist destinations depends on their ability to create inter-sectoral local networks.

Wine and food tourism

The wine and food tourism industry is of growing importance globally in terms of overall number of wine and food tourist flows, revenues, occupancy and territorial development (Atsuko & Telfer, 2003; Bruwer, 2003; Getz & Brown, 2006).

The phenomenon interests Europe as like as the rest of the world: the number of wineries opening to tourists is growing (O'Neill & Charters, 2000); wine trails are a significant tourist attraction in the main wine producing countries – France, Italy, Spain and the USA, that bring into the market more than half of total world wine production and its consumption – but also in countries that produce smaller quantities – like Portugal, Canada and Australia – (Jaffe & Pasternak, 2004).

The conceptualization of wine tourism has not resulted in a uniform way. However, traveller's motivations and experiences are mentioned in most definitions of wine tourism, between which one of most popular is: 'visitation to vineyards, wineries, wine festivals and wine shows for which grape wine tasting and/or experiencing the attributes of a grape wine region are the prime motivating factors for visitors' (Hall et al., 2000). Other researchers underlined the existence of three major perspectives on this topic: that of wine producers, tourism agencies and consumers (Getz, 2000). That is why wine tourism can be considered simultaneously a form of consumer behaviour, where wine lovers or interested people travel to preferred destinations; a strategy by which destinations develop and market wine-related attractions and imagery; finally, a marketing opportunity for wineries to educate consumers and to sell their products directly to them (Getz & Brown, 2006).

The wine and food tourism industry's growth attracted marketing interest and studies especially at the turn of the new Century, together with the growing attention to crafts tourism, creative tourism and the general emphasis on symbolic products. In the last few years there has been a number of studies on wine regions (Skinner, 2000), wine routes (Bruwer, 2003) and wine festival and events (Carlsen, 2000, 2004). According to some researchers, this industry is becoming one of the most promising segments of the tourism sector (Atsuko & Telfer, 2003; Brower, 2003). It is interesting to underline how a deep evolution has interested the sector: in the past rural tourism was considered a second choice product, retained only by people who could not afford more attractive and expensive destinations; on the contrary, today the re-discovery of traditions, based on typical products and rural lifestyle, let the rural tourism become a high-standard segment, in terms of prices/spending patterns and quality of services delivered (Antonioli Corigliano, 1996; Mottironi, 2005; Getz & Brown, 2006; Ab Karim & Chi, 2010).

The advantages and benefits of the move to wine and food tourism for wineries and producers are plentiful: increasing consumer exposure to products, brand awareness and loyalty, increasing margins, providing additional sales outlets, developing marketing intelligence on products and consumers, and heightening consumer awareness and understanding of wine products. Moreover, besides the direct benefits to wine producers, wine tourism also provides a wider range of returns, at a higher level, like the creation of many full and part-time jobs, foreign exchange earnings, the generation of secondary economic activities, tourism and corporate investments (O'Neill & Charters, 2000). Therefore, the wine tourism industry is now considered an essential regional economic development strategy.

In this perspective, wine tourism can play a significant role in regional promotion and tourism plans through its contribution to sustaining the economic and social bases of regions. It can be an important factor in providing horizontal and vertical linkages within the rural areas and in many cases new activities are explicitly made in order to strengthen those back-linkages (Antonioli Corigliano & Mottironi, 2013). The interrelations between tourism and food/beverage have been increasingly considered also by policy makers and planners engaged in regional economic development: those 'can represent the shifting emphasis in the way in which governance for rural development is being reconceived from a sectorally based approach, to a territorially-based one' (Boyne et al., 2003, p. 143).

One of the most important benefits offered by wine tourism is its capability of promoting the regional image. According to Peters (1997) – who calls the wine region 'winescape', when viticulture is successful, it can transform the local landscape into something more: a combination of agriculture, industry and tourism. Hall (2002) underlines the key role of region in marketing, arguing that wine, food and tourism industries support the regional brands, critical sources of differentiation and value added for rural regions.

Regional branding is the basis for both wine and tourism industries. Wine routes – 'usually a designed itinerary through the wine region' (Hall et al., 2000), 'involving an interaction between different material and immaterial components, facilities, services, environment and local communities' (Antonioli Corigliano, 2002) – give an important contribution to this process; most wine routes, in fact, bounded in 'an officially demarcated wine region or geographical indication (GI) that has an identity in the form of a branded descriptive name, such as Champagne (France) or Stellenbosch (South Africa)' (Bruwer, 2003), express typical regional attributes, and environmental, cultural and social features and therefore give the region a distinctive trademark or brand identity (Moran, 1993).

This is clearly linked to the new kind of motivations and desires that move tourists: the wish of having a noteworthy experience to remember and talk about, the desire of experiencing the region as a whole, discover its identity and traditional values and come into direct contact with the local community. At a higher level, the wine and food industry could be also viewed as an important cultural embodiment (Bernard & Zaragoza, 1999; Handszuh, 2000; Hjalager & Antonioli Corigliano,

2000), a significant feature of national identity. Especially in countries like Italy, extremely rich of artistic heritage, different cultural expressions and plentiful typical regional culinary products, wine and gastronomic tourism can make a contribution to relating the distinctive culture of a region to the wider social, economic and environmental context of the location.

Therefore, wineries and all the different regional stakeholders have to support the wine tourism industry and to exploit its opportunities, enhancing the link between territory and wine and designing appropriate marketing strategies. If the discovery and tasting of typical wine and gastronomic products is a relevant motivation for rural tourism, this calls for the adoption of appropriate strategies to exploit this potential. Two aspects are here relevant: the enhancement of the wine and food identity of a place and the ability of the local stakeholders to implement a common entrepreneurial approach, integrating wine and gastronomy into the global tourism market. The two aspects are deeply interrelated, since tourism is a key driver for wine and food identity in terms of marketing and sustainable development, but this depends on the tourism destination management strategies and actions developed at a local level. It is also a self-reinforcing process: tourism destination management supports the enhancement of wine and food identity and a stronger identity attracts tourists in the area.

In particular, wine and food routes are an example of collective tourism products created in order to exploit the tourism potential of rural areas with an oeno-gastronomic value (see, e.g., Antonioli Corigliano, 1999; Bruwer, 2003; Jaffel & Pasternak, 2004). They developed globally, but the Italian experience is particularly significant because of its considerable number of wine and food routes.

Italian wine and food routes

The Italian context is worth to be studied, since it is rich of wine and gastronomic resources that are considered an integral part of the national cultural heritage. Moreover, initiatives to promote wine and food tourism have been encouraged since the 1980s: the first law dedicated to farm tourism was promulgated in 1985 (Law No. 730/1985), in order to help farmers to remain in rural areas while improving their living conditions and fostering the development and balance of the agricultural region through tourism. A law on Wine Routes followed in 1999 (Law No. 268/1999), in order to incentive the creation of this type of tourism itineraries, considered a relevant way to promote the knowledge and experience of rural areas. In those same years two national associations were also founded and, nowadays, they are still key actors: the Wine Tourism Movement *(Movimento Turismo del Vino)* and the Wine Town Association *(Associazione Città del Vino)*. They both have largely contributed to the creation of a wine and gastronomic tourism culture and have facilitated connections among local and national operators.

After the national law 268/99, around 150 wine and food routes (the Italian denomination is *Strade del vino e dei sapori*) have been created. To understand their diffusion, it is worth noticing that they interest the 14% of the Italian municipalities. Wine and food routes are defined by the Italian law as itineraries created in the geographical areas where protected wines and foodstuffs are produced. A partnership of agricultural and tourism operators has to be created in order to develop common projects and implement joint actions. The main goal of wine and food routes is to communicate and market rural areas as tourism destinations.

Identity, cooperation and management are therefore key assets of wine and food routes and they underpin the reason why of the law. Identity, as Italian wine and food roots can be created just within geographical areas characterized by the production of 'denominated' (protected) agricultural products, thus areas where the identity of the local productions and the deep connection with the territory are guaranteed. Cooperation, as wine and food routes are a formal partnership among the local stakeholders, generally through the creation of either a no-profit association or a consortium. Management, as the main task of wine and food roots is to facilitate the management of rural areas as tourist destinations and to enhance territorial development and cohesion. The consequence is that wine and food roots are more than an itinerary. They are a model of destination management.

Within this common framework, the Italian context is variegated: its several wine and food routes have different life cycles and just some of them have been able to effectively manage the local tourism development. This is because a wine and food route is a complex tourist product, involving an interaction between different tangible and intangible components: facilities, services, environment and local communities. Moreover different stakeholders are involved, such as local authorities, tourism and agricultural enterprises, investors, residents and so on. Networks are essential to build an efficient and competitive tourism destination, to market high quality products and to take advantage of the synergies that can be created through a systemic approach. However in order to manage this complexity and achieve positive results, appropriate strategies and actions need to be undertaken by the routes.

Local tourism networks

In general the development of the tourism sector has demonstrated the need for a systemic, or district, approach to its management. This for several reasons starting from its collective nature and the relevance of the territorial assets, arriving to the various economic advantages that derive in terms of economies of scale, economies of scope and creation of positive externalities. Interestingly, the advantages arise for the tourism industry and also for the communities involved as a consequence of the relevant local impacts that distinguish the tourism sector. The advantages of a tourism district are several but the main are identified in the following ones: uphill economies of scale and for the internal management of common services and local assets (destination price policies and costs reduction); economies of specialization and of scale for communication and promotional activities also through an increase of the bargaining power towards intermediation, the creation of centralized reservation systems and the management of independent demand; economies of specialization and of scale for information handling, overcoming asymmetric information issues affecting the sector; and finally, the creation of economic links with other economic sectors at local level and the reduction of economic leakages (Antonioli Corigliano, 1999).

The essence of a tourism district approach lies in the ability to put into operation a system of coordinated relational networks among the various decision-makers and the various public and private operators of a destination. It has to be remained that the tourist experience is a composed one and refers to a combination of structures, infrastructures, services and resources. All of them refer to different actors that generally do not act together as a finalized organization. As a consequence, the tourist product is structured just after a process of organization based on the coordination of the single decisions and intervention tools and, finally, on the activation and management of an effective network (Mottironi & Antonioli, 2012).

However, the creation of these types of networks and synergies is complex and often represents a key obstacle to the progress of tourism territories. Main difficulties derive from the management of these multifaceted networks that cannot be framed either in a corporate logic or in a relationship between companies one (as it is in manufacturing districts). The extra-economic networks – meaning the relationships between public sector, private operators and local community – have a significant influence in tourism. The understanding of the underlying dynamics of these types of relations is crucial and must be based on a concrete and clear definition of specific roles for the subjects involved and on the choice of common strategic objectives, identified on the acceptance of stakes and advantages that are necessarily different for the various groups involved.

Moreover, the complexity of the tourist product imposes to act not just in a cooperative way enhancing territorial resources and competences, but requires also the adoption of integrated management tools or the implementation of the so-called destination management.

Over the last decade the relevance of managing the destination has emerged significantly and has represented a main stream of interest for both practitioners and researchers involved in tourism. The literature has stressed in particular how, in order to benefit from the economic outcomes of tourism, organizations and firms have had to increase their efforts to promote and sell their products, basically reinforcing marketing activities, striving to enhance their differentiation and image, and focusing on the quality and value of the destination product. These issues are central also for wine and food routes that – as seen above – are deeply grounded in the territorial identity of their location and are in their essence a form of networking. As such, these issues are also the basis for the study reported in the following pages.

Local networking in practice: an analysis of Italian wine and food routes

The study aims at investigating key aspects of cooperation and destination management through the analysis of nine wine and food routes located in Northern Italy. The agricultural area under consideration is the most important in Italy with around 70,000 agricultural and alimentary farms. In addition, it has invested significantly in quality products with around 30 protected designation of origin (PDOs) and PGIs (protected GI) products and over 85 million bottles of CDOs (Controlled Designation of Origin), and GCDOs (denomination of controlled and guaranteed origin) wines a year. The nine wine and food routes under investigation were created starting from 2000, just after the national law. Besides matching the minimum standards required by law, they are managed independently and this makes it interesting to compare the main strategies they have adopted. In addition, the wine and food routes under investigation – after a long start-up period – have been operating regularly for more than a decade now. As such, more recent wine and food routes in the same or similar areas have been excluded from the analysis.

The objective of the analysis is to understand the strategic choices of the wine and food routes under investigation when confronted with their ability to be effective collective agents of development of rural areas. In order to explore this issue, the following two aspects are investigated:

1   First, wine and food routes are a case of cooperation of different stakeholders (private and public, related both to the agricultural and the tourism sectors) with different interests and competences. It is then relevant to understand the functioning of this network, meaning the real degree of cooperation, the strategies and tools used to involve the stakeholders, the difficulties encountered in activating local cooperation and the types of joint actions implemented.

2   Second, wine and food routes are a case of collective business at a local level. As such, we may argue that they are effective if they are able to develop a district approach, leading to system economies

(Antonioli Corigliano, 1999). It is then relevant to evaluate if they are able to operate in this perspective, creating added value for the rural territory and the stakeholders involved. Integrated quality management, knowledge transfer, product innovation and destination marketing are assumed as key collective strategies that wine and food routes can implement to sustain the small-medium enterprises that typically operate in rural areas.

To investigate the two aspects, a survey was conducted through in depth interviews to privileged stakeholders and decision makers followed by a questionnaire submitted to a larger sample of stakeholders. Overall, 324 questionnaires were submitted to different types of stakeholders of the wine routes under investigation (managers, partners and others how have a stake) and 232 resulted valid for the purpose of the study. The sample was asked to report and evaluate various aspects related to the activity of the wine and food routes under investigation in order to analyse issues related to local cooperation and to their ability to operate as effective destination management organizations (DMOs). When an evaluation was required, a Likert scale 1–5 was used; otherwise the results are reported in percentage.

Coherently with the aspects under investigation, the questionnaire was divided into two sections: section one was dedicated to the management of cooperation or networking issues while section two was dedicated to the ability of wine and food routes to implement destination management tools in order to leverage on system economies. It has to be reminded that wine and food route partners are for the most part micro-small firms that can take advantage from networking. The aspects surveyed in the two sections through different variables are summarized in Table 15.1. The items included in the survey were confronted with experts of the sector before being delivered to the sample.

Table 15.1 The survey

Section 1: Cooperation
(1a) Perceived level of cooperation
(1b) Joint actions promoted by the route
(1c) Barriers to cooperation
(1d) Actions to overcome barriers to cooperation

Section 2: Destination management
(2a) Tourist services
(2b) Marketing tools
(2c) Market knowledge
(2d) Quality improvement

Main results of the analysis

Some of the main evidences that emerged from the case studies under analyses are here summarized around the issues of Table 1. First co-operation, in terms of cooperation at a local level, the wine and food routes surveyed have not reached an optimal situation yet. The degree of cooperation cannot be considered satisfactory, since it is evaluated – on average – from very low (1.5) to fairly good (3.3) by the stakeholders interviewed, while the actions undertaken to overcome the obstacles to cooperate (see Figure 15.1) are sporadic and often limited to meetings (54.5%). However strategic and tactical planning are increasingly used, even though their percentage remains around 30%, showing a margin of improvement, also considered the very low frequency (6.4%) of monitoring practices to verify the results obtained.

However a real agreement on the main obstacles or barriers to cooperation did not emerge from the survey: there is clearly a need to better understand the dynamics of cooperation in order to overcome the scarce attitude towards networking. Also in terms of joint actions implemented by wine and food routes to enhance rural areas (Figure 15.2), the survey indicates that the external links are not exploited to the utmost, since the highest percentage of answers just refer to the promotion of events (wine and cultural events, exhibitions). The positive impacts of events are widely recognized, however they are not sufficient: these wine and food routes have been operating since 2000, but their role within the territory seems to be too restricted; moreover, they are not catalysing different competencies in order to use them to promote local development.

The second aspect under investigation is the ability of wine and food routes to create added value for their partners through the achievement of a proper destination management system. Different aspects were

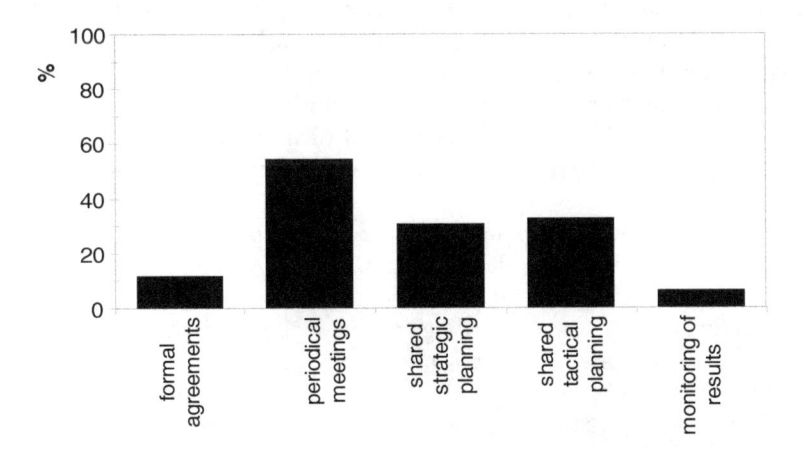

Figure 15.1 Actions of wine and food routes to enhance cooperation.

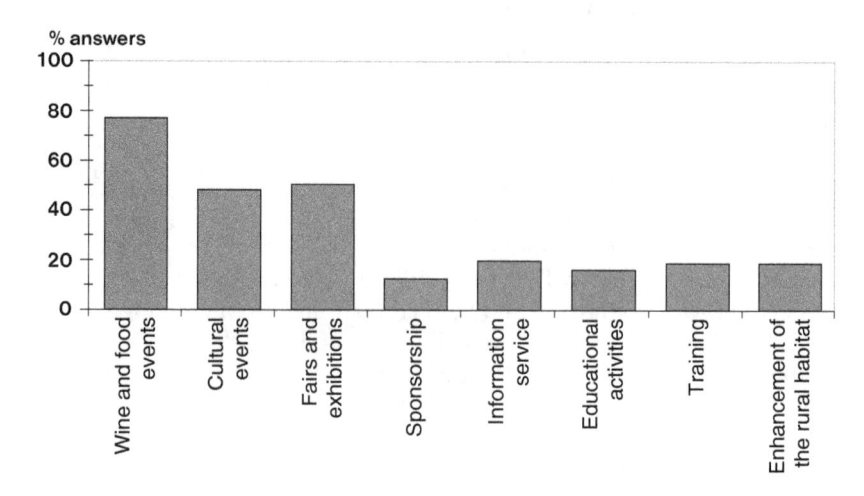

Figure 15.2 Joint actions promoted by the routes to enhance rural areas.

evaluated ranging from management and marketing tools adapted to the degree of product innovation achieved, and knowledge and information transfer. The route can act as a DMO, providing the expertise and logistic support that allows its partners to benefit system economies that are not available to individual enterprises (Porter, 1998; Schmitz, 1998; Pearce, 2013). Information management, improvement of the quality level of the destination, training and specialized communication channels are just some examples (Antonioli Corigliano, 1999, 2003; Ivaniš, 2011). In terms of marketing tools and tourist services offered (see Figure 15.3), they are quite standardized among the nine wine routes. Some services are typical tourist services (such as packaging, information offices and wine exhibitions), while others are more oriented to enhance the knowledge of the rural habitat (such as courses on the local cuisine, museums and educational programmes). We may notice that, while the variety of services provided is positive, the level of innovation is low: as a result the product offered by the routes seems to be appealing but yet not diversified.

If wine and food routes seem to operate as typical DMOs, providing services to experience the destination and doing destination marketing, their role in creating the conditions to generate other system economies is questionable. If we refer to Figures 15.4 and 15.5, we can evaluate three key determinants of territorial competitiveness (see, e.g., Ritchie and Crouch, 2003; Dwyer et al., 2004): market knowledge and information transfer, quality improvement and human resources. Demand knowledge is not a common and diffused practice among the wine routes surveyed: some actions have been undertaken to improve it but their

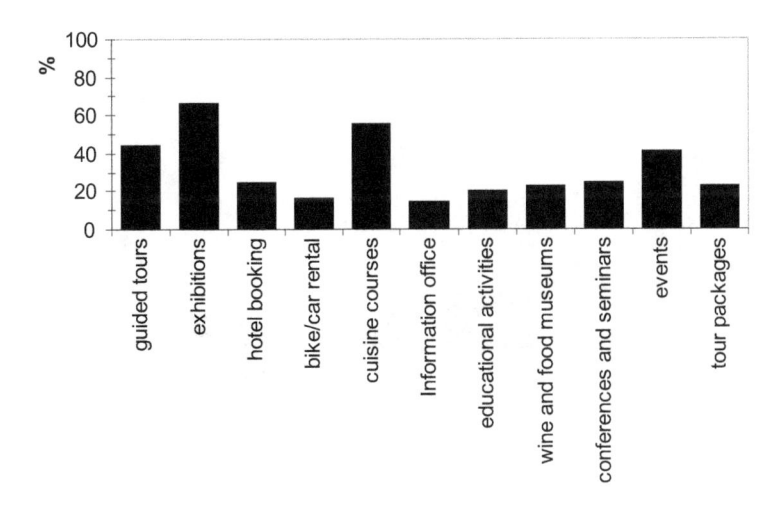

Figure 15.3 Tourist services implemented by the wine and food routes.

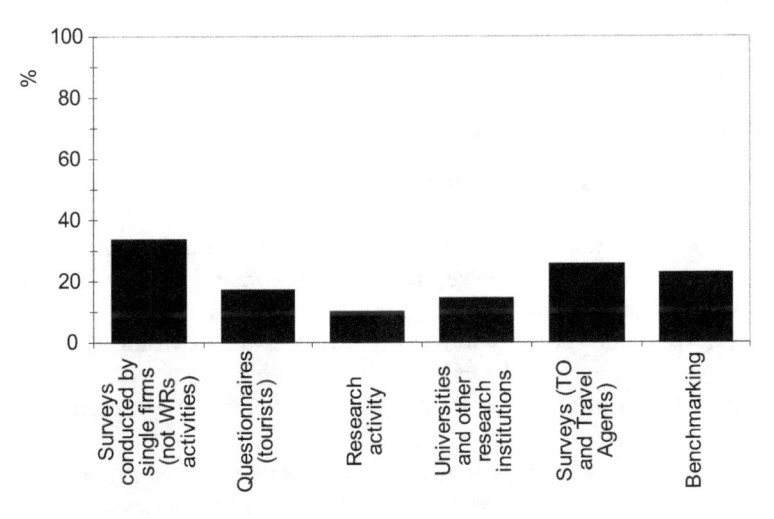

Figure 15.4 Actions to improve demand knowledge.

frequency is quite low. The highest percentage (30%) refers to surveys conducted by single companies, not even by the route. This is particularly meaningful if we consider that the sample was not able to provide any basic information about their tourists: arrivals, main markets and average stay.

Also in terms of actions to improve quality, the potential of having created a network is not exploited: for instance, complaints are almost not collected, common quality standards for all the partners are adopted

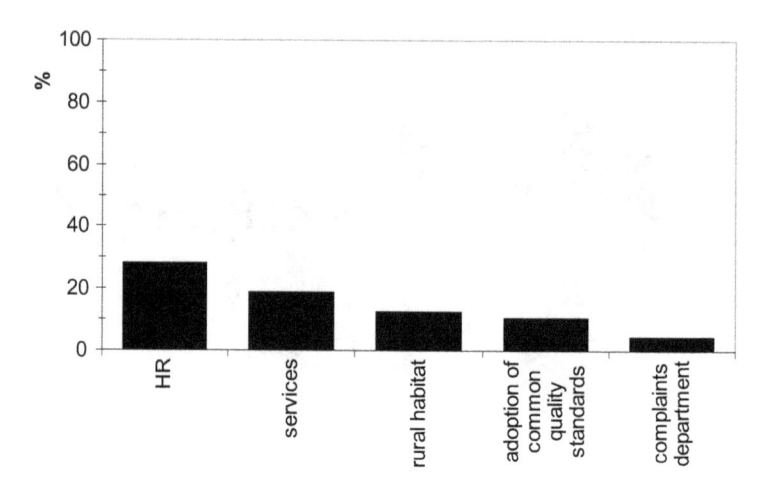

Figure 15.5 Actions to improve quality.

just in few cases (10%). Finally, human resources are the main field of action (28%); however, the 57.3% of the sample has not attended any training course in the last 2 years.

Future research directions

The study shows how some Italian local routes have been operating effectively in terms of exploiting the identity and positive image of the production areas in which they operate in order to market various tourism activities and services. However, local innovation and a wider process of creation of various system economies are still lacking.

If this applies to the networks under investigation, it would be relevant to enlarge the sample and verify if differences exist in a wider comparison, mainly at international level, with the objective to benchmark and cluster wine and food routes with different strategic levels.

Another relevant issue would be to investigate the typologies of organizational forms that different wine routes have implemented and verify if this has an impact on their operativity and on their ability to create and exploit system economies locally.

Finally, the allocation of resources to these networks is paramount, and a specific focus on the investments and different budget allocations the local stakeholders make would help in understanding the functioning of the wine and food routes as DMOs.

Conclusion

Wine and food routes have a high potential to be a link among tourism, agriculture and rural habitat, acting as effective DMOs and developing networks – both internal and external – at a local level. The literature on networks and clusters underline how they can promote local development and competitiveness creating system economies that generate benefits for local firms. Operators, local authorities and organizations, however, should enhance such opportunities by implementing a planned development process based on synergies between public and private sector and by adopting an appropriate strategic positioning. This is particularly important once the start-up phase is over, as it is the case of the wine and food routes surveyed.

The cases here investigated show how a shift is required in order to meet the objectives above mentioned. Wine and food routes demonstrate a low level of innovation, since they offer an interesting variety of services but that tend to be standardized. Competitive factors such as training and quality are not exploited enough, and the level of knowledge of the actual and potential demand is not sufficient. As a consequence the promotional tools are not differentiated and their efficacy may be notably reduced.

While having typical and high-quality food and wines are paramount in order to attract visitors and enhance the place identity of rural areas, their role in terms of long-term competitiveness may be questionable. Destinations relying too heavily on the quality and image of their resources (here typical wines and foodstuff) may not be able to upgrade true underlying tourism competitiveness and long-term prosperity: wine and food routes may be promoter of sustainable and competitive rural development through tourism, but they have to understand the real potential of networking and put it into practice.

Key construct definitions

Wine and food tourism: a form of tourism that is primarily motivated by wine and food related activities such as the visitation to vineyards, wineries and food producers, or the participation to wine and food festivals and shows, or the participation to wine and food tasting/workshops. The experiencing of the attributes of a production region is a relevant factor of this form of tourism.

Geographic indication (GI): a label, recognized as intellectual property, used on products that have a specific geographical origin and possess qualities or a reputation that are due to that origin. As such, the products with a designation or appellation of origin are intrinsically linked with the place in which they are made. In Europe, wine and foods have the following GIs: PDO for the products with the strongest link to their production area (all the production and transformation takes place in a specific region); Protected geographical indication (PGI) for products with a particular quality or reputation related to a territory; GI of spirit drinks and aromatised wines (GI), similar to the PGIs; and traditional speciality guaranteed for traditional food and agricultural products.

Wine and food routes: it is a concept made of three layers. First, itineraries that allow the discovery of a territory through the visit to production and transformation firms. Second, a proper cooperation among the various tourism and agricultural stakeholders of a production area, formalized by the creation of a partnership (often public-private). Third, a district characterized by both economic and socio-cultural bounds. They can be considered as local DMOs (see below). Wine and food routes are often promoted in territories characterized by the presence of products with GI labels.

Destination marketing/management organizations (DMOs): organizations officially dedicated to the marketing and management of tourism destinations for the well-being of the local businesses and community. They coordinate the various components of the tourism experience, provide visitor services, develop destination marketing strategies and develop services for the local players. DMOs increasingly integrate tourism and other local economic sectors.

Tourism district economies: advantages that derive from the proximity, agglomeration and cooperation of the various players of the tourism system. Because of the specific nature of the tourism system, a tourism district is made of horizontal and vertical linkages and includes various extra-economic aspects and it is the result of the interplay of both public and private players. The advantages may range from innovation and know-how transfer, economies of scale and economies of agglomeration. Wine and food routes are a specific case of a mixed tourism and rural district.

References

Ab Karim, S., & Chi, C. G.-Q. (2010). Culinary tourism as a destination attraction: An empirical examination of destinations' food image. *Journal of Hospitality Marketing and Management, 19*(6), 531–555.

Antonioli Corigliano, M. (1996). *Enoturismo. Caratteristiche della domanda, strategie di offerta e aspetti territoriali e ambientali*. Milano: Franco Angeli.

Antonioli Corigliano, M. (1999). *Strade del Vino ed enoturismo. Distretti turistici e vie di comunicazione*. Milano: Franco Angeli.

Antonioli Corigliano, M. (2002). The route to quality: Italian gastronomy networks in operation. In A.M. Hjalager, & G. Richards (Eds.), *Tourism and gastronomy*. London: Routledge, 166–185.

Antonioli Corigliano, M., & Mottironi, C. (2013). Planning and management of European rural territories. In C. Costa, P. E., & D. Buhalis (Eds.), *European tourism planning and organisation systems Vol. I. New perspectives and emerging issues* (pp. 33–46). Bristol: Channel View Publications.

Atsuko, H., & Telfer, D. J. (2003). Positioning an emerging wine route in the Niagara Region: Understanding the wine tourism market and its implications for marketing. *Journal of Travel and Tourism Marketing, 14*(3/4), 61–76.

Bernard, A., & Zaragoza, I. (1999). Art and gastronomy routes: An unexplored tourism proposal for Latin America. *Proceedings of the first Pan-American conference*, Panama City.

Boyne, S., Hall, D., & Williams, F. (2003). Policy, support and promotion for food-related tourism initiatives: A marketing approach to regional development. *Journal of Travel & Tourism Marketing, 14*(3/4), 131–154.

Bruwer, J. (2003). South African wine routes: Some perspectives on the wine tourism industry's structural dimensions and wine tourism product. *Tourism Management, 24*, 423–435.

Carlsen, J. (2002). Segmentation and profiling of the wine festival visitor market. In C. Cullen, G. Pickering, & R. Phillips (Eds.), *Baccus to the future: The inaugural Brock University Wine conference* (pp. 257–278). St. Catharines, Ontario: Brock University Press.

Carlsen, J. (2004). A review of global wine tourism research. *Journal of Wine Research, 15*(1), 5–13.

Dwyer, L., Mellor, R., Livaic, Z., Edwards, D., & Kim, C. (2004). Attributes of destination competitiveness: A factor analysis. *Tourism Analysis, 9*(1/2), 91–101.

Getz, D. (2000). *Explore wine tourism: Management, development and destinations*. New York: Cognizant Communication Corporation.

Getz, D., & Brown, G. (2006). Critical success factors for wine tourism regions: A demand analysis. *Tourism Management, 27*, 146–158.

Hall, C. M. (May 16–18, 2002). Local initiatives for local regional development: The role of food, wine and tourism. *Proceedings of the 2nd tourism industry and education symposium*. Jyvaskyla, Finland: Jyvaskyla Polytechnic.

Hall, C. M., Longo, A. M., Mitchell, R., & Johnson, G. (2000). Wine tourism in New Zealand. In C. M. Hall, L. Sharples, B. Cambourne, & N. Macionis (Eds.), *Wine tourism around the world: Development, management and markets* (pp. 150–176). Oxford: Elsevier.

Handszuh, H. (2000). Local food in tourism policies. *Proceedings of the international conference on local food and tourism*. Larnaka, Cyprus.

Hjalager, A. M., & Antonioli Corigliano, M. (2000). Food for tourist-determinants of an image. *International Journal of Tourism Research, 2*, 281–293.

Hjalager, A. M., & Richards, G. (2002). *Tourism and gastronomy*. London: Routledge-ATLAS.

Ivaniš, M. (2011). General model of small entrepreneurship development in tourism destinations in Croatia. *Tourism and Hospitality Management, 17*(2), 231–250.

Jaffel, E., & Pasternak, H. (2004). Developing wine trails as a tourist attraction in Israel. *International Journal of Tourism Research, 1*(6), 237–249.

Montanari, M. (1992). *Convivio oggi*. Bari: Laterza.

Moran, W. (1993). Rural space as intellectual property. *Political Geography, 12*, 263–277.

Mottironi, C. (2005). Turisti verso un prodotto o verso un luogo? In M. Antonioli Corigliano, & G. Viganò (Eds.), *Turisti per gusto. Enogastronomia, territorio, sostenibilità* (pp. 91–138). Novara: DeAgostini.

Mottironi, C., & Antonioli, M. (2012). Tourist destination competitiveness: The role of cooperation. *Rivista Italiana di Economia, Demografia e Statistica, LXVI*(2), 156–167.

O'Neill, M., & Charters, S. (2000). Service quality at the cellar door: Implications for Western Australia's developing wine tourism industry. *Managing Service Quality, 10*(2), 112–122.

Pearce, D. (2013). Toward an integrative conceptual framework of destinations. *Journal of Travel Research, 20*(10), 1–13.

Peters, G. L. (1997). *American winescapes*. Boulder, Colorado: Westview Press.

Ritchie, J. R., & Crouch, G. (2003). *The competitive destination. A sustainable tourism perspective*. Cambridge, MA: CABI Publishing.

Scarpato, R. (1999). Food globalisation, new global cuisine and the quest for a definition. In R. Dare (Ed.), *Cuisines: Regional, national or global?*. Adelaide: Research Centre for the history of Food and Drink.

Scarpato, R. (2003). Sustainable gastronomy as a tourism product. In A. M. Hjalager, & G. Richards (Eds.), *Tourism and gastronomy* (pp. 51–70). London: Routledge-ATLAS.

Skinner, A. (2000). Napa valley, California: A model of wine region development. In C. Hall, L. Sharples, B. Cambourne, & N. Macionis (Eds.), *Wine tourism around the world* (pp. 283–296). Oxford: Butterworth-Heinemann.

16 Moving beyond the "traditional Kodak moment"? Examining virtual data collection in place research

Kathryn Swanson, Dominic Medway, and Gary Warnaby

Learning outcomes

At the end of this chapter, readers should be able to

1 Understand the common virtual data collection techniques used by place researchers
2 Demonstrate how virtual data collection techniques can be applied to qualitative methodological approaches in place research
3 Appraise virtual techniques with reference to a technology acceptance model for consumers
4 Identify issues raised through the use of virtual data collection in place research, including spatial and temporal considerations
5 Understand the role virtual data collection techniques can play in capturing the embodied experience in a place context.

Research background

The rapid development of Internet-based capabilities and associated virtual platforms over the past 20 years has greatly expanded the methodological possibilities available to social science researchers (Deakin & Wakefield, 2014). For place research in particular, where potential participants may be geographically dispersed, such technological advances have the potential to overcome spatial and temporal barriers to gaining insights from populations. Data collection via virtual platforms has relevance for quantitative and qualitative methods. Regarding the former, Internet applications such as Survey Monkey and Qualtrics allow accessibility to populations for surveys, without the need for the researcher to be physically present at the point of data collection, and avoiding reliance on the time and costs (e.g., postage) associated with mail survey techniques (Malhotra & Birks, 2007).

However, with a growing focus on qualitative methods for gaining insight into place consumers' affective states and behaviours (Jamal & Hollinshead, 2001), the potential for virtual platforms is broadened beyond web-enabled survey techniques into a variety of social media applications that are ideally suited to capturing place consumers' discourses in the form of their narratives and stories about places. This paper is primarily concerned with these more qualitative forms of enquiry, and draws on a multiple-case research study of tourists' attachment to destinations and their associated destination brand "'love," which relates to issues of affective state. However, the specific findings of this study are not the focus of discussion; rather, we are concerned with examining *how* this work was done by using the study as an exemplar.

Specifically, in undertaking our research, it became clear that there were several methodological issues requiring attention in terms of research design, which were relevant to place research more generally. The aim of this methodology paper, therefore, is to critically examine the collection and use of data from, and using, virtual platforms—or put more simply, "virtual data"—in place research. (For purposes of this article, we define "virtual data" as *using some aspect of the Internet to facilitate data collection.*) In undertaking this, our contribution is threefold: First, we provide an analysis of common virtual data collection techniques used by place researchers. Second, we use our exemplar research study to demonstrate how virtual data collection techniques can be applied to qualitative methodological approaches in place research. Third, we offer a detailed appraisal of these virtual techniques with reference to the unified theory of acceptance and use of technology (UTAUT) model for consumers (Venkatesh, Thong, & Xu, 2012). In the discussion, we identify a number of the potential issues raised through the use of virtual data collection in place research. These include spatial and temporal considerations, and, most notably, capturing the embodied place consumer experience, beyond what has been termed the "traditional Kodak moment."

It should be noted that the specific focus of our exemplar research study was in a tourism context, and thus there is a preponderance of tourism journals in the reference list. However, the issues raised are applicable not only in this specific tourism context but could be widened to incorporate such issues as strong feelings of place attachment and place love in other contexts (e.g., residents and how they might communicate these feelings). Thus, the research is relevant for tourism and place researchers alike.

Literature review

The development of Internet technologies over the last two decades has led to the growth of data collection on virtual platforms, and the use of virtual data (Deakin & Wakefield, 2014), both in academic and corporate contexts. The following literature review is organised into three broad virtual data categories, termed "pre-existing," "real-time occurring" and "solicited." Pre-existing and real-time occurring data are secondary to the researcher, whereas solicited data would be considered primary, and therefore involves direct interaction with the participant and their awareness of participation in research.

Pre-existing data

Studies using pre-existing data typically rely on information that is available through the Internet at the point at which the research process begins. Such research does not involve direct interaction with participants and pulls data from sources such as online review websites (Liu & Park, 2015), travel blogs (Magnini, Crotts, & Zehrer, 2011), and online communities (Arsal, Woosnam, Baldwin, & Backman, 2010). Depending on the purpose of the study, some researchers have analysed this type of data quantitatively through modelling, analytics, etc. (Duverger, 2013; Phillips, Zigan, Santos Silva, & Schegg, 2015), and others have employed qualitative approaches such as thematic coding of textual data (Arsal et al., 2010; Cong, Wu, Morrison, Shu, & Wang, 2014). Other studies combine both qualitative and quantitative analysis (Cabiddu, Carlo, & Piccoli, 2014; Crotts, Mason, & Davis, 2009). Some studies also utilise big data from sources such as web traffic, search engine queries, and social media activity to predict tourist demand or behaviour (Mariani, Di Felice, & Maura, 2016; Pan & Yang, 2016; Yang, Pan, & Song, 2014), and this data is analysed quantitatively through modelling and forecasting. Overall, pre-existing data appear to provide valuable, quickly accessible, inexpensive, and non-directed insights into individuals' opinions, emotions, and behaviour. However, the non-directed nature of these data may also be restricting for researchers, in that the data may not necessarily assume the content or format preferred. This is analogous to some of the disadvantages of using secondary data more generally (Cowton, 1998).

Real-time occurring data

The distinction between pre-existing data and real-time occurring data is a subtle one concerning the timing of data production in relation to the research process. The former, as already indicated, represents an information source that is always fully available at the point at which the research process begins. By contrast, we would argue that real-time occurring data continues to emerge from virtual sources as it is studied. A popular utilisation of such data is in the form of netnographies—a term developed by Kozinets (2002) to capture the application of ethnography to social networking sites such as Facebook and Twitter. In a specific tourism context, Mkono (2013) reinforces the distinction between a "lurker" approach in netnographies, which involves simply the passive observation of online communities, and a more active mode of observer as participant within the online community under study. In many cases, the netnographic dimension of these studies involves the analysis of social media via data mining exercises, within the specific time frame of the research study. Such works arguably are more about the "net" of netnography, than the "ography" —i.e., ethnography in the more established understandings of the term, which would typically involve researcher immersion within the community being studied (Mkono, 2013).

The advantages of real-time occurring data captured through approaches such as netnography include the fact that these data emerge in a relatively organic sense from participants, and in doing so may reveal things about perceptions of their experience and affective state that might not be gained through more formally structured data collection methods (Rageh, Melewar, & Woodside, 2013). The collection of such data is also cost-effective and efficient (Kozinets, 2002). Such data are usually best suited to qualitative analysis approaches such as thematic coding and discourse analysis (Kozinets, 2002). A downside to real-time occurring data collected through approaches such as netnography is that the researcher does not overtly prescribe the topic/content of participants' contributions (Wu & Pearce, 2014a), and is therefore dependent on the natural course of online interactions. However, some netnographic studies partially offset this issue by also incorporating solicited data involving online (Tavakoli & Mura, 2015; Wu & Pearce, 2014b) or offline (Janta, Lugosi, Brown, & Ladkin, 2012) interviews/chats. It is also worth considering that if the researcher acts as participant, as opposed to lurker, in a netnographic context, then their presence within an online community may influence its dynamics and, by implication, the nature of any data that subsequently emerge.

Solicited data

A third category of data is solicited by researchers, and *necessarily* involves a degree of interaction with participants. A common means of collecting these data is through online surveys. Such studies often use e-mail or social media to recruit participants (Amaro & Duarte, 2015; Dijkmans, Kerkhof, & Beukeboom, 2015), and analyse data through quantitative approaches involving statistical manipulation (Liu & Park, 2015; Lu & Stepchenkova, 2012). Another form of solicited data collection is GPS tracking, where researchers typically ask participants to carry GPS devices and study their behaviour and movement patterns (Shoval & Isaacson, 2007; Tchetchik, Fleischer, & Shoval, 2009), and these data are typically subject to quantitative analysis and often represented through mapping. A feature of such approaches is that the researcher can solicit data directly from participants, and do so during consumption of the place experience, if this is important for the research questions under investigation. Solicited data can also be collected via online experiments and simulations to study participants' behaviour (Sparks & Browning, 2011; Sparks, Perkins, & Buckley, 2013), the results of which are also usually analysed using quantitative approaches. As indicated earlier, solicited data can also involve online interviews/chats, usually subject to qualitative analysis approaches involving thematic coding and/or narrative analysis (Tavakoli & Mura, 2015; Wu & Pearce, 2014b).

An advantage of soliciting data virtually is that study participants can, theoretically, take part from almost anywhere in the world (Hung & Law, 2011). Counter to this, however, not everyone has equal access to the Internet, which could exclude relevant voices from participating (Hung & Law, 2011). Indeed, lack of online access has implications for the production and representative validity of all categories of virtual data in place research.

Mixed virtual formats

As already illustrated, some studies involving virtual data collection adopt a mixed format in which researchers use pre-existing or real-time occurring data, but also engage with participants to comment on that data (i.e., a solicited approach). For example, Lo and McKercher (2015) accessed tourists' photos from social media, and then interviewed them offline regarding that data. We have also discussed above how netnographies of real-time occurring data can be combined with solicited primary data collection such as online interviews/chats (Tavakoli & Mura, 2015; Wu & Pearce, 2014b), or online surveys (Janta et al., 2012). It appears that these mixed format approaches could achieve the benefits of both real-time occurring data (in terms of its organic nature), and solicited data (in terms of the ability to ask participants specific questions relating to the research objectives of the study in question).

Reasons for virtual data collection

The literature retrieved for the above review reveals five key reasons for using virtual data collection in place research:

Volume/diversity—One reason cited for using virtual data collection is related to the volume and diversity of available information on the Internet (Cong et al., 2014; Lu & Stepchenkova, 2012), which makes it an efficient resource for place researchers looking for a critical mass of data on a wide variety of topics.

Access—A second reason for employing virtual data collection relates to access. Much Internet-based data is easily accessible and publicly available (Cong et al., 2014; Lu & Stepchenkova, 2012), which is highly convenient for researchers. Furthermore, in place research, where participants are often geographically dispersed, it may be easier to access participants virtually than in person, emphasising the relative geographical/spatial flexibility of virtual data collection approaches. On the downside, however, there may be an issue with trying to collect data from participants at the point of consumption of the place experience in remote locations, where Internet access may be poor.

Efficiency—Another common reason mentioned for the employment of virtual data collection relates to efficiency. Given the Internet's large volume and diversity of easily accessible data, this makes collecting virtual data time-efficient, and it can facilitate rapid insights on new topic areas (Wu & Pearce, 2014b) through search engine capabilities.

Budget—Related to efficiency is budget. It can be more cost-effective to utilise virtual data collection than more traditional approaches (Illum, Ivanov, & Liang, 2010), which may require significant travel costs to conduct in-person research, or postage costs for survey work.

Research Question—A fifth identified reason for using virtual data collection is that the research question relates specifically to participant behaviour online. For example, Luo and Zhong (2015) looked at communication characteristics of electronic word-of-mouth, and Schroeder and Pennington-Gray (2014) investigated international tourists' use of social media during a crisis.

In summary, common reasons cited for using virtual data relate to practical matters such as efficiency, ease of access, and budget constraints. Less frequently mentioned are the benefits that virtual data collection may have over other approaches. For example, Guimarães et al. (2015) incorporate virtual data collection to avoid "coverage bias" through being better able to reach certain members of the target population. Another study discusses the environmentally conscious appeal of virtual data collection, which cuts down on travel between researcher and participants (Hanna, 2012). Both of these studies hint at a potential for virtual data collection to serve a wider purpose than is often recognised in place research. There is an absence of discussion in the literature on temporal flexibility; specifically being able to interrogate the participant at different times *throughout* the process of experiencing a place (Smith, Xiang, Pan, Witte, & Doherty, 2015). Virtual data collection arguably increases this flexibility compared to non-virtual data collection methods. For example, it may be easier to invoke a Skype call than to arrange a face-to-face interview offline. Clearly, there is an opportunity to explore how such applications and associated virtual technologies can enhance qualitative research inquiry generally (Moylan, Derr, & Lindhorst, 2015), which could have particular relevance to tourism and place research (Hanna, 2012).

Methodological context

As noted above, the research study informing this paper explored the concept of tourists' "love" for destination brands. Carroll and Ahuvia (2006, p. 81) define "brand love" as "the degree of passionate emotional attachment a satisfied consumer has for a particular trade name." Whilst tourists' emotions relating to destinations have been researched (Hosany & Gilbert, 2010; Hosany, Prayag, Deesilatham, Causevic, & Odeh, 2014), the concept of love for destination brands has not. Academic enquiry into brand love has a predominantly positivistic and quantitative focus (e.g., Albert, Dwight, & Valette-Florence, 2008; Batra, Ahuvia, & Bagozzi, 2012; Bergkvist & Bech-Larsen, 2010; Carroll & Ahuvia, 2006; Sarkar, Ponnam, & Murthy, 2012). However, taking the view that emotions such as love should be studied using phenomenological modes of enquiry (Sturdy, 2003), we determined an inductive, exploratory approach involving qualitative methods would be appropriate to research the love of destination brands in a tourism context. This would potentially deliver richer insights and "thicker" descriptions (Geertz, 1973) than would be possible with quantitative methods alone.

The research study employed a contrasting case study approach (Yin, 2009), involving tourists of three vacation destinations in the United States: Orlando, Florida; Las Vegas, Nevada; and Minneapolis, Minnesota. As appropriate for qualitative research (Saunders, 2012), participants were selected in a snowball manner. Six participants took part in the research as tourists of Minneapolis, seven as tourists of Orlando and seven as tourists of Las Vegas, making a total of 20. All were adult residents of the United States (60% female/40% male), with ages ranging from 23 to 86 years. Participants were required to have been a tourist visiting the relevant destination for non-business purposes, and needed to initially agree that they "love" the destination. In short, this research aimed to explore whether (and if so how) love for a tourist destination might (or might not) translate into love for the destination's brand identity. However, as noted above, the findings of this actual enquiry are not the focus of the discussion below; rather, the current paper is concerned with *how* the research for this study was done, and specifically its use of virtual data sources. Thus, we move to our paper's second and third contributions: using this exemplar study to demonstrate how virtual data collection techniques can be applied in qualitative methodological approaches to place research, and offering a detailed appraisal of these virtual techniques with reference to the UTAUT model (Venkatesh et al., 2012).

In qualitative tourism research the triangulation of methods is a common strategy for developing empirical validity (Decrop, 1999). Accordingly, three different data collection tools were employed: semi-structured tourist interviews, volunteer-employed photography (VEP), and tourist collage creation. All data collection was carried out by the first author. Most critical to the focus of the current paper, at an early stage it was decided that the use of virtual technologies and platforms would be useful in maximising the engagement of the study's tourist participants in the completion of research tasks, particularly as they were often located in geographically distant locations at the time of data collection, both from each other, and from the researcher.

Tourist interviews

Interviews were conducted at participants' homes. Nine interviews involved the researcher visiting the participant to conduct the interview, whilst 11 were undertaken virtually via Skype. This was purely dependent on the researcher's geographical propinquity to a participant's home at the time an interview was scheduled to take place. The Skype-enabled interviews arguably fit into the broad category of solicited virtual data in place research (see above). The interviews followed a semi-structured format and used, as a general guide, a list of questions informed by the literature and trialled and revised in a pilot interview (not reported). Interviews lasted 45 to 75 minutes each.

Volunteer-employed photography (VEP)

Emotions can be difficult to express in words (Sturdy, 2003), so asking participants to produce images of their "loved" tourist destination with a camera (i.e., engage in VEP—see, Garrod, 2008) provided a "different way in" (Guillemin & Drew, 2010, p. 178) to investigating the research question. Photography is also a common way for tourists to capture their relationships with destinations (Edensor, 2000) and, equally, can be used by consumers to record their relationships with brands (Hollenbeck & Kaikati, 2012). Participants were asked to take photos on their next trip to the destination in question and return them electronically as soon as possible with a "brief commentary" explaining "the main subject of the photo and the reason it was taken." Instructions regarding the commentary were based on insights from MacKay and Couldwell (2004) and were critical in identifying participants' affective state and emotions, including potentially love, when the picture was taken. Most photos and comments were requested and provided in virtual formats via e-mail or text message (only two participants chose to return photographs as hard copies), again fitting into the broad category of solicited virtual data. Unlike the interviews, VEP represented participant data collected *during* as opposed to *after* the tourism "experience." We discuss later in the paper the potential benefits of virtual methods undertaken in this manner—i.e., by bringing the point of researcher enquiry closer to the point of place consumption.

Tourist collages

Again, considering the potential difficulties for people to express emotions verbally, collage creation was used. This technique has been used in brand and tourism research (Koll, von Wallpach, & Kreuzer, 2010; Prebensen, 2007), and results suggest that collages, and subsequent discussion of their contents with their creators, can tap into knowledge that might not be revealed in more direct enquiry techniques such as interviewing. Indeed, as a projective technique, collages are identified as effective at revealing information about consumer-brand bonds and tapping into consumers' "subconscious desires, wishes or feelings" (Gordon & Langmaid, 1988, p. 94). It has also been suggested that collage-based research is particularly useful at exploring people's relationships with experiential brands (Koll et al., 2010), which would include tourism destination brands.

For the collage creation, participants were asked to participate in a group session made up of others from the same tourist destination. They were asked to bring with them copies of photos of previous vacations to the destination being researched. Reflecting the fact that respondents lived in geographically dispersed areas, group sessions were conducted in a mixed in-person/virtual, or entirely virtual, format through the use of Skype or Google Hangout. Participants were provided with a variety of magazines on topics such as tourism and travel, entertainment, general interest, etc. (these were mailed to the virtual participants ahead of time) and paper, glue sticks, sticky tape, scissors, and pens (virtual respondents provided these other items themselves).

Participants were instructed to create a collage that demonstrated and encapsulated the love they felt for the destination. On the back of their collage, they were asked to reflect, in writing, on why they chose and used the images within it. Other studies have asked participants to identify pictures (Koll et al., 2010) or to explain their choices (Prebensen, 2007) in this manner. When collages were finished, each participant presented their creation to the others, after which all respondents discussed it. During presentations and discussion, participants held up their collages to the computer camera so that there was mutual sharing of information between those occupying virtual and non-virtual space.

Participant feedback on virtual method

All 20 tourist participants completed their interviews and collages, and 18 provided photos. After the research process, they were asked to provide written feedback via e-mail on the advantages and disadvantages of using Skype and/or Google Hangout during their interview and/or group session. They were also asked to provide their general reactions to using these virtual technology interfaces as research participants. This feedback was analysed thematically and showed strong resonance with the UTAUT model for consumers (Venkatesh et al., 2012), which in tourism research has been previously applied in the context of airline ticket purchasing (Escobar-Rodríguez & Carvajal-Trujillo, 2014). Accordingly, in Table 16.1, respondent feedback is organised according to the constructs that can affect acceptance of technology: performance expectancy, effort expectancy, social influence, facilitating conditions, hedonic motivation, price value, and experience and habit (Venkatesh et al., 2012). The second column provides a definition of each of these constructs. The third column includes potential positives of the virtual method used in the study, and the fourth column consists of explanations and participant quotes regarding such positives. The fifth and sixth columns respectively include the potential negatives of the virtual method used in the study and explanations/participant quotes relating to these.

Researcher reflections on virtual method

For the research detailed in this paper, the researcher was also a "consumer" of the technology applications used. Thus, researcher reflections on the virtual data collection can also be categorised according to the UTAUT model (Venkatesh et al., 2012) as has been done in Table 16.2, using the same structure as Table 16.1.

Discussion

This paper has provided an indicative review and categorisation of various types of virtual data employed in place research, before demonstrating how virtual data collection was used in a qualitative study exploring tourists' love for destination brands, and appraising such virtual techniques from participant and researcher perspectives using the UTAUT model (Venkatesh et al., 2012). Drawing the strands of the discussion together, we suggest it may be beneficial for place researchers more broadly to think about virtual data collection in terms of the methodological challenges it helps resolve, whilst at the same time being cognisant of the paradoxical tensions it creates.

One methodological challenge potentially resolved by virtual data collection relates to spatial dispersion. Place research can often, though not always, involve multi-site contexts. This may occur between participant and researcher locations, with the latter traveling to study the former *in situ* (Varley & Medway, 2011), as well as between participants at different locations in the same study (Swanson, 2015). Virtual technologies expand the realm of methodological possibilities in these instances.

Table 16.1 Participant feedback on virtual methods organised by UTAUT model constructs

	Definition (Venkatesh et al., 2012)	Positives	Explanation/participant quote	Negatives	Explanation/participant quote
Performance expectancy	Benefits consumers will receive in terms of performing activities when using a technology	Facilitates communication using visual and verbal cues	"I think Skype is almost to the point of being like an interview in the same room."	Operational issues: computer connectivity, video resolution, sound quality	Two participants had microphone problems during a group session, could not be heard, and thus were distanced/marginalized
Effort expectancy	A consumer's ease of use of a technology	Low effort needed to use virtual interfaces	"User-friendly," "convenient," "efficient."	Effort needed to set up an account and initially learn about a program	"Since I am not Internet savvy, it was time-consuming to open an account and become familiar with using it."
Social influence	Consumers' belief that others wish them to use a technology with which they may not be familiar	Satisfaction gained from pleasing others	Participants appeared to feel satisfied that they were being "good" participants and pleasing the researcher	Sense of peer pressure; ethical implications regarding ensuring participants do not feel pressured by the process of virtual data collection	No direct evidence, yet some participants appeared nervous regarding using the virtual interface and mentioned their "bad hair day" or lack of make-up when discussing the fact their participation was being recorded
Facilitating conditions	Consumers' perceptions of the support and resources available to them in relation to the technology used	N/A – training not provided to participants	N/A	Absence of technology support may have led some to feel ill-at-ease	A participant reported feeling initially distracted during a collage session because she was unfamiliar with the platform and afraid she was doing something wrong

(Continued)

	Definition (Venkatesh et al., 2012)	Positives	Explanation/participant quote	Negatives	Explanation/participant quote
Hedonic motivation	The extent that consumers enjoy using a certain technology	Pleasure derived from the educational and skill-building nature of trying out a virtual interface with which they were not familiar	"Google hangouts (*sic*) was also a cool thing to use. This was my first time being introduced to this program and I liked it. It really was great to be able to see everyone as we made the collage. I really enjoyed listening to the others when they presented [too]."	Some participants alluded to enjoying the chosen platforms less than other, similar platforms	"I like Skype overall, but iChat is better."
Price value	Consumers' perceptions of the benefit of using certain technologies compared to their cost	Participants appeared to perceive the cost of the technology as free since they all already had computers and Internet connections; use of technology also appeared to reduce the perceived cost of time	Participants alluded to the "convenience" and "efficiency" of their virtual sessions with the researcher, and that the chosen platforms are "cost-efficient."	N/A – none reported	N/A
Experience and habit	Experience relates to the amount of time that has passed since a consumer first used a technology, and habit relates to the consumer's prior behaviour and the extent to which s/he views that behaviour as automatic	Some participants indicated prior experience with the virtual applications, even to the extent of habitual usage	These individuals appeared to view the technologies favourably	Some participants indicated no prior experience, down to a degree of resistance or "laggardism" (after Rogers, 2010)	"Probably just me and the way I am, but: I am a telephone person."

Table 16.2 Researcher reflections on virtual methods organized by UTAUT model constructs

	Positives	Explanation/Example	Negatives	Explanation/Example
Performance expectancy	Enhanced viability of the study Being able to read body language and visual cues Fewer potential distractions in the conversation. Participants may be more engaged and focused on the task at hand than in non-virtual, in-person formats	Due to geographical distance, without Skype and Google Hangout, it would have been impractical to include many of the participants if the visual interaction/face-to-face component of the research was to be retained Analysis was enhanced by being able to draw on the visual subtleties (Hanna, 2012) of a physical as well as spoken narrative Participants took Skype as an opportunity to remove themselves from potential distractions so they could concentrate fully on the technology and the interview at hand. During in-person interviews, by contrast, there were many interruptions such as spouses entering the room	Technology failures negatively impact the flow and momentum of virtual data collection and distract the narrative focus of participants. The virtual platform can become a disruptive force if it underperforms technically	One Skype interview transcript had four breaks in the conversation when the connection was interrupted
Effort expectancy	Virtual data collection was efficient for the researcher	The researcher saved time by not having to make travel arrangements, and physically travel, to participants' locations	Some additional organization and pre-planning was required to coordinate participants' use of virtual platforms (particularly in a group context)	The researcher spent some time sending materials to virtual participants and ensuring they had access to, and knowledge of, the appropriate technology programs. This required less time than travelling to participants' locations
Social influence	Virtual data collection techniques are becoming more commonplace	Researchers may receive encouragement to explore virtual data collection and take advantage of its benefits	Sense of peer pressure	Researchers may feel obligated to use virtual data collection even if it is not best suited to their research questions

(Continued)

	Positives	Explanation/Example	Negatives	Explanation/Example
Facilitating conditions	N/A – training not provided to researchers; researchers already had experience with the technologies used	N/A	Lack of knowledge and training may impact the speed with which new virtual data collection approaches are adopted in a field such as tourism	If no training is provided to researchers, they may feel uncomfortable using virtual data collection due to their own lack of knowledge and the necessary reliance on participants' abilities to navigate the virtual technologies used and participants' access to quality equipment and Internet connections
Hedonic motivation	Enhanced level of interest/excitement for the researcher over engagement with non-visual technologies such as the telephone. Avoidance of negative researcher feelings relating to their possible infringement on participants' personal, physical space (Hanna, 2012)	It was rewarding for the researcher to connect virtually with participants with whom visual interaction would otherwise be impractical	There may be a reduced level of engagement for the researcher in connecting virtually with participants when compared to in-person contexts	It can be quite enjoyable to visit participants in person in their home environments, and such visits may provide valuable contextual data on those participants
Price value	Virtual technologies often have a low cost. Reduced environmental impact of the research, in terms of fewer "fieldwork miles" travelled	The research budget was very limited and the participants were geographically dispersed, so using low-cost virtual technologies to collect data was beneficial	Equipment costs (e.g., computer, Internet connection, etc.)	Costs of equipment were fixed rather than varying according to the number of participants
Experience and habit	The researcher had experience with, and habitually used, the technologies used in the study	The researcher felt comfortable during data collection. As virtual technologies become more commonplace and mainstream, it is likely more researchers will be naturally inclined to incorporate them into their studies	Researchers who do not have experience with virtual technologies may be more hesitant to use them	A bifurcation of research studies could occur, between those which use and do not use virtual data. It is potentially problematic if this split is governed by researcher experience and habit, rather than research objectives

Specifically, researcher and participant are more able to communicate regardless of their location, which may effectively expand the respondent pool from which a sample can be drawn. However, tensions arise over the fact that certain participants may find it difficult to access virtual technologies due to reasons relating to the cost/affordability of, and/ or connectivity or familiarity with, the technology itself. These difficulties could be more prevalent amongst certain age groups and cultural backgrounds. We therefore suggest that place researchers should carefully consider the characteristics of their population under investigation in determining whether virtual data collection is entirely appropriate.

Another methodological challenge which might be resolved through virtual data collection relates to temporal issues, particularly in situations when places are experienced as tourism destinations. It can be argued that it may be more effective to study tourism as it is occurring (Smith et al., 2015), rather than afterwards, when tourists' perceptions of their vacation experiences might be affected by any cognitive dissonance arising from the time between a tourism "event" and questions asked about it by a researcher. Virtual data collection can provide the means to gather information closer to the point at which tourism occurs and is experienced. For example, although the research study detailed above utilised Skype and Google Hangout in post-travel contexts, the inclusion of the VEP task began to explore data collection nearer the moment of tourism consumption, and while tourists were at the destination in question. Similarly, some researchers have begun to integrate smartphones into methodological design, including asking tourists to record videos, comment on them, and send them to researchers *during* their tourism experience rather than afterwards (Smith et al., 2015). The critical issue here is that tourists' perceptions of a destination may change at different points in time, both during and after a trip (Smith et al., 2015). Collecting data virtually may facilitate a connection with tourists as and when these changes are occurring. This could be beneficial in enhancing both academic and practitioner understanding of what drives tourists' behaviours and what affects or moderates their consumption experiences of a place.

Furthermore, there has been growing interest in the topic of embodiment and tourism (Crouch, 2000; Giovanardi, Lucarelli, & Decosta, 2014; Jensen, 2016; Jensen, Scarles, & Cohen, 2015; Mordue, 2009; Varley & Medway, 2011); embodiment being "a process of experiencing, making sense, knowing through practise as a sensual human subject in the world" (Crouch, 2000, p. 68). There are obvious links here to non-representational theory (Thrift, 1996), which emphasises the "half-second delay" between a sensory stimulus and conscious thought, also referred to as the "bare life," "simple living body" or "... fleeting space of the moment ... utterly wrapped up with its context, and most especially the object world" (Thrift, 2004, p. 152; see also Macpherson,

2010). For a place, one might imagine the potential for such a moment on, say, a boat trip when a whale breaches the water. In that instant the viewing individual can experience a fleeting sense of visceral and embodied awe, before cognition and conation set in to rationalise the event and set it in a wider temporal and spatial context. In such instances, virtual data collection provides an ability to capture data closer to the moment of embodiment. Researchers have already asked place visitors to take photos to communicate their feelings and perceptions (Robinson & Picard, 2009). Virtual data collection could take this a step further. For example, a participant could take a photo and post it to Instagram, or send a message via Twitter, for the researcher, as they experience what they consider to be significant events. Admittedly, by the time a participant thinks of doing this, the moment of embodiment, or "bare life" has arguably passed. Nevertheless, if a participant sends data virtually as soon as possible after an experienced event, then it at least helps the researcher get a closer connection to that moment, especially compared to alternative data collection methods such as interviewing, focus groups, or even diary keeping, either during or after experiencing a place—although this does not deny that post-embodiment reflection by participants might sometimes be what the researcher is seeking.

Emphasising this potential benefit of virtual technologies, the founder of Snap chat has noted that it "isn't about capturing the traditional Kodak moment" but "about communicating with the full range of human emotion" (www.snapchat-blog.com). Put otherwise, virtual data collection may have the ability to better record participants' somatic and affective experiences of a place, as opposed to their semantic and cognitive appreciations of such an experiential event. However, using virtual platforms to try and deliver such insights to the researcher could paradoxically distance the participant from somatic sensitivity due to technological interference. Thus, in just the same way that photography can be used by individuals to mediate their identities (Robinson & Picard, 2009), introducing a layer of technology via virtual data collection could potentially disrupt the embodied experience, not least if participants are asked to record key moments within their place experience through the lenses of Instagram, Twitter and similar. Indeed, there is a concern in studies using the experience sampling method of participants feeling burdened or annoyed when repeatedly interrupted to provide data (Quinlan Cutler, Doherty, & Carmichael, 2016).

Another methodological challenge for future researchers, particularly those following lines of phenomenological inquiry using qualitative methods and interpretivist approaches, relates to hermeneutics. On the one hand, data interpretation may be enhanced when researchers are able to see participants and their facial expressions and body language, which makes virtual video-conferencing platforms such as Skype arguably preferable to the telephone when interviewing or undertaking focus groups. On the other hand, platforms such as Skype may be subject to technological malfunctions. More critically, virtual video-conferencing might paradoxically hinder the participants' responses to research questions if they are unfamiliar with the technology, or feel nervous about being in front of a camera, as was the case with some of the participants in our study reported above.

Clearly, the range of virtual technologies now available can deliver numerous opportunities for methodological creativity in place research, provided this is suitably matched to research questions. Of course, ethical considerations should always be taken into account when undertaking such work. Online research requires certain special considerations (Elgesem, 2002), which have been discussed in detail elsewhere (see, for example, Bassett & O'Riordan, 2002; Elgesem, 2002; Madge, 2007; Walther, 2002). These include informed consent, data confidentiality, participant privacy, debriefing (i.e., following-up with participants after the research process), and "netiquette" (i.e., online etiquette). However, Madge (2007) notes that we should be beware of going too far in this regard and imposing higher expectations on researchers adopting online methods. Going forward, it may be appropriate to include a consideration of the value of the research being conducted (Elgesem, 2002), and not simply apply a rigid structure of ethical standards across the board, but rather take a more flexible approach to online research ethics that considers the specifics of each research study (Berry, 2004).

Future research directions

Potential future research streams are numerous and include investigating the optimum means of operationalising online technologies and applications while participants are at a place being studied. This may involve evaluating different means of virtual participant engagement and data capture at various points during place experiences, determining what works well (and less well) in terms of, for example: virtual data as a *product* (i.e., the quality and volume of data obtained, and its suitability with regard to the research questions asked and the participant population and context under study); and data-related *process(es)* (i.e., access to data sources, ease of data capture and analysis).

Conclusion

Future research aside, the existing literature, discussed earlier in this paper, indicates that virtual technologies and applications offer significant potential for enhancing the study of the behaviours of those who experience places. In undertaking such research, considerations should be given to participant, as well as researcher, acceptance of technology. Furthermore, methodological issues, including space, time, embodiment, hermeneutics, and ethics, should be taken into account.

Key construct definitions

Brand love—the degree of passionate emotional attachment a satisfied consumer has for a particular trade name (Carroll & Ahuvia, 2006, p. 81)

Embodiment—a process of experiencing, making sense, knowing through practise as a sensual human subject in the world (Crouch, 2000, p. 68)

Pre-existing data—data that are available through the Internet at the point at which the research process begins. Such research does not involve direct interaction with participants

Real-time occurring data – data that continues to emerge from virtual sources as it is studied

Solicited data – data that are solicited by researchers, and necessarily involves a degree of interaction with participants

UTUAT model—Unified theory of acceptance and use of technology model which includes the constructs: performance expectancy, effort expectancy, social influence, facilitating conditions, hedonic motivation, price value and experience and habit (Venkatesh et al., 2012)

Virtual data—using some aspect of the Internet to facilitate data collection

References

Albert, N., Dwight, M., & Valette-Florence, P. (2008). When consumers love their brands: Exploring the concept and its dimensions. *Journal of Business Research, 61,* 1062–1075.

Amaro, S., & Duarte, P. (2015). An integrative model of consumers' intentions to purchase travel online. *Tourism Management, 46,* 64–79. doi: 10.1016/j.tourman.2014.06.006

Arsal, I., Woosnam, K. M., Baldwin, E. D., & Backman, S. J. (2010). Residents as travel destination information providers: An online community perspective. *Journal of Travel Research, 49*(4), 400–413. doi: 10.1177/0047287509346856

Bassett, E. H., & O'Riordan, K. (2002). Ethics of Internet research: Contesting the human subjects research model. *Ethics and Information Technology, 4*(3), 233–247.

Batra, R., Ahuvia, A., & Bagozzi, R. P. (2012). Brand love. *Journal of Marketing, 76*(March), 1–16.

Bergkvist, L., & Bech-Larsen, T. (2010). Two studies of consequences and actionable antecedents of brand love. *Journal of Brand Management, 17*(7), 504–518.

Berry, D. M. (2004). Internet research: Privacy, ethics and alienation: An open source approach. *Internet Research, 14*(4), 323–332.

Cabiddu, F., Carlo, M. D., & Piccoli, G. (2014). Social media affordances: Enabling customer engagement. *Annals of Tourism Research, 48,* 175–192. doi: 10.1016/j.annals.2014.06.003

Carroll, B. A., & Ahuvia, A. C. (2006). Some antecedents and outcomes of brand love. *Marketing Letters, 17*(2), 79–89.

Cong, L., Wu, B., Morrison, A. M., Shu, H., & Wang, M. (2014). Analysis of wildlife tourism experiences with endangered species: An exploratory study of encounters with giant pandas in Chengdu, China. *Tourism Management, 40,* 300–310. doi: 10.1016/j.tourman.2013.07.005

Cowton, C. (1998). The use of secondary data in business ethics research. *Journal of Business Ethics, 17*(4), 423–434. doi: 10.1023/a:1005730825103

Crotts, J. C., Mason, P. R., & Davis, B. (2009). Measuring guest satisfaction and competitive position in the hospitality and tourism industry: An application of stance-shift analysis to travel blog narratives. *Journal of Travel Research, 48*(2), 139–151. doi: 10.1177/0047287508328795

Crouch, D. (2000). Places around us: Embodied lay geographies in leisure and tourism. *Leisure Studies, 19*(2), 63–76.

Deakin, H., & Wakefield, K. (2014). Skype interviewing: Reflections of two PhD researchers. *Qualitative Research, 14*(5), 603–616.

Decrop, A. (1999). Triangulation in qualitative tourism research. *Tourism Management, 20*, 157–161.

Dijkmans, C., Kerkhof, P., & Beukeboom, C. J. (2015). A stage to engage: Social media use and corporate reputation. *Tourism Management, 47*, 58–67. doi: 10.1016/j.tourman.2014.09.005

Duverger, P. (2013). Curvilinear effects of user-generated content on hotels' market share: A dynamic panel-data analysis. *Journal of Travel Research, 52*(4), 465–478. 10.1177/0047287513478498

Edensor, T. (2000). Staging tourism: Tourists as performers. *Annals of Tourism Research, 27*(2), 322–344.

Elgesem, D. (2002). What is special about the ethical issues in online research?. *Ethics and Information Technology, 4*(3), 195–203.

Escobar-Rodríguez, T., & Carvajal-Trujillo, E. (2014). Online purchasing tickets for low cost carriers: An application of the unified theory of acceptance and use of technology (UTAUT) model. *Tourism Management, 43*, 70–88. doi: 10.1016/j.tourman.2014.01.017

Garrod, B. (2008). Exploring place perception: A photo-based analysis. *Annals of Tourism Research, 35*(2), 381–401.

Geertz, C. (1973). Thick description: Toward an interpretive theory of culture. In C. Geertz (Ed.), *The interpretation of cultures: Selected essays* (pp. 3–30). New York, NY: Basic Books.

Giovanardi, M., Lucarelli, A., & Decosta, P. L. E. (2014). Co-performing tourism places: The "Pink Night" festival. *Annals of Tourism Research, 44*, 102–115. doi: 10.1016/j.annals.2013.09.004

Gordon, W., & Langmaid, R. (1988). *Qualitative market research: A practitioner's and buyer's guide*. Aldershot, England: Gower Publishing Company Limited.

Guillemin, M., & Drew, S. (2010). Questions of process in participant-generated visual methodologies. *Visual Studies, 25*(2), 175–188.

Guimarães, M. H., Nunes, L. C., Madureira, L., Santos, J. L., Boski, T., & Dentinho, T. (2015). Measuring birdwatchers preferences: A case for using online networks and mixed-mode surveys. *Tourism Management, 46*, 102–113.

Hanna, P. (2012). Using Internet technologies (such as Skype) as a research medium: A research note. *Qualitative Research, 12*(2), 239–242.

Hollenbeck, C. R., & Kaikati, A. M. (2012). Consumers' use of brands to reflect their actual and ideal selves on Facebook. *International Journal of Research in Marketing, 29*(4), 395–405.

Hosany, S., & Gilbert, D. (2010). Measuring tourists' emotional experiences toward hedonic holiday destinations. *Journal of Travel Research, 49*(4), 513–526.

Hosany, S., Prayag, G., Deesilatham, S., Causevic, S., & Odeh, K. (2014). Measuring tourists' emotional experiences: Further validation of the Destination Emotion Scale. *Journal of Travel Research, 54*(4), 482–495.

Hung, K., & Law, R. (2011). An overview of Internet-based surveys in hospitality and tourism journals. *Tourism Management, 32*(4), 717–724. doi: 10.1016/j.tourman.2010.05.027

Illum, S. F., Ivanov, S. H., & Liang, Y. (2010). Using virtual communities in tourism research. *Tourism Management, 31*(3), 335–340. doi: 10.1016/j.tourman.2009.03.012

Jamal, T., & Hollinshead, K. (2001). Tourism and the forbidden zone: The underserved power of qualitative inquiry. *Tourism Management, 22*, 63–82.

Janta, H., Lugosi, P., Brown, L., & Ladkin, A. (2012). Migrant networks, language learning and tourism employment. *Tourism Management, 33*(2), 431–439. doi: 10.1016/j.tourman.2011.05.004

Jensen, M. T. (2016). Distorted representation in visual tourism research. *Current Issues in Tourism, 19*(6), 545–563. doi: 10.1080/13683500.2015.1023268

Jensen, M. T., Scarles, C., & Cohen, S. A. (2015). A multisensory phenomenology of interrail mobilities. *Annals of Tourism Research, 53*, 61–76. doi: 10.1016/j.annals.2015.04.002

Koll, O., von Wallpach, S., & Kreuzer, M. (2010). Multi-method research on consumer-brand associations: Comparing free associations, storytelling, and collages. *Psychology & Marketing, 27*(6), 584–602.

Kozinets, R. V. (2002). The field behind the screen: Using netnography for marketing research in online communities. *Journal of Marketing Research, 39*(1), 61–72.

Liu, Z., & Park, S. (2015). What makes a useful online review?. Implication for travel product websites. *Tourism Management, 47*, 140–151. doi: 10.1016/j.tourman.2014.09.020

Lo, I. S., & McKercher, B. (2015). Ideal image in process: Online tourist photography and impression management. *Annals of Tourism Research, 52*, 104–116. doi: 10.1016/j.annals.2015.02.019

Lu, W., & Stepchenkova, S. (2012). Ecotourism experiences reported online: Classification of satisfaction attributes. *Tourism Management, 33*(3), 702–712. doi: 10.1016/j.tourman.2011.08.003

Luo, Q., & Zhong, D. (2015). Using social network analysis to explain communication characteristics of travel-related electronic word-of-mouth on social networking sites. *Tourism Management, 46*, 274–282. doi: 10.1016/j.tourman.2014.07.007

MacKay, K. J., & Couldwell, C. M. (2004). Using visitor-employed photography to investigate destination image. *Journal of Travel Research, 42*(May), 390–396.

Macpherson, H. (2010). Non-representational approaches to body-landscape relations. *Geography Compass, 4*(1), 1–13.

Madge, C. (2007). Developing a geographers' agenda for online research ethics. *Progress in Human Geography, 31*(5), 654–674.

Magnini, V. P., Crotts, J. C., & Zehrer, A. (2011). Understanding customer delight: An application of travel blog analysis. *Journal of Travel Research, 50*(5), 535–545. doi: 10.1177/0047287510379162

Malhotra, N. K., & Birks, D. F. (2007). *Marketing research: An applied approach* (3rd ed.). Harlow: FT Prentice Hall.

Mariani, M. M., Di Felice, M., & Mura, M. (2016). Facebook as a destination marketing tool: Evidence from Italian regional destination management organizations. *Tourism Management, 54*, 321–343. doi: 10.1016/j.tourman.2015.12.008

Mkono, M. (2013). African and Western tourists: Object authenticity quest?. *Annals of Tourism Research, 41*, 195–214. doi: 10.1016/j.annals.2013.01.002

Mordue, T. (2009). Angling in modernity: A tour through society, nature and embodied passion. *Current Issues in Tourism, 12*(5–6), 529–552. doi: 10.1080/13683500903043244

Moylan, C. A., Derr, A. S., & Lindhorst, T. (2015). Increasingly mobile: How new technologies can enhance qualitative research. *Qualitative Social Work, 14*(1), 36–47.

Pan, B., & Yang, Y. (2016). Forecasting destination weekly hotel occupancy with big data. *Journal of Travel Research.* doi: 10.1177/0047287516669050

Phillips, P., Zigan, K., Santos Silva, M. M., & Schegg, R. (2015). The interactive effects of online reviews on the determinants of Swiss hotel performance: A neural network analysis. *Tourism Management, 50*, 130–141. doi: 10.1016/j.tourman.2015.01.028

Prebensen, N. K. (2007). Exploring tourists' images of a distant destination. *Tourism Management, 28*, 747–756.

Quinlan Cutler, S., Doherty, S., & Carmichael, B. (2016). The experience sampling method: Examining its use and potential in tourist experience research. *Current Issues in Tourism*, 1–23. doi: 10.1080/13683500.2015.1131670

Rageh, A., Melewar, T. C., & Woodside, A. (2013). Using netnography research method to reveal the underlying dimensions of the customer/tourist experience. *Qualitative Market Research: An International Journal, 16*(2), 126–149.

Robinson, M., & Picard, D. (2009). Moments, magic and memories: Photographing tourists, tourist photographs and making worlds. In M. Robinson & D. Picard (Eds.), *The framed world: Tourism, tourists and photography* (pp. 1–37). Surrey, England: Ashgate.

Rogers, E. M. (2010). *Diffusion of innovations* (4th ed). New York, NY: Simon and Schuster.

Sarkar, A., Ponnam, A., & Murthy, B. K. (2012). Understanding and measuring romantic brand love. *Journal of Customer Behaviour, 11*(4), 325–348.

Saunders, M. N. K. (2012). Choosing research participants. In G. Symon & C. Cassell (Eds.), *Qualitative organizational research* (pp. 35–52). London, UK: SAGE.

Schroeder, A., & Pennington-Gray, L. (2014). The role of social media in international tourist's decision making. *Journal of Travel Research.* doi: 10.1177/0047287514528284

Shoval, N., & Isaacson, M. (2007). Tracking tourists in the digital age. *Annals of Tourism Research, 34*(1), 141–159. doi: 10.1016/j.annals.2006.07.007

Smith, W. W., Xiang, L., Pan, B., Witte, M., & Doherty, S. T. (2015). Tracking destination image across the trip experience with smartphone technology. *Tourism Management, 48*, 113–122.

Snap Inc. (2012, May 9). Let's chat [web log comment]. Retrieved from http://snapchat-blog.com/post/22756675666/lets-chat

Sparks, B. A., & Browning, V. (2011). The impact of online reviews on hotel booking intentions and perception of trust. *Tourism Management, 32*(6), 1310–1323. doi: 10.1016/j.tourman.2010.12.011

Sparks, B. A., Perkins, H. E., & Buckley, R. (2013). Online travel reviews as persuasive communication: The effects of content type, source, and certification logos on consumer behavior. *Tourism Management, 39*, 1–9. doi: 10.1016/j.tourman.2013.03.007

Sturdy, A. (2003). Knowing the unknowable?. A discussion of methodological and theoretical issues in emotion research and organizational studies. *Organization, 10*(1), 81–105.

Swanson, K. (2015). Place brand love and marketing to place consumers as tourists. *Journal of Place Management and Development, 8*(2), 142–146.

Tavakoli, R., & Mura, P. (2015). 'Journeys in second life' – Iranian Muslim women's behaviour in virtual tourist destinations. *Tourism Management, 46*, 398–407. doi: 10.1016/j.tourman.2014.07.015

Tchetchik, A., Fleischer, A., & Shoval, N. (2009). Segmentation of visitors to a heritage site using high-resolution time-space data. *Journal of Travel Research, 48*(2), 216–229. doi: 10.1177/0047287509332307

Thrift, N. (1996). *Spatial formations.* London, UK: Sage.

Thrift, N. (2004). Bare life. In H. Thomas & J. Ahmed (Eds.), *Cultural bodies: Ethnography and theory* (pp. 145–169). Malden, MA & Oxford, UK: Blackwell Publishing Ltd.

Varley, P., & Medway, D. (2011). Ecosophy and tourism: Rethinking a mountain resort. *Tourism Management, 32*, 902–911.

Venkatesh, V., Thong, J. Y. L., & Xu, X. (2012). Consumer acceptance and use of information technology: Extending the unified theory of acceptance and use of technology. *MIS Quarterly, 36*(1), 157–178.

Walther, J. B. (2002). Research ethics in Internet-enabled research: Human subjects issues and methodological myopia. *Ethics and Information Technology, 4*(3), 205–216.

Wu, M.-Y., & Pearce, P. L. (2014a). Appraising netnography: Towards insights about new markets in the digital tourist era. *Current Issues in Tourism, 17*(5), 463–474.

Wu, M.-Y., & Pearce, P. L. (2014b). Chinese recreational vehicle users in Australia: A netnographic study of tourist motivation. *Tourism Management, 43*, 22–35. doi: 10.1016/j.tourman.2014.01.010

Yang, Y., Pan, B., & Song, H. (2014). Predicting hotel demand using destination marketing organization's web traffic data. *Journal of Travel Research, 53*(4), 433–447. doi: 10.1177/0047287513500391

Yin, R. K. (2009). Case study research design and methods. In L. Bickman & D. J. Rog (Series Eds.), *Applied social research methods series*, Vol. 5. Retrieved from www.amazon.com

Part V
Conclusions

17 Place branding in context

Current challenges, global changes and future trends

Cristina Fona

As we leave this decade to enter the year 2020, we can look back with a certain interest at the last 30 years of studies on place branding. The previous chapters in this collection present a critical overview of this past and offer substantial contributions to the current development of the discipline. Despite recurrent criticisms regarding its legitimacy (Anholt, 2006; Blichfeld, 2005; Medway et al., 2015; Stubbs & Warnaby, 2015) and the lack of a commonly accepted theoretical framework (Ashworth, Kavaratzis & Warnaby, 2015), the study of place branding is now widely acknowledged and recognised inside (Anholt, 2007; Dinnie, 2017; Ermann & Hermanik, 2017; Govers, 2018) and outside of academia (Klijn, Eshuis & Braun, 2012; Zukin, 2014; Salzman, 2016; Subramanian, 2017) and can leverage an extended literature that encompasses several academic domains (Hankinson, 2010, 2015; Vuignier, 2017).

The various contributions in this book highlight the role that research can play in assisting destinations—cities, regions, countries—to analyse the experience of individuals and groups that consume, manage, and co-create them. This final chapter aims to go a step further as it seeks to uncover current challenges and future trends that will change our approach to place branding research. It aims to do so by analysing recent socio-economic and political upheavals that are affecting the way in which we think of and relate to places.

Current challenges in place branding

Given its relatively young age, contested role and fragmented past (Ashworth, Kavaratzis & Warnaby, 2015) place branding has often been subject to criticisms (Zenker & Braun, 2017). The majority of these critiques derive from the very nature of places. Place brands greatly differ from corporate brands due to the multiplicity of stakeholders involved and the lack of control over the place entity and the process (Kavaratzis & Kalandides, 2015). This is strictly connected to terminological issues regarding the notions of place, space, and brand as well as legitimacy issues that undermine the development of place branding initiatives. An informed analysis of current challenges cannot disregard this complex historical background that still represents a motive for debate. At the moment of writing, we can leverage a significant number of studies that assess these criticisms. Compared to 30 years ago, we are certainly wiser (Kavaratzis, 2015). Nonetheless, the practice of place branding is still confronted with limitations that could threaten the future of the field. The first of these concerns relates to leadership. Place brand managers are now required to adapt to a new environment in which their role is reduced to facilitators. This threatens the power of dominant groups that leverage "visual and spatial strategies to impose their views" (Broudehoux, 2001, p. 272), thus causing frictions among stakeholders regarding the management of the place brand (Bennett & Savani, 2003). This and the lack of an appropriate strategy (Kavaratzis & Hatch, 2013; Kavaratzis, 2016) are often the cause of the "toponymic commodification and place related sloganising" (Medway et al., 2015, p. 64) that leads to a "one size fits all" approach (Zenker and Brown, 2017, p. 271), ultimately hinders differentiation and limits the potential of participatory branding (Govers, 2013). The same idea of participatory branding, often discussed in academic research, is not unproblematic. While some authors question "the ways in which consumer participation is converted into added value for brands" (Kaneva, 2018, p. 184), others call for more research concerning its implementation and particularly the coordination and engagement of different stakeholders (Kavaratzis, 2016). Another key issue that emerges from the literature is the lack of clarity regarding the effectiveness of place branding and the evaluation of brand performance (Hankinson, 2010; Cleave et al., 2017; Govers, Kaefer & Ferrer-Roca, 2017). "There is an expectation that the promotional actors in place branding should quantitatively and qualitatively demonstrate that the work makes a major difference in awareness, attendance, acceptance and adoption of images and messages into wider discourse" (Warren & Dinnie, 2018, p. 312). Failure to appropriately measure the outcome of a strategy has a negative impact on (public and private) funding and often causes the implementation of short-term marketing activities, as already reported by Hankinson (2010). This again reflects negatively on promotional actors and contributes to the general feeling of mistrust towards branding practices (Warren & Dinnie, 2018). Leadership, management, and measurement are only some of the issues that emerge after a careful review of the literature. Reflecting on them reveals the complexity of the systems that surround the branding practice and that can be solved only by a closer collaboration between practice and research and a clinical look at the current market environment.

Emerging issues and trends

Economic instability, political uprisings, and the increased use of technology are some of the factors that are changing the fundamental structure of modern society. By observing this dynamic setting, the following section will explore the future of research in place branding. The analysis will focus on four major themes: contested places and identities, new and emerging place brands, un-sustainable destinations, and digital place brands.

Contested places and identities

"We live in a global system in transition; a system that is still a 'system' but is constantly under attack in terms of its legitimacy and its capacity to impose a clear mandate" (Lopez-Alves & Johnson, 2018, p. 3). If the increased level of interconnectedness of social, economic, and technological exchanges has partially changed the geography of real and virtual places (Amin, 2002; Antonsich, 2010), it has certainly failed to fulfil the promise of a borderless world. Alienation (Xue, Manuel-Naverrete & Buzinde, 2014) and loss of sense of place are two of the consequences of the growing mobility of people and goods (Hay, 1998), partly exacerbated by the instability of the world's economy (Collins, 2019; IMF, 2019). A general sense of insecurity (Govers, 2018; Brende, 2019), a growing mistrust of experts (e.g., vaccination crisis, global warming denial) and institutions (Kauppi, 2018; Rutjens et al., 2018), the immobility and loss of power of old democracies, and the rise of populist nationalism (Lopez-Alves & Johnson, 2018; Rodrik, 2018) and post-truth politics (Davies, 2016; Lockie, 2017) characterise the Western world. Individuals are closer than ever to the ideal of the "global citizen"—through consumption of global goods and media—and yet they feel the need to re-affirm their sense of belonging to a place. In this arena, the identity of entire territories, their boundaries, values, and responsibilities are contested. Recent examples include the debates surrounding political crises (e.g., Brexit, Catalonia's bid for independence) and controversial executive decisions concerning issues such as immigration and climate change (e.g., US, UK, and Italian political agendas). Globalisation and its undesirable consequences have therefore marked "a new ontology of place/space relations" that urges researchers to re-think "territories and their delimitations" (Amin, 2002, p. 385). Future investigations should reflect on this complexity by focusing on the nature of contested place identities and the conflict generated by the creation of multiple senses of the same place. The analysis should examine both the internal and external consequences of these political and social crises that affect place brands by leveraging the benefits of longitudinal and comparative studies. As geo-political and economic tensions intensify (Collins, 2019), special attention should also be paid to institutional and mediatic discourses that surround contested places on- and offline (Kaneva, 2018) and their impact on internal and external place branding. Finally, scholars could explore in more depth the wide-spread feelings of loss of sense of place and insecurity by looking at the impact they exert on the consumption and management of places. In addition to commonly used surveys, ethnographic and netnographic approaches could prove particularly useful in these inquiries. If place narratives and the collective construction of the meaning of a place are key to its very existence, reflecting on the impact that marketing and branding can have on such narratives and constructions is proving more urgent than ever.

Un-sustainable destinations

Climate change, mass migrations, over-tourism, and the increased exploitation of natural resources are slowly transforming the geography of the world. The consequences of unchecked economic growth, widely acknowledged by policy makers (UNWTO, 2008, 2018; EEA, 2015), and the academic community (Hall et al., 2015; Seraphin, Sheeran & Pilato, 2018), have placed a spotlight on issues regarding sustainable development. High on the political agenda (WCED, 1987; UN, 2019; WEF, 2019), these issues have fuelled academic production and led to the creation of alternative forms of production and consumption of places and destinations, including sustainable tourism (often associated with slow, responsible, eco, and alternative tourism) (Ruhanen et al., 2015; Bramwell et al., 2016) and sustainable urban design and governance (Satterthwaite, 1997; Jenks, Jenks & Dempsey, 2005; Larco, 2016). Nevertheless, despite more than 30 years of studies, the possibility of a sustainable society is still at the centre of heated debates (Buckley, 2012). A closer look at the literature, in fact, reveals major challenges. Although the increased "awareness of the consequences of excessive consumerism" (Hanna et al., 2018, p. 36) has led to higher levels of green consciousness amongst consumers (Carrington, Zwick & Neville, 2015; Kang & Namkung, 2017), these pro-environmental attitudes rarely lead to meaningful behavioural changes (attitude–behaviour gap) (Carrigan & Attalla, 2001; Juvar & Dolnicar, 2016; Park & Lin, 2018). In fact, "the direct correlation between increased interest in sustainability in tourism and greater demand for tourism products that are embedded with sustainability principles has yet to be directly proven through research" (Hanna et al., 2018, p. 36). This over reliance on altruistic forms of consumption has fuelled the green marketing myopia (Hanna et al., 2018) and created an empty rhetoric (Prothero & Fitchett, 2000; Lansing & de Vries, 2007) partly responsible for the theoretical divide already mentioned by Sharpley (2000) and for increasing levels of scepticism (Insch, 2011). Further challenges concern the difficult implementation of sustainable programmes due to divergent views and conflicts of interests since "different understandings of what sustainable [tourism] development should mean [often] emerge among the various destination stakeholders" (Wickens, Bakir & Alvarez, 2015, p. 2). As we fast approach the next deadline set by the United Nations for the 2030 Sustainable Development Goals, it is imperative to reflect on the position that place branding research occupies in this arena. Although initial enquires have found that nation branding can be used to guide businesses towards sustainability, "providing qualifications for sustainable business, legitimizing these qualifications, and attaching national aspirations to business conduct that meets these qualifications" (Frig & Sorsa, 2018, p. 1), further studies examining the role of place branding as a driver of sustainable development are warranted (Maheshwari, Vandewalle & Bamber, 2011; Dinnie, 2017). Specifically, researchers could compare the strategies and narratives used in contexts characterised by extensive (e.g., Nordic countries) versus less structured nation branding programmes (e.g., BRIC countries). The analysis can take into consideration a wider range of communication tools and pay attention to different governmental bodies and place entities. In addition, scholars could benefit from unfolding the concept of sustainability to focus on specific environmental or social aspects that influence place brand image and reputation. For instance, referring to the work of Vallaster, von Wallpach and Zenker (2018), Kavaratzis (2018) encourages colleagues to further analyse the consequences of the refugee crisis on place brands (Kaneva, 2018). Similarly, Dioko claims that destination marketing will have an important part to play in connection with over-tourism and the preservation of "residents' locus of identity" (Dioko, 2016, p. 8). Also, partly connected to the above topic of contested places is the examination of how place brands known as multicultural and tolerant (Hassen & Giovanardi, 2018) manage their internal contradictions in spite of contrasting political discourses, rising discrimination, and cultural and religious intolerance. How does branding deal with the multiplicity and diversity of these voices? Last, place marketing literature might prove helpful for solving some of the controversies rooted in sustainability outlined above. Can place marketing be the real engine of the green commodity discourse (Prothero & Fitchett, 2000)? Or will it only contribute to fuel the green marketing propaganda (Insch, 2011)?

New and emerging place brands

In the wake of the world's financial crisis, changes in global economic governance are shifting attention from old to new and emerging place brands. Although the definition of emerging markets differs, the focus is mainly placed on the BRICS (Brasil, Russia, India, China, South Africa) (Li & Marsh, 2016; Dinnie, 2017). The acronym refers to Brazil, Russia, China and South Africa. It is estimated that these countries could soon represent a serious threat to the G7, the world's most advanced economies (Dhiman, 2017).

Their competitiveness, however, seems to be undermined by recent micro and macro changes that are affecting their socio-political stability (Mostafa & Mahmood, 2015), not least the recent Brazilian elections

(Casaroes, 2018). Although some scholars have opened the way to debate the application of nation branding strategies to BRICS countries (Niesing, 2013; Fang, 2015; Li & Marsh, 2016; Ageeva & Foroudi, 2019; Bose, Roy & Nguyen, 2019), there is a clear need for more empirical research to support practice. Given the enormous differences amongst the players in the region, researchers could benefit from comparing their approaches. Furthermore, studies could examine how branding processes are used to address BRICS individual and common fragilities (Li & Marsh, 2016; Saran, 2017). In addition to BRICS, other areas have recently captured the attention of economists, Middle East and Northern Africa, particularly the Middle East, and the ASEAN-5 (Indonesia, Malaysia, Philippines, Singapore, and Thailand). The literature on the Middle East is fragmented and mainly focuses on emblematic cases such as the UAE, Dubai, and Abu Dabhi (Freire, 2012; Govers, 2015; Zeineddine, 2017; Allagui & Al-Najjar, 2018; Rutter et al. 2018). Taking advantage of the complex nature of its socio-political situation, qualitative and quantitative studies that analyse place brand management in other Middle Eastern countries, regions and cities could offer an interesting contribution to current knowledge. The analysis of these markets would help assess whether we are witnessing a real shift from the anglocentric paradigm to new forms of place brand management (Dinnie, 2017) or to a mere adaptation of Western formulas (Li & Marsh, 2016). Whilst emerging markets strive under the weight of a limping global economy, another important shift promises to change the geography of place branding as citizens move from real to virtual places. The Bitnation (Decentralized Borderless Voluntary Nation (DBVN)) (https://tse.bitnation.co/), the Estonian E-Residency project and The Good Country are amongst the most interesting and ambitious experiments (Govers, 2018) that might lead the way for the creation of other virtual place brand initiatives. Researchers should work alongside policymakers and communities to explore the opportunities but also the risks involved in the creation of e-places, particularly in times of socio-political instability. How can collective actions lead to the co-construction of e-place brands? What negative/positive influence would this exert on nation state identities? Moreover, this virtual migration that affects residents might soon exert more attractive power in tourism. If virtual reality (VR) holidays are already a reality for some (Libert, 2017; Reuters, 2018), what future can we envisage for e-destinations? The following section will elaborate on this and on new digital advances.

Digital place brands

As digital places aspire to become the new acropolis, technology will have an even more important part to play in years to come. "The digital presence of place brands is arguably more important than that of other types of brands, since potential and existing investors, visitors and residents increasingly use the web to explore and research places" (Hanna & Rowley, 2015, p. 86). This is also reflected in some of the studies included in this book that investigate the use of technology in place branding. The Web 2.0 revolution and the consequential democratization of consumption have empowered place brand stakeholders to become co-producers of meanings (Oliveira & Panyik, 2015; Deng et al., 2019). Place identities are now constructed and experienced through real and digital encounters via online platforms (websites, blogs, social media, mobile apps, and online media platforms such as Netflix and Amazon Prime) and content (videos, images, animations, web series, and web games). In academia, this is evidenced by the increased interest in studies on participatory forms of place branding (Kavaratzis & Kalandides, 2015) and value co-creation (Cabiddu, Lui & Piccoli, 2013; Buhalis & Foreste, 2015; Lin, Chen & Filieri, 2017). Social media and user-generated content have already fuelled academic production and will continue to represent an important stage in social exchange in the following years. Although mobile video/image sharing platforms (e.g., YouTube, Instagram, Flickr, and Snapchat) and live streaming apps (e.g., Periscope and Facebook Live) will dominate the scene, interesting marketing opportunities will also be provided by online virtual worlds (e.g., second life) (Huang et al., 2013, 2016). Strictly connected to this is the use of immersive technologies such as VR and augmented reality (AR) by means of wearable devices (e.g., Samsung Gear, Google Cardboard, and Oculus Rift). Both have shown the potential to revolutionise the marketing of places (Marasco et al., 2018; Tussyadiah et al., 2018), as they "facilitate the encounters amongst tourists and destinations" (Pantano & Servidio, 2011; Marasco et al., 2018, p. 139; Bogicevic et al., 2019) influencing all the stages of the customer journey (Neuburger, Beck & Egger, 2018). Analysed in the broader context of smart technologies, VR, and AR represent only two applications of ICT. As cities and destinations are competing to become "smarter," researchers bet on cloud computing, the Internet-of-Things, artificial intelligence (Wang et al., 2016), and machine learning (Deng et al., 2019) to radically change the way residents and visitors relate to place and space. Research in these areas is only in its early stages, mainly conceptual and still accompanied by criticisms. Technology's fast-paced development, however, urges academics to reflect on the opportunities that these applications offer to place branding. There is therefore scope for empirical studies that investigate stakeholders' awareness, expectations, and attitudes towards the use of smart technologies. Specifically, researchers should focus on place brand managers' concerns regarding the use of these devices for the promotion and management of places as well as the challenges, not least the costs, level of usability and threats to data protection. The concept of "smart" and the phenomenon of "smart-washing" (Place Brand Observer, 2018) also deserve attention. Is being "more intelligent" enough to be unique and competitive in a market already full of smart cities? How can branding guide the development and promotion of places that aim to become smarter? Finally, technology offers researchers a real chance to rethink the management of place brands in terms of efficiency, sustainability, and accessibility. This, however, comes at a cost. Adapting technological advances to meet place branding needs will require a new set of technical skills as well as a good dose of imagination. Are we ready to jump on the bandwagon of the next technological (r)evolution?

Conclusion

Global dynamics are causing disruptive changes in our society and the places where we live. This chapter briefly outlined how these external factors will influence place branding research and the type of challenges academics will face in the near future. Far from being exhaustive, the analysis highlights the significance of the role that branding research plays in shaping the socio-political layers of a place. Leveraging studies on new social and technological developments, researchers have the potential to become drivers of positive change and empower communities to manage and measure the process of reconstruction and deconstruction of places. The author hopes that this research agenda will inspire future generation of researchers to answer this call.

References

Ageeva, E. & Foroudi, P. (2019). Examining the destination website: a case of Visit Tatarstan. In P. Foroudi, C. Mauri, C. Dennis, & T. C. Melewar (Eds.), Place Branding. New York, NY: Taylor & Francis Group.

Allagui, I. & Al-Najjar, A. (2018). From women empowerment to nation branding: A case study from the United Arab Emirates. *International Journal of Communication*, 12, 68–85.

Amin, A. (2002). Spatialities of globalization. *Environment and Planning A*, 34, 385–399.

Anholt, S. (2006). Editorial. Why brand? Some practical considerations for nation branding. *Place Branding*, 2(2), 97–107.

Anholt, S. (2007). *Competitive identity. The new brand management for nations, cities and regions*. London: Palgrave Macmillan.

Antonsich, M. (2010). Grounding theories of place and globalisation. *Tijdschrift voor Economische en Sociale Geografie*, 102(3), 331–345.

Ashworth, G.J., Kavaratzis, M. & Warnaby, G. (2015). The need to rethink place branding. In G.J. Ashworth, M. Kavaratzis & G. Warnaby (Eds.), *Rethinking place branding: Comprehensive brand development for cities and regions* (pp. 1–11). London: Springer.

Bennett, R. & Savani, S. (2003). The rebranding of city places: An international comparative investigation. *International Public Management Review*, 4(2), 70–87.

Blichfeld, B.S. (2005). Unmanageable place brands?. *Place Branding*, 1(4), 388–401.

Bogicevic, V., Seo, S., Kandampully, J.A., Liu, S.Q. & Rudd, N.A. (2019). Virtual reality presence as a preamble of tourism experience: The role of mental imagery. *Tourism Management*, 74, 55–64.

Bose, S., Roy, S. K. & Nguyen, N. (2019). Developing a 'customer based place brand equity – destination branding' instrument. In P. Foroudi, C. Mauri, C. Dennis, & T. C. Melewar (Eds.), Place Branding. New York, NY: Taylor & Francis Group.

Bramwell, B., Higham, J., Lane, B. & Miller, G. (2016). Twenty-five years of sustainable tourism and the Journal of Sustainable Tourism: looking back and moving forward. *Journal of Sustainable Tourism*, 25(1), 1–9.

Brende, B. (2019). *Preface—The global risks report 2019 14th edition.* Geneva: The World Economic Forum.

Broudehoux, A.M. (2001). Image making, place marketing and the aesthetization of social inequality in Rio de Janeiro. In N. Alsayyad (Ed.), *Consuming tradition, manufacturing heritage* (pp. 273–297). London: Routledge.

Buhalis, D. & Foreste, M. (2015). SoCoMo marketing for travel and tourism: Empowering co-creation of value. *Journal of Destination Marketing & Management*, 4(3), 151–161.

Buckley, R. (2012). Sustainable tourism: Research and reality. *Annals of Tourism*, 39(2), 528–546.

Cabiddu, F., Lui, T. & Piccoli, G. (2013). Managing value co-creation in the tourism industry. *Annals of Tourism Research*, 42, 86–107.

Carrigan, M. & Attalla, A. (2001) The myth of the ethical consumer – Do ethics matter in purchase behaviour?. *Journal of Consumer Marketing*, 18(7), 560–577.

Carrington, M.J., Zwick, D. & Neville, B. (2015). The ideology of the ethical consumption gap. *Marketing Theory*, 16(1), 21–38.

Casaroes, G. (2018). Brazilian elections and the future of the BRICS—ISPI—Istituto per gli Studi di Politica Internazionale. Retrieved from: www.ispi online.it/it/pubblicazione/brazilian-elections-and-future-brics-21347

Cleave, E., Arku, G., Sadler, R. & Gilliland, J. (2017). Is it sound policy or fast policy? Practitioners' perspectives on the role of place branding in local economic development. *Urban Geography*, 38(7), 1133–1157.

Collins, A. (2019). Are we sleepwalking into a new global crisis?—World Economic Forum. Retrieved from: www.weforum.org/agenda/2019/01/is-the-world-sleepwalking-into-a-new-global-crisis/

Davies, W. (2016, August 24). The age of post-truth politics. Retrieved from: www.nytimes.com/2016/08/24/opinion/campaign-stops/the-age-of-post-truth-politics.html

Deng, N., Liu, J., Dai, Y. & Li, H. (2019). Different cultures, different photos: A comparison of Shanghai's pictorial destination image between East and West. *Tourism Management*, 30, 182–192.

Dhiman, M.C. (2017). *Opportunities and challenges for tourism and hospitality in the BRIC region.* Hershey: IGI Global.

Dinnie, K. (2017). *Nation branding: Concepts, issues, practice.* London: Routledge.

Dioko, L. (Don) A.N. (2016). Progress and trends in destination branding and marketing—A brief and broad review. *International Journal of Culture, Tourism and Hospitality Research*, 10(1), 1–17.

EEA (2015, February 18). Tourism—A report of the European Environment Agency. Retrieved from: www.eea.europa.eu/soer-2015/europe/tourism

Ermann, U. & Hermanik, K. (2017). *Branding the nation, the place, the product.* London: Routledge.

Fang, Y. (2015). *Faked in China: Nation branding, counterfeit culture, and globalization.* Bloomington: Indiana University Press.

Freire, J. (2012). Special section: Place branding in the Middle East. *Place Branding and Public Diplomacy,* 8(1), 46–47.

Frig, M. & Sorsa, V. (2018). Nation branding as sustainability governance: A comparative case analysis. Business & Society. Published online February 20, 2018 https://doi.org/10.1177/0007650318758322.

Govers, R. (2013). Why place branding is not about logos and slogans, *Place Branding and Public Diplomacy,* 9(2), 71–75.

Govers, R. (2015). Rethinking virtual and online place branding. In G.J. Ashworth, M. Kavaratzis & G. Warnaby (Eds.), *Rethinking place branding: Comprehensive brand development for cities and regions* (pp. 1–11). London: Springer.

Govers, R. (2018). *Imaginative communities: Admired cities, regions and countries.* Antwerp: Reputo Press.

Govers, R., Kaefer, F. & Ferrer-Roca, N. (2017). The state of academic place branding research according to practitioners. *Place Branding and Public Diplomacy,* 13(1), 1–3.

Hall, C.M., Amelung, B., Cohen, S., Eijgelaar, E., Gössling, S. Higham, J., Leemans, R., Peeters, P., Ram, Y. & Scott, D. (2015). On climate change skepticism and denial in tourism. *Journal of Sustainable Tourism,* 23(1), 4–25.

Hankinson, G. (2010). Place branding research: A cross-disciplinary agenda and the views of practitioners. *Place Branding and Public Diplomacy,* 6(4), 300–315.

Hankinson, G. (2015). Rethinking the place branding construct. In G.J. Ashworth, M. Kavaratzis & G. Warnaby (Eds.), *Rethinking place branding: Comprehensive brand development for cities and regions* (pp. 13–31). London: Springer.

Hanna, P., Fonta, X., Scarlesa, C., Weedenb, C. & Harrisona, C. (2018). Tourist destination marketing: From sustainability myopia to memorable experiences. *Journal of Destination Marketing & Management,* 9, 36–43.

Hanna, S.A. & Rowley, J. (2015). Rethinking strategic place branding in the digital age. In G.J. Ashworth, M. Kavaratzis & G. Warnaby (Eds.), *Rethinking place branding: Comprehensive brand development for cities and regions* (pp. 85–99). London: Springer.

Hassen, I. & Giovanardi, M. (2018). The difference of 'being diverse': City branding and multiculturalism in the 'Leicester Model'. *Cities,* 80, 45–52.

Hay, R. (1998). Sense of place in developmental context. *Journal of Environmental Psychology,* 18, 5–29.

Huang, Y., Backman, K.F, Backman, S. & Chang, L.L. (2016). Exploring the implications of virtual reality technology in tourism. *International Journal of Tourism Research,* 18, 116–128.

Huang, Y., Backman, S., Backman, K.F. & Moore, D. (2013). Exploring user acceptance of 3D virtual worlds in travel and tourism marketing. *Tourism Management,* 36, 490–501.

IMF (2019). The global economy: A delicate Moment—IMFBlog (International Monetary Fund) insights & analysis on economics and finance. Retrieved from: https://blogs.imf.org/2019/04/09/the-global-economy-a-delicate-moment/

Insch, A. (2011). Conceptualization and anatomy of green destination brands. *International Journal of Culture and Hospitality Research*, 5(3), 282–290.

Jenks, M., Jenks, M. & Dempsey, N. (2005). *Future forms and design for sustainable cities.* Burlington, VT: Elsevier.

Juvar, E. & Dolnicar, S. (2016). Measuring environmentally sustainable tourist behaviour. *Annals of Tourism Research*, 59, 30–44.

Kaneva, N. (2018). Between brand utopias and lived experience. In M. Kavaratzis, M. Giovanardi & M. Lichrou (Eds.), *Inclusive place branding: Critical perspectives on theory and practice* (pp. 182–190). London: Routledge.

Kang, J. & Namkung, Y. (2017). The effect of corporate social responsibility on brand equity and the moderating role of ethical consumerism: The case of Starbucks. *Journal of Hospitality & Tourism Research*, 42(7), 1130–1151.

Kauppi, N. (2018). *Democracy, social resources and political power in the European Union.* Manchester: Manchester University Press.

Kavaratzis, M. (2015). Place branding scholars and practitioners: "Strangers in the night"?. *Journal of Place Management and Development*, 8(3), 266–270.

Kavaratzis, M. (2016). The participatory place branding process for tourism: Linking visitors and residents through the city brand. In N. Bellini & C. Pasquinelli (Eds.), *Tourism in the city* (pp. 93–107). London: Springer.

Kavaratzis, M. (2018). Place branding: Are we any wiser?. *Cities*, 80, 53–60.

Kavaratzis, M. & Hatch, M.J. (2013). The dynamics of place brands: An identity-based approach to place branding theory. *Marketing Theory*, 13(1), 69–86.

Kavaratzis, M. & Kalandides, A. (2015). Rethinking the place brand: The interactive formation of place brands and the role of participatory place branding. *Environment and Planning A*, 47, 1368–1382.

Klijn, E.H., Eshuis, J. & Braun, E. (2012). The influence of stakeholder involvement on the effectiveness of place branding. *Public Management Review*, 14(4), 499–519.

Lansing, P. & de Vries, P. (2007). Sustainable tourism: Ethical alternative or marketing ploy?. *Journal of Business Ethics*, 72, 77–85.

Larco, N. (2016). Sustainable urban design—A (draft) framework. *Journal of Urban Design*, 21(1), 1–29.

Li, H. & Marsh, L.L. (2016). Building the BRICS: Media, nation branding, and global citizenship. *International Journal of Communication*, 10, 2973–2988.

Libert, L. (2017, November 7). Exploring Egypt's great pyramid from the inside, virtually—Reuters. Retrieved from: www.reuters.com/article/us-science-pyramid-virtualreality/exploring-egypts-great-pyramid-from-the-inside-virtually-idUSKBN1D72UB

Lin, Z., Chen, Y. & Filieri, R. (2017). Resident-tourist value co-creation: The role of residents' perceived tourism impacts and life satisfaction. *Tourism Management*, 61(C), 436–442.

Lockie, S. (2017). Post-truth politics and the social sciences. *Environmental Sociology*, 3(1), 1–5.

Lopez-Alves, F. & Johnson, D.E. (2018). *Populist nationalism in Europe and the Americas.* New York: Routledge.

Maheshwari, V., Vandewalle, I. & Bamber, D. (2011). Place branding's role in sustainable development. *Journal of Place Management & Development*, 4(2), 198–213.

Marasco, A., Buonincontri, P., van Niekerk, M. & Orlowski, M. (2018). Exploring the role of next-generation virtual technologies in destination marketing. *Journal of Destination Marketing & Management*, 9, 138–148.

Medway, D., Swanson K., Delpy N.L., Pasquinelli C. & Zenker S. (2015). Place branding: Are we wasting our time?. *Journal of Place Management and Development*, 8(1), 63–68.

Mostafa, G. & Mahmood, M. (2015). The rise of the BRICS and their challenge to the G7. *International Journal of Emerging Markets*, 10(1), 156–170.

Neuburger, L., Beck, J. & Egger, R. (2018). The 'Phygital' tourist experience: The use of augmented and virtual reality in destination marketing. In M.A. Camilleri (Ed.), *Tourism planning and destination marketing* (pp. 183–202). Bingley: Emerald.

Niesing, E. (2013). Latin America's potential in Nation Branding: A closer look at Brazil's, Chile's and Colombia's practices. Hamburg: Anchor Academic Publishing.

Oliveira, E. & Panyik, E. (2015). Content, context and co-creation: Digital challenges in destination branding with references to Portugal as a tourist destination. *Journal of Vacation Marketing*, 21(1), 53–74.

Pantano, E. & Servidio, R. (2011). An exploratory study of the role of pervasive environments for promotion of tourism destinations. *Journal of Hospitality and Tourism Technology*, 2(1), 50–65.

Park, H.J. & Lin, L.M. (2018). Exploring attitude–behavior gap in sustainable consumption: comparison of recycled and upcycled fashion products, *Journal of Business Research*. Available online August 20, 2018.

Place Brand Observer (2018). Smart cities and place branding: Opportunities and challenges. Retrieved from: https://placebrandobserver.com/smart-cities-place-branding-opportunities-challenges/

Prothero, A. & Fitchett, J.A. (2000). Greening capitalism: Opportunities for a green commodity. *Journal of Macromarketing*, 20(1), 46–55.

Reuters (2018, February 15). Japanese tour firm offers virtual reality holidays—With a first-class seat. Retrieved from: www.theguardian.com/world/2018/feb/15/japanese-tour-firm-offers-virtual-reality-holidays-with-a-first-class-seat

Rodrik, D. (2018). Populism and the economics of globalization. *Journal of International Business Policy*, 1, 12–33.

Ruhanen, L., Weiler, B., Moyle, B.D. & McLennan, C.J. (2015). Trends and patterns in sustainable tourism research: A 25-year bibliometric analysis. *Journal of Sustainable Tourism*, 23(4), 517–535.

Rutjens, B. T., Heine, S. J., Sutton, R. M., & van Harreveld, F. (2018). Attitudes towards science. *Advances in Experimental Social Psychology*, 57, 125–165.

Rutter, R., Nadeau, J., Lettice, F., Lim, M. & al Shamaisi, S. (2018). Place branding of seaports in the Middle East. *Place Branding and Public Diplomacy*, 14(3), 197–212.

Salzman, M. (2016, May 24). *Why place branding is becoming place doing (consider Austin)*. Retrieved from www.forbes.com/sites/mariansalzman/2016/05/24/why-place-branding-is-becoming-place-doing-consider-austin/#4932408661bf

Saran, S. (2017). The next ten years of BRICS—Will the relationship last?—World Economic Forum. Retrieved from: www.weforum.org/agenda/2017/10/brics-first-next-ten-years/

Satterthwaite, D. (1997). Sustainable cities or cities that contribute to sustainable development?. *Urban Studies*, 34(10), 1667–1691.

Seraphin, H., Sheeran, P. & Pilato, M. (2018). Over-tourism and the fall of Venice as a destination. *Journal of Destination Marketing & Management*, 9, 374–376.

Sharpley, R. (2000). Tourism and sustainable development: Exploring the theoretical divide. *Journal of Sustainable Tourism*, 8(1), 1–19.

Stubbs, J. & Warnaby, G. (2015). Rethinking place branding from a practice perspective: Working with stakeholders, In G.J. Ashworth, M. Kavaratzis & G. Warnaby (Eds.), *Rethinking place branding: Comprehensive brand development for cities and regions* (pp. 101–118). London: Springer.

Subramanian, S. (2017, November 7). How to sell a country: The booming business of nation branding. Retrieved from: www.theguardian.com/news/2017/nov/07/nation-branding-industry-how-to-sell-a-country

Tussyadiah, I.P., Wang, D., Jung, T.H., tom Dieck, M.C. (2018). Virtual reality, presence, and attitude change: Empirical evidence from tourism, *Tourism Management*, 66, 140–154.

UN (2019). The sustainable development agenda. Retrieved from: www.un.org/sustainabledevelopment/development-agenda/

UNWTO (2008). *Climate change and tourism. Responding to global challenges*. Madrid: World Tourism Organization.

UNWTO (2018). *'Overtourism'?—Understanding and managing urban tourism growth beyond perceptions*. Madrid: World Tourism Organization.

Vallaster, C., von Wallapach, S. & Zenker, S. (2018). The interplay between urban policies and grassroots city brand co-creation and co-destruction during the refugee crisis: Insights from the city brand Munich (Germany). *City*, 80, 53–60.

Vuignier, R. (2017). Place branding & place marketing 1976–2016: A multidisciplinary literature review. *International Review on Public and Nonprofit Marketing*, 14(4), 447–473.

Wang, X., Lin, X.R., Zhen, F. & Zhang, J. (2016). How smart is your tourist attraction?: Measuring tourist preferences of smart tourism attractions via a FCEM-AHP and IPA approach. *Tourism Management*, 54, 309–320.

Warren, G. & Dinnie, K. (2018). Cultural intermediaries in place branding: Who are they and how do they construct legitimacy for their work and for themselves?. *Tourism Management*, 66, 302–314.

WCED (1987). *Our common future. World commission on environment and development*. Oxford: Oxford University Press.

WEF (2019). *The global risks report 2019 14th edition*. Geneva: The World Economic Forum.

Wickens, E., Bakir, A.& Alvarez, M.D. (2015). Sustainable destination development: Issues and challenges. *Tourism Planning & Development*, 12(1), 1–5.

Xue, L., Manuel-Navarrete, D. & Buzinde, C.N. (2014). Theorizing the concept of alienation in tourism studies. *Annals of Tourism Research*, 44, 186–199.

Zeineddine, C. (2017). Employing nation branding in the Middle East—United Arab Emirates (UAE) and Qatar. *Management & Marketing*, 12(2), 208–221.

Zenker, S. & Braun, E. (2017). Questioning a "one size fits all" city brand: Developing a branded house strategy for place brand management. *Journal of Place Management and Development*, 10(3), 270–287.

Zukin, S. (2014, May 6). *Postcard-perfect: The big business of city branding*. Retrieved from: www.theguardian.com/cities/2014/may/06/postcard-perfect-the-big-business-of-city-branding

Index

Taylor & Francis eBooks

www.taylorfrancis.com

A single destination for eBooks from Taylor & Francis
with increased functionality and an improved user
experience to meet the needs of our customers.

90,000+ eBooks of award-winning academic content in
Humanities, Social Science, Science, Technology, Engineering,
and Medical written by a global network of editors and authors.

TAYLOR & FRANCIS EBOOKS OFFERS:

A streamlined
experience for
our library
customers

A single point
of discovery
for all of our
eBook content

Improved
search and
discovery of
content at both
book and
chapter level

REQUEST A FREE TRIAL
support@taylorfrancis.com

 Routledge
Taylor & Francis Group

 CRC Press
Taylor & Francis Group